The Structure of Economic Systems

The Structure of
Economic Systems

John Michael Montias

New Haven and London, Yale University Press, 1976

Library of Congress catalog card number: 75-43327
International standard book number: 0-300-01833-9

Designed by John O. C. McCrillis
and set in Baskerville type.
Printed in the United States of America by
The Vail-Ballou Press, Binghamton, New York.

Published in Great Britain, Europe, Africa, and Asia
(except Japan) by Yale University Press, Ltd., London.
Distributed in Latin America by Kaiman & Polon,
Inc., New York City; in Australia and New Zealand by
Book & Film Services, Artarmon, N.S.W., Australia;
in Japan by John Weatherhill, Inc., Tokyo.

To my son John Luke

Contents

Foreword

The title of this book, especially if emphasis is placed on the definite article that begins it, sounds more comprehensive and ambitious than I meant it to be. The French *La Structure des Systèmes Economiques* comes closer to my meaning, inasmuch as the definite article in French does not imply a particular structure —let alone a unique one—but only structure in the abstract. On the other hand, "Structures of Economic Systems" would also have fallen short of the mark, since I did not intend to list, exhaustively or otherwise, the possible structures that might occur. What the book is about is the study of structure in economic systems and of its effects on efficiency, equity, and other outcomes of interest, where structure is interpreted narrowly to mean the formal and informal rules that constrain individuals in making their economic decisions. Even though the word "institution" (almost) never appears in the book (chiefly because I could not give it a precise meaning that would fit into the constructive vocabulary I tried to develop for the analysis of economic systems), the reader will recognize that my study deals with institutional economics in comparative perspective. A justification (and apology) for this approach forms the subject of the first chapter.

My initial debt is to Tjalling C. Koopmans, who originally proposed some of the ideas in this book (particularly the notion of a system-free vocabulary and the basic framework for macroeconomic comparisons) when we were working together on the paper "On the Description and Comparison of Economic Systems."* Although most of our interaction took place at the Center for Advanced Study in the Behavioral Sciences in 1968–69, I have profited from his comments and advice since that time, especially in connection with the problem of the aggregation of controls and the autonomy of subordinates analyzed in chapter 14. Needless to say, neither he nor any of the scholars mentioned below is in any manner whatsoever responsible for any errors that may remain in the book.

I am grateful to Frederic L. Pryor, who did me the favor of reading the whole manuscript with great care and from whose numerous comments I have greatly benefited. I am also beholden to Richard R. Nelson, Egon Neuberger, Stephen R. Sacks, Herbert Scarf, and Gary Yohe, who read and commented on various parts of the manuscript. I have been particularly

*Published in A. Eckstein, ed., *Comparison of Economic Systems* (Berkeley: University of California Press, 1971).

influenced by conversations with Richard R. Nelson (on the description and modeling of institutional processes) and with Herbert Scarf (on general equilibrium analysis). Such knowledge as I have of the Japanese economic system was in large measure acquired from my colleague Hugh Patrick. As I have acknowledged in the footnotes, I have found a number of dissertations and papers written by students (graduate and undergraduate) in my courses in "comparative systems" to be valuable sources of knowledge and inspiration. I trust that my summary presentation of their findings will not discourage them from publishing their ideas in full (especially in the cases of Gary Yohe and Andrew Feltenstein, whose doctoral dissertations deal in greater depth with problems discussed in sections 14.3 and 17.8, respectively).

I am especially grateful to Ms. Cheryl Hunt for typing several drafts of the manuscript. She deserves a degree in paleography for deciphering my handwriting and for transcribing the mathematical notation.

Finally, I wish to thank Mr. Alexander Metro for his painstaking editing, which corrected a number of oversights and stylistic errors.

Part 1
Method and Outline of Problems

1

An Introduction and an Apology

Les sciences psychologiques resteront où elles gisent, c'est à dire dans les
ténèbres et la folie, tant qu'elles n'auront pas une nomenclature exacte,
qu'il sera permis d'employer la même expression pour signifier les idées
les plus diverses.

Gustave Flaubert
to George Sand, 1866

The psychological sciences will continue to lie in darkness and in folly,
Flaubert wrote over a century ago, as long as they do not develop a precise
vocabulary, as long as they continue to use the same expression to denote
the most disparate ideas. Are not "planning," "socialism," "centralization,"
"market economy," "competition," and many other terms we use in economics—one of the sciences that Flaubert would have considered "psychologiques"—words and expressions that mean different things to many
people living in the "American system," let alone to people educated in
different systems? Is it any wonder that the comparison of economic systems
has made so little progress when economists have not proposed—let alone
agreed on—an exact nomenclature to describe individual systems?

This book was initially conceived as a framework for comparing systems.
But as work on the book progressed, it became increasingly evident to me
that no serious attempt at system comparison could be made until a fairly
extensive vocabulary had been developed with which one would be able to
describe each system with precision. This was also the underlying principle
of a recent paper written jointly with T. C. Koopmans, whose ideas on this
and on many other subjects dealt with in the present work exerted a pervasive
influence on my thinking.[1]

If I had been entirely consistent in my approach, I should have limited
the contents of my study to the description and comparison of system structures. But differences in structures are supposed to be reflected in differences
in the outcomes of economic processes, and the quantitative comparison of
outcomes—particularly of national incomes and aggregate factor productivities—presents fascinating problems that I could not force myself to ignore.

1. T. C. Koopmans and J. M. Montias, "On the Description and Comparison of Economic
Systems," in A. Eckstein, ed, *Comparison of Economic Systems: Theoretical and Methodological Approaches* (Berkeley: University of California Press, 1971).

3

When I wrote, a couple of paragraphs above, that the comparison of systems had made little progress, I did not mean to imply that the field was all "ténèbres et folie." Nevertheless, it is remarkable how little impact efforts in this direction have had on the behavioral sciences at large. Symptomatic perhaps is the fact that the comparison of systems failed to chalk up a single entry in the index of the *International Encyclopedia of the Social Sciences*, published in 1968, let alone a separate article.[2] If courses on the subject were offered at all in colleges and universities at the beginning of the 1970s, they were taught chiefly as one-at-a-time descriptions of the market and centrally planned economies and lacked systematic comparisons beyond the contrast of extreme centralization in Soviet-type economies with more or less idealized competitive systems.[3] By the beginning of the 1970s, in short, the field had barely gotten past the stage that psychologists studying infantile behavior call "parallel play." In view of this backwardness in the state of the art, even the partial fulfillment of modest aims may be a contribution.

My aims, in any event, are these:

1. To supply a value-free vocabulary with which to describe and compare economies and systems, or, more precisely, to describe and compare the structures or "working arrangements" of systems and their outcomes.

2. To propose a framework for organizing data gathered from different economies with a view to drawing comparisons.

3. To consider analytical methods, drawn chiefly from economics and organization theory, that may help construct models relevant to comparisons.

4. With the help of analytical models, to suggest hypotheses ("conjectures") that might be tested on cross-national data.

5. To review some recent quantitative comparisons made by empirical researchers in the field in the light of the methodological considerations discussed in the book.

---

2. Comparative government, history, politics, psychology, and law all received separate treatment. All in all there were 21 separate mentions in the index of applications of the comparative method to a variety of subjects, none of them economic.

3. The bright spots in the comparisons of economic systems in the 1960s and early 1970s were chiefly the incidental work of "outsiders," mathematical economists such as Leo Hurwicz and Thomas Marschak, or of specialists in Soviet economics such as Abram Bergson, Egon Neuberger, and Gregory Grossman. Valuable empirical work in the field has been done by Frederic L. Pryor (*Public Expenditures in Communist and Capitalist Nations* [Bloomington: Indiana University Press, 1968], and *Property and Industrial Organization in Communist and Capitalist Nations* [Bloomington: Indiana University Press, 1973]). The theoretical description of system structure has also been advanced by the interesting and thought-provoking work of the outstanding Hungarian economist Janos Kornai (see his *Anti-Equilibrium: On Economic Systems Theory and the Tasks of Research* [Amsterdam: North–Holland, 1971]). When the present work was already in galleys, there appeared a textbook for undergraduates by Egon Neuberger and William Duffy (*Comparative Economic Systems: A Decision-Making Approach* [Boston: Allyn & Bacon, 1976]), which propounds an analytical framework similar, and related, to the one developed in the Koopmans–Montias paper referred to in n. 1 above and in the text of this book.

6. To write a book on economic systems that anthropologists, political scientists, and sociologists might read with the feeling that the author was not completely oblivious to their methods, ideas, and approaches.

Although I have no "theory of economic systems," I can at least lay claim to an individual point of view. My interest, along the lines that were already traced out in the Koopmans–Montias paper, lies in the interaction of individuals *within* and *across* organizations in different systems. I propose to study the interface between organization theory and economics in the belief that some of the most significant differences among systems can be brought to light and analyzed by combining the techniques developed in these two disciplines.[4] The idea that it is necessary to look at the interests of groups of individuals within any large organization in order to generate realistic hypotheses about the behavior of the organization as a whole has become increasingly popular of late among students of industrial organization. Comparers of systems must now follow their lead and look into the organizational black box for an understanding of how diverse interest groups interact in the pursuit of their separate goals under different environments and system rules.[5]

This study will focus on the *structures* of systems, by which I mean the laws, rules, taboos, and other man-made restrictions on the decisions of participants in one or more systems. We shall compare economic systems and their structures across nations as well as across time within one or more nations. In keeping with the tradition of normative economics, I have not abandoned the hope that this analysis may be of help to those desirous of influencing system change by evolutionary or revolutionary means.

We shall think of comparisons of economies as being made up of *models* of these economies or systems. That is, instead of comparing two economies directly, models will be abstracted from our knowledge of these economies and then the models will be compared with each other, as well as with the realities whose relevant features they embody. This premise holds for quantitative comparisons based on a sample of commodities and services aggregated according to some notion of relative preferences, just as it holds for the postulation of enterprise managers' behavior and its logical consequences for the economics of production. We can never consider all commodities and services and all the preferences that govern them. Neither can we investigate the behavior of every enterprise manager. We may, however, take a sample of the goods produced in an economy that we have reason to believe is representative of all the goods turned out, and we may weight them with prices

4. Herbert Simon, *The Sciences of the Artificial* (Cambridge, Mass.: MIT Press, 1969), chap. 2.

5. For a good recent example of an attempt to develop testable hypotheses about the behavior of economic organizations from the special interests of intraorganizational groups and from their relative powers, see Marc J. Roberts, "An Evolutionary and Institutional View of the Behavior of Public and Private Companies," *American Economic Review* 65 (May 1975): 415–27. See also sec. 9.5.

that we think reflect more or less faithfully the relative preferences of the consumers or of any other group of decision makers in this economy. Similarly, we may not believe that every capitalist manager maximizes profits or the net worth of his enterprise, or that every workers' council presses the management council of its firm to earn the highest possible net income per employee, but such behavior may be regular enough to warrant postulating it as the norm and investigating its effects methodically.

Models in this book are highly simplified; most of them seriously distort the reality of a complex, rapidly evolving world. Faced with a choice between the clear articulation of a simple relationship and a realistic description of a complex process, I have generally opted for the former. I take my cue from Bertrand Russell in the belief that scientific progress is made "by analysis and artificial isolation." I am open therefore to many of the objections that Ludwig von Bertalanffy has leveled against the "mechanistic view" of the world.[6] Even when I discuss interaction among individuals (chapter 8) or price and nonprice competitive processes (chapter 10), where I make at least a stab at viewing the system as a whole, I stick fairly close to a mechanistic view. Except for an occasional genuflection, I ignore entrepreneurship, innovation, and other interesting, important, but hard-to-model concepts.[7]

Aside from the relative merits of the mechanistic and organic approaches, I incline toward simplified representations because I believe that the scientific comparison of systems suffers far more at present from a lack of precise concepts and of clearly articulated relations among system components than it does from any failure to describe system traits in comprehensive detail.

Some of the models developed in this book are highly abstract and replete with mathematical terms. Some are very simple and verbal, leaning toward the loose paradigm rather than the logically precise axiomatic approach. Even when mathematics is used (even then never involving material more complicated than elementary set theory or simple vectors and matrix algebra), the purpose is not to prove abstruse theorems but to provide precise definitions and a neater formulation of certain problems than might be possible verbally. Also, in specific cases I hope to develop propositions with a greater degree of generality than I could if I used only elementary algebra and differential calculus. Chapter 17 forms the main exception to this restrained employment of mathematical methods. It should be read—if it is read at all—by readers acquainted with the basic mathematical notions of general equilibrium.

To justify my attempt to construct an analytical framework that may be more useful for organizing my own thinking than the reader's, I must first

6. The Russell citation is taken from von Bertalanffy's *General System Theory: Foundations, Development, Application* (New York: Braziller, 1968), pp. 67–68.

7. Cf. William J. Baumol, "Entrepreneurship in Economic Theory," *American Economic Review* 58 (May 1968): 64–71.

state my objections to three competing methodological approaches to the description and comparison of systems. They are (1) invidious comparisons with an all-purpose ideal, (2) unique principles of comparison, and (3) measurement without theory, or "fishing for hypotheses."

The first two approaches are by no means mutually exclusive; the third, however, is the particular province of aberrant empiricists endowed with an ample allowance for computing expenses. They are all, of course, caricatures that no serious economist would ever fully identify himself with, but their conscious or unconscious effect on the methodology of some comparers is sufficiently strong to warrant at least a brief discussion.

1. Invidious comparisons. The invidious comparer rates all systems according to a trait that he considers ideal, which among Western economists is most frequently the extent to which that system satisfies the requirements of atomistic competition in free markets. Since, under assumptions that he does not always specify, perfect competition is conducive to efficiency in both production and distribution ("Pareto optimality"), and since centralized decision making, for lack of information and computing capabilities, cannot match this efficiency, he concludes that the more widely the system departs from these optimal measures, the greater will be its lapse from full efficiency. One inference sometimes drawn from this line of reasoning is that, starting from a centralized system, the creation of markets for *some* goods or the delegation of less basic production or distribution decisions to lower levels in the hierarchy managing the economy must necessarily raise the level of efficiency attained by the system.

I need only remind the reader that the efficiency of decentralized production decisions is only guaranteed if (1) the decentralized units maximize profits at parametric prices, (2) they take into account all the costs they inflict and all the benefits they confer on one another or on the public, and (3) indivisibilities and economies of scale in production processes are not sufficiently strong to make the competitive behavior of these units unprofitable ("convexity of production sets"); and (4) consumers' preferences satisfy transitivity and the requirement of increasing marginal rates of substitution (more generally, "convexity of consumption sets"). Even if all these conditions were met, which is unlikely in the modern world, a more dispassionate comparer might ask whether the putative loss in "static" (single period) efficiency of a more centralized allocation might not be warranted by the gains in "dynamic" (multiperiod) efficiency rendered possible by higher levels of investment, research and development, or both, or even by a distribution of incomes that he or some important group within that society might hold to be more desirable. (Some of these concepts, used in their conventional ambit in the statement of these three conditions, will be refined in the following chapters.)

2. Unique principles of comparison. Centralized controls versus markets, public versus private ownership of the means of production, national economic planning versus laissez-faire, control of firms by the workers' collective versus control by the bureaucracy—all these are examples of alternative institutional arrangements that some economists hold to be quintessential to the nature of any system. There would be more justification for this ontological approach if there were only two kinds of systems, say, centralized and decentralized, and all other traits fell in with one or the other of these alternatives—if, for example, all economies in which the means of production were publicly owned were also centrally controlled and planned and their enterprises managed by workers' representatives.[8] But the most casual observation of system traits in the actual world reveals that this is not the case. Even if we were to grant that system characteristics can be so sharply dichotomized, we should still be faced with examples of almost every combination of these traits, including one socialist, decentrally managed, centrally planned state where workers are *not* in control of their enterprises (Hungary). Which trait we select as essential is then a matter of values and judgment, of what we shall call the "norms" used for analyzing and comparing systems.[9]

In any event these system dichotomies are much too coarse. To throw communist China and Poland into the same class of centralized economies, except as a preliminary step toward a more sophisticated classification, is more likely to obscure than to illuminate the way these two economies actually operate (or, to be more precise, since we are always supposed to be comparing models rather than the infinite-dimensioned reality that underlies them, the way a more realistic model of these economies would represent their operation). Not that all talk about the great "isms" should forthwith be ruled out of our universe of discourse. Capitalism, communism, socialism, and kindred terms, whatever system traits they may in actuality represent, have a life of their own. They live as symbols or clusters of symbols in the minds of the participants in all modern systems (where most people are sufficiently educated to entertain such notions), and they may have a profound influence on the way actual systems change or on the reasons why they fail to change.

The increased variety of systems, incidentally, provides opportunities for comparisons between economies that are alike in most respects and differ notably in only one or two dimensions—comparisons that may permit tracing the effects of specific traits on outcomes with greater confidence. For instance,

8. Pryor calls this the "seamless web" hypothesis (*Property and Industrial Organization*, op. cit., p. 12).

9. A more sophisticated variant of this unique-principle approach is Karl Polanyi's attempt to classify economies according to three principal forms of "integration": "reciprocity," "redistribution," and "exchange" (see his "The Economy as Instituted Process" in *Primitive, Archaic and Modern Economies: Essays of Karl Polanyi*, ed. J. Dalton (Boston: Beacon Press, 1968); also, below, sec. 8.1.

it may be easier to compare the role of market prices on government controls in Belgium and the Netherlands or of investment policies in Poland and Rumania—in both cases the two countries have many common traits— before proceeding to the more complex comparisons of the total systems of countries that are more disparate in their institutions, sizes, and resources.

3. *Measurement without theory.* This approach, as T. C. Koopmans observed in another context, emphasizes the number and wide coverage of observations to the virtual exclusion of explicit a priori specification.[10] No behavioral equations are postulated; no hypotheses based on a priori reasoning are tested on available data. This lack-purpose accumulation of data deprives the observer of the analytical power that formal techniques of statistical inference can provide. One variant of this aberration consists of "fishing for hypotheses" by correlating every variable that can be observed with every other variable and by extracting one's hypotheses from the "statistically significant" rela- tions. The observer following this approach runs the risk of accepting as significant associations that are really due to chance, especially if the number of correlations is very large. The method is also enfeebled by its inability to distinguish among various possible explanations of the associations observed.[11]

By carefully defining the terms employed in the description of a system and by laying the groundwork for the a priori specification of the variables that affect outcomes in each system, I hope that the present work may help pave the way to measurement *with* theory in the comparison of systems.

10. Tjalling C. Koopmans, *Three Essays on the State of Economic Science* (New York: McGraw-Hill, 1957), p. 199.

11. Cf. Franklyn M. Fisher, "Statistical Identifiability," in *International Encyclopedia of the Social Sciences*, ed. David L. Sills (New York: Macmillan Co. and the Free Press, 1968), 15: 201–06.

2

A Basic Vocabulary for System Description

2.1 METHOD

A series of clear operational definitions describing the elements of a system and their modes of interaction is a first but essential step toward understanding how such a system works. The more accurate the definitions, the better we should be able to simulate the system's behavior when different environments or behavioral rules are assumed.

An objective description of an economic system—one that will lend itself to comparisons—must be couched as much as possible in system-free terms.[1] The ideal is that the *primitive* (undefined) terms entering into these definitions be few in number and universal in applicability and meaning. Preferably, these terms should be drawn from disciplines dealing with other (non-economic) parts of the larger system, such as engineering, psychology, and physiology, that have a relatively system-free status, at least from the viewpoint of economics. Terms such as "individuals," "preferences," "stimulus," "intensity," "perception," "communication," and "constraints on behavior" almost meet this requirement. Terms such as "prices," "supervision," "organization," "planning," and "decentralization" do not. Their meanings are frequently influenced by the ideology of the system's participants. If possible they should be defined with the aid of primitives originating outside the economic system or at least from terms that have already been defined with the help of primitives.[2]

Occasionally I shall confer specialized meaning on terms, such as "information," in common usage outside the field of economics although I shall also try to build up definitions from terminologies external to economics. Henceforth, insofar as possible, undefined terms will be enclosed in quotation marks and terms newly defined will be italicized.

Although a value-free terminology is necessary to compare systems, it is not sufficient. We must also define terms in such a way as to make quantifica-

---

1. This is a necessary but not a sufficient condition for "objectivity." It must be recognized that any conceptual approach to the description or comparison of systems is likely to be influenced by the observer's or analyst's values and, more generally, by his *Weltanschauung*.

2. Koopmans and Montias, "On the Description and Comparison of Economic Systems," in A. Eckstein, ed., *Comparison of Economic Systems*, p. 9.

tion of the phenomena we are talking about possible. If, for example, we are interested in "economic activities," we must define the concept with such precision that it will allow an observer, with the requisite information about the characteristics of the activities he is examining, to decide whether a particular activity is or is not economic. I do not think the definitions in this chapter would satisfy a statistician embarking on a survey. But I should hope at least that they would be clear and precise enough to serve as a basis from which a statistician could refine the concepts in the light of the particular problem he wished to study. In addition to the statistician surveying the "real world," I have tried to keep in mind the problems of simulating the behavior of one or more systems on a computer. One criterion of the precision of a definition is whether or not it could be used as a basis for working out a program or a routine that the computer would "understand" and that would bear a reasonable resemblance to the "real-life" phenomena that were meant to be represented.

An example of the constructive method of defining terms that we shall henceforth follow will give the reader an idea of our approach. Consider an "order by a superordinate in a hierarchy to decentralize production decisions by subordinates," a concept requiring so many other terms (both primitive and derived) to define it that it will only be introduced at a much later point in this book. The definition may be derived as follows:

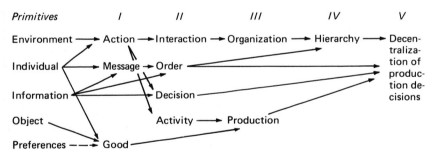

The terms originating outside the economic system are listed in the first column. All the others are directly or indirectly derived from these primitives. An arrow indicates the direct "input" of a term into a definition. The definition of our complex term calls for primitives plus at least four layers of terms of increasing degree of complexity.

The reader will note that all the arrows point to the right, in the direction of terms of increasing complexity. This means that there are no "circular interdependencies" among these definitions: no two terms are defined with reference *to each other*. It is my intention to proceed according to such a unilinear progression, starting from as few primitives as possible, although I cannot guarantee that progress from one layer of definitions to the next will always be as systematic and as sparing in its use of primitives as it should be.

2.2 AN INITIAL VOCABULARY

To illustrate the method of deriving definitions from a limited number of primitives, some undefined terms were introduced in the first chapter to convey to the reader a rough notion of my use of the term "economic system" (from outside which the primitives are supposed to stem). We shall now start again, from the ground up, to define these and other terms that will be used in subsequent chapters.

In addition to logical, mathematical, and statistical concepts, such as set, number, and probability distribution, our basic set of primitives consists of *time, space, individual, object, quantity, perception, preferences,* and *information*.[3] This list will be used as the basis for most of the definitions in this chapter, although it will have to be supplemented in a few cases by primitives borrowed mainly from psychology ("routine," "habits," and so on). The primitives above and all the terms that will be derived refer to aggregated or otherwise simplified *representations* by the observer or comparer of the elements belonging to the items alluded to.

At any one time there is a finite set of individuals (the world's population). There is an infinite (but countable) number of objects (animate, excluding man, and inanimate) that individuals can perceive. A dog, a television signal, and a sun ray are all such objects. Wherever two or more objects are so similar to each other that their difference cannot be perceived by an individual (e.g., drops of milk in a quart), we conceive of them as aggregated into a single object. One of the characteristics of an aggregated object is its quantity (weight, number, and so forth).[4] We can distinguish objects and individuals existing before, during, and after the finite period of time selected by the observer for his intended description or comparison called *period of observation.*

An individual's *initial environment* comprises (1) his personal characteristics —age, sex, preferences, and so on—at the beginning of the period[5] and (2) all objects and individuals, together with their observable characteristics, and all items of information that are external to him at that time. Objects, individuals, and external items of information present during the period make up his

---

3. In the Appendix an attempt is made to derive the term "information" from terms such as "outcome" and "action" that can themselves be derived from our basic set of primitives (excluding "information").

4. For a related but distinct concept, see "homogeneous goods" in chap. 9.

5. In effect we regard the individual's characteristics as inherited from a previous period and therefore external to the period of observation.

contemporary environment,[6] those present at the end of the period his *terminal environment.* An environment for an individual is thus a countable and exhaustive, although for almost any purpose infinite, list of objects, individuals, and items of information.

To simplify the vocabulary, whenever there is no room for ambiguity I shall use the term "environment" without qualifier to denote a contemporary environment. The attribute "initial," if not otherwise qualified, refers to the beginning of a period of observation.

An *action* by an individual, either by itself or in conjunction with actions by one or more other individuals, changes his contemporary or terminal environment in some way. Depending on the "decision-making" model adopted by the observer, the *outcome* of the action may be defined as the perceived change in the environment of the individual performing the action, as the new environment resulting from the action, or as elements in the initial environment that have undergone a change "resulting" from the action.[7] In general, the context will make clear which of these definitions we have in mind. Whichever definition we choose, we may define an action more precisely as a function from the set of states of an individual's environment to the set of outcomes.

When we write that the individual perceives his environment in a particular way (or with the aid of a particular instrument), we mean that to each state e in E there corresponds an image, or *message,* y. The function η mapping E into the set of all possible messages Y is called an information-gathering function.[8] We may associate with each instrument for observing individual i's environment (a telephone, a microscope, and so forth) and with each distinct individual from whom he may obtain messages a distinct information-gathering function. The set of messages that an individual has collected in all past periods is his *information set.*

The action of *choosing* from among the elements of the finite set S may be represented as a function associating with the entire set S a single element of S, if only one element is chosen at a time, or a single element of ζ, the set of all possible subsets of S, if any number of elements of S may be chosen at a time.[9] In either case, the chosen element is an image of the choice function.[10]

---

6. If the period is long enough for these objects, individuals, and items of information to undergo change, there may be many sets of these environmental elements in a contemporary environment.

7. For details, see below, pp. 73–76.

8. See Appendix A.

9. The set ζ is called the *power set* of S.

10. We may extend this concept to a *choice correspondence*, which associates with the set S a particular subset of S or of ζ normally containing more than one element. It then remains to be seen how the individual chooses—perhaps by random methods—a single element from that subset.

If an individual in period t can choose in his information set an element perceived in a previous period, he may be said to have *remembered* it. To remember every element j ($j = 1, \ldots, n$) in his (finite) information set, he would have to have a different choice function $f_j (S)$ for every element j in S.[11] All information that can be remembered in period t is contained in an individual's *memory* for period t.

The memories of other individuals are included in each individual's environment. Since all surviving information about the past is contained either in the memories of individuals or in objects (e.g., books, computer tapes), the environments of individuals at any time preceding the period of observation can be ignored, except insofar as they are reflected or contained in contemporary objects or memories.

A *decision* by individual i is a choice among the actions or the sequences of actions that i considers feasible. The decision is *contingent* if the choice is limited to the subset of all actions considered feasible for a particular future state or for a subset of the possible states of the environment.

Given a number of rather strong assumptions about the behavior of individuals, their "preferences" regarding the outcomes of their alternative actions and their "subjective expectations" about future states of their environment can be inferred from the actions they actually undertake.[12] In the framework of this model we say that an individual i *does not prefer* action a' to action a if, under environmental state e, he would undertake a rather than a'. The strong assumption is then made that if outcome o is not preferred to o' given environmental state e, then o is not preferred to o' given any state e' distinct from e. The implication is that preferences over outcomes can be dissociated from the states in which they occur. This assumption will be reconsidered in chapter 6.

An *event* is a subset of E (the set of all possible states), each element of which is associated with the same outcome for a given action a in A (the set of all possible actions for an individual). In other words, if both e and e' belong to event z and if action a leads to outcome o under e, it will also lead to outcome o under e'. The set Z of all possible events is a partition of E (i.e., every element e in E belongs to one and only one element z in Z).

Suppose that action a by individual i results in outcome o with the occurrence of event z, a subset of the set E of possible states, and in outcome f in

---

11. If he can no longer distinguish j from originally distinct elements in a subset J of S, we may write that J is the image-set of a choice correspondence $\phi_J (S)$ (for every subset J of indistinguishable elements). In that case the individual may be said to have an *imperfect memory*. Complete *amnesia* occurs when J is identical to S. The concept of an imperfect memory is similar to that of a *coarser partitioning of the elements of S* in the information theory outlined in Appendix A.

12. For details, see Jacob Marschak and Roy Radner, *Economic Theory of Teams* (New Haven: Yale University Press, 1972), chap. 1 and Appendix A.

case z does not occur. Suppose also that i prefers o to f, so that o may be called "success" and f "failure." These outcomes, which are ranked in the decision maker's preference ordering, are then the alternative *payoffs* of action a. Let some other action a' result in the same successful outcome o as before if z', an event distinct from z, occurs and in the same failure f if it does not. Clearly, as long as the values of o and f to the individual concerned are independent of the states in which they occur, he will only choose a over a' if he believes z to be at least at probable as z'. If this is so, it may be said that i attaches a higher *subjective probability* to event z than to z'. Provided that the individual's beliefs are independent of his tastes, it should not matter what payoffs o and f happen to stand for (amounts of money gained or lost, target achieved or not achieved, or any other reward).

Given a sufficient number of possible actions and states (to ensure continuity), these and some other (weaker) assumptions[13] imply the possibility of representing an individual i's preferences by means of two functions, one associating a subjective probability with each event and another—called *utility function*—mapping his preference ordering over outcomes into the set of real numbers.[14]

The *expected utility* of action a depends on the utility of the possible outcomes of a. Let z be an event that, given a, generates outcome o. The utility of the outcome may then be written $u(z, a)$. The expected utility Ω of action a is defined as follows:

$$\Omega(a) = \sum_{z \in \mathcal{Z}} u(z, a) \, \pi(z), \tag{2.1}$$

where $\pi(z)$ is the subjective probability the individual attaches to event z and $\mathcal{Z}$ is the set of all possible events. "$z \in \mathcal{Z}$" signifies "for any event z in the set $\mathcal{Z}$ of all possible events."

One version of the model of decision making under uncertainty summarized above supposes that each individual behaves in such a way as to maximize $\Omega(a)$ over the set of his possible actions. It is also compatible, however, with a model which assumes that decision maker i *satisfices* in the following sense. There is some number α that leaves i "indifferent" among all actions for which $\Omega(a) \geq \alpha$. "Indifferent" may be taken to mean that if there are n actions that satisfy the above inequality, the "objective probability" that any one of them will be carried out will be $1/n$.

Both these versions presuppose that the decision maker is "indifferent toward risk" or "risk neutral." This means that if both a and a' yield the same expected utility, he will be indifferent between the two actions, even

13. One critical assumption is that preferences under uncertainty be *transitive*: if, under state e, a is not preferred to b and b is not preferred to c, then a is not preferred to c (under this state).
14. Marschak and Radner, op. cit., p. 15.

though the expected variances and higher moments of a and a' may appreciably differ. A *risk-averse* individual, on the other hand, will prefer a to a' when $\Omega(a) = \Omega(a')$, provided that the expected variance associated with the outcomes of a is smaller than that associated with the outcomes of a'. Risk preference is defined by substituting "larger" for "smaller" in the preceding sentence. Risk aversion must be postulated to explain the behavior of individuals *insuring* themselves against certain large losses or relinquishing a part of their payoff to other individuals willing to assume this risk. The success of lotteries organized in such a way that the combined value of all prizes given out is smaller than the value of the participations sold can only be explained by the risk preference of the participants, at least on the assumption that their subjective probabilities correspond precisely to the objective chances of receiving prizes and that they can correctly evaluate the expected payoffs.

Individuals' attitudes toward risk can easily be incorporated into a model of decision making by assuming that their utility depends not only on the first moment of the subjective probability distribution of utility payoffs but on the second and possibly higher moments as well (e.g., on the expected variance, the expected bias of the distribution). For example, in certain models decision makers are supposed to choose the action that will yield their preferred combination of expected payoff and expected variance out of the set of all attainable combinations of these two moments, given the possible states of the environment and their variability.[15] From now on, when I speak of an individual's choice of an action maximizing his expected utility, I shall mean that he expects his action to maximize his utility, including his preference or aversion to risk.

Individuals typically satisfice under conditions of imperfect or limited information; satisficing also occurs when it would be too costly or time consuming for the decision maker to calculate all the possible outcomes and their probabilities necessary to choose an action or a sequence of actions maximizing his expected utility as defined above. The first constraint on utility maximization has been called "information impactedness" and the second "bounded rationality" (by Oliver E. Williamson).[16] Analytical convenience largely determines whether one wishes to think of an individual as satisficing by reason of these limitations or as utility maximizing while subject to constraints on the availability of information and the time or cost necessary to achieve an optimum. In either case it is evident that these limitations are very serious

15. These models were originally developed in connection with the analysis of financial portfolios. The basic reference here is to Harry M. Markowitz, *Portfolio Selection: Efficient Diversification of Investments* (New York: John Wiley, 1959). See also Donald Hester and James Tobin, eds., *Studies of Portfolio Behavior* (New York: John Wiley, 1967).

16. "Markets and Hierarchies: Some Elementary Considerations," *American Economic Review* 63 (May 1973): 317.

in the real world and should, insofar as possible, be explicitly recognized in any description of decision-making processes pretending to a degree of realism. The system comparer in particular must be alert to the various ways whereby system rules facilitate or impede the flow of information to decision makers. Many examples of such effects will be discussed in the course of this book. The influence of system rules on the bounds to rational calculation, on the other hand, is more devious and subtle and cannot always be captured. How far and deep an individual chooses to calculate before making a decision or adopting a policy may depend on who will be affected by it and on the extent to which the decision maker "identifies" with the persons who are likely to be affected. The system structure may then impinge on the bounds to rationality via the rules governing the extent of the decision maker's "responsibility" for the benefactions he may confer and the harm he may inflict on others.

The formula for maximizing expected utility shown in equation 2.1 may be modified to allow for limitations on the information available to the decision maker. We may model his behavior in this situation as follows. We assume that his decisions will be based on messages, denoted y, drawn from his environment E via an information-gathering function η. A decision function α determines the action a that the individual will take on receipt of message y, so that $a = \alpha\,(y)$. Since, by the definition of an event, all the states in event z will generate the same outcome when action a is taken, we may, as in equation 2.1, aggregate states into events as arguments of the decision maker's utility function. The utility of the outcome resulting from state z and action a taken on receipt of message $y\,[=\eta\,(e)]$ may be written as: $u\{z, \alpha[\eta\,(e)]\}$. The (conditional) probability that event z actually occurred when information y was obtained is denoted $\pi[z|\eta\,(e)]$. The individual's expected utility is

$$\sum_{e \in E} u\{z, \alpha[\eta\,(e)]\}\pi[z|\eta\,(e)]. \tag{2.2}$$

This expression will be maximized when the optimal decision rule α^* and the optimal information structure η^* available to the decision maker have been selected. If the individual satisfices rather than utility-maximizes, he may stick to a decision rule α and a structure η that are not optimal so long as they generate a satisfactory utility level, given the probability distribution on E. A perceived change in the probability distribution over the states of his environment may then trigger a search for a better decision rule, for more accurate information, or for both.

When one or more of the assumptions of the model inferring utility and subjective probability from individual behavior cannot be maintained (especially when the assumption that an individual's preferences over outcomes are independent of his beliefs is inconsistent with observed evidence), it may be necessary to introduce "preferences" and "subjective probabilities" as primitives. For instance, we may associate an individual's preferences and subjective probabilities with possible states (defined to include the outcomes resulting from an individual's actions), even though neither these preferences nor these subjective probabilities could possibly be "read off" from his actions. My guess is that the behavioristic theory of decision making under uncertainty may be more readily applied to decisions made by "producers," whose actions result in outcomes such as "output," "profit," or "market share" (the preference ordering over which may be invariant to the states of the environment in which they occur), than to the decisions of "consumers," for whom this assumption is less likely to hold. (This problem will be considered again in section 6.1.)

The formula for expected utility under limited information in equation 2.2 may be deemed unrealistic in another way. It may be argued that "certainty about events" has merely been displaced by "certainty about the probability distribution of these events." But this would be an inaccurate (and unfair) interpretation of the formula. An individual may have only the vaguest notion about the probability of occurrence of different states and still behave as if he were maximizing expected utility in the sense of equation 2.2. If his information is extremely poor, he may assume that all events that are likely to occur at all have the same chance of occurring. He may, particularly if he is risk averse, play safe by choosing the action that will yield the maximum utility upon occurrence of the least advantageous event. (This is sometimes called a "maxmin" strategy.)

We now revert to our constructive sequence of definitions, most of which fortunately will not raise the conceptual problems that we have just encountered with preferences, subjective probabilities, and expectations.

When individual i chooses action a for individual i' to perform, the message from i to i' informing him of i's choice is an *order*, provided that (1) i believes that the set of possible actions open to i' contains more than one possible action (not necessarily including a!), and (2) i expects that i' will perform action a (that he will "comply" or at least that he would comply with other similarly worded messages from i).

A *rule* is a message stipulating or constraining the actions of a set of participants for an indefinite period and under specified states of these individuals' environments.

A *policy* is a class of contingent decisions, frequently announced (conveyed by message to other, not necessarily designated, participants) with a view to creating stable expectations about the future decisions of the policy maker.

The *intention* or *goal* of an action is the preferred state of an individual's environment, which he expects to bring about as a consequence of this action.

An *interaction* is a set of actions, simultaneous, sequential, or both, such that each participant in the interacting subset of individuals changes the perceived environment of *some* participant(s) in the subset. The interaction is said to be *reciprocal* when every participant in the subset affects every other participant.[17]

An *activity* is a repeatable action. *Production* is an activity that during the course of a certain period transforms one collection of objects, individuals, or both, called *inputs*, into another collection of these objects and individuals, called *outputs*.[18]

A *technology* is a list of activities transforming inputs into outputs according to information available to some set of individuals. It may be thought of as a long list of commodity specifications together with a long list of descriptions of possible activities.

An *organization*, defined with reference to a specific set of activities, is a set of regularly interacting individuals called the *members* of the organization, whose actions are constrained by the formal or informal rules specific to that organization. For any two members of the organization, we require that there be a *chain* of interactions connecting them, that is, a sequence $i, k, l, \ldots, p, q$ of different members such that $(i, k), (k, l), \ldots, (p, q)$ are interacting pairs (not necessarily for the same activities or activities in the set).[19] Among the basic rules of any organization are those that determine how its membership shall be composed and how the potentially different interests of its members shall be aggregated (e.g., through voting procedures).

Members of certain organizations issue rules and orders concerning certain activities that normally call forth compliant actions not only from their own members but also from individuals, defined by their residence, place of birth, or some other principle, who do not belong to that organization.[20] These order-and-rule-issuing organizations are called *ruling organizations* (federal government, Supreme Court of the United States, and so on).

17. Interaction, as defined in Koopmans and Montias (op. cit., p. 21), corresponds to "*reciprocal* interaction" in the present text. I have chosen this definition because it circumvents the problem of finding a convenient term for nonmutual interactions.

18. If different outputs are obtained from a given collection of inputs (depending, e.g., on the various possible states of the environment of the individuals performing the activity), the transformation may be viewed as a stochastic process.

19. For a refinement of this definition, see sec. 11.1.

20. In primitive tribes the ruling organization may include all adult members of the organization constituting the entire "society." In accordance with our definitions of "polity," "economy," and "system," which are meant in general to apply to both primitive and modern "societies," we assume that some of the most basic "institutions" and patterns of regular interaction among individuals in a system normally last through at least the period of description or comparison— an assumption that may not be valid for primitive societies. Some of these societies, for example, may not even be "clearly bounded in territory or in membership in the sense that more advanced societies are" (Talcott Parsons, *Societies: Evolutionary and Comparative Perspectives*, [Englewood Cliffs, N.J.: Prentice-Hall, 1966], p. 33.)

Consider a set of individuals responding with a compliant action, if only by a message acknowledging an order received, to all the ruling organizations affecting their behavior (e.g., from the fire department of their township to the ministry of interior of their federal government) but who themselves are not members of these ruling organizations. Now enlarge the set of these individuals to include every individual complying to some degree with the rules and orders of this set of ruling organizations, which we shall term collectively the *polity* of these individuals.[21] These individuals, now including the members of the ruling organizations, are said to constitute its *subjects*. (It should be evident that the polity may encompass more ruling organizations than the "nation," a term we may borrow from political science without definition.)

The *participants* in a system may include all the subjects of a polity or a subset of them, such as those that correspond to a region, a political subdivision, or a city.

The *structure of the system* to which the set of individuals selected belongs consists of all the formal and informal rules constraining the actions of these participants. The refinement and interpretation of rules by individual bodies are also part of the system structure, which includes both the rules initially in effect and those introduced during the period of description or comparison. The provisions for creating or dissolving organizations, modifying relations between organizations, amending the rules, and otherwise influencing patterns of interaction are themselves considered part of this structure.

Not all rules in a given system structure have the same "status." Certain rules take precedence over others in the sense that the latter cannot be "legitimately" imposed if they infringe on the former. Rules stipulating how other rules can be made may be termed *constitutional*. The order of precedence of rules is also part of the system structure.

We now have a set of individuals I "participating" in an undefined "system" and a system structure s. Let $a_t, a_{t+1}, \ldots, a_{t+\tau}$ be the sequence of "economic" actions[22] undertaken by a set of individuals in a period of ob-

---

21. Note that religious organizations qualify as ruling organizations only if they are able to govern or at least influence by their rules or orders the behavior of individuals who are not their members. Thus, if the Pope prohibits or permits eating fish on Friday and practicing American Catholics comply with his order, this does not mean that they are the subjects of a polity with its headquarters outside the United States, at least as long as we allow that they are members of the (international) Catholic organization. The same applies to orders by the top management of multinational corporations to officials operating in various countries. Our definitions might break down for the study of medieval society, in which the Church's rules and orders did influence the behavior of nonmembers (Jews, heretics, and so forth). It is not clear in this case whether the polity of a nation could be unambiguously defined, an ambiguity that is inherent in this historical situation.

22. The term "economic" will be defined in chap. 6.

servation of duration τ, and denote this sequence a.[23] Let o stand for $o_t, \ldots,$ $o_{t+\tau}$, the sequence of outcomes observed in the period.

We may wish to define an economic system during period t to $t + \tau$ as the quadruple (I, a, o, s) for the period. However, this definition is a mere amalgam; it does not even suggest what *might* be the relations among I, a, o, and s. A more ambitious definition of system can be constructed by analogy with "functional systems" used in engineering. We again denote by A the set of all the conceivable sequences of action vectors (such as a) that individuals in I might undertake and by O the set of possible outcomes of these actions. The *system* may be defined as a particular subset of $A \times O$, that is, a subset of all possible pairs (a, o), where a is in A and o in O. If a system S is functional, the pairs (a, o) and (a, o') will only occur in S if o is identical to o' (i.e., if o is a proper function of a).[24]

To understand a system we must find out why action–outcome pairs belonging to a particular subset of $A \times O$ can occur but no others. This means that we must (1) study the restrictions on individuals' choices of actions imposed by their preferences, system-structure rules, and environments, and (2) ascertain the relation between the actions these individuals undertake and their outcomes in given environments.

An example of a highly simplified economy, described as a system, will illustrate the above definitions.[25] The period of observation τ is divided into n subperiods $1, \ldots, n$. The only stimulus observed in the environment of this hypothetical economy is an external "price" p_j $(j = 1, \ldots, n)$, a real nonnegative random number, for a good g that may be imported or exported. The m individuals in I are constrained by their system structure s to act in such a way as to satisfy the following equation:

$$a_j = \sum_{i=1}^{m} a_{ij} = \alpha(\bar{p} - p_j) \qquad (j = 1, \ldots, n), \qquad (2.3)$$

where a_{ij} is the action of individual i in the time period j, and α and $\bar{p}$ are positive real numbers. Interpretation: when p_j is lower than $\bar{p}$, the individuals in I collectively buy (import) an amount $\alpha(\bar{p} - p_j)$. When p_j is higher than $\bar{p}$, they sell (export) the amount $\alpha(\bar{p} - p_j)$.

In each period j, the economy's outcomes are determined as follows:

$$o_j = o_{j-1} + a_j \qquad (j = 1, \ldots, n), \qquad (2.4)$$

where o_j is the stock of good g in period j.

---

23. In every vector $a_{t+\tau}$, there will be m subvectors, each with a potentially different number of elements, where m is the number of individuals in I.

24. M. D. Mesarovic, D. Macko, and Y. Takahara, *Theory of Hierarchical Multi-level Systems* (New York: Academic Press, 1970), p. 62.

25. This example is elaborated from a simple system in ibid., pp. 69–70.

Equation 2.3 maps every n-tuple of prices $(p_1, \ldots, p_n)$ into an n-tuple of actions $(a_1, \ldots, a_n)$. Given an initial stock o (i.e., an initial environment $e_0 = \bar{o}$), equation 2.4 maps every n-tuple of actions into an n-tuple of outcomes $(o_1, \ldots, o_n)$.

If we let $A \equiv A_1 \times A_2 \times \ldots \times A_n$ and $O \equiv O_1 \times O_2 \times \ldots \times O_n$ where the sets of possible actions A_1 to A_n and of possible outcomes O_1 to O_n comprise all real numbers, then clearly

$$S_{\bar{o}} \subseteq A \times O,$$

where $S_{\bar{o}}$ is the set of pairs (a, o) satisfying equations 2.3 and 2.4 given the initial condition $e_0 = \bar{o}$.

$S_{\bar{o}}$ is a functional system because for every n-tuple of actions $(a_1, \ldots, a_n)$ there is one and only one n-tuple of outcomes $(o_1, \ldots, o_n)$.

Suppose now that e_0 was allowed to take on any value in set E_0. Then we have

$$S = \bigcup_{e_0 \in E_0} S_{e_0} \subseteq A \times O.$$

S, the union of all the sets of pairs determined by initial environments e_0 in E_0, is still a system but no longer a functional one, since, for a given n-tuple of actions, there will be as many n-tuples of outcomes as there are distinct elements e_0 in E_0.

Every economy will be analyzed as if it could be described as a system, although of course we may never know precisely how a given system is "put together" (just as one may believe that a watch in working order can be represented as a functional system, at least in a "normal" environment, although one might not know precisely how to do so).

We are now ready to define the *environment of an economy*, which was used as a primitive in the above example. We consider the entire sociopolitical system of an economy, including its political constitution and all its rules insofar as they are not already regarded as part of its economic structure, as belonging to its environment.[26] The *initial environment* of an economy includes the resources (capital stock, population, natural resources) and information, *including technology*, available to participants at the beginning of the period.[27] The initial population is composed of individuals with a given age and sex distribution, endowed with preferences, attitudes, habits, memories, beliefs,

26. The dividing line between the political and the economic structure of a system is arbitrary and may be adjusted to the problem of comparison at hand. Criminal laws and the police and judicial apparatus for enforcing them may be regarded as part of the environment for a comparison of national incomes in one system and as part of the system structure for a comparison of economic losses due to crime in another.

27. Note that the resources and information "available" at the beginning of the period become endogenous variables during the period.

and all other "internal" determinants of their behavior. The information contained in an incomplete interaction—one whose initial actions antedate the beginning of the period—is also part of the initial environment (example: an obligation incurred from the previous period).

The *contemporary environment* of the economy comprises external technologies perceived by any of the system's participants, actions by individuals outside the system, and states of the world strictly exogenous to the system insofar as they affect economic activities within the system.[28] Noneconomic actions (political, social) taken by participants in the total system may be considered a part of the economy's contemporary environment insofar as they have any impact on activities going on within the economic system. However, to the extent that we may be describing and comparing economic systems from their simplified models, the influence or impact of an external agent should be significant enough to be considered in the model before it can be included in the economy's environment. Two economies will only have the same contemporary environment if the probability distributions of the states of the world affecting both sets of participants are the same. Even though such a coincidence could never occur in the real world, this criterion of "ideal coincidence" will serve to remind us that the environments of two economies will only be similar if they face not only similar exogenous states but if the variance, range, or other measure of variation of these states is similar (e.g., if the fluctuations in the world prices for their imported and exported products are approximately the same). Finally, the *terminal environment* may be defined as the initial environment of the economy for the period following the termination of the period of description or comparison.

2.3 A Campaign Plan

Our fundamental concern, we stress again, is with the comparison of system rules and of their effects on outcomes. We do not presume that every rule will be obeyed by all the individuals to whom it is meant to apply. However, every rule of interest to us will, to some extent at least, be enforced and will be associated with certain negative payoffs or *penalties* for transgression, ranging from the deprivation of life to social disapproval, which, whatever the individual's attitude toward risk may be, will affect the distribution of the payoffs associated with each of his possible actions and hence will influence

---

28. In most cases weather conditions would be strictly exogenous to the system and hence would constitute part of the environment. But an insect plague might be endogenous to the system since it might be significantly affected by the rules of the system structure concerning the use of DDT or other insecticides. Strictly speaking, the insect population as it existed at the beginning of the period of observation would be a part of the initial environment, but the insect population *during* the period of observation would be an endogenous variable affected by the policies pursued by participants (as well as by exogenous variables such as weather conditions).

his decisions. In general we may safely assume that most individuals are risk neutral or risk averse when they consider illegal actions that may trigger penalties. This implies that rules—whether they be system-wide or limited in their application to the members of an organization, whether they prescribe or proscribe—do place restraints on people's behavior. The system analyst, concerned with the impact of rules on outcomes, may of course have to take into consideration the extent to which rules are actually enforced by the courts, the executives of ruling organizations, and other guardians of the law. No one can understand why "planning" is largely deprived of influence or why there is no mortgage banking in many developing countries if he does not realize that these countries lack effective machinery for enforcing the plans in one case and for assisting banks in the repossession of assets held by defaulting debtors in the other.

This book might have been organized along the lines of a scheme for classifying rules according to their impact on basic types of decisions such as will be outlined below. But this principle of organization could not be reconciled with the idea of developing complex from simple terms in building a vocabulary for system description and of investigating methodically the component parts of systems. Still, I think it may be useful to sketch a broad classification of rules, without pretending to an exhaustive listing, and to indicate where each class will be discussed in subsequent chapters.

All rules govern (1) interactions among individuals, (2) the relations of individuals to objects, or (3) both. Technically, most rules belong to the first or third group because there are relatively few rules prescribing or proscribing individual actions regarding objects that do not involve some interaction among different individuals. (A counterexample is a rule prohibiting the manufacture of alcohol in homemade stills.) However this may be, in the following tentative classification I shall aggregate with group 2 all rules that chiefly affect man's relation to objects, irrespective of the interactions that may accompany the actions concerned.

    I. Rules governing interactions among individuals
        A. Organizational rules: who may belong to what organization (creation, mergers and liquidation of organizations, nationalization, and so on) (chapters 11–12)
        B. Informational rules: who may tell what to whom
            1. Orders (chapter 8)
            2. Proposals (chapter 8)
            3. Advertising and propaganda (chapter 8)
            4. Secrecy laws (chapter 7)
        C. Benevolent or malevolent actions (other than externalities) (not covered)

   II. Rules governing the relation of individuals to objects
      A. Consumption rules (e.g., sumptuary laws) (chapter 6)
      B. Production rules (inputs, outputs, technology) (chapters 7, 15, 16)
      C. Laws regulating foreign trade (not covered)
  III. Rules governing interactions among individuals and the relation of individuals to objects
      A. Exclusion rules
         1. Custody, property and terms on which it may be exchanged (including price controls) (chapter 9)
         2. Lending and borrowing (chapter 18)
      B. Rules setting goals and purposes of organizations (chapter 11)
      C. Regulation of externalities (chapter 9)
      D. Distribution of organizational payoffs
         1. Taxation and subsidies (chapter 17)
         2. Incentive systems (chapter 13)
         3. Distribution of dividends, reinvestment, and other disposal of payoff (chapter 17)
         4. Rationing of consumer goods and services (not covered)
         5. Laws regulating insurance and lottery activities (not covered)
      E. Planning systems (chapters 14 and 17)

Before resuming our constructive sequence of definitions and our discussion of rules in chapter 6, we shall devote three chapters to what may be called the "macroeconomics" of system comparison: the criteria for comparing and evaluating according to a common norm the outcomes of different systems (chapter 3), the desiderata (common and specific) pursued by decision makers in each system that have a decisive influence on system outcomes and their relation to efficiency in the use of resources (chapter 4), and the statistical problems bound up in the quantitative comparison of outcomes and in efforts to disentangle the effects of system rules from other determinants of outcomes (chapter 5).

Part 2
The Macroeconomics of the Comparison of Systems

3

System Structure and Normed Outcomes

3.1 NORMS AND OUTCOMES[1]

In this chapter we shall focus on the measurable outcomes of system-wide rules and policies. A system's outcomes for our purposes will comprise all those aspects or consequences of the system structure and of the policies, decisions, or actions of the system's participants that are positively or negatively valued either by individuals within the system or by observers without.

In order to be measured and compared across systems, outcomes must be highly aggregated. Furthermore, if we wish to disentangle the separate effects on outcomes of environment, system rules, and policies, these separate factors must also be measured in broad aggregates or described in summary terms. We cannot consider the preferences of every decision maker; neither can the policies of every organization be taken into account. Even the complex of laws and traditions that impose constraints on individual decisions in every system must be greatly simplified if we wish to single out a few rules that are likely to have a discernible effect on aggregate outcomes.

No meaningful comparison of systems or of their structures is possible without at least the implicit application of some *norm* for evaluating their outcomes. Such a norm may be a function that maps vectors of outcomes into scalars (sometimes called "levels of aggregate welfare"). Or it may be a rough rule that will in effect convert a short list of perceived outcomes into a system rating such as "good," "bad," or "indifferent."

Norms are often implicit, as are those that guide us in the selection of certain system traits in preference to others in a seemingly descriptive comparison. A norm may also be limited by the perception of the comparer, or its presence and nature may escape the perception of some or most of his readers. But the conscious and unconscious motivations of the investigator and the natural selection by which individual studies enter into the cumulative record of social science results tend to introduce the underlying norms and make them apparent over time.

---

1. Parts of this section, with minor changes, are taken verbatim from Koopmans and Montias, "On the Description and Comparison of Economic Systems," in A. Eckstein, ed., *Comparison of Economic Systems*, pp. 41–50.

Norms become more visible when observed intersystem differences in various system traits are brought together and weighed against each other. An *explicit norm* (hereafter often briefly a *norm*) is defined as an evaluation function (welfare function, goal attainment function) of all outcomes that represents the preferences of some individual or group pertinent to the comparison.

For any given norm, we shall call *desiderata* those outcomes on which the norm depends positively at observed levels of these outcomes.[2] *Odiosa* are those on which the norm depends negatively at observed levels of the outcomes. The *common* desiderata for all modern economic systems, defined at the level of the nation-state, include (1) a high level of per capita consumption of goods and services, (2) growth in per capita consumption, (3) equity, (4) the increased provision of social services and public goods, (5) stability of employment and incomes, and (6) national strength. A common odiosum is the pollution of air, water, and other natural resources. We shall describe these and other desiderata in greater detail in the next chapter.

If we denote by o_i the column array (vector) of outcomes that we have selected as significant for system i, the norm n we deem appropriate to the evaluation and comparison of the outcomes observed in this system is some function of all these outcomes yielding a single number $n(o_i)$ for *each* system $i(i = 1, \ldots, H$, where H is the total number of systems to be compared).

Suppose, for instance, that o_i consisted of only three elements, consumption per head (C_i), the percentage rate of growth of national income during the period of comparison ($\dot{Y}_i$), and the fraction of disposable national income accruing to the bottom quartile of the income distribution ($\bar{Q}_i$). Then our norm function for system i might be represented as follows:

$$n(o_i) = n(C_i, \dot{Y}_i, \bar{Q}_i).$$

Since all three arguments of the function may be considered desiderata at normally observed levels in modern systems, we may write

$$\frac{\delta n(o_i)}{\delta C_i} > 0, \frac{\delta n(o_i)}{\delta \dot{Y}_i} > 0, \frac{\delta n(o_i)}{\delta \bar{Q}_i} > 0 \text{ for all } i.$$

Small increments in any of these variables will yield a positive increment in the norm function or welfare indicator for that system. The form of the norm function (e.g., linear or nonlinear, arithmetic or geometric sum of the arguments) as well as the weights attached to each argument will be determined by the nature of the preferences entering the norm, the information available on these preferences, and the compromise that must normally be made be-

---

2. On policy outcomes that may be desirable at some levels and undesirable at others, see Henri Theil, *Economic Forecasts and Policy* (Amsterdam: North–Holland, 1961), pp. 406–07.

tween precision on the one hand and manipulative ease or convenience of representation on the other. We shall return to these alternative norms in 3.4.

3.2 RELATION OF OUTCOMES TO ENVIRONMENT, SYSTEM STRUCTURE, AND POLICIES

If one compares observed outcomes in different systems or economies, differences in outcomes will generally reflect such differences as are present in all components of environment, system structure, and policy.

Symbolically, if e denotes the environment, s system structure, p_s policies pursued by the participants under system structure s, and o the outcomes observed during the period of comparison, we then may write

$$o = f(e, s, p_s) \qquad (3.1)$$

for the grand relationships we should all like to know and understand. Even though our actual knowledge is pitifully small compared with the complexity of the relationships in question, writing them out in this explicit way may help in their discussion. The implied assumption is that, in a manner subject in principle to objective inquiry and explicit description, the laws of physics, chemistry, technology, agronomy, human and animal physiology circumscribe what can be achieved by the individuals in a system with a given structure.[3]

We recall that the initial environment of a system in the period of observation or comparison includes the preferences of its participants at the end of the preceding period. The rules of organizations (a part of the system structure), together with the preferences of their members, including their attitude toward risk, may be thought to determine the goals pursued by the decision makers in these organizations (e.g., the maximizing behavior of enterprise managers). In chapter 15 we shall consider some simple models designed to predict certain outcomes of systems characterized by different modes of organizational behavior.

The goals pursued by organizations, the initial capital/labor ratio, mineral wealth, climate and soil, the geographical location of other nations important for trade, national security, or influence, are all examples of environmental variables that codetermine, say, the consumption–growth–security locus attainable with the "best" rules, customs, and traditions making up a system structure. The use of observations on economies with markedly different environments for the empirical comparison of systems therefore requires the econometric estimation of the vector function f, or at least of the first and possibly second derivatives of important outcomes in f with respect to significantly different environmental variables.

---

3. Koopmans and Montias, op. cit., p. 35.

A similar problem arises in regard to the policy variables p_s. The very nature (as distinct from the numerical values) of these variables will in general depend on the system structure. This is particularly true for the policies of ruling organizations. It may well be true also for those of other participants. One may take the view that one wishes to compare systems under the policies actually or typically in use in each system during the period(s) of the comparison. In that case, there is no new econometric problem of separating the effects of policies from those of system structure. However, the principal reason for the distinction between system structure and policies is that the latter can be changed more easily than the former. One may therefore wish also to compare systems on an assumption that, at least on the level of ruling organizations, the best policies available within the institutional and normative constraints of the system are applied in each system. To do this would require —in addition to estimation of the values $f(e_0, s_i, p_{s_i})$ of the outcome vectors f for some standardized environment e_0 and for the (s_i, p_{s_i}) combinations observed in the systems labeled $i = 1, 2, \ldots, H$—the further estimation of first and second derivatives of important outcomes in f with regard to important components of p_{s_i} in those countries where policy is deemed clearly nonoptimal.[4]

So far most comparative studies have singled out the impact of environment on outcomes, neglecting system structure and policies. When economists have attempted to measure aggregate production functions from cross-section data by relating gross national product in each economy to its supply of capital, labor, and other factors, they have implicitly assumed that system structure and policies mattered less, at least for this particular outcome, than the initial conditions in the environment of these economies. Is this neglect justified? For some studies, the "signal" emitted by system rules may be so dominated by the "noise" of the other arguments in the outcome function that it cannot be detected. In other words the system structure must sometimes be considered part of the error term in the regressions. However, the comparer whose main concern is with system differences ought to try to set up his statistical tests in such a way that the impact of the system structure on at least some outcomes can be separated out from the other arguments.

3.3 EFFECTS OF ENVIRONMENT ON SYSTEM STRUCTURE AND POLICIES

In grand equation 3.1 we specified that policies were constrained by system rules. Another significant interdependency is that of the system structure itself on the environment. We readily observe that certain rules will be appropriate or suitable only in a given environment. Economies characterized by specific environmental features will then generally be associated with a

4. Ibid., pp. 36–37.

narrow range of system rules. This complicates the task of disentangling the effects of system rules from the environment since, in a comparison of a number of distinct economies, we may totally lack observations that would allow us to infer how an economy might perform under an alternative set of rules. This difficulty is recognizable to econometricians as an extreme case of multicollinearity.

A few examples will show that this phenomenon is by no means a curiosum of comparative economics. Suppose we were interested in the effects of (1) level of development (e_1) and size of country (e_2); (2) centralization of decision making (s); and (3) propensity to trade with foreign countries (p_s) on an outcome related to efficiency such as gross domestic product per unit of combined labor and capital (o).[5] In our sample of countries to be compared, we might discover that every country that was highly developed and small in size was relatively decentralized and had a high propensity to trade. If so, we should not have a single observation at our disposal that would indicate how highly developed small countries might perform on our efficiency scale under a set of highly centralized system rules. Under extreme environmental conditions, the rules actually in effect may be the only ones that will allow the system to survive or at least to perform sufficiently well to forestall a political upset.

An example of two contiguous systems each of which may be viable because of the presence of the other in its environment is that of Hong Kong and communist China. I should think that the Chinese leaders would not be able to run their economy in precisely the same manner if they could not depend on yearly earnings amounting to several hundred million dollars in foreign exchange from Hong Kong. Similarly the British Crown Colony of Hong Kong might not be able to run such an open and laissez-faire operation if it did not have the Chinese hinterland to provide it with cheap immigrant labor and material inputs. We have an instance here of what may be called the symbiosis of contrasting system structures.

One might also wonder whether the Communist party leaders of Yugoslavia could have decentralized the Yugoslav economic system in the early 1950s without United States aid or whether Castro could have continued, as long as he did, to infuse romantic and utopian elements in the management of the Cuban economy if it had not been for the subsidies he received from his Soviet allies. These are rather loose speculations that probably cannot be subjected to statistical testing. More systematic, though still controversial, evidence on this issue has been brought forward by Wittfogel,[6] who suggests that in certain environments special forms of hierarchic organization, run by bureaucracies with virtually unlimited power over the participants in their system, may

5. For a discussion of this measure of total factor productivity, see below, sec. 4.3.
6. Karl A. Wittfogel, *Oriental Despotism* (New Haven: Yale University Press, 1957), chap. 3.

have arisen in response to the need for coping with drought (through irrigation), with floods (through flood control), and with other negative factors in their environment. That the relation is not one-to-one, however, may be shown by invoking the example of the Netherlands, where a rather permissive and decentralized economic system developed in the seventeenth century in the face of recurrent incursions by the sea and of invasions by foreign armies.

The problem of tracing an economy's structure to its environment would be difficult enough if we could assert that observed system structures represented the best adaptation to a given physical environment. Yet as we have seen, the preferences of decision makers, at least as they stand in the beginning of a period of comparison, are also part of an economy's (initial) environment. Thus if individuals in leading positions have strong preferences for certain system rules over others, irrespective of their impact on desiderata such as growth of consumption or efficiency, the structure actually adopted may not be optimal with respect to these other outcomes. With this difficulty in mind, I have chosen to take system structure as given in the following chapters, with the exception of an occasional digression on the relation of an organization's rules to its environment.[7]

These remarks apply perhaps with even greater force to policies that surely depend on preferences and other components of an economy's initial environment. But again the difficulties of tracing the policies in effect at a particular time to an economy's environment may be too great statistically to enable us to eliminate the intermediate policy variable.

In sum, although we recognize that both s_i and p_{s_i} may be functionally related to e_i in any system i, and hence that all the differences among the observed outcomes of systems may ultimately be traceable to differences in their environments, our ignorance of the true nature of these functional relations will generally compel us to take policies and system rules as givens, independent of environment for the period of observation.

3.4 Interaction among Prevailing Norms, Other Norms, and Systems

The concept of a prevailing norm differs between systems. In a highly centralized system the prevailing norm is essentially the norm of those exercising power in the system. Interest groups may exercise influence, but the process by which they do so generally escapes any but conjectural and inferential analysis.

In pluralistic societies, by contrast, most interest groups are clearly visible and in explicit competition through political processes, collective bargaining, strikes, advertising, demonstrations, and the means of bringing their "message" to the public. The prevailing norm may be altered as parties

7. Section 9.1.

Table 3.1 Influence of Policy Makers in the Pursuit of Selected Objectives in Eight European Countries (circa 1960)

Policy area

Degree of influence	*Expansion of production*	*Improvement in income distri- bution*	*Protection of regions, industries, special interests, farmers*
Dominant	—	—	—
Dominant or significant	Government, ministries	Government, farmers, trade unions	—
Significant	Employers, political parties[a]	Employers, ministries	Government, employers
Significant or minor	Central bank	Political parties	Political parties, paraliament, ministries
Minor	Trade unions	Parliament	Foreign or inter- national organs
Minor or negligible	Parliament, political parties[b]	—	Trade unions
Negligible	Farmers, foreign or inter- national organs	Central bank, foreign or inter- national organs	Central bank

[a] In Belgium, Italy, and Norway.
[b] In France, West Germany, Luxembourg, the Netherlands, and the United Kingdom.
Source: E. Kirschen and Associates, *Economic Policy in Our Time* (Amsterdam: North–Holland, 1964), Vol. 1, p. 234.

succeed one another in power or as, in the process of integrating conflicting interests, they shift their priorities to reflect the changing moods and desiderata of their constituents.

The extent of diffusion of economic power in Western Europe at the national level may be gathered from table 3.1, taken from a major study of European policy by Etienne Kirschen and Associates. This aspect of the Kirschen investigation was confined to three proximate desiderata, or "objectives"[8]: (1) "expansion of production," (2) "improvement in income distribution," and (3) "protection of priorities" (accorded to special industries or regions). The "degree of influence" on these three objectives was ascertained from the answers given in a questionnaire addressed to a panel of

8. On proximate desiderata, see below, sec. 5.1.

experts on the countries concerned (Belgium, Luxembourg, France, West Germany, Italy, the Netherlands, Norway, and the United Kingdom).

For the most part, the influence exercised by the various organizations listed was of the same general magnitude in all eight countries. The principal exceptions were (1) the influence of political parties on the expansion of production, which was significant in one group of countries and minor or negligible in another, (2) the influence of the central bank on production (significant in one group, minor in the other), (3) the influence of political parties on income distribution (significant or minor), and (4) the influence of political parties, parliament, and ministries on the protection of regions, industries, or other special interests (significant or minor).

The relative preferences for conflicting policy objectives of the political parties that have been in and out of power in Europe are known to diverge significantly. For example, as a general rule, socialists put a very high value on achieving full employment and on improving the distribution of incomes, whereas center and conservative parties are more concerned with price stability, national strength, and (for center parties) the expansion of production.[9] What are we to conclude from this about the prevailing norms of countries where socialist, center, and conservative parties have taken their turn repeatedly at the helm of the state? One might argue that in a country such as France the electorate, directly or via the General Assembly, has acted as a servomechanism correcting the excesses of the party last in power by handing over the reins of government to the party on the other side of the policy continuum. Thus conservative governments are called in to suppress or contain the inflation released by their left-of-center predecessors and to improve the balance of payments, whereas the latter, when they assume power, take measures to step up the rate of increase of GNP at the cost of increased tension in the economy. One is tempted to infer from this "dialectical process" that France's prevailing norm, which might be used to aggregate such desiderata as the growth of consumption, equity, and stability in different systems, should be expressed as a combination of the revealed preferences for these desiderata on the part of French political parties from the moderate left to the right of center.

Systems and norms influence each other in many ways. The most important example concerns *system change*, which itself may be included among the outcomes to be compared. System change (more precisely, change in system structure) tends to be resisted by those participants on whom the system bestows wealth, influence, power, or both, a resistance aided by traditional values and the advantages of stability. The ideology of the dominant group,

---

9. Etienne Kirschen and Associates, *Economic Policy in Our Time* (Amsterdam: North–Holland, 1966), vol. 1, p. 227.

which may be spread among the participants through propaganda, advertising, proselytization, or other vehicles of persuasion, reinforces these conservative tendencies. It follows from this bias that comparison between two systems *with similar factor endowments and technologies* on the basis of the prevailing norm of either will tend to favor the system whose prevailing norm instructs the comparison.[10] Even if the list of desiderata were to be the same in the two prevailing norms, any difference in the weights given to the desiderata in the respective prevailing norms will make either system bend the outcomes to its own norm, other things being equal. Changes in system structure nevertheless occur either when those in situations of power are dissatisfied with the performance of the system and are desirous of bringing about its reform or overhaul, or when a group of individuals who are not among the top power holders and feel disadvantaged or otherwise dissatisfied with the structure of the system can force a modification of it that gives greater effect to their own norms. The pressure for change on the part of persons in and out of power depends on the information generated by the system about its performance, itself a system characteristic. It has been conjectured, for instance, that the amount and quality of information percolating to power holders will vary inversely with the political coercion and restrictions they impose upon society.[11]

The change effected in the system is said to be *evolutionary* if it takes place clearly within the framework and procedures recognized in the system structure. This requires that the prevailing norm give weight to the provision for change in the system's structure. A *revolutionary* change takes place if a group has ways to force such a change according to its own norm, which then supersedes the previous norms outright. These are extremes on a scale, and intermediate forms of changes in system structure are frequent. In revolutionary change, the parts of the system that change most are the institutions, organizations, and laws and rules, while the regular patterns of behavior are not generally capable of abrupt change. (There is an analogy here with technological change. Important new knowledge can become available overnight. Its incorporation in new capital stock and [re]trained labor force takes much longer.)

Neither the partisans nor the opponents of revolutionary change are given to make explicit the norms governing their attitudes toward these grand

10. Just as a comparison of aggregate outputs in two economies with similar factor endowments and technologies but made up of individuals harboring substantially different preferences will tend to favor the economy whose relative prices are used to weigh outputs, provided these prices are based on the marginal rates of substitution for consumers at points of the production surface corresponding to the actually observed output mix in this economy.

11. David Apter, *The Politics of Modernization* (Chicago: University of Chicago Press, 1965), p. 40.

social options. Yet such explicitness may be necessary if there is to be any rational discourse between the two groups—a first step toward abating their mutual animosity.

The component of the norm that may matter most here is the social rate of discount for reducing future payoffs to their present value. There is usually also a serious disparity between the subjective probability attached by revolutionaries to the state of affairs they wish to bring about by the overturn of the system and that attached by those who oppose them. As a general rule, "revolutionaries" and "conservatives" attach very different weights to the levels of the desiderata the former look forward to in the indefinite future and in the transition period linking the present to this state of bliss. The revolutionaries place their wager on the future and neglect the transition; the conservatives discount this future heavily, not only by reason of their "impatience" —their preference for present enjoyment of the desiderata—but because of their doubts regarding its attainment. Revolutionaries are generally unwilling to accept "consumers' sovereignty," at least for the period including the transition, and are prepared if necessary to sacrifice certain interests, and even lives, to bring about the desired state. Conservatives and "evolutionaries" apparently value the shells of the eggs that revolutionaries are willing, if not eager, to break in order to "make an omelet."

4

Common Desiderata and Efficiency

4.1 COMMON DESIDERATA[1]

An explicit norm was defined in the last chapter as a function of all outcomes representing the preferences of some individual or group pertinent to the comparison. Desiderata and odiosa are outcomes on which the norm depends, respectively, in a positive or negative manner.

The limited number of arguments that can be encapsuled in an evaluation function suggests that a norm depends only on the *subset* of all outcomes that the individual or group happens to be interested in. Any trait of a system or policy can itself become an outcome, and hence a desideratum in some norm, if value is attached to it in that norm, possibly because of its presumed non-economic effects. "Decentralization of economic decision making," for example, may be valued in itself because it is looked upon as strengthening the self-reliance of individuals. In contrast, in another system "centralization" may be valued in itself because it is thought to help maintain political control. In comparisons the fact that these system traits appear as outcomes valued in opposite ways in different norms must be taken into account.

The inclusion in a norm or the giving of extra weight to a desideratum merely because of its presumed relation to some unnamed, perhaps non-economic, desideratum introduces into the norm an assumption about causal relationships that may be mistaken. This element of speculation is present, to a smaller or larger degree, in almost all adoption and weighting of desiderata. It is increased in importance by the fact that the more ulterior desiderata are often harder to quantify and are therefore represented by more quantifiable proximate desiderata believed to serve the ultimate ends in question.[2]

We now proceed to list desiderata that appear to be present in the prevailing norms of most systems in the modern world. That the same desiderata appear in the norms of two or more systems should not be taken to imply that they hold the same importance, and hence that they should be assigned the same relevant weights, in those norms. Neither is the desideratum recognized as

1. The bulk of secs. 4.1 and 4.2 is taken verbatim from Koopmans and Montias, op. cit., pp. 26–39.
2. See below, sec. 5.1.

39

"common" necessarily expressible in the same form—for example, by the same indicator(s)—in different systems. Nevertheless, a list of common desiderata is a first step toward a methodology of comparison of economic systems that may gain acceptance by economists living under different systems. In this listing I shall have occasion to refer to various groups of countries generally identified with a particular system structure, a high or low level of development, or both. As in the Koopmans—Montias paper already referred to, I shall avoid terms such as "communist" and "capitalist" in order not to crystallize the reader's ideas around these ideologically loaded "gestalts." Reaching into geography for substitute labels, I shall use "East" for the diverse groups of countries in which a communist party is the leading political organ; "West" for the developed "capitalist" and mixed "capitalist–socialist" countries; and "South" for the less developed non-"communist" countries, regardless of their individual locations. It will then be understood that Cuba is in "East," whereas Australia and Finland are in "West." Yugoslavia, which does not seem to fit with either "East" or "West" in its economic institutions, will be mentioned separately when the need arises.

We begin our list with

> y_1 a high level of *per capita consumption*
> of goods and services desired *by* or *for*
> consumers.[3]

Although some individuals seek or have sought a life of austerity and self-denial, for most system participants, including "dictators" and "ruling parties," this desideratum enters the norm with a significant weight. It is practically universal in the modern world, without as yet any signs of an approach to saturation even in the wealthiest economies.

This definition may be extended to include leisure among the "services" consumed. Similarly, we may consider a reduction in the level of bads inflicted on consumers (e.g., by pollution) as an increase in the level of per capita consumption.

In measuring consumption over a period of comparison, its components— the goods and bads available at different times within the period—should be properly aggregated, presumably by means of weights reflecting the marginal rates of substitution among those goods and bads in the corresponding norms. Unless the period is quite short, the same good available at different times will not be valued equally (at least in most norms). A rate of discount must then be adduced to permit the valuation of all the components of the consumption bundle at a precise point in time. In systems marked by the absence

---

3. The words "by or for" allude to a system difference to be discussed further in connection with desideratum y_*.

of free markets for "futures" or for other assets maturing at different dates, an arbitrary interest rate must frequently be invoked to calculate the "present value" of goods available at later dates, with adverse effect on the precision of the comparison. In addition, where the prices of the goods consumed are a poor reflection of either consumers' or planners' "marginal rates of substitution" (a state of affairs normally met with in centralized economies), the difficulties of measurement and comparison are compounded.

Almost as universal is the desire for

y_2 *growth* in the per capita consumption of
goods and services.

This is in part a matter of intertemporal distribution of consumption and of dissatisfaction with present consumption levels, especially in the less developed countries.

It sometimes competes with and sometimes reinforces another desideratum:

y_6 national strength or the desire to hold
one's own in the competition for influence
and power in the world,

which is mentioned here somewhat out of sequence in anticipation of further comment.

Growth in per capita consumption is achieved mainly through technical advances and the accumulation of human and physical capital. In the more affluent countries with private property and enterprise, a given population growth produces at least a corresponding growth in capital almost painlessly through the desire for continuity of income into the retirement period. Additional sources of capital accumulation and technical advance include the desire of the young to acquire skills and knowledge that have market value besides their personal value; the competition among business firms, nation-states, and systems in the technological race; and the pressure from scientists for funds to pursue their intellectual interests.

The three desiderata listed so far introduce the major contenders for the use of resources in modern systems. Subsequent desiderata deal more with their apportioning by types of goods and by recipients. It is therefore appropriate here to make the point that simultaneous pursuit of these desiderata, whatever their (positive) weights in the pertinent norm, implies a "derived desideratum" of

y_* *efficiency* in the use of resources.

Efficiency in production is defined as a choice of the kinds and levels of production activities in use such that, within the bounds of the given resource availabilities, it is not technologically possible to produce more of any good or service desired by some participant in some period except at the opportunity cost of producing less of some good or of inflicting more of some bad on one or more participants in this or another period.[4]

An efficiently produced bundle of goods and services may or may not be satisfactory from the viewpoint of decision makers (consumers, "central planners," or others). A more inclusive concept of efficiency, called "Pareto optimality," requires that "it not be possible to increase the utility of any one individual without decreasing that of another" when the individuals in question are those who, according to the rules of the system, are directly or indirectly responsible for determining the bundle of goods and services produced. At one extreme we may have a group of "central planners" acting in concert who are responsible for setting targets for the outputs of goods and services. In this case Pareto optimality would be achieved if these central planners could not cause a bundle of goods and services to be produced that would be more desirable to them (under existing resource constraints). At the other extreme, consumers are the sovereign determinants of the allocation of resources, and Pareto optimality requires that it not be possible to increase the utility of any one consumer without decreasing that of another. When consumers' sovereignty prevails, Pareto optimality calls for efficiency in distribution as well as in production.[5] In the definition of desideratum y_1, a high level of per capita consumption of goods and services is then "desired *by* consumers." In the absence of consumers' sovereignty, efficiency in production needs to be supplemented by a specification of the quantities, marginal rates of substitution, or ratios[6] determining the consumption of individual goods "desired *for* consumers." In section 4.3 below we shall extend the definition of efficiency to take into consideration desiderata other than consumption and growth (y_1 and y_2) and examine the implications for efficiency in this broader context of uncertainty in the outcomes.

Single-period efficiency (in any of the alternative definitions of efficiency above)

4. Definitions of efficiency usually apply to the opportunity cost of increasing the *utilization* of exogenous inputs such as labor or natural resources. Inasmuch as we treat leisure as a good or labor time expended on economic activities as a bad, there is no need to refer specifically to exogenous labor inputs. Similarly, the more intensive utilization of natural resources may either be thought of as the infliction of a bad in the definition of the text or as an opportunity cost in terms of goods forgone in some future period if the resources are consumed now.

5. Efficiency in production, assuming nonsaturation, is implied in Pareto optimality. Note that, in a world without uncertainty and with perfect information, planners bent on maximizing consumers' satisfaction might make decisions consistent with Pareto optimality *for* consumers. In this case the two extremes of decision making would converge, at least with respect to this desideratum.

6. See, for instance, L. V. Kantorovich, *Ekonomicheskii raschet nailushchego ispol'zovania resursov* (Economic Calculation of the Best Use of Economic Resources), Academy of Sciences of the USSR, 1959, p. 276 and passim.

is obtained if all the inputs and outputs (or utilities) in the definition apply to a single time period.[7] In this interpretation, one must specify in the definition of efficiency that, in comparisons with other allocations (and distributions), the amount of all goods to be held over for use in later periods be kept constant. *Intertemporal efficiency* is obtained if the same good available in different periods is interpreted as so many different goods, while holding the initial and (for a finite horizon) terminal capital stocks constant. This concept implies single-period efficiency in all periods in question, but the converse is not true. Hence intertemporal efficiency is the stricter and indeed more meaningful desideratum. For long-run decisions it also requires efficiency in choosing the size and composition of investment. However, it suffers from an implication of perfect foresight as to technology, preferences, and actual allocation and distribution for an idefinite number of periods ahead.

Whereas single-period efficiency does in turn imply in some sense maximal consumption y_1 in that period compatible with the stipulations in its definition, intertemporal efficiency is of course compatible with high or low growth, stationarity, decline, or fluctuating per capita consumption. The growth desideratum y_2 adds to this a specific preference for *aggregate* intertemporal distribution of consumption.

A concern with distribution among individuals is expressed by

y_3 *equity* in the distribution of the conditions
of living, or at least of opportunity in that
regard, among contemporaries,

which is more strongly held, particularly by individuals in positions of power in East and West than in many parts of South. The "conditions of living" include consumption levels (current as well as lifetime prospects), health care, protection from adverse working conditions, absence of nonfunctional discrimination, and dignity in human interactions. The ethical term "equity" is preferable in this context to the term "equality," which ignores differences in need arising, for instance, from different states of health or from different numbers of dependents or providers.

Particularly in West and South, social services and public goods are largely provided by mechanisms different from those by which other consumption goods are supplied. For this reason we should recognize as a separate desideratum

y_4 *provision of social services and public goods.*

---

7. This concept is also somewhat inaccurately named "static efficiency," a term better reserved for efficiency attained in a hypothetical stationary state with all variables constant over time.

This desideratum, which amounts to a further stipulation within the consumption desideratum y_1, rates higher by and large in East than in South and West in relation to resources. However, the modern emphasis on rising levels of increasingly widespread education, observed already in connection with the growth desideratum y_2, is almost universal.

The following intertemporal aspect of the conditions of living deserves separate mention:

y_5 *stability* of employment and incomes.

In West policy makers use monetary and fiscal policy toward this goal. With respect to South, efforts are made to protect the value of exports against price fluctuations and "overproduction" by arrangements modifying the operation of markets in important raw materials. In East direct controls over investments and bank restrictions on short-term credits are used to maintain macroeconomic stability when such stability does not conflict too markedly with the other goals of the ruling party.

There remains the crucial desideratum y_6 already mentioned. We extend its definition here:

y_6 (*national strength*) to ensure the continuation
of national existence and of national and/or
ideological independence; where possible to
extend national and/or ideological influence,
prestige, and power.

As between different countries or systems this desideratum is *similar* rather than common. It has the same definition except that in each case a different name of country or system is written in.

The economic significance of this largely political desideratum is very great. It competes with most of the foregoing desiderata by the absorption of resources in military preparedness and, if the case arises, in armed international conflict. Nevertheless, a lesser but noticeable complementarity relation may arise from the benefits to production for civilian consumption spun off by military research. A definite contribution to the satisfaction of other desiderata stems from some primarily nonmilitary activities motivated by y_6. This includes the emphasis on rapid industrialization in South and East and ventures in oceanographic or space research in the most highly developed countries.

Another, largely political desideratum influencing policy in a number of countries is

y_7 the achievement of a desirable size and
structure of the population.

This desideratum may in part be derived from others, including the desiderata for a high level of consumption per capita and for national strength, but it may also have an autonomous place in the list. For some participants, for example, a larger population in at least some regions of the country they inhabit may be desirable in and of itself ("the more the merrier"). For others, a stable population (zero population growth) may be an end in itself, although it is more commonly derived from y_1 broadly interpreted to include the consumption of an unspoiled environment.

Another primary desideratum, similar in intent but possibly quite different in form of application between different systems, is

> y_8 *provision for orderly change in system structure*
> to permit adjustment to changing circum-
> stances without endangering its essential
> continuity.

Changes in system structure were noted among possible outcomes in chapter 3. Normally, within the same economy system-change desiderata differ considerably between prevailing and other contending norms. The prevailing norm tends to be for little or no change, and the contending norms favor a variety of not necessarily compatible changes. We return to these relationships in section 4.4.

4.2 DESIDERATA SPECIFIC TO VARIOUS NORMS

In general, West favors and practices

> y_9 *widely dispersed economic decisions* through
> inheritable private property, through individual
> and corporate enterprise, and through
> a legal framework enforcing contracts while
> permitting "limited liability."

In different degrees in different countries of West and possibly South the concern for business enterprise is carried to the point of

> y_{10} *commercialism*, a tolerant attitude toward
> uninformative competitive advertising,
> sales pressure, and the influencing of
> essentially educational and cultural
> activities by business interests,

in some comparers' norms the tolerance of an odiosum rather than a positively valued desideratum.

The traditional desideratum of East,

> y_{11} *centralized*[8] *decisions and control* over
> the composition of output and consumption,

has been explicitly abandoned in Yugoslavia and is currently up for reconsideration in most East European countries because of its perceived conflict with y^* (efficiency in the use of resources).

Some desiderata and odiosa are specific to comprehensive views of society and its processes usually associated with "ideologies." "Alienation," for example, is an odiosum shared by many individuals sympathetic to, or influenced by, Marxist ideology. In Marx, it refers to the inability of man to become a "totally self-realized individual" with fully developed productive powers under the capitalist mode of production with its concomitant division of labor, which compels him to specialize his production activities to an extreme extent.[9] In Yugoslavia the overcoming of workers' alienation has become a distinct desideratum in the prevailing norm, but it is interpreted in a special way as

> y_{12} *the removal of workers' alienation through
> their control of production decisions.*[10]

The comparer may also wish to propose as pertinent desiderata not previously given expression.

An example of a newly proposed desideratum is the coexistence characteristics of various mixtures of economic system. The comparer might wish to propose the study of unilaterally initiated or mutually agreed self-reforms of coexistent systems to

> y_{13} *reduce both the cost of the balance of
> deterrence and the probability and/or
> destructiveness of armed conflict* between
> countries having similar or different
> systems.

The crucial importance of this (proximate rather than ultimate) desideratum for the future of mankind contrasts sharply with the difficulties of obtaining clarity and, if needed, agreement on policies promoting this desideratum. It is not even clear what bearing economic policies may have on its attainment, except for a general presumption that the increasing interdependence of

---

8. Again, "centralization" as understood in East.

9. Cf. Robert C. Tucker, *The Marxian Revolutionary Idea* (New York: Norton, 1969), p. 22.

10. For a theoretical analysis of the effects on decision making of workers' identification with the interests of the enterprise he is supposed to co-own, see Jaroslav Vanek, *The General Theory of Labor-Managed Economies* (Ithaca, N.Y.: Cornell University Press, 1970), chaps. 12 and 13.

economies in the modern world is likely to increase the importance of various system characteristics to coexistence problems.

Obviously the list of desiderata could be extended and the individual desiderata disaggregated indefinitely. It may be mentioned in passing that in a recent listing of the "aims" of policy in Western Europe, where a number of the aims coincided with our desiderata, E. Kirschen and L. Morrissens included the "reduction of social tensions," "ethics and religion," (the pursuit of) "political power" (presumably by power holders), and the promotion of international solidarity.[11] These aims are only tangentially expressed in some of our desiderata, and perhaps each deserves a separate status.

4.3 SYSTEM ASPECTS OF ECONOMIC EFFICIENCY[12]

In section 4.1 we set forth alternative definitions of "efficiency in the use of resources." A still broader concept will now be introduced that explicitly recognizes the fact that decision makers influencing the outcomes of economies to be compared may pursue desiderata other than per capita consumption of goods and services (y_1) and growth (y_2). Efficiency, according to this broader concept, requires that:

The choice of kind and levels of activities in use be such that within the bounds of given environmental variables it should not be possible to increase the level of any desideratum without decreasing that of another.

Hereafter we shall refer to this variant of the efficiency requirement as "general efficiency."

Before citing conditions under which efficiency in production, Pareto optimality, or both are likely to be sacrificed for the sake of competing desiderata (without impairment to general efficiency), we should make clear what we mean, in the context of our broader definition, by "a choice of kind and levels of activities in use." Needless to say, these activities are not limited to the production of goods qua tangible objects. They also encompass any activities decision makers may engage in that will affect the outcomes that an observer might wish to analyze or compare. Suppose, for example, that a decision maker sought by his actions to influence income equality, which, via equity, entered as an argument in the observer's norm function. If he is a legislator he might do so by sponsoring a new tax law; as an official of a ruling organization operating at a local level, he might opt to spend a greater part of his budget on a direct welfare program benefiting the poor or on a special work scheme for the unemployed. The newly promulgated law or the

11. "The Objectives and Instruments of Economic Policy," in B. G. Hickman, ed., *Quantitative Planning of Economic Policy* (Washington, D.C.: The Brookings Institution, 1965), pp. 116–17.

12. Parts of this section are reproduced from J. M. Montias and P. H. Sturm, "System Aspects of Economic Efficiency," a paper prepared for the conference on "Measurement of Factor Productivities: Theoretical Problems and Empirical Results," Reisenburg, Germany, June 1974.

budget policy actually adopted may entail an appreciable opportunity cost in terms of other desiderata, including efficiency in the use of resources. If the decision maker had the "capacity" to choose an alternative technique or activity for redistributing incomes that did not require the sacrifice of competing desiderata, the law or budget decision he actually chose can be said to have been inefficient in the general sense.

But this amplification of our definition raises a further question: How should we interpret a decision maker's "capacity" to choose among alternative activities? If the information needed to choose an efficient activity is costless, why should an inefficient solution ever be adopted? If it is costly, the lapse from efficiency may be more apparent than real when opportunity costs are fully reckoned. In empirical comparisons of systems it is generally difficult or impossible to make an allowance for discrepancies in the information available to decision makers operating in different systems, and there may be no alternative to calling more efficient the system that, in a more or less comparable environment, performs better according to a given norm.

Difficulties in interpreting apparent lapses in efficiency are compounded when we consider that basic system outcomes may be the product of complex interactions among individuals, none of whom may be pursuing the desiderata that an observer deems important enough to enter his norm. Alternatively, the outcomes may significantly differ from those that decision makers are pursuing because a process of interaction is going on that they cannot fully comprehend, let alone master. Income distribution, both in market and in socialist economies, may be regarded as an instance of such an "epipheno-menon"—the unplanned outcome of a complex process of interaction.[13] Economic instability, insofar as it is reflected in strikes and other interruptions of the work process, is the resultant of complex forces, especially in market economies where labor union leaders bargain decentrally with representatives of private enterprises. It is safe to assert that the number of working days lost to work stoppages is not a decision variable under any one's control.

The looseness of the link between individual decisions and aggregate outcomes should be kept distinct from uncertainty and the inability of decision makers to predict with precision the states of the environment that will affect the outcomes of their decisions. For an individual facing uncertainty, the efficiency of his decisions may be restated in terms of *expected* outcomes. In the case of phenomena resulting from the interaction of multitudes of individuals pursuing different goals, one cannot meaningfully assign subjective probabilities to the decision makers and compute their expectations regarding aggregate outcomes unless they are personally concerned about these out-

13. Cf. Charles E. Lindblom, "Epiphenomenal Planning," paper prepared for the research conference on "Economic Planning, East and West," Bellagio, 1973.

comes. We can conceive, however, of an observer making predictions about the outcomes of multitudinous decisions, just as a stockbroker may have expectations about tomorrow's Dow–Jones average.

These arguments suggest that we should abandon our counsel of perfection and move away from a focus on individual decision making in defining efficiency at the economy- or system-wide level. Our primary concern after all is with the effect of system rules on normed outcomes. We shall be satisfied if we can claim in any actual comparison that system rule A is *more* efficient than system rule B. We may define this superiority to mean that, under comparable environmental conditions, rule A is statistically associated with a set of outcomes that register at least as high as rule B in all dimensions of desired-outcome space and higher in at least one dimension. There is no presumption here that decision makers in *any* of the economies to be compared will generate an efficient set of outcomes, however defined.

When it comes to actual measurement, the above definition of *relative* efficiency is also beyond our statistical grasp. In order to satisfy the requirement of "comparable environmental conditions," we face the insuperable task of calculating what outcomes would have been attained by economy A, under its system rules, if it had been constrained by the environment of economy B, and vice versa. Environment, as we have defined the concept, includes initial technology and preferences as well as the capital stock, population, education, skills, and other more or less measurable inputs at the beginning of the period of observation.

What is actually done to measure relative efficiency in production—the introduction of desiderata such as equity and stability into the measure is still out of the question at this time—is to construct a ratio of measurable inputs (usually capital and labor) in the two economies in terms of the prices for these inputs prevailing in one or the other of these economies and a ratio of their aggregate outputs weighted with the output prices prevailing in either economy.[14] The ratio of the relative outputs of the two economies to their relative inputs is a measure of "total factor productivity," which has been used as a gauge of relative efficiency in production.[15]

14. There are thus two sets of output prices and two sets of input prices. The theoretical implications of these alternative price systems for the measurement of relative efficiency in production were first explored by Richard H. Moorsteen in his pioneering article, "On Measuring Productive Potential and Relative Efficiency," *Quarterly Journal of Economics* 75 (Aug. 1961): 451–54, 467. For applications of this technique to the comparison of Soviet and U.S. aggregate inputs and outputs, see Abram Bergson, "Comparative Productivity and Efficiency in the USA and the USSR," in Eckstein, ed., op. cit., pp. 161–218; A. Bergson, "Productivity under Two Systems: The USSR Versus the West," in *Optimum Social Welfare and Productivity: A Comparative View* (New York: New York University Press, 1972), pp. 55–152.

15. There are four such measures, two for the alternative input prices and two for the alternative output prices.

How good a gauge of relative efficiency does this ratio of ratios afford? It clearly does not segregate the effects of differences in system structure on aggregate outputs from the effects of disparities in the level and kind of technology in use. Neither does it make adequate allowances for differences in preferences.

Even if one were to make the extreme assumption that the adoption of an inferior technology by one of the two countries was a consequence of its system structure, we should still have to allow for possible differences in scale between these economies that would affect their relative factor productivity, irrespective of their relative efficiencies.[16] With regard to preferences on the output side of the ratio, the measure suffers from a defect already noted by Richard Moorsteen, namely, from its implicit assumption that the output mix of either country would remain unchanged if its input mix were shifted to the input proportions of the other. In reality, we should expect that if, say, United States outputs were constrained by the labor and capital available in the Soviet Union, the U.S. output mix would shift away from capital-intensive toward more labor-intensive products, which would be relatively cheaper to produce under these hypothetical conditions. On the input side the measure ignores the possibility that one set of system rules may be better than the other at coaxing out labor services and other factors of production. A stronger work ethic or a smaller aversion to the participation of women in the labor force may also have effect of raising the number of individuals employed in a given population. In either case, when higher levels of variable inputs are applied to a comparable capital stock in one economy than in the other, then, owing to the effects of diminishing returns, the ratio of measured outputs to inputs may be reduced (depending on the price system used to compare the combined inputs). If factor productivity is actually lower in the economy where labor is more successfully mobilized, this discrepancy should not lead us to conclude that this economy is necessarily any less efficient than the other.

Suppose that country A registered a higher total factor productivity than country B and that we had sufficient reason to infer from this observation that

16. A smaller country with a limited domestic market can realize economies of scale by engaging in international trade. If it fails to do so, the reason may lie in an aversion to trade motivated by a stability or national-strength desideratum. Strictly speaking then, diseconomies of small scale could be ascribed to "inefficiency in production," although there would be no lapse from general efficiency.

For a discussion of this point, which is critical to a comparison of the relative efficiencies of system structures in East and West Germany, the reader is referred to Montias and Sturm, op. cit., pp. 29–31. Peter Sturm, in his systematic comparison of system effects on productivity in East and West Germany, found that the scale parameter in the production functions fitted separately for the two countries ranged from 1.01 to 1.28, depending on the specification of the functions assumed.

the system structure of B was indeed less efficient in production than the system structure of A. Our next task should be to ascertain whether desiderata competing with per capita consumption and growth, or more generally with production in B, might account for this inferiority. A few examples will now be cited in which the adoption of system rules apt to cause significant inefficiency in production was motivated by competing desiderata. It should be noted in perusing these cases that the trade-off between efficiency and competing desiderata is rarely recognized as such by the rule maker, who will frequently deny that any efficiency loss need ensue from the measures he introduces. The critic within the system, or the observer of the rule maker without, is the one most apt to perceive the conflict among the desiderata pursued.

1. Important conflicts frequently arise between efficiency and noneconomic desiderata, such as the desire of decision makers to conserve or strengthen their own power or the power of their political party. "Red versus expert" is the form that this opposition assumes in many countries ruled by a communist-type party. Factory managers, despite their lack of education, competence, or both, are often appointed or maintained in their posts because they are known to be loyal to the party, with obvious implications for efficiency in production.

2. Efficiency and equity collide in many situations in both East and West. Rent controls that remain in force for many years after an initial, more or less equitable allocation of space has taken place frequently generate flagrant inefficiencies in distribution (e.g., 7–8-room apartments in Paris or Berlin that were once occupied by a large family but now are owned by widows or widowers without children who may not sell their rights of occupancy even though they would prefer to trade them for other goods and services). Military conscription in countries where only a fraction of the population in given age groups is actually drafted (after selection by lottery or otherwise) also pits efficiency in distribution against equity because, if the law permitted, some of the wealthier individuals selected would be willing and able to pay poorer individuals with no obligation to serve the price the latter would demand to take their place. Many economists would argue that the emphasis on moral at the expense of material incentives for the workers and staff of factories in China is likely to have an adverse effect on efficiency in production.[17]

3. Central governments frequently set or adjust prices on imported or exported goods in the pursuit of self-sufficiency (usually a proxy for national strength) or of stability, as in the case of developing countries where export taxes are levied on primary products to encourage a more diversified export mix aimed at reducing the variance of export earnings. This behavior may of course be perfectly compatible with general efficiency.

17. For a discussion of moral versus material incentives, see secs. 13.1 and 13.4.

4. Among the rules in effect in almost all systems are restrictions on "who may give what information to whom." In some instances these rules may conflict with efficiency in production. For example, rules prohibiting the diffusion of technical secrets in defense industries may be imposed for fear other nations might latch onto this information, even though the other segments of the economy might benefit significantly from the spin-off.

5. The ideological attachment of decision makers to one or more rules in the system structure that have become desiderata in themselves sometimes explains observed lapses from efficiency in the use of resources. The unwillingness on the part of the rule makers in certain socialist countries to license private shops that would operate in competition with state retail establishments has at times undoubtedly contributed to inefficiency in distribution. Their reluctance to decentralize production decisions in the socialized sector—whether it be motivated by political reasons or by the failure to perceive the potential gains of a reform—may have had a similar effect in periods during which the system was hypercentralized (e.g., in the early 1950s).

To move forward with the comparison of systems, we need to recognize the reasons why decision makers are at times willing to tolerate inefficiencies for the sake of pursuing desiderata that are either incompatible with full efficiency in the use of resources or that can only be made compatible with efficiency by profound changes in the political-economic system structure.

5

From Theory to Measurement

5.1 PROXIMATE VERSUS ULTIMATE DESIDERATA

Any politician, from East, West, South, or Erewhon, confronted with the list of common desiderata in chapter 4 might easily deny that any of them were precisely the goals he pursued in behalf of his actual or symbolic constituency. He would understand better and be more attracted to goals such as rapid industrialization, the defense of the balance of payments, price stability, a high rate of growth of national income, or the extension of social security. If an observer sought to infer the preferences prevailing in the Soviet Union in the early 1930s from the allocation decisions that were made at that time, he would be led to conclude that consumption per capita in the immediate future was a goal less pursued by the planners than a constraint imposing an upper bound on the rate of investment (and indirectly on the growth rate of industrial output). High rates of investment and low levels of consumption in this initial period of rapid industrialization can probably be explained and justified by the extraordinarily heavy weight given in the prevailing norm to consumption (or its rate of increase) in a very remote period. But it may be more fruitful to speculate that the ultimate desiderata regarding consumption had been *displaced* in the planners' preferences by more proximate goals, including a high growth rate for the output of heavy industry and a high rate of investment. This is an instance of a phenomenon described by March and Simon, who observe that the repeated choice of specific means to a valued end often causes a gradual transfer of the preference from the end to the means adopted when the means may be a proximate goal or an institutional device for reaching such a goal.[1] The displacement may go so far as to leave only a tenuous link between the original and the proximate goal, as when politicians in West strive for a balanced budget or even for the reduction of the national debt in the (often mistaken) belief that the achievement of these goals will necessarily help to generate high and stable levels of consumption.

In this connection it is instructive to compare the list of policy objectives for some West European countries in the postwar period, as drawn up by

1. J. G. March and H. Simon, *Organizations* (New York: Wiley, 1958), p. 38.

E. Kirschen et al. on the basis of observed policies and government statements, with the ultimate desiderata defined in the preceding section. In table 5.1 a cross appearing in any cell relating an objective in the Kirschen list with an ultimate desideratum should be interpreted to mean that the attainment of the objective in question has the presumed effect of promoting that desideratum. (Only the most obvious of these links are shown in the table).

Table 5.1. Ultimate Desiderata

Policy objectives	y_1	y_2	y_3	y_4	y_5	y_6	y_7
Major							
Full employment	×	×			×		
Price stability	×		×				
Improvement in the balance of payments					×		
Expansion of production	×	×					
Improvement in the allocation of factors of production	×	×				×	
Satisfaction of collective needs			×	×		×	
Improvement in the distribution of income and wealth			×				
Protection of and priorities given to particular regions or industries			×		×		
Minor							
Improvement in the pattern of private consumption	×						
Security of supply					×	×	
Improvement in the size or structure of the population	×					×	×
Reduction in working hours	×		×				

Source: E. Kirschen and Associates, *Economic Policy in Our Time* (Amsterdam: North–Holland, 1964), vol. 1, pp. 5–6. A similar table but with a somewhat different list of policy goals may be found in E. Kirschen and L. Morrissens, "The Objectives and Instruments of Economic Policy," in B. G. Hickman, ed., *Quantitative Planning of Economic Policy* (Washington, D.C.: The Brookings Institution, 1965), pp. 116–17.

Note: y_1 = a high level of consumption per capita
     y_2 = growth in per capita consumption
     y_3 = equity
     y_4 = provision of social services and public goods
     y_5 = stability of employment and incomes
     y_6 = national strength
     y_7 = achievement of a desirable size and structure of the population.

5.2 Indicators

Whether we wish to compare economies with the apparatus of the econo-metrician or with the simpler tools of the casual observer, we cannot help working with remote surrogates, or "proxies," for the desiderata we have in mind. If we focus on equality, for example, as a proximate desideratum for equity, we can do no better than find a summary indicator, such as a percentile, a variance, or a Gini index, that will give us a rough measure of equality. Are the indicators good proxies for the desiderata and are they strictly comparable for the sample of economies we wish to compare? In routine comparisons the answer is often negative, although such shortcomings do not necessarily invalidate the comparison. A physician trained in India who for economic reasons chooses to practice in the United States may have available to him only very poor indicators of the relative standards of living of doctors in India and the United States, but the disparity to the advantage of the latter may loom large enough in his mind to warrant his emigration. The "economic refugees" from East to West Germany, before the Berlin wall went up in 1961, may have made their move on the basis of the most slender comparative evidence. Yet the overwhelming majority of these refugees stayed in the Federal Republic after they had a better chance to compare levels of living in the two Germanies.

Even casual comparisons may be improved if the indicators are chosen with a minimum of care and effort to understand their relation to the goals they are supposed to represent. To take an extreme case, I remember asking a few years ago a U.S. government official who had lived in both Bulgaria and Turkey whether, on the basis of his observation, the Bulgarians enjoyed a higher level of living on the average than the Turks. He answered that the Turks seemed better off, and he cited as evidence the greater abundance of goods in Turkish stores. He may well have been right, but his evidence was poor. He was judging consumption by inventories, on the implicit assumption that the ratio of the "stock" to the "flow" was roughly the same in the two countries. In fact, my impression based on casual observation in the two countries was that inventories in Turkey moved very slowly—a man might spend a whole day selling a case of dried figs, a box of oranges, and a few cans of dried milk—whereas most desirable goods were snapped up in Bulgaria as soon as they were put on sale in the stores.[2] Differences in systems—hidden

---

2. Without detailed study, I could not rule out the possibility that the ratio of total retail inventories to sales was roughly the same in the two countries, considering that Bulgarian stores decorated their windows with less salable items such as canned goods. My guess is, however, that the ratio of inventories to sales *for the items most commonly purchased in both countries* was much lower in Bulgaria than in Turkey.

unemployment in service occupations and a "sellers' market" in one country and full employment and a "buyers' market" in the other—distorted the significance and the comparability of the indicator.

Mismatching indicators and goals is a danger to which even respectable scholars are hardly proof, as witness the following, partly hypothetical example. The ultimate desideratum in this case was a high and sustained growth rate of consumption over time. The derived desideratum was the intertemporal efficiency of resource allocation. One element of this is the efficiency of research and development (R & D) expenditures. Now, as Pryor has shown in a recent study,[3] the East European socialist economies, including Yugoslavia, have a significantly higher ratio of R & D expenditures to GNP than Western and Southern Europe and North America, after controlling for GNP per capita and population. According to another study, the "rate of invention is substantially lower in Eastern than in Western Europe,"[4] as measured by the number of inventions registered per 100,000 inhabitants in 1964. From this it might easily be inferred that the efficiency of R & D expenditures must be lower in Eastern than in Western Europe. The obvious question is whether registered inventions are an acceptable indicator of R & D *output*. Do inventors have the same incentives to register innovations in the two sets of countries?[5] Are innovations in priority sectors in Eastern Europe, such as defense, registered at all? If not, is the relative importance of defense R & D to total R & D expenditures roughly the same in Eastern and Western Europe?

These are slippery assumptions to make. I would contend, to the contrary, that both system structure and policy affect registration of inventions in Eastern and Western Europe. Without further careful study, in my opinion, this indicator should not be used even as an approximation of R & D output.[6] It goes without saying that comparing this output indicator with an input indicator obtained by a different method would yield no reliable intelligence about the relative efficiency of R & D in different systems.

The equality of earnings, already referred to as a proxy for equity, is only loosely linked to the desideratum it is meant to represent. In the study of

3. Frederic L. Pryor, "Research and Development Expenditures in Eastern Europe," in *East-West Trade and the Technology Gap: A Political and Economic Appraisal*, ed. S. Wasowski, (New York: Praeger, 1970), p. 76.

4. R. V. Burks, "Technology and Political Change in Eastern Europe," in Chalmers Johnson, ed., *Change in Communist Systems* (Stanford, Calif.: Stanford University Press, 1970), p. 272.

5. Burks recognizes this problem (ibid., sources to table 2) but claims that the "gap between the two sets of countries would still be large even if the figures were strictly comparable." This is plausible, but only qualitative evidence is available to support the contention.

6. Note also that the comparison of registered inventions per 100,000 inhabitants in the paper by Burks is not controlled for differences in GNP per capita and population, both of which, according to Pryor, have a significant impact on R & D *inputs*.

income inequality discussed in section 5.5, the conclusion emerges that "communist" systems have a less unequal distribution of wage and salary income than do "capitalist" countries, other things equal. The addition of property incomes to wages and salaries would make for still greater inequality of total incomes in "capitalist" than in "communist" countries (since property incomes are very unequally divided in the former). On the other hand, in many societies access to goods, services, influence, and power is determined by "status" (who a person is) as well as by "contract" or "achievement" (what a person does). Inequality of privileges may be as serious a form of inequity, according at least to some norms, as inequality of incomes. The "yellow-curtain stores," to which only high officials, security officers, and other privileged members of the communist élite had access in Poland in the early 1950s, introduced an element of inequity that offset to some extent the relative equality of incomes that prevailed at the time.

It is hardly necessary to remind the reader that, in measuring aggregate output or such inputs as "the labor force" or "capital," not only should the sample of goods (or bads) contained in the indicator be representative but the bundle of objects and actions making up each included good or service should be more or less comparable across economies. Among the several dimensions of a good must be cited its quality, length of service life, terms of delivery, and cost of maintenance or service. A good that one has spent three hours queuing up for is not the same as one that was sold with a smile and delivered to one's door. Another dimension, which used to be neglected but is now coming to the fore, is the eventual disposability of the object, that is, its fate after its service life has been terminated. A beer can made of quick-rusting tin-coated iron is not the same as one made of long-lasting, hard-to-disintegrate aluminium, even though the utility of the contents to a hypothetical customer might be the same. This suggests that the problem of international comparability is bound up in the norm we wish to adopt. The two beer cans may be treated as identical if only the utility of the drinker is taken into account and as different goods if the relative social costs of disposal are also considered.

Both the example of the object for which one must queue up in at least one system and the can that becomes a nuisance after use involve the unjustified commingling of goods and bads. Perhaps the best way out of the quandary would be to aggregate all goods and all bads separately in such a way that both the hours wasted in queues and the marginal costs of disposing of the cans were tallied up in the final accounting.[7] An indicator of output for each country might then consist of a pair of numbers (the aggregate of goods and the

7. The aggregate of bads would of course include labor, accidents of all kinds, and morbidity rates. The problem of aggregating bads is briefly alluded to in Larry E. Ruff, "The Economic Common Sense of Pollution," *The Public Interest* 19 (Spring 1970): 73–77.

aggregate of bads), each of which might in turn be weighted in the norm, along with equity, security, stability, and other basic desiderata. (The indicator of bads would presumably be assigned a negative weight.)

Another problem in comparability crops up when two or more countries have a desideratum in common but different paths to attain it.[8] Most societies, for example, wish to minimize economic strife and to preserve a reasonable degree of stability in the distribution of income. In economies where labor is autonomously organized, man-days lost by strikes may be used as an indicator of strife and tension. But no measure is available for economies in which strikes are prohibited by law or otherwise repressed. In Yugoslavia, where strikes are on the fringes of legality, statistics on work stoppages were published until 1966, when they were suddenly discontinued.[9]

Another example is the volume of unfinished construction, an indicator that is likely to be relevant for comparing the intertemporal efficiency of alternative systems. Data on this variable can be obtained on a comprehensive basis only for the Soviet Union and for the East European economies. In market economies these data, if they are collected at all at the level of the construction enterprise, are generally not aggregated, presumably because neither the decision makers in the governmental hierarchy nor those in any nongovernmental organization have felt, or articulated, a need for them in reaching their decisions.

5.3 Estimation of the Impact of System-Structure Variables on Outcomes

We now take a closer look at our "grand relation" to bring to light the statistical problems inherent in any effort to isolate the effects of system rules on key outcomes.

For any economy i we have

$$o = f(e_i, s_i, p_{s_i}) \quad (i = 1, \ldots, H). \tag{5.1}$$

We recall that o_i, e_i, s_i and p_{s_i} may all be multielement vectors. If there are m distinct outcomes, there will be m equations *for each system* relating these outcomes to environment, system rules, and policies. By omitting the i subscript from f we are in effect implying that we can use our H sets of observations to derive a set of m equations with a *common structure*. Differences in observed outcomes between economies i and i' are attributed to differences in the values assumed by the variables e, s, and p_s in economies i and i', but in no way to differences in the structural coefficients through which these variables are linked in the grand relationship.

8. This discussion follows Koopmans and Montias, op. cit., pp. 27–28.

9. Joel B. Dirlam and James L. Plummer, *An Introduction to the Yugoslav Economy* (Columbus, Ohio: Merrill, 1973), pp. 36–37.

Relation 5.1 shows outcomes on the left-hand side exclusively. In many situations, though, certain outcomes will affect other outcomes, perhaps after a time lag or, if the period of observation is fairly extended, without one.

Suppose that the interdependencies can be expressed as a system of m linear equations in m endogenous variables with a vector of error terms u_i. When outcomes affect one another, this system may then be written as

$$B o_i = \Gamma x_i + u_i \quad (i = 1, \ldots, H), \tag{5.2}$$

where B is an $m \times m$ matrix of coefficients of endogenous variables, Γ is an $m \times n$ matrix of coefficients of exogenous variables, and $x_i \equiv (e_i, s_i, p_{s_i})$ is an n-dimensional vector whose elements are the values of the exogenous variables for system i.[10]

Provided that the determinant of B does not vanish, we can premultiply both sides of equation 5.2 by B^{-1} and obtain the "reduced form" of the system, where only endogenous variables appear on the left-hand side:

$$o_i = \Pi x_i + v_i \quad (i = 1, \ldots, H), \tag{5.3}$$

where $\Pi = B^{-1} \Gamma$ and $v_i = B^{-1} u_i$.

We have in effect H sets (one for each economic system) of observations, with m endogenous variables and n exogenous variables in each set. For the grand relation to assume the form of equation 5.1 in a linear system with interdependent outcomes, the matrix of coefficients B must be invertible, which was ensured in the development of equation 5.3 by assuming that the determinant of B did not vanish.

Can we move from the estimation of the coefficients in matrix Π of the reduced form back to the "structural coefficients" of equation 5.2? In general, in the absence of any a priori restrictions on B or Γ, there will be any number of these pairs of matrices that will satisfy the condition $\Pi = B^{-1} \Gamma$. A priori restrictions are needed to solve the "identification problem," that is, to extract a unique set of parameters B and Γ from Π. By positing certain coefficients in equation 5.2 to be zero, that is, by omitting specific variables from the structural equations, we introduce a priori restrictions necessary to satisfy the "identification conditions" and solve our problem of extracting the structural parameters from the parameters of the reduced form.[11]

---

10. We shall assume for the sake of simplicity that there is no interdependence between systems. If the error terms u_i and u_{i+j} ($j \neq 0$) are actually correlated, the concept of exogenous variables has to be replaced by that of "predetermined variables."

11. For a full and lucid treatment of this problem, see Thomas J. Rothenberg, *Efficient Estimation with A Priori Information* (New Haven: Yale University Press), pp. 59–86. A simpler but equally illuminating treatment is to be found in J. Johnston, *Econometric Methods* (New York: McGraw-Hill, 1960), pp. 230–74.

In the following, clearly hypothetical example, the flow variables are expressed on a yearly basis. The three endogenous variables are y_i, gross domestic product per capita; d_i, days lost to labor strikes; and c_i, consumption per capita. The three exogenous variables are k_i, capital per capita (average value of capital per capita during the year); t_i, gross investment per capita; and s_i, a system rule affecting the number of days lost to strikes, such as the right (de facto or de jure) of local union "shops" to strike without the concurrence of the national union leadership. u_{1i} and u_{2i} are error terms. The sample of H sets of observations is drawn from H market economies where strikes are actually known to occur.

The structural relations, which are assumed to be linear, are specified as follows:

$$
\begin{aligned}
y_i + \beta_{12}d_i &= \alpha_1 + \alpha_{11}k_i && + u_{1i} && (5.4.1) \\
d_i + \beta_{23}c_i &= \alpha_2 && + \alpha_{22}s_i && + u_{2i} && (5.4.2) \\
y_i \qquad - \qquad c_i &= && t_i && && (5.4.3)
\end{aligned}
$$
$$(i = 1, \ldots, H).$$

In the above system, $B \equiv \begin{bmatrix} 1 & \beta_{12} & 0 \\ 0 & 1 & \beta_{23} \\ 1 & 0 & -1 \end{bmatrix}$

and $\qquad \Gamma = \begin{bmatrix} \alpha_1 & \alpha_{11} & 0 & 0 \\ \alpha_2 & 0 & \alpha_{22} & 0 \\ 0 & 0 & 0 & 1 \end{bmatrix}.$

We see from the first relation that y_i is jointly determined by d_i, an endogenous variable, and by k_i; from the second, that d_i is a function of per capita consumption (a proxy for real wages) and the system rule. In the last relation we have an identity linking y_i to c_i and t_i.

The structural relations in equation 5.4 can be recast in reduced form since matrix B is normally nonsingular.[12]

12. The determinant of B, denoted Δ, is equal to $\beta_{12}\beta_{23} - 1$. Since β_{12} should be negative (days lost to strikes have a depressing effect on GDP per capita) and β_{23} should be positive (consumption and national income are positively correlated), the product $\beta_{12}\beta_{23}$ will generally be negative. But there is no reason, except in freakish cases, that it should be equal to 1. The inverse of B is equal to

$$
\frac{1}{\beta_{12}\beta_{23} - 1} \begin{bmatrix} -1 & \beta_{12} & \beta_{12}\beta_{23} \\ \beta_{23} & -1 & -\beta_{23} \\ -1 & \beta_{12} & 1 \end{bmatrix}.
$$

The reduced form of equations 5.4 is shown below:[13]

$$y_i = \frac{-\alpha_1 + \alpha_2\beta_{12}}{\Delta} - \frac{\alpha_{11}}{\Delta} k_i + \frac{\alpha_{22}\beta_{12}}{\Delta} s_i + \frac{\beta_{12}\beta_{23}}{\Delta} t_i + v_{1i}$$

$$d_i = \frac{\alpha_1\beta_{23} - \alpha_2}{\Delta} + \frac{\alpha_{11}\beta_{23}}{\Delta} k_i - \frac{\alpha_{22}}{\Delta} s_i - \frac{\beta_{23}}{\Delta} t_i + v_{2i} \qquad (5.5)$$

$$c_i = \frac{-\alpha_1 + \alpha_2\beta_{12}}{\Delta} - \frac{\alpha_{11}}{\Delta} k_i + \frac{\alpha_{22}\beta_{12}}{\Delta} s_i + t_i + v_{3i}.$$

We shall now verify from equations 5.5 that the conditions for exact identification are satisfied for the first relation (i.e., that the coefficients in the first of equations 5.4 can be deduced from the estimated coefficients of equation 5.5).

We first observe that the only nonzero coefficients in the first of equations 5.4 are for the first and second endogenous variables and for the first and second exogenous variables (counting the intercept as the first exogenous variable). We now write the submatrix, denoted $\Pi_{\Delta,**}$, of the matrix Π of coefficients of the reduced form, where the rows of $\Pi_{\Delta,**}$ correspond to the *included* endogenous variables in B (i.e., y_i and d_i) and its columns to the coefficient in Π of the *excluded* exogenous variables in Γ (i.e., s_i and t_i):

$$\begin{bmatrix} \alpha_{22}\beta_{12} & \beta_{12}\beta_{23} \\ -\alpha_{22} & -\beta_{23} \end{bmatrix}.$$

The determinant of this matrix being equal to zero, its rank, on the assumption that at least one coefficient differs from zero, is equal to 1. Because the number of included endogenous variables in the first of relations 5.4 is 2, the identification condition is exactly satisfied:

$$\rho\,(\Pi_{\Delta,**}) = 1 = G_\Delta - 1,$$

where $\rho\,(\Pi_{\Delta,**})$ is the rank of $\Pi_{\Delta,**}$ and G_Δ is the number of endogenous variables included with nonzero coefficients in the first of equations 5.4. It is

13. An error term now appears in equation 5.5, which is no longer an identity as in the structural form of equations 5.4. That v_{3i} depends on u_{1i} and u_{2i} may be inferred from the fact that B^{-1} has no zero elements. Multiplying the third row of B^{-1} by $(u_{1i}, u_{2i}, 0)'$, we obtain

$$v_3 = -\frac{u_{1i}}{\Delta} + \frac{\beta_{12}}{\Delta} u_{2i},$$

where $\Delta = (\beta_{12}\beta_{23} - 1)$.

easily verified that this same condition for exact identification is satisfied for the second and third relation as well.[14]

Inasmuch as the identification conditions are exactly satisfied, the regression coefficients may be calculated by any one of three familiar methods (indirect least squares, limited information single-equation technique, and two-stage least squares). The indirect least-squares method, for instance, calls for the calculation of all the coefficients of each equation of the reduced form by ordinary least squares (using the H sets of observations). Once these estimated coefficients are obtained for all three equations, it is an easy matter to derive the coefficients of the structural equation from these estimates by solving the requisite number of simultaneous equations (in this case by solving seven equations for the seven unknown parameters of equations 5.4).

The main point the comparer may wish to retain from this technical discussion is that when a system of interdependent relations is misspecified as a single-equation system, the coefficients obtained by the least-squares method from the latter will give biased estimates of the "true" coefficients in the correctly specified system. For example, were we to regress days lost to strikes on consumption per capita and the system structure variable, omitting the other relations, we would find the error term u_i correlated with consumption (because of the simultaneous nature of the system) and $E(u_i, c_i)$, the covariance between u_i and c_i, would no longer be zero, as must be the case to obtain "best linear unbiased estimates" from least-squares regressions. If the coefficient α_{22} of the system-structure variable were positive, it would be *overestimated* inasmuch as the single-equation regression ignores the depressing effect on GNP per capita of days lost to strikes (equation 5.4.1), of a lower GNP per capita on consumption, given exogenous investment (equation 5.4.3), and, hence, the indirect negative influence of s on c via equations 5.4.1 and 5.4.3, which partly offsets its direct positive impact in equation 5.4.2. The negative correlation of s and c is not captured by the least-squares estimate of the regression coefficient α_{22}, since c is treated as an exogenous variable in this misspecified system.

---

14. Note that the identification conditions could have been checked directly from equations 5.4. For example, if we exclude the rows and columns of B and Γ corresponding to the variables included in the first relation, we are left with

$$\begin{bmatrix} \beta_{23} & \alpha_{22} & 0 \\ -1 & 0 & 1 \end{bmatrix}.$$

The rank of this matrix is 2, which is equal to the number of endogenous variables in the entire structure minus 1, so that the condition for exact identification of the first relation is satisfied (see Johnston, op. cit., pp. 250–52).

5.4 System Structure and Efficiency Revisited[15]

In international comparisons the effect of the system structure can theoretically be determined in either of two ways, which can be formally stated, using "grand relationship" 5.1 expressed in reduced form. Provided all variables are continuous and possess derivatives of at least the first order, we can totally differentiate equation 5.1 to obtain

$$do = f_e \cdot de + f_s \cdot ds + f_p \cdot dp, \tag{5.6}$$

where do represents observed differences among countries or systems; de, ds, and dp stand for differences in the vectors of explanatory variables e, s, and p; and f_e, f_s, and f_p are matrices of partial derivatives of all functions in the equation system $f(\ )$ with respect to the explanatory variables e, s, and p.

The direct method determines the effect of the system structure on outcomes (do_s) by directly computing the vector $f_s \cdot ds$ equal to do_s. The indirect method consists of computing

$$do_s = do - f_e \cdot de - f_p \cdot dp.$$

Here we take the observed differences in outcomes and adjust for the presumed impact of observed differences in the environment and policies in order to derive the impact of the system structure on outcomes as a residual. This residual will also contain the effects of errors in the model (due to omitted variables, inaccuracies in measuring the explanatory variables, or both) and should therefore be calculated as a confidence interval (subjective, if necessary) rather than as a point estimate. Which of the alternative ways for the computation of do_s is adopted will depend at least in part on the information available about the various partial derivatives and about the differences in the explanatory variables observed in the countries compared.

In the previous section we illustrated the use of the direct method, to which we shall presently return (in sec. 5.5). The calculations of total factor productivity discussed in section 4.3 rest on the indirect approach. As we argued in that section, the differences in capital-and-labor productivity between two countries are likely to be caused by more factors than merely the differential effect of alternative system rules on production. Gaps in technological knowledge, divergent preferences, disparities in scale, and the effects of suboptimal policies in one or more of the economies compared are all potentially entangled in the skein of the residuals. Conclusions about the relative efficiencies of alternative system arrangements should only be drawn from the calculation of these residuals with the greatest diffidence and with appropriate modesty about the significance of the results.

---

15. This section is in part reproduced from Montias and Sturm, op. cit., sec. III.

5.5 Dummy Variables

The question that we have glossed over so far is how the variable, or the set of variables, subsumed under the term "system structure" ought to be measured. In some but by no means all cases, elements of the system structure may be measured if not on a continuum, at least on an integer scale. In a socialist economy of the Soviet type, for instance, rules determine which materials and machines will be rationed to producers by the Council of Ministers (or in effect by the Planning Commission), which by ministries, and which by the enterprises themselves. The proportion of the value of all materials and machines sold to domestic producers represented by materials and machines that are "centrally distributed" by the Council of Ministers may be taken as an index of centralization of a socialist economy. In market economies where strikes are permitted, the percentage of strikes decided on at the local trade union level is a quantifiable indicator of the decentralization of the union movement.

At times also, where a direct measure of a system rule cannot be effected, a rough proxy for the rule may be devised by introducing its presumed direct effect as an explanatory variable in a regression. Rules discriminating against "native" and "colored" workers in South Africa, for example, may be represented by a difference in wages between whites and nonwhites. However, suitable care should be taken that the proxy not be influenced by variables other than discrimination rules, in this case such as the educational level of the workers, their acquired skills, experience, and reliability. Since such proxies to rules are likely to be contaminated by the effects of environmental variables, no matter how hard we may try to purge them thereof, it is probably safer in most empirical studies to rely on direct indicators of the system structure even though they may not be continuous.

In recent years the use of binary $(0, 1)$ variables has gained wide currency. These variables, generally called "dummy variables" in regressions, are used to record the presence or absence of a particular system trait or even of an entire system structure, such as "communist" and "noncommunist," "centralized" and "market," "colonial rule" and "independence," and so forth.

The following example, based on the work of Frederic L. Pryor on the international determinants of income distribution,[16] illustrates the technique, along with some of the thornier problems encountered in its use. The dummy variable here is meant to capture the effect of "the system as a whole," that is, of both system rules and policies. It should be clear from the outset that, to the extent system rules and policies differ within the two groups of countries into which the sample of observations is divided ("communist" and "capital-

16. From his book *Property and Industrial Organization in Communist and Capitalist Nations* (Bloomington: Indiana University Press, 1973), pp. 82–83 and Appendix B9, pp. 448–49.

ist"), there will be "errors of measurement" in this explanatory variable similar to the errors introduced by aggregating heterogeneous variables.

Pryor posits the following functional relation between an index of income distribution and three explanatory variables:

$$X_{per} = f(P, Y/P, S), \qquad (5.7)$$

where X_{per} is the selected measure of income distribution (a percentile), P is total population, Y/P is GNP per capita, and S (basic system structure) $= 1$ for "communist countries" and 0 for "capitalist countries."[17] All observations are based on national statistics pertaining to the late 1950s or early 1960s. Earnings refer to pretax wages and salaries of full-time male workers outside agriculture.

The first two arguments in equation 5.7 represent environmental variables, GNP per capita standing as a proxy for the capital stock and other initial conditions. Owing to the strictly cross-sectional nature of the analysis, the policies available under each system could not be separated out from the system itself. To prevent the statistics for the largest countries (the United States and the Soviet Union) from dominating the regression and to increase the likelihood of normal distribution of the error terms in his regression, Pryor expressed all the variables in equation 5.7 in terms of natural logarithms. His results for the index of income distribution represented by the 75th percentile[18] in relation to the median income for each country were as follows:

$$\ln(X_{75}) = 4.138 - .041 \ln P + .068 S + .083 \ln(Y/P)$$
$$\phantom{\ln(X_{75}) = 4.138} (.009) \qquad (.023) \quad (.027) \qquad\qquad (5.8)$$

$$R^2 = .67 \qquad N \text{ (size of sample)} = 21,$$

where the data in parentheses are the standard deviations of the coefficients shown above and R is the coefficient of determination in this regression. All coefficients differ significantly from zero at the 95 percent probability level.

According to these results the effect of a larger population is to decrease the earnings per head that 75 percent of the population earn in excess of (measured in relation to the median) and hence to augment *inequality*. This is presumably due to the fact that, other things equal, larger countries may have a relatively wider range of regional disparities in earnings than smaller

17. The "communist countries" are the Soviet Union, Bulgaria, Czechoslovakia, East Germany, Hungary, Poland, and Yugoslavia. The "capitalist countries" are the United States, New Zealand, Australia, Sweden, Canada, Belgium, France, United Kingdom, West Germany, Denmark, the Netherlands, Austria, Finland, Spain, and Japan.

18. The "75th percentile" is defined here as the labor earnings per capita that were surpassed by 75 percent of labor earners. Earnings are expressed per job, not per person, and therefore exclude wages from moonlighting (important in certain communist countries).

countries do (vide East and South in the United States, Siberia and Tadzhi-kistan in the Soviet Union). Increases in national income per head have the opposite effect of reducing inequality. This may be attributed to the broader spread of education and technical training in richer countries, which would tend to reduce the premium paid for the possessions of these skills relative to untrained workers. The impact of the communist system is, apparently, to increase by 7 percent the relative earnings that 75 percent of the population earn in excess of.[19] It therefore decreases inequality.

The regression for the 5th percentile is

$$\ln (X_5) = 5.81 + .057 \ln P - .163S - .137 \ln (Y/P)$$
$$(.019) \qquad (.05) \quad (.058)$$
$$R^2 = .55 \qquad N = 21,$$

which again shows that population size increases inequality, while system and income per head tend to reduce it. All coefficients are again significantly different from zero at the 95 percent probability level.

All sorts of objections may be raised against these results. One may impugn the data, the regressions, or both. The data, as far as I could ascertain, are the best obtainable at the present time. This, however, is not a strong re-

---

19. The approximate antilog of .068 is .07. To see why the coefficient of S measures the ratio of the expected values of the dependent variable X_{75} in the two groups of countries, consider the basic equation (5.8) on which the regression is based:

$$\ln (X_{75}) = \alpha + \delta \ln P + \gamma S + \beta \ln (Y/P),$$

where δ, γ, and β are the regression coefficients of the natural logarithms of P, S, and Y/P, respectively, and α is the intercept of the regression line.

Let us assume that all coefficients except α are drawn from the same universe for both groups of countries. Then for the communist group of countries alone, the explicit form of the equation is

$$\ln (X_{75})_1 = \alpha + \delta \ln P + \gamma + \beta \ln (Y/P) \qquad (5.2')$$

since $S = 1$ for this group.

For the capitalist group we have

$$\ln (X_{75})_2 = \alpha + \delta \ln P + \beta \ln (Y/P) \qquad (5.2'')$$

since $S = 0$.

Subtracting equation 5.2' from 5.2'' yields

$$\ln (X_{75})_1 - \ln (X_{75})_2 = \gamma.$$

Hence $\dfrac{(X_{75})_1}{(X_{75})_2} = $ antilog γ.

If some of the other coefficients γ differ significantly for the two groups of countries, other dummy variables must be introduced to register these differences (see J. Johnston, op. cit., pp. 222–23). To test whether coefficients differ in two groups of observations, see George C. Chow, "Tests of Equality Between Sets of Coefficients in Two Linear Regressions," *Econometrica* 28 (July 1960): 591–605.

commendation. The regressions appear reasonable in the sense that none of the alternatives that come to mind seems any better.

It may be urged, for example, that "system" is highly correlated with some other explanatory variable that is actually influencing the dependent variable. At my suggestion, Pryor introduced the yearly change in GNP per head as an explanatory variable on the basis of the following reasoning: A rapid rate of growth might be expected to (1) turn the urban–rural terms of trade in favor of the farm sector, (2) raise the supply price of off-farm unskilled labor relative to intramarginal skilled workers, and hence (3) reduce income inequality in industry. The coefficient of regression for this variable did not turn out to be significant. A jointly conducted analysis of the residuals in equation 5.8—the difference between expected and observed values of the dependent variable—failed to reveal any pattern that could be attributed to conspicuous nonlinearity or to any omitted explanatory variables.

It is not obvious, at least to specialists in the West, why the income distribution in communist countries should be more even than in capitalist countries. Pryor's study of access to education and training in East and West led him to reject the hypothesis that the lower differentials in earnings in communist countries might be due to more widespread, less expensive facilities for acquiring skills. For the time being, we have no tenable hypothesis other than that some combination of the system rules and policies in effect in communist countries tends to make for a relatively egalitarian income distribution.

The use of dummy variables may be extended to more complex system phenomena than the one we have just examined. For instance, instead of one dummy variable representing "centralized" or "decentralized" economies, we may introduce a number of these variables, one for each important dimension along which centralization–decentralization may be defined (e.g., output setting, price determination, investment project-making, decisions on welfare budgets). We may also have indicators for different *degrees* of decentralization along any one of these dimensions. Suppose, for example, that investment decisions may be made at the level of (1) the plant, (2) the enterprise, (3) a regional organ, or (4) a federal agency. Dummy variables may then be defined as in the table below:

Level at which investment decisions are chiefly made	X_1	X_2	X_3	X_4
Plant	1	0	0	0
Enterprise	0	1	0	0
Region	0	0	1	0
Federal government	0	0	0	1

We might be interested in explaining the regional dispersion of investments[20] in a group of countries according to their observed degrees of centralization of investment decisions and their GNP per head. The regression might then be written in the following form:

$$\ln D = \beta_1 X_1 + \beta_2 X_2 + \beta_3 X_3 + \beta_4 X_4 + \beta_5 \ln (Y/P) + u, \quad (5.9)$$

where D is some appropriate measure for the regional dispersion of investments,[21] β_1 to β_4 are the regression coefficients on the dummy variables, β_5 is the coefficient for GNP per head, and u is an error term.

The assumption underlying this form of the regression is that the coefficient of the quantified explanatory variable [ln (Y/P) in equation 5.9] does not differ significantly for the different groups, in this case for the four levels at which investment decisions are chiefly made. If this assumption did not hold for one or more groups,[22] new dummy variables would have to be introduced to take these differences in slope into account.

Unfortunately, the addition of dummy variables entails a cumulative loss in degrees of freedom. As the confidence intervals around the regression coefficients become wider as a result of this loss, the chances of finding any of these coefficients to be significantly different from zero become slimmer.

The remedy for this loss may perhaps be found in alternative ways of augmenting the sample size of systems represented. The first is to pool cross-section data for various periods; the second is to break country data down into regions, states, constituent republics, or any other subaggregates of national systems.

To obtain any leverage from pooling cross-sectional data for various periods, it must first be shown that the coefficients of regression for these periods do not differ significantly. Otherwise, still more dummy variables must be introduced, and the observer may again be stymied by insufficient degrees of freedom.[23] Another difficulty often encountered with this technique is that the dependent variable in one period may be an explanatory variable in a subsequent period or at least may be highly correlated with an explanatory variable. This is almost certain to be the case when GNP per head is a dependent variable. In a model where GNP per capita was an explanatory variable and income distribution a dependent variable, the latter could have

20. One of the many conceivable indicators of equity.

21. One such measure would be the coefficient of regional variation. This would be computed from the sum of squared deviations from the per-region average of investments per head (calculated for each region), which sum would then be divided by the per-region average.

22. For a test of this assumption, see the reference to Chow, op. cit.

23. Note, however, that significant differences in regression coefficients for the different time periods may reflect important differences in the policy carried out in these periods in various countries (for instance, in the case of the United States as well as in the countries that are at present said to be "communist," differences in monetary and fiscal policy in the 1930s and in the postwar period). This may in and of itself be of interest to the comparer.

a statistical effect on the former via efficiency. If such a mutual dependence were observed, one would have to resort to a simultaneous-equation model, which, as we have seen, must then be properly identified to yield significant results. This is not to say that the mutual dependency of explanatory and dependent variables is ruled out in cross-section analyses but that it is likely to present a more serious problem in case data for various periods are pooled.

The technique of breaking down national data into subaggregates also has its drawbacks. The principal one is the doubtful availability of comparable data at the subnational level for a reasonably broad sample of countries. Another is that regions that are parts of larger economies cannot be expected to behave in precisely the same way as independent states with the same environment, policy, and system structure. Bulgaria and Belorussia may be broadly similar with regard to system structure, population, and GNP per head, but the fact that one is an independent state and the other a region of a much larger aggregate subject to allocation and distribution decisions taken at the federal level would lead one to suspect substantial differences in the behavior of these "communist systems." To avoid this difficulty, one may introduce another set of dummy variables, again at the cost of a loss in degrees

Region or country	Independent nation (I), state of the U.S. (U), Republic of Yugoslavia (Y), or Republic of the Soviet Union (S)	Dummy variables			
		X_1	X_2	X_3	X_4
Slovenia	Y	1	0	0	0
.	.	.	.	.	.
.	.	.	.	.	.
Macedonia	Y	1	0	0	0
Alabama	U	0	1	0	0
.	.	.	.	.	.
.	.	.	.	.	.
Washington	U	0	1	0	0
Belorussia	S	0	0	1	0
.	.	.	.	.	.
.	.	.	.	.	.
Ukraine	S	0	0	1	0
Hungary	I	0	0	0	1
.	.	.	.	.	.
.	.	.	.	.	.
Switzerland	I	0	0	0	1

of freedom. The comparer will incur a smaller loss if he classifies all elements in the sample as either independent states or regions and a larger loss if he wishes to associate each region with the particular aggregate of which it is a part. The following example illustrates the former approach.

Alternatively, in the above example, a fifth dummy variable (X_5) might be introduced that would denote whether a region was an independent state or part of a larger aggregate.

The system structure might also be disaggregated into a number of basic characteristics, such as the scale of centralization–decentralization of investment expenditures we already referred to, and a dummy variable might then be attached to each such attribute.

The number and kind of dummy variables introduced in an econometric model should not in principle depend merely on the likelihood of obtaining significant regression coefficients. The warning against "fishing for hypotheses," expressed in the first chapter definitely applies here. As far as possible, the model ought to be specified before the data are subjected to testing. We must have some theoretical reason for inserting an explanatory variable before we plug it into a regression. For if we allow the data to suggest the hypotheses, we run the risk of spurious or chance correlations. That the associations are due only to chance may be discovered—to our discomfiture—only when another observer tries to replicate the testing of the model with another set of observations.

In the next chapter we return to the microeconomics of system comparisons. Comparisons of system traits and the analysis of their effects on efficiency and on other outcomes may be interesting in and of themselves but we should always keep in mind that, wherever possible, the conjectures they suggest should be confronted with the evidence thrown up by actual systems, whether contemporary or historical. The testing of hypotheses based on the implications of models of systems differing from each other in one or more elements of their structure may at times seem a long way down the road; we shall try at least to start traveling down the right road.

Part 3
Microcomparisons: Elements of System Description

6

Consumption and Distribution

6.1 INSTRUMENTAL AND CONSUMMATORY ACTIONS

System rules may affect "consumption" decisions in direct ways ("only noblemen are entitled to carry swords") or in indirect ways ("cigarette ads may be posted but not televised"). Neoclassical economics, if it recognizes these effects at all, would relegate them to the general category of "changes in tastes." Greater precision in defining our concepts will allow us to make useful distinctions among these "changes in tastes" and enable us to analyze more methodically the impact of different system rules on consumption decisions. It will incidentally help us to construct definitions of "goods" and "bads," "economic activities," and other basic building blocks in our system description.

A basic distinction may be made between an individual's "instrumental" and "consummatory" actions. Consider an individual who may either carry out action a_1 with outcome o_1 under state e_1 and o_2 under state e_2 or action a_0 with outcome o_3 in state e_1 and outcome o_1 in state e_2. (These states are considered to be "exogenous" components of his environment beyond his power to affect them, at least by the actions considered.) His alternatives are described in the following table.

	State e_1	State e_2
a_1	o_1	o_2
a_0	o_3	o_1

To infuse the example with concrete imagery, suppose that a_1 stands for "i buys a turkey at the store at time t" and a_0 for "i watches television at t." The distinct outcomes at $t + 1$ are (1) o_1, "a turkey is in the refrigerator," (2) o_2, "two turkeys are in the refrigerator," and (3) o_3, "the refrigerator is empty." State e_1 is "no other individual has put a turkey in the refrigerator" and e_2 "i's wife has put a turkey in the refrigerator." If i would choose a_1 in case he were *a priori* certain that state e_1 would occur but would choose a_0 if he knew e_2 would occur, then a_1 is "instrumental" to outcome o_1. In general, an individual's action is strictly *instrumental* to a given outcome if he would carry

73

it out only if he knew for sure that the outcome would *not* occur unless this particular action was undertaken. Such actions are said to be *irksome*. (Whether or not an action is irksome for him clearly depends on i's alternatives and on his expectations.)

An action by individual i is *consummatory* when (1) its outcome cannot occur unless i himself performs the action or (2) if the outcome were certain to occur independently of i's action, i would undertake it anyway. Example 1: "i eats a piece of the turkey," where the outcome is "the turkey is chemically transformed inside i's body into nutritive ingredients and waste matter." Example 2: "i enjoys shopping and would buy a turkey even if he knew his wife had already gotten one."

As a third example, consider a man who gives to charity because he would like to relieve poverty but who would cease his benefaction if he heard that some individual or organization was about to assume the burden. His charitable action is then instrumental. So is an eleemosynary act by a person who wishes to set an example for others to follow in the expectation that if everyone were as generous as he was, the world would be better off. However, if the benefactor were ready to give the same amount to charity, irrespective of the actions of others, his actions would be consummatory.[1]

Many actions have both "consummatory" and "instrumental" aspects. Although a man may go shopping mainly to bring goods home that will later make it possible for him to engage in consummatory actions, he may also enjoy the shopping itself. One way to identify and to describe these "enjoyable instrumental actions" is as follows. At time t an individual is taken to be indifferent between some consummatory action a with an immediate and final outcome at t, and such a mixed action, denoted $\tilde{a}$. If he were to receive information at this time that the consummatory action he counted on performing as a sequel to $\tilde{a}$ at a later time were unlikely to be possible, his preference ordering over actions at t would change and he would prefer a to $\tilde{a}$. Example: at time t a man is indifferent between going out to shoot wild ducks

---

1. These three cases correspond to Kenneth Arrow's three-way classification of the motives for charity ("Gifts and Exchanges," *Philosophy and Public Affairs* 1 [Oct.–Dec. 1972]: 348). Consummatory and instrumental actions were already sharply distinguished in Plato's *Republic*. Glaucon, Socrates' protagonist, was of the opinion that there were three kinds of "goods": (1) a kind "we should be glad to have for its sake alone, not because we desire what comes from it"; (2) a kind "that we love both for its own sake and for what comes from it"; and (3) "a kind of good which athletic sports belong to, and to be cured by treatment when sick, and the art of healing, and the other ways of making money. These are laborious...but they give us benefit; we should not care to have them alone for their own sakes, but for the sake of the wages and the other things which come from them" (*Great Dialogues of Plato*, trans., W. D. H. Rouse [New York: Mentor Classic, 1956], p. 155). To enjoy the first kind is to perform a consummatory action, the second kind is a mixed instrumental and consummatory action, the third a pure instrumental action.

in the bay, action $\tilde{a}$, and watching TV, action a. He reads in the newspaper at t that his shotgun pellets are likely to poison the meat of ducks, which therefore should not be eaten. If duck hunting is a mixed action—owing to the added dividend, after the pleasure of the hunt, of eating wild duck—the new information he has received should cause him to opt for watching television instead of hunting. Pure consummatory actions are then those that have no such "instrumental component."

The outcome (corresponding to a particular exogenous state) of an instrumental action performed at or before t may be deemed part of the initial environment for period $t + 1$. For a vast class of instrumental actions, the outcome makes it possible to engage in one or more consummatory actions in $t + 1$ for at least some of the exogenous states that might occur in that period. Suppose that if an individual could predict state e with certainty he would prefer action $a(e)$ to all other actions in $A(e)$, the set of possible actions in $t + 1$.[2] We may extend our assumption about the measurable utility of outcomes to the utility of *consummatory actions carried out under given states*. We also posit, in case a consummatory action has an "instrumental component," that it can be assigned a utility number *as if* the consummatory actions consequent upon its outcome(s) in later periods were predicted to be impossible (i.e., as if hunting generated only immediate utility, none being anticipated from eating its possible products).

The expected utility of an instrumental action a would then be the sum, over all consummatory actions rendered possible by a, of the utilities assigned to these actions under given states, weighted by the subjective probabilities that the individual attaches to the (exogenous) states of the world in which they would be chosen over all others. For example, an individual's expected utility from renting a convertible car for the weekend may depend on his subjective probability of the occurrence of weather warm enough to enjoy riding with the top down. Let this probability be $\frac{1}{2}$. If the utility of riding with the top down is u_x and of riding in poor weather with the top up is u_y, where this action is still preferred to all other alternatives for that state, the expected utility $\bar{u}$ of renting the convertible will be $\frac{1}{2}u_x + \frac{1}{2}u_y$.

We can rank according to preference the instrumental actions that an individual might undertake to achieve a given expected utility $\bar{u}$ as if $\bar{u}$ were an outcome under certainty (i.e., under a given state). The individual will then choose the instrumental action that he prefers over all others in order to achieve $\bar{u}$.

Stronger assumptions are needed (1) to assign utility numbers to the instrumental actions such that the utility (if negative, the "disutility") of each

---

2. The definitions below are easily modified to accommodate the case where $a(e)$ belongs to a set $\{a(e)\}$ of actions preferred to all others but among which the individual is indifferent.

instrumental action can be compared to $\bar{u}$ and (2) to argue that no instrumental action resulting in $\bar{u}$ will be performed unless its utility is larger or its "disutility" smaller than $\bar{u}$.

This behavioral "ye-shall-know-them-by-their-acts" approach does not require us to assume that an individual can rank according to his preferences all possible states of his environment.[3] If he regularly gives to charity or votes for a candidate to public office who is known to favor income-redistributive policies and if he is consistent in his actions, we may infer that he prefers his poorer fellow-citizens to be better off than they are now. We need not assume that he attaches a different utility number to each possible income distribution, let alone to each of the bundles of "goods and services" that his fellow citizens might be able to "consume." Neither need we assume that a "central planner" responsible for making decisions that will affect most citizens' welfare has a well-defined preference ordering over all possible direct and indirect outcomes of his actions. It may be more fruitful to assume that he will choose among the instrumental actions open to him in such a way as to maximize the expected utility of the outcomes that these actions will make possible (e.g., a 10 percent increase in industrial output or possibly even a promotion to a higher political post).[4]

The analysis of "externalities",[5] however, will require us to assume that individuals have preferences over states of their environment that cannot necessarily be inferred from their actions. If a factory emits smoke that deposits soot on the paint of neighboring houses, the preference of these neighbors for states of their environment where this pollution would not occur may be expressible only in words, not in actions. Their negative preference would be just as real whether they were moved to repaint their house or just to deplore their loss.

The rules and laws in a system structure constrain individuals' decisions with respect to the instrumental or consummatory actions they could conceivably undertake; they may also affect their expectations and hence the expected utility of the instrumental actions they contemplate.

The system structure of most modern economies severely restricts the choices individuals can make among certain instrumental actions of critical importance to their livelihood. The length of their working day, for instance, is most frequently determined by the rules of ruling organizations, by the rules of the organization for which they work, or by both. It would be unrealistic to suppose that a majority of the individuals in these economies can match the

---

3. The behavioral approach of course can only be adopted if the assumptions about the independence of "tastes" and "beliefs" are warranted. If not, as we have already argued (p. 18), we may have to assume individual utility functions on the domain of outcomes or of states.

4. Cf. S. Wellisz, "Lessons of 20 Years of Planning and Developing Countries," *Economica* 38 (May 1971): 121–35.

5. On externalities, see sec. 9.4.

disutility of an extra hour of work against the expected utility of the consummatory actions they would be able to perform if they put in the additional
effort. A less unrealistic supposition is that individuals may choose to work for
an organization in which the intensity of their effort and the length of the working day will be most suitable, given their expected earnings and the expected
utility they may hope to derive from them. Even family farms have formal or
informal rules—imposed by the owner, patriarch, or head of household—that
may make it difficult for any member to work only as long and as hard as his
expected utility of the extra payoff might warrant.

Sumptuary laws, which were commonly enacted in Europe in the fourteenth
to sixteenth centuries, regulated the clothes and apparel that individuals were
permitted to wear. The laws could prohibit the acquisition of certain items,
thus restraining consummatory actions associated with their wear or display.
However, a restraint bearing specifically on consummatory actions did not
necessarily rule out the acquisition of these items: a sword, for instance, might
be bought by a man who was not noble and therefore could not wear it in
public, but it could be kept in his house for defensive purposes or for decoration.
Sumptuary laws have a modern equivalent in the unwritten rules of certain
corporations that make it inadvisable for an underling to drive a Cadillac
when his boss drives a Ford or to wear an open shirt at the office when the boss
wears a collar and tie.

The administrative rules in the USSR that prohibit foreign citizens from
traveling beyond a prescribed distance from the capital without permission
may have effects similar to those of sumptuary laws. A foreign diplomat, we
may surmise, would be less inclined to buy a station wagon and to bring it to
Moscow for his personal use if he knew he would not be allowed to travel
freely over long distances (as was the case in Stalin's era).

Ruling organizations, virtually in all periods of history and in all the
economies one could name, have attempted to restrain individuals from
perpetrating "fraud" in their dealings with other individuals. The notion
here is that if individual i acquires an object from individual j, then i's instrumental action must be guided by subjective probabilities of the future
consummatory actions this object will render possible that are reasonably
accurate, or at least that do not differ too markedly from the expectations that
j may entertain about the possibility of i's performing these actions. The law
will not allow a man to insert razor blades in the apples he will give to children
at Halloween. In recent years in the United States, cigarette manufacturers
have been compelled to state the possible health risks to which their customers
may be exposed. In this instance the ruling organization may be suggesting
to consumers that the risks are even greater than the manufacturer believes
to be the case (assuming that the latter really has faith in the reports of the
Tobacco Institute).

Advertising may be aimed at changing individuals' expectations regarding the nature, range, or duration of the consummatory actions they will engage in if they buy the advertised product or it may be aimed at modifying their preferences directly. "Our razor blades last longer" is an example of the first category, "our cigarettes *taste* good" of the second.

In modern economies the objects an individual acquires from a manufacturer or dealer are not "one of a kind" but are representatives of a population of very similar objects produced or distributed by the seller. A "label" or "brand name" is usually attached to all these similar objects. The expectations of future utility that an individual will form about a particular object belonging to such a population will depend in part on the consummatory actions that he previously engaged in with other objects in this same population (or what he believes to be the same population). His expectations will be most realistic if the differences among these objects are indeed very small and he has frequently sampled from the population. By sticking to a brand, an individual may then hope to minimize the number of decisions he will regret. As the individual samples these objects, he accumulates information about their typical properties, including their possible deviations from the norm. Knowledge of the history of an individual's consumption of a particular "product" is often essential to an understanding of how he will react to changes in its "price" or other exogenously given characteristics.

Repeated sampling, it should be remarked, may affect an individual's preferences as well as his subjective probabilities. He may get tired of the product or like it increasingly well (for a given quantity "consumed" per period). A particular instance of a repetition that is preference enhancing is when each consummatory action "reveals" characteristics that had not been perceived before. An individual may have a very different sensation from hearing a Bartok quartet for the first time and for the tenth. A rationale for the "subsidization" by ruling organizations of musical performances is that they will induce people to listen to music which they would not otherwise have heard and that eventually the change in a listener's tastes brought about by repeated exposure will make it possible to remove the subsidy and put the activity on a self-sustaining basis.[6] In this instance, policy rather than system rules would be used to achieve the outcome desired by the decision makers in the ruling organizations. Formally, we may call *educative* a sequence of consummatory actions of a given type each of which enhances the utility of the next above what it would have been in its absence.[7]

To recapitulate, we have focused on the advantages for system description

6. The parallel with "infant industry" arguments for subsidizing manufactures in developing countries is self-evident.

7. It is assumed that the actions in the sequence are sufficiently spaced out in time to rule out diminishing marginal utility due to satiation (e.g., hearing the same Bartok quartet four times the same evening).

of the behavioristic model which posits that individuals choose among instrumental actions in such a way as to maximize the expected utility of the consummatory actions that they render possible (or, if they satisfice, in such a way as to secure an expected utility equal or superior to some satisfactory level). The rules of a system may influence individuals' choices among instrumental actions by modifying their expectations or by altering their preference ordering over the consummatory actions these instrumental actions will render possible. The policies of ruling organizations may also affect individuals' preference orderings by inducing them to expose themselves to educative sequences of consummatory actions.

6.2 CUSTODY AND ITS RELATION TO CONSUMPTION AND PRODUCTION ACTIVITIES

We now propose to use the definitions developed in the last section to break down into their constituent elements such complex operations as "consumption" and "distribution" as they are carried out under the restraints set by the rules, customs, and traditions of a system structure.

When an individual performs a consummatory or instrumental action, the objects that are "used" (perceived, transformed, and so on) in performing this action as well as the actions by other individuals that contribute to its performance may be called the *inputs* of the action. The (expected) utility associated with the action may be thought of as its *output*. An object or another individual's action is *consumed* when it enters as an input into a pure consummatory action.[8] (The object may or may not be transformed in the process.) A *good* is an input into a consummatory or an instrumental action with the following properties: (1) One or more of its characteristics, including possibly its location, must be the outcome of an individual action, and (2) it must be positively valued in the individual's utility function. A *bad* is defined identically, with the exception of the second property, where the word "negatively" should be substituted for the word "positively." A *service* (resp. *disservice*) for individual i is a good consisting of an action positively (resp. negatively) valued by i, where this action is performed by some other individual on his behalf (resp. to his detriment). A service, unlike most goods, cannot be stored for future use.

Let object j[9] enter as an input at a given point in time in the consummatory action of individual i. Object j may be of the type that for technological reasons cannot be shared, in the sense that it may enter as an input into an action for

---

8. This is in accord with everyday usage of the word *consumed*. We are not used to thinking that a businessman "consumes" his office and his secretary's services when he enjoys the instrumental activity of working.

9. We recall that an object may be a television signal or any other source of stimuli that can be perceived by an individual's senses.

only one individual at a time (a clarinet in the action "playing a clarinet," a cigarette in the action "smoking a cigarette," and so forth). Or it may be of the type that the utility to i will be lowered for every additional individual who shares in its use (a swimming pool on a hot summer day).[10] Or it may be a collection of objects such that the utility to i will be higher the more individuals share in its use, at least up to a certain number (example: most people prefer a full concert hall or theater to an empty one for a live performance). Finally, certain objects or amalgams of objects can be shared among any number of individuals without affecting the utility of any of them. Whether or not these objects are produced by a ruling organization, they are called *public goods* (or *public bads* if they affect the utility of individuals adversely). The same classification may be made of actions whose benefic or malefic effects may or may not be shared by a variable number of individuals.[11]

Consider now *all* the goods and services entering as inputs into consummatory or instrumental actions performed by individuals belonging to the system in period t. A *distribution* is a complete description of these inputs including a listing of the individuals sharing in the benefic or malefic effects of each of these inputs.[12] System rules in all known systems place significant restrictions on (1) the class of acceptable distributions ("who may have access to what") and (2) the class of actions that will result in a legitimate change in distribution ("who may transfer custody for what to whom").

Custody is a relation between the individuals in a system and the objects whose physical characteristics, location, or other properties these individuals can affect by their actions. One or more participants in a system are said to have *custody* over an object if, by virtue of a formal or an informal rule of the organization to which they belong or of a ruling organization to which they are subject, they may change the physical characteristics, the location, or the custody itself of that object within the time period and other limits set by this rule. (The rule may be a matter of convention or custom, as when a mother normally has custody of her own child or a boy of the snowman he has built.)[13]

Custody rules make it possible for the individual desirous of consuming a nondurable object in his custody to do so without fear of retaliation by other individuals who would also have liked to consume it. If the object is more or less durable or reusable and if his enjoyment is significantly reduced by its simultaneous consumption by other individuals, most systems grant him

---

10. If an individual buys a clarinet (an instrumental action), the expected utility of the action is likely to be lower if he knows he will have to share it *in the course of time* with a certain number of individuals.

11. More precise definitions of public goods will be found in sec. 17.2.

12. For details, see sec. 9.2.

13. Disposition over objects and ownership will be studied in sec. 9.2.

custodial rights restricting its access.[14] These rights may or may not be exclusive. In the case of production activities, custodial rights are necessary to prevent unauthorized individuals from consuming other individuals' inputs or outputs —for obvious reasons. This derivation reveals the "social character" (to borrow an expression from the Marxist vocabulary) of consumption and production activities.

For technological reasons, many public goods are such that their consumption by individuals either cannot be restricted at all or can be restricted only at a prohibitive cost with existing technology. Unrestrictable public goods include security from invasion from abroad, freedom from contagious diseases, and the privilege of living in a society where *other individuals* do not die of hunger in the streets. An example of a restrictable public good is a cable-television signal. A park may be thought of as a *semipublic good* insofar as the sharing of its benefits will not, up to a certain point, reduce the utility of the sharers.

We are now ready to discuss the notion of scarcity. Suppose that good j can be divided into units that are small relative to the ability of most individuals to discriminate in the perception of the characteristics of these individual units. Such a good will be *scarce for a set of individuals in a system* if either (or both) of the following conditions prevail: (1) Irksome actions by one or more members of the set are required to increase by one unit the supply from the environment or from a production activity of this good or of its close "substitutes" (e.g., goods or services with characteristics similar to j and ranked approximately as high in the preference ordering of at least one of these individuals) *and* at least one individual would prefer to consume that extra unit rather than not to consume it; (2)(a) member i has exclusive or custody rights over a unit of j permitting him to consume a unit of this good "all by himself" or partial rights of custody allowing him to share its consumption with a list of individuals specified by order or by rule, (b) he would prefer consuming this unit of the good or the service rather than do without it, and (c) some other individual(s) in the set would prefer an alternative situation where exclusive or partial custody rights would be transferred to him (or to them).

14. The extent to which access to the consumption of an object or a bundle of objects and services is restricted varies from system to system depending in part on the importance that individuals place on exclusive or nearly exclusive access. In most places nowadays, for example, restaurants offer exclusive custody to their patrons of the food they serve but restricted, non-exclusive custody of the locale. In the United States, if the table has a tablecloth, a customer and his guests have exclusive temporary custodial rights over it; in the Soviet Union, generally speaking, they do not (anyone can be seated at "your" table). In the late nineteenth century many patrons of French restaurants preferred not to share the restaurant's locale with other individuals and were served in special rooms or isolated booths, where they could engage in a broader range of consumption activities.

Some examples may help clarify our use of this familiar concept. Consider the canvasses of a man painting for his own pleasure. Suppose that all his products are of the same quality and are enjoyed equally by those who view them. If neither he would be made better off if he could enjoy one more of his own paintings nor would anyone else prefer to have one more than he currently has access to rather than do without it for his own enjoyment, the man's paintings are *not* scarce. A priest may enjoy saying mass or he may do it from sheer habit without any sense of irksomeness. But if the church is packed on a particular Sunday and someone is frustrated in his desire to get in or even to obtain a better view of the altar, the sequence of actions that the priest performs for the faithful *is* a scarce service.

Rain needed to humidify a parched agricultural region is not normally a scarce good, since human actions that would increase its supply are usually technically infeasible. However, if rain clouds can be seeded with a significant chance of success, rain becomes a scarce good in terms of our definition.[15]

It is generally true, in the sense of a fact frequently observed rather than a proposition that can be derived from the above definitions, that when a good under an individual's custody is scarce there is usually some individual willing to perform an irksome action or to give up some quantity of another scarce good to obtain access to it. (Counterexample: a man gathers crayfish from a river at considerable trouble to himself; nobody he knows likes crayfish but him.)

In most systems an individual i wishing to consume good j must normally perform an irksome action or give up some good j' desired by one or more individuals with custody over j to induce him or them to give up custody over j in his favor. He must then choose between a collection of objects or actions $(x_1, \ldots, x_j, \ldots, x_k, \ldots, x_n)$ and another collection $(x_1, \ldots, x_j + \Delta x_j, \ldots, x_k - \Delta x_k, \ldots, x_n)$, where Δx_j is the amount of j desired from individual i' and Δx_k is the amount of x_k that i expects i' will accept "in exchange for" Δx_j.[16] Even though the characteristics of good k may already have been perceived by i (since some quantities are already in his custody), the choice between the two collections may be fairly complicated. If, for example, he is extremely uncertain about the characteristics of j—he is not sure whether j will turn out to be a good or a bad—he may still be willing to accept some units of j, if only to experiment with its consumption, but he may not be able to tell how much k he should give up to obtain Δx_j.

---

15. Suppose that the individuals in a system *believe* they can influence the rainfall by implorations to the deity, rain dances, and so on. Then the logic of the above definition would compel us to admit that, if these implorations or dances were irksome—the individuals concerned would rather be doing something else—rain would be a scarce good.

16. This example assumes that individuals barter goods. Once "price" and "income" have been defined, it is possible to treat Δx_k as the decrement in good k that i prefers to give up when his income is diminished by the price he has to pay to i' or to anybody else to obtain Δx_j.

Economic activity may now be defined as a production or distribution activity performed with the intention of increasing the availability to some individual(s) of a scarce good or service or of transferring its custody from one set of individuals to another.[17]

6.3 TASTES AND VALUES

So far we have used individuals' preferences at decision points to classify objects and actions as goods or bads. Nothing was said about whether or not

17. Two alternative approaches to the definitions of "economic" and "economics" may briefly be considered. Karl Polanyi argues that economics has a formal meaning that "derives from the logical character of the means-ends relationship" and a "substantive meaning [that] derives from man's dependence for his livelihood upon nature and his fellows." The substantive meaning "refers to the interaction with his natural and social environment, insofar as this results in supplying him with the means of material want satisfaction" (Polanyi, *Semantics of General Economic History*, rev. ed. [New York, 1953], p. 162). Polanyi rejects the notion that the logic of choice "between different uses of means induced by an insufficiency of the means," is relevant to all concrete, observable situations where man interacts with his environment in supplying himself with the means of material want satisfaction. Indeed, he points out further (p. 163) that "some of the most important physical and social conditions of livelihood such as the availability of air and water or a loving mother's devotion to her infant are not, as a rule, so limiting" (i.e., scarcity generating). I have two main objections to the "substantive definition" (which is basic for Polanyi's study of historical systems). (1) "Material wants," if they could be defined precisely, would probably be too narrow a category. (Art and religion do not satisfy "material wants" but are bound up with economic activities that may be a proper subject of study.) (2) Nonscarce goods such as air and water may be inputs to economic activities, the products of which *are* scarce. But I doubt whether there is anything to be gained by considering as economic such activities as swimming for pleasure or walking in fresh air (where there is no scarcity, "on the margin," of either fresh water or air). A "loving mother's devotion to her infant" may or may not be sufficient to ensure that all services the infant would enjoy or that the mother would like to have performed on his behalf are actually carried out by the mother without becoming irksome to her. If some of these activities become irksome, there is proper reason to consider them economic. They may indeed be performed differently in different systems: by nurses or by automatic rockers at home, or in day-care centers.

Kenneth Boulding in his presidential address to the American Economic Association wrote that "economics specializes in the study of that part of the total system which is organized through exchange and which deals with exchangeables. This to my mind is a better definition of economics than those which define it as relating to scarcity or allocation, for the allocation of scarce resources is a universal problem which applies to political decisions and political structures through coercion, threat, and even to love and community, just as it does to exchange" ("Economics as a Moral Science," *American Economic Review* 59 [March 1969]: 4). One obvious objection to Boulding's definition is that it excludes all Robinson Crusoe-type situations where individuals must budget scarce resources, including time, among different activities without interacting with other individuals at all. The key word "exchange," furthermore, is not defined. According to a plausible definition, if individual i has custody over good j and i' over good j', an exchange occurs when, as a result of an interaction between i and i', individual i ends up with j' and i' with j. "Exchange" then excludes non-quid pro quo transactions, where i ends up with j *and* j' and i' with nothing. If so, Boulding surely rules out a great many interesting interactions about which economists might have something useful to say. (Boulding himself considers a number of problems in his address that would be out of bounds if this strict definition were applied.)

some other individual i' would prefer i to have access or to be exposed to one or another collection of objects or actions. For the purposes of defining a "good j for i" then, the preferences of i for j mattered; those of i' for the consumption of j by i did not. There is some gain in clarity to be made by calling the preferences of i among the objects and actions he might have access or be exposed to his *tastes*, whereas his preferences among the objects and actions *other* individuals might have access or be exposed to may be called his *values*.[18] Here of course the collection may include bads or disservices for these other individuals, such as poison or capital punishment, as well as goods and services. Also what i' may consider a good for himself may be considered by i a bad for i' (e.g., i' is a drug addict, i is not, and a dose of morphine is the object that i would like i' *not* to consume).

When many individuals in a system share the same value (e.g., that all individuals in the system should be free from starvation), it is said to be a *common value*. The "legitimacy" of the ruling organizations and of the rules they issue often rests on these common values. Loosely speaking, societies "come unglued" when the set of individuals with common values concerning a number of basic propositions shrinks below a certain minimum.

---

18. Boulding, op. cit., p. 1.

7

Technology and System

7.1 INTERACTIVITIES

Anyone taking the trouble to look out of the window of his train (wherever this particular technique of transportation can still be used by the itinerant comparer) will notice differences in technology as he travels from one economy to another. The combination of land, labor, machinery, and structures used to breed cattle, to plant or to harvest potatoes, or to transport these products from farm to village differs conspicuously, even in neighboring countries such as Bulgaria and Turkey. Economists are given to attribute these differences in technology to differences in resource endowment, including available machinery and labor of varying skills, or more generally, if we may revert to the vocabulary developed in chapter 2, to differences in the environments of the economies undergoing comparison.[1]

As a first approximation and in a majority of cases, this environmental explanation is probably correct. Nevertheless, it may be instructive to consider an important category of cases where the structure of the system or the preferences of decision makers influence, or even determine, the technology adopted in individual economies.

The definition of an activity in chapter 2—essentially a repeatable action that transforms one collection of individuals and objects, called inputs, into another, called outputs—was broad enough to range from a detailed process for making a small valve in an automobile to the manufacture of the entire automobile itself up to and including delivery to a customer. For purposes of this analysis it will be useful to distinguish two classes of activities: *elemental activities* and *interactivities*.

Elemental activities associate a given set of individuals with the transformation process. Except for buying–selling and other transfer activities, no change of custody takes place as inputs are transformed into outputs.

1. Attempts to construct aggregate production functions from countries with different capital/labor ratios and relative wages and returns to capital rest (ever so uncomfortably) on the assumption of a uniformly available "technology," in the sense of a large bundle of activities from among which each country's decision makers choose those subsets that are most profitable to utilize, given the relative scarcities of capital, labor, and other inputs prevailing therein.

Interactivities (which bear much the same relation to activities as interactions to actions) are combinations of interdependent elemental activities, each of which is associated with a distinct set of individuals. The interdependence of the activities in question will occur whenever the efficiency of allocation, as perceived by the individuals making the relevant decisions, requires at least one of the following.

1. The activities make use of the same indivisible input(s) (example: different tasks to be carried out on one lathe in the same day).

2. They contribute to the same indivisible output(s) (building a house).

3. They must be carried out jointly (one man holds the horse, the other shoes it) or simultaneously (individuals whose travel converges on a common meeting place).

4. They must be carried out in a particular sequence because an output of one activity becomes an input to another (transferring liquid iron from a blast furnace to a foundry).

5. Their levels must stand in a certain proportion because two of their respective inputs originate from, or two of their respective outputs are required for, a single activity characterized by constant proportions of outputs or inputs.

The interdependencies 1–3 are often absolutes. Interdependencies 4 and 5 become a matter of degree if alternative sources of input or uses of output exist at moderate cost differentials. On the other hand, chains of pairwise interdependencies of types 4 and/or 5 create secondary, tertiary, . . . interdependencies of a similar type that attenuate further as the number of links in the chain increases.[2]

The "coordination problems"[3] of production, transportation, distribution, and consumption take their form in large part from the nature of the interdependencies among the activities involved. The literature on activity analysis can be drawn upon for a formalization of these coordination problems; it also provides a background against which the solutions offered by different systems can be compared. The following section contains further observations toward such a marriage of activity analysis and organization theory.

7.2 Custody and Transfers of Custody[4]

We may conjecture that in most modern systems almost any resource, item of equipment, or good in process is at any time in the custody of some entity (operator, foreman, plant department, sales department, owner, manager,

---

2. Koopmans and Montias, op. cit., pp. 54–55.
3. For a definition of "coordination," see sec. 10.4.
4. The greater part of this section is taken from Koopmans and Montias, pp. 52–53.

trader, and so on). In the case of a machine, the *custodial entity* controls its use in time and between claimants. In the case of a material, good in process, or finished good, the custodial entity determines the next disposition of the good, such as leaving or placing it in inventory, continuing its processing, entering it into the next stage of processing, while in some of these cases transferring its custody to another entity.

Transfers of custody tend to occur, for good and rather obvious efficiency reasons, in those states of each good between processing stages, to be called *transfer states*, in which one or more of the following applies.

a. The good is capable of being handled (automobiles) and/or stored (steel billets) and/or delivered (electric power) without serious loss of quality.

b. The specifications describing the transfer state are standardized.

c. The transferrer or the transferee or both can expect to have a choice between more than one transferee or transferrer, respectively, who may belong to different entities engaged in the same production activities or who may differ in the processing activity that preceded transfer or that is to take place after transfer (coal).

If a custodial entity is an organization, efficiency often requires that it be clear to all concerned to which member of the organization the custody of which good is delegated, even if subject to reversal by a supervisor for the custodial activity in the case of a "hierarchy."[5] For goods not in continuous use (television set in the family) delegation may extend to all members of an organization on a first-come-first-served basis, again subject to reversal.

In any system in which one or more of the above types of goods or resources are privately owned, custody normally goes with ownership or is delegated by the owner.[6] For this and other reasons, private ownership of resources and of man-made means of production is usually regarded as a major system characteristic.

Transfers of custody, or of delegated custody, may take place between entities embedded in the same organization or between entities not belonging to the same organization for the activity or set of activities in question. Whether the transfer of a given type of good of similar specification in two systems falls in one or the other of these two cases will in general depend on the system. The relative frequency of transfers within as against between organizations is indeed an important system characteristic. However, we conjecture that there is a very substantial similarity and overlap between systems in the specifications not only of finished goods and services but also of the unfinished transfer states in the production of these commodities. We surmise further that the particular bundle of production activities taking

5. On hierarchies, see sec. 12.1.
6. Further remarks on the relation of custody and ownership are given in sec. 9.3.

place between two successive transfer states that two systems have in common depends less on their system structure than on the scale of the economy or of the enterprise, and, given a modicum of efficiency, on the environment. Among pertinent environmental factors, the relative scarcities of aggregate basic inputs such as labor, resources, and capital (produced means of production) to the economy as a whole are especially significant.

We adduce three reasons for these conjectures. The first is that technology does not stop or change much in character at the boundaries between systems. Acceptability of technology is usually unrelated to the system of origin, and information on advanced technology circulates widely and is given constant attention. The second reason follows from the first. The economies inherent in the characteristics a, b, and, c of transfer states listed above are rather apparent, and their perception is not much affected by system characteristics. Finally (the third reason), both scale and factor proportions are likely to enter into the bundle of production activities occurring between successive transfer states, scale because of the indivisibilities of human operators and pieces of equipment, factor proportions because even moderate efficiency demands reasonably full use of available factors.

While the above reasoning has been largely in terms of production of goods, similar reasoning applies, *mutatis mutandis*, to most industrial services as well, if performance of a service is substituted for transfer of custody of a good. This includes transportation, in which case only transport-relevant characteristics of the goods shipped need to be taken into account.

A *counterexample* to the above conjecture may be helpful in illustrating its portent. Pig iron in most economies is produced in an integrated steel mill. It is transferred from the blast furnace to the open hearth in a hot state. If it is shipped from one mill to another it must be reheated at a significant expense. In Poland in the mid-1950s, owing to errors in investment policy and short-falls in the realization of investment plans, a good deal of pig iron had to be shipped from iron-surplus to iron-deficit mills. The transfer in a cold state was an indirect consequence of the system—perhaps ultimately traceable to overcentralization of investment decisions—that, however, was eliminated as soon as a balance between the supply and demand for pig iron in each mill could be effected.

We now list some typical interactivities that may differ from one system to the other.

> Assigning, directing, and/or coordinating tasks for elemental activities requiring simultaneous or successive actions by two or more individuals.

> Arranging the transfer of custody of a specific batch, quantity, or item of a specific good to a specific next using, processing, or consuming entity, which has a demand for it.

Arranging for the use of a given resource, or fraction thereof, by a specific producer or household during a given time.

(Within a household) determining which quantity of which consumption good available to it is consumed by which member of the household.

7.3 System-bound Activities

Whereas the interactivities in the above list need to be performed under any system, their character depends on the organizational structure and operating procedures of the system more than do most elemental "technological" activities, which bear directly on the physical transformation of inputs into outputs. However, in most systems the activities listed are only a part of the organizational activities required by the system. One could, it is true, imagine a command system capable of perfect coordination, in which both elemental technological activities and the interactivities in the list were implemented by commanded actions of individuals belonging to one large hierarchy. In that case, the commanded transfers of custody would themselves define the demands they meet and the supplies from which they are made. In all systems of record, many other activities intervene to determine these demands and supplies and serve various other desiderata. The nature of these activities depends strongly on the system in which they occur. For this reason some of the terms we will use, although perfectly familiar to the reader, have not yet found a place in the framework of concepts developed so far, because they anticipate essentially organizational concepts to be introduced in subsequent chapters.

Examples of specific system-bound activities are:

Activities determining capabilities to acquire custody of additional means of production through credit from financial intermediaries that absorb savings by individuals and organizations or from governmental credit institutions drawing on tax revenues for the purpose.

Activities that spread risk by pooling.

Protection of individuals from ill effects of adverse conditions of labor (for instance, as provided by labor unions in interaction with employers).

Education and training for managerial and other system-bound activities.

The *provision* of health services.[7]

The collection of interactivities actually used by a set of individuals to produce a given product or bundle of joint products and to deliver it to its utimate consumer(s) is obviously a subset of the entire technology for these

7. Koopmans and Montias, op. cit., p. 55.

products, which comprises, in addition, the activities that are potentially available to the producer and that might actually be adopted if changes occurred in his environment (e.g., changes in prevailing input prices in a "market economy"). The collection involved may be called the *actual technology* of these individuals or of the organization they belong to. The broader the range of activities in this collection, the more likely it is to be influenced by the system. Thus, while the elemental activities for producing oil drills in Romania and in France or Coca-Cola in Soviet Georgia and in Bulgaria may be very much the same (or may differ mainly by reason of differing input scarcities in these pairs of countries), the entire sequence of activities from the procurement of the raw materials to the sale of the final product will exhibit definite system characteristics, which will be familiar to any one with the least knowledge of the way things are done in the economies of East and West. The special importance and the high intensity of activities devoted to the procurement of materials used as inputs in the former and to marketing in the latter are symptomatic, along with many other factors, of these differences. In the sequence of interactivities defining a given product technology, those activities requiring contacts among individuals belonging to different organizations are particularly susceptible to being affected by variations in system structures. These activities, in addition to procurement and marketing, would include financial activities and certain types of R & D activities calling for interorganizational contacts (e.g., between enterprises or government departments on the one hand and universities on the other). Other activities in a sequence likely to be affected by the structure of a system are those occurring outside the plant, factory, farm, or other physical plant in which the main process takes place. Such activities, even though they may be critical to a sequence, are often not prescribed or even listed when a "technology" is transferred across system boundaries. For example, a technology for teaching children how to read that was successful in the suburbs may flounder in ghetto schools because children are hampered in their learning ability by the fact that they had no breakfast before starting out for school or because their home environment did not contain the reading materials that would boost the prestige of the printed word in the eyes of the child or increase his familiarity with its existence—necessary conditions for the program to catch on. Here the inability to give children an adequate breakfast and the absence of books are interpreted as (social) system characteristics. If these failures can better be accounted for by the low-income level of the ghetto population, the example is clearly inappropriate.

In the Cameroons, to cite another example, cocoa is grown on family farms with relatively primitive techniques of cultivation compared to the Ivory Coast, where farms are most often run by local owners or managers with hired help from alien tribes. The Ivorian type of organization permits the implantation of techniques of cultivation and management that would not be feasible in the Cameroons. The disparity in techniques may be attributed as a first approximation to differences in factor proportions. But if one goes back one step further, one observes that the people of the Cameroons are much less hospitable to members of alien tribes than Ivory Coast farmers and that they do not seem to be able to absorb hired labor "from abroad" successfully—an inability that may be interpreted as a system trait.[8]

7.4 INFLUENCE OF SYSTEM TRAITS ON PRODUCERS' CHOICE OF TECHNIQUES

A producer's choice of technique is usually said to be "rational" when his choice minimizes the expected cost of producing a particular good or service for any desired scale of its output. This notion of rationality presupposes that (1) the producer is permitted by the rulers of the system to make a choice, (2) he is seriously concerned with costs, (3) he knows the prices of his inputs, (4) he is sufficiently informed about the probability distribution of the possible states of his environment to make an intelligent choice, and (5) the combination of inputs that minimizes expected costs does not entail an intolerable risk (e.g., of bankruptcy). Lurking in the background, also, is the assumption that the producer has made a reasonable search for the technique most likely to minimize costs.

System traits may render invalid one or more of these assumptions. Moreover, a choice that may be deemed rational for the producer in the light of his objectives need not be efficient for the system as a whole, since the prices of his inputs may not reflect relative scarcities and the information in his possession about available technologies and about the probability distribution of the possible states of his environment may be systematically distorted. We shall consider in the rest of this chapter several illustrations of these various possibilities.

A study by the British economist C. C. Gallagher, specifically aimed at detecting the "influence of different economic systems on detailed technology," compares the choice of engineering techniques in a British and in a Polish plant manufacturing cutting tools around 1970.[9] He concludes that Polish engineers design for "optimum performance" regardless of cost considerations, essentially "because there is no effective motive for cost reduction." In contrast, the British manufacturer eliminates "non-essential features" in his design "possibly at some risk" (presumably to the user) in order to cut down on costs. Polish designers are constrained in their choices because supplies of

8. This example is based on my own, admittedly rather casual, observations in the Cameroons and the Ivory Coast in 1964.

9. "The Influence of Different Economic Systems on Detailed Technology," *Soviet Studies* 26 (Oct. 1974): 604–09. This short article is a summary of the author's thesis, "Polish Factory Organization" (Birmingham, England, 1971).

raw materials and components are limited and because there are virtually no alternative sources of supply (other than those offered in the course of official distribution). Finally, because design, manufacture, and use of the metal-cutting equipment are more or less isolated from one another in Poland, compared to British practice, there is no "unified outlook" toward the improvement of the product that would effectively reconcile the points of view of designers, manufacturers, and final users.[10]

The first two items of comparison illustrate the points made earlier about constraints on decision makers' choices and about their possible lack of cost-consciousness. The third, concerning the difficulty of integrating the points of view of designers, makers, and consumers, is an example of the possible divergence between the rationality of individual decision makers and the system-wide efficiency of the sequence of interdependent decisions.

On the subject of risk (of technical failure), which is apparently thrust on the user in the British plant and averted by the incurrence of higher costs in the Polish plant, it is by no means certain which is the more efficient solution for the economy as a whole. (The answer would depend on whether the user was aware of these risks to begin with and on whether he had a chance to choose between more-expensive-and-more-reliable equipment and less costly equipment that was more subject to failure.)

Again on the subject of risk, it has frequently been observed that the system may impinge on the choice of techniques through its influence on the willingness or ability of decision makers to assume risks. Peasants in less developed countries are given to reject the introduction of techniques that could *on average* be expected to increase the profitability of their operations but that increased the risk of being completely wiped out in the event of harvest failure or other natural calamity (e.g., the purchase of fertilizer or hybrid seed on credit pledged against the value of the farm in case of failure to repay). Here a change in the laws on bankruptcy and foreclosure, the creation of a superior institution for channeling credit, or any other system change having the effect of diminishing the peasant's subjective estimate of the risks he faces should facilitate the introduction of the new technology.

Observable differences in the technologies actually in use in various economies can in many cases be traced to the preferences of relevant decision makers, which in turn are often shaped or perpetuated by the system structure prevailing in each of these economies.

The indirect impact of preferences on the choice of alternative activities for producing the same output (via obstacles to the flow of capital goods or of information) is easier to illustrate by examples than the "far out" category of cases where the selection of techniques hinges, not so much on their relative

10. Ibid., p. 608.

efficiencies (given prevailing scarcities), as on the preferences of the relevant decision makers for these techniques in and of themselves. The eccentric preferences and aversions of Academician Trofim Lysenko for and against various plant- and animal-breeding techniques and their imposition on Soviet farms through command and persuasion offer the most interesting set of examples of this behavior. Lysenko influenced both the choice among existing techniques (e.g., his insistence on the "vernalization" of seed grain, a preparation that probably had no beneficial effect on the growth of the seedlings) and the development of new techniques (e.g., his opposition to genetically grounded experiments with hybrid varieties of corn and other plants).

It might be argued that the techniques advocated by Lysenko and his aides were *thought* to be more efficient than those they fought against and hence that the choice of techniques was motivated by efficiency considerations within the limits imposed by the perception of these individuals. But these pseudoscientists also opposed the use of formal statistical methods to determine the veracity of their claims and used the system to bias results in their favor. (For instance, if kolkhoz chairmen had more than one kind of seed to sow, they knew it was a "good idea" to plant the vernalized grain on the best land.) Thus, at the very least, the structure of the system impinged on the choice of techniques through the *perception* of their relative efficiencies.

Lysenko's influence on Soviet agricultural technology was so aberrant that its adverse effects on efficiency eventually became manifest to virtually the entire scientific and technological community in the Soviet Union. In most other cases where it is suspected that techniques have been selected for reasons other than their superior efficiency in the light of prevailing resource scarcities, the evaluation of the relative performances of the competing techniques is so fraught with uncertainty that only the most tentative conclusions can be drawn. In many developing countries, both centrally directed and market oriented, it seems that the techniques borrowed from more advanced economies are more capital intensive than they should be, given the prevailing abundance of labor. But then all sorts of plausible arguments can be advanced to justify this policy. Among other such arguments, one may invoke the shortage of *skilled* labor (which may be economized with automatic capital-intensive equipment), the advantage of using modern equipment to train a work force, and the shortage of engineers and other trained personnel necessary to design, run, and maintain equipment adapted to take advantage of the local abundance of unskilled labor. These arguments are often unquantifiable, and the possibilities of experimentation with alternative techniques to arrive at an objective judgment of their relative merits are usually quite limited (if the need for such experimentation is perceived at all). Uncertainty about the performance characteristics of alternative techniques in some systems is compounded by uncertainty about the relative scarcity of the inputs utilized, particularly in calculations of relative efficiency made for projects that do not need to be self-sustaining in terms of prevailing domestic prices. Labor, foreign exchange, and capital may be assigned "shadow prices" that seriously diverge from prevailing transfer prices. Unless these alternative prices are grounded on calculations that are accepted as valid by all persons concerned with a project, it may not be possible to reconcile the conflicting opinions of advocates of competing techniques, whose advocacy in the last analysis often rests on motives extraneous to efficiency. In Poland, for example, the partisans of thermal plants to generate electric power used to argue their case on the basis of the official (low) prices for coal, the partisans of hydraulically generated power in terms of the (high) opportunity cost of coal in foreign trade. Each group had its "vested interest" in its preferred technology. Their attitudes can perhaps be explained by pecuniary motives, but I suspect that *esprit de corps* provides the main psychological motivation: engineers and project designers will be inclined to favor the hydraulic techniques they are familiar with because their own prestige and self-respect are bound up with them (just as navy men tend to favor naval power and airmen air power, whatever may be the "objective" merits of these alternate means of defending or extending their country's military power).

If these examples are at all susceptible of generalization, they suggest the hypothesis that the influence of the system structure or of the decision makers' preferences on technology will be less in systems or subsystems where there is a generally agreed measure of relative efficiency (such as "money costs and returns") than in those where this condition does not obtain. Granted the validity of this hypothesis, we would expect to find that in an economy such as that of the United States "irrational" technological biases flourish mainly in nonmarket areas such as health care (the treatment of cancer), education (teaching children how to read), and R & D programs, where performance is hard to gauge by objective standards (some types of military and space research).[11]

The indirect impact of preferences on the choice of economic activities manifests itself chiefly through interruptions in the free flow of capital goods embodying new technology, scientific magazines, patents, licenses, and other vehicles of technological information. Restraints on international trade in capital goods or their spare parts (whether through export or import controls) obviously constrain the choice of techniques available to the would-be

11. In all matters regarding the generation and diffusion of new technologies, I have greatly profited from the writings of Richard R. Nelson and from conversations I had with him on this subject.

borrowers of foreign technologies. These restraints are generally imposed by national governments to protect domestic producers of capital goods or to stimulate the development of home-grown technologies. The desiderata prompting such policies generally include the wish to conserve or increase a nation's power or prestige or to reduce its economic dependence on other nations for ultimately the same reasons. Similarly, the United States embargo on trade with communist China and Cuba was designed to reduce the economic and, withal, the political power of these countries and, as a consequence, to increase or maintain American power. The restrictions imposed by Great Britain on exports of machinery in the early nineteenth century were meant to prevent the growth of competition and to preserve British supremacy in this field because this was thought to be economically beneficial to British nationals (or a group or "class" thereof), because supremacy contributed to the power of the British state, or for a combination of these reasons.

The system structure may also directly impede the flow of technological information by restricting the contacts between potential suppliers of technologies abroad and domestic users. This may take the form of laws against direct investments by foreign nationals, of restrictions on the employment of foreign technicians, or of system-induced limitations on the kind and frequency of possible interactions with foreigners. The structures of the economic systems of COMECON members[12] in particular were rife with such restrictions, at least until the later 1960s. The economic reforms initiated in these countries a few years ago were in part directed toward renewing or otherwise facilitating these contacts, which had been interrupted for years by the virtual ban on the interactions of citizens belonging to enterprises, research institutes, or project-making organizations with nationals of other countries.

Finally, as we already noted in the comparison of British and Polish engineering practices, decisions on the selection of elemental technological activities frequently have side effects on interdependent activities. When a policy of favoring domestic technology or the technology of "friendly countries" is pursued for some time, it may have the effect of complicating unwittingly the import of any outsiders' technology, to the extent that the latter will violate the norms, measures, tolerances, and other characteristics that have gradually come to be accepted in the country. The disintegration of Germany into two independent economies after World War II was long retarded by the prevalence of common norms and measures. However, after the German Democratic Republic had discriminated for many years in its trade in capital goods, licenses, and patents in favor of countries belonging to

---

12. The countries that are currently members of the Council for Mutual Economic Assistance are Bulgaria, Cuba, Czechoslovakia, the German Democratic Republic, Hungary, Mongolia, Poland, Romania, and the USSR.

COMECON, the economy's integration into this relatively autarkic bloc was facilitated by the adoption in the GDR of norms and measures common to the bloc.

8

Interactions

8.1 Interactions and the Classification of Systems

The idea of classifying systems according to the prevailing mode of interactions among its members has attracted a number of comparatists in recent years. It is relatively easy to identify each mode empirically—whether it be interactions through "exchange," "reciprocity," or "redistribution" as in Polanyi's classification or through "exchange," "threats," and "interactions contributing to the integrative system" (gifts or other benefactions) as in Kenneth Boulding's.[1] The classes are few in number, and each class contains a sufficient number of "important" examples to deserve a separate status. As a principle of classification it falls short chiefly by reason of the tenuous, if not totally absent, link between classes of interactions and system outcomes, including efficiency, equity, and stability, that economists with a normative inclination are interested in. The weakness of this link is due in part to the lack of an underlying theory of individual motivation that would explain why certain types of interactions and not others occur in a given system structure. Nevertheless, if we keep in mind the need for forging these links and study classes of interactions in conjunction with the rules of the system structure determining who will interact with whom and for what purpose, we shall have made a sound beginning toward a useful classification of systems.

We start with some remarks on the conceptual measurement of actions and on their classification. Every individual may be said to have a *decision space*, each dimension of which is identified with a particular type of action. For each dimension the level of the action may be measured either along a continuum (e.g., the price he may set for a good in his custody) or on an integer scale (e.g., inviting one's boss to dinner so many times a year).[2] When in a process of interaction with one or more individuals a participant must make a series of m decisions affecting the individuals he is interacting with, the sequence of decisions he will make is said to be contained in his *strategy space*, which may by thought of as an ensemble of m decision spaces. We have already defined

1. Karl Polanyi, *Semantics of General Economic History*, rev. ed. (New York, 1953); Boulding, "Economics as a Moral Science," *American Economic Review* 59 (March 1969): 4.

2. The integer scale may be limited to two values (0 and 1) in case the decision comes down to an either/or proposition (e.g., accept or refuse to fight a duel).

a *policy* as a series of contingent decisions. An individual's policy must therefore belong to his strategy space.

Our initial distinction is between *informational* and *effective* actions. An informational action changes the environment of other individuals in a system only insofar as it affects the information set of the recipient(s). We call all other actions effective, including those associated with the process of carrying out the information activities.[3]

Informational actions comprise (1) *proposals*, defined as messages suggesting a set of effective actions that might be undertaken by the recipient. An important class of proposals includes offers and acceptances concerning transfers of custody, with or without payment in return; (2) rules and orders and responses thereto; (3) *communications*, which we define here as messages containing information about the environment of the sender (e.g., his technology, preferences, or resource endowment) or that of other participants;[4] (4) "threats," "appeals," and other messages aiming to exert influence on the recipient's actions.

Individual h *threatens* i in a message when he announces that if the action undertaken by i after receiving his message falls in a particular subset of i's decision space,[5] h will carry out an effective action intended to lower i's expected utility. An *appeal* from h to i is a message attempting to increase i's expected utility, and hence his motivation, for carrying out one or more actions that h would like to have carried out by alluding to i's own tastes or values.

8.2 Who Interacts with Whom

At one end of the spectrum we have *anonymous interactions*, which are constrained neither by the system structure nor by the tastes or values of the interactors as to who their interacting partners may be. An interaction between i and i' is anonymous *for i* whenever i *expects* the same utility or disutility from the good, bad, service, or disservice that i' might provide or inflict as he would if i'' or any other individual in the system were to provide this good or service or inflict this bad or disservice. Similarly, it is anonymous *for i'* if he expects

---

3. If individual i calls i' on the telephone and tells him that i'' is coming to see him, the conveying of the message is an informational action. The use of the telephone to convey it is an effective action. (The message would presumably have been the same if it had been transmitted by radio or by private messenger.)

4. Hurwicz defines *privacy* in an information structure as a situation where each participant's response function "depends only on its own environmental component, but not on those of other units." Hence if he receives communications at all, his responses ignore them (see Hurwicz, "Centralization and Decentralization in Economic Processes," in Eckstein, ed., *Comparison of Economic Systems*, p. 93).

5. The possibility of inaction ("doing nothing") is normally included in the recipient's decision space.

the same utility from the goods, bads, services, or disservices that i might provide or inflict as he would from any other individual in the system.[6] We emphasize that in an anonymous interaction each interactor *expects* to derive the same utility from the good or service supplied by any other individual in the system at the point when he acquires ownership rights over this good or service or otherwise achieves the possibility of enjoying or deriving profit or other benefits from it. Thus when a housewife hires a cleaning woman, both individuals expect certain standards of performance from each other. The interaction is anonymous as long as each is indifferent among various possible individuals who would be expected to perform according to the same standards. But it may easily turn out that either of the individuals or both may give more or less satisfaction than expected, at which point they may no longer be interchangeable with other employers or employees.[7]

An interaction between i and i' will be *partially anonymous* for i if there is a subset of the individuals in the system who could be substituted for i' without affecting the utility, profit, or other benefits that i' expects from the interaction. Examples of partially anonymous interactions are the cutting of hair by barbers who are willing to serve only white customers, parochial schools that accept only baptized children, and the exchange of confidential technological information among the members of an organization. Finally, an interaction between i and i' is termed *personal* for i if the utility or disutility he expects out of the interaction differs for any interacting partner other than i'.

Insofar as the rules, customs, or traditions of the system structure concerning who-may-interact-with-whom-for-what influence individuals' behavior, we may surmise that they affect the utility or disutility of their engaging in sanctioned or forbidden interactions. *Other things equal*, we expect an individual to prefer to engage in an interaction with an individual with whom he is permitted by rules, traditions, or customs to interact for a given purpose than with an individual who is proscribed for that purpose.

The impact of the system structure on the marriage of adult men and women will illustrate these definitions. I know of no system where interactions leading to marriage are strictly anonymous, since there are always rules, customs, or traditions discouraging marriage with specific adult individuals,

6. This definition of anonymity differs in several respects from that of Hurwicz, who focuses on the nature of messages exchanged rather than on the expected utility to the individuals concerned of the effective interactions they contemplate.

7. Tastes and values regarding individuals may creep into the choice of interacting partners via expectations, which will in part be shaped by the perception of previous interactions, by prejudices, by myths, and so forth. There is obviously a thin line between the refusal to interact with an individual because of his race or religion and the refusal to interact with him because the goods or services he is supplying are expected, for no "objective" reasons, to be inferior.

and these taboos are powerful enough to affect individuals' expected utility from entering into these forbidden transactions. When the marriage is arranged by his or her parents without the individual's advice or consent, the interaction from the individual's point of view will be personal. From the parents' point of view it is likely to be partially anonymous. For the individual who is free to choose his or her mate, we must distinguish at least two stages in the sequence of interactions leading to marriage. His search process will normally involve partially anonymous interactions. The final interaction— the marriage ceremony—will presumably be a personal type of interaction.

When rule, tradition, or custom allows individual i to interact only with a very narrow group of individuals defined according to criteria that are not directly related to their capacity to supply goods or perform services useful to i, this personal or quasi-personal interaction is termed *ascriptive*. The criteria for defining the individuals with whom i may interact are said to be *particularistic* if they depend on who these individuals are (their family origin, political connections, or status in the system) rather than what they can do for i.[8]

In traditional or "primitive" systems, interactions involving the transfer of custody of goods or the performance of services are rarely anonymous. They are typically ascriptive in character whether the system is based on "reciprocal" or "redistributive" relations, concepts that we have yet to define.

8.3 DIRECTED GRAPHS

A directed graph provides a convenient and instructive way of describing interactions among individuals belonging to an organization or to a system. To construct such a graph, we must single out a particular type of informational or effective action that will serve as the basis for relating the individuals in the set under consideration. The relation between two individuals i and j belonging to a finite set S may be of a general character (e.g., i's informational action affects j), or it may be very precisely defined (e.g., i issues an order to j concerning activity k).

In a directed graph the relation is always defined in such a way that for any pair of individuals (i, j), the informational or effective action is initiated by i, who through this action affects j in some way. The pair (i, j) is called an *ordered pair*.

Let there be m individuals in S. We can construct an $m \times m$ table showing all the possible ordered pairs matching any individual i in S with another individual in S for a given relation r. The set of these possible pairs for r is the Cartesian product of S or $S \times S$. The subset of $S \times S$ consisting of actually interacting pairs is denoted V. A *directed graph* G is a pair of sets (S, V), where

---

8. These terms are Talcott Parsons's.

the elements of S are called *vertices* and the elements of V are called *arcs*. The set V itself is the *network* of interactions for a given relation. An example of a graph describing the interactions among six persons is shown below. The set S consists of $(x_1, x_2, x_3, x_4, x_5, x_6)$, where x $(i = 1, \ldots, 6)$ represents a person. The set V consists of $(V_{12}, V_{13}, V_{16}, V_{26}, V_{34}, V_{35}, V_{45}, V_{56}, V_{64})$, each element V_{ij} representing an actual interaction between x_i and x_j where i initiates the informational or effective action affecting j according to relation r. The directed graph G for (S, V) is shown below.

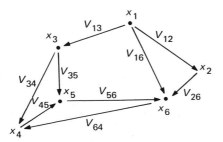

The adjacent matrix of G, denoted $A(G)$, is an $m \times m$ matrix where the cell corresponding to the kth row and lth column is assigned a value of 1 if (k, l) is in V and 0 if it is not.

The adjacent matrix for the above directed graph is:

	1	2	3	4	5	6
1	0	1	1	0	0	1
2	0	0	0	0	0	1
3	0	0	0	1	1	0
4	0	0	0	0	1	0
5	0	0	0	0	0	1
6	0	0	0	1	0	0

A *chain* or *path* from i to j in a graph G is a sequence of ordered pairs (i, k) $(k, \cdot), \ldots, (\cdot, l)$ (l, j) in V. A *loop* is a chain from i to i. In the above example there is a chain $(V_{12}, V_{26}, V_{64}, V_{45})$ linking persons 1, 2, 4, 5, and 6. If we add V_{56} and V_{61}, which are both in V, to form a longer chain, we generate a loop from 1 to 1. If a relation is reciprocal, every pair (i, j) in V is matched with another pair (j, i) also in V. Only the most loosely defined relations such as "i initiates an effective action affecting j's environment" have the characteristic of automatic reciprocity. The response of j to an action initiated by i is not usually "in kind." To analyze situations that are not fully reciprocal we may form the union of two directed graphs (S, V) and (S, V') for the distinct relations r and r'. Such a union is called a *bigraph* for r and r'. The relations r and r' are said to be reciprocal when for every pair (i, j) in V, the pair (j, i) is in V'. As an important example we may cite the relations "i sells a good to j" and "j makes a payment to i." The adjacent matrix for a system where individuals acted exclusively as sellers or buyers of goods might look like this:

	1	2	3	...	m
1	0/0	1/0	1/0	...	0/1
2	0/1	0/0	1/0	...	0/1
3	0/1	0/1	0/0	...	0/1
.	.	.	.		.
.	.	.	.	...	.
.	.	.	.		.
m	1/0	1/0	1/0	...	0/0

Every cell of this matrix has been divided by a slash into an upper part showing the relation in V and a lower part showing the relation in V'. To indicate, for instance, that the pair $(1, 3)$ is in V and the pair $(3, 1)$ is in V', a 1 has been entered in the upper half and a 0 in the lower half of the cell located in the first row and third column and a 0 in the upper half and a 1 in the lower half of the cell in the third row and first column.

As we shall see below, reciprocal interactions are by no means the only important type of interdependent effective actions, but they do play a particularly significant role in social and economic life. All exchanges of goods and services, including "favors," involve reciprocal actions.[9] So does retaliation, as in vengeance or vendettas.[10]

A sequence of three or more interdependent effective actions initiated by i need not involve any reciprocity to affect i. This will be the case if there is a

9. Karl Polanyi makes a distinction between "reciprocity" and "exchange" that I cannot follow. According to him, "reciprocity denotes movements between correlative points of symmetrical groupings in society . . . exchange refers to vice-versa movements taking place as between 'hands' under a market system" (op. cit., p. 169). Now "points of symmetrical groupings" in a "primitive" tribe might be the father of a boy and the father of a girl, not related by close blood ties, who may if they wish arrange the marriage of their children and confer on each other ceremonial gifts. I fail to see in what sense this change in custody fails to qualify as an exchange. The distinction between reciprocity and exchange that Polanyi had in mind seems to be related to the degree of "mutuality" of the transaction, which will be discussed in sec. 4 of this chapter.

10. Individuals acting in the framework of organizations may be affected by the actions of the individuals with whom they interact via the payoff of the organization or via the sentiments they may harbor for their comembers. Whether we wish to treat entire organizations (enterprises or families) as "persons" (as if the organization acted like a single individual) or as sets of distinct individuals may depend on the degree of "cohesiveness" of the organization (the extent to which all its members are affected by changes in its joint payoff). It may also depend on the type of problem or comparison considered. These considerations are further elaborated in chaps. 11 and 12.

loop from i to i in the graph (S, V). This interdependency may be termed *circular*.

A classic example of circular interdependency among effective actions is the Kula ring of Papua's Trobrianders, as it was observed by B. Malinowski shortly after World War I. In one major type of interaction, ceremonial goods were given by the members of one village to those of another, often situated on a different island, who in turn made gifts—sometimes consisting of the very same objects—to members of a third village. Eventually, members of some nth village would confer gifts on those of the first, and the ring was closed.[11] Certain sequences of minor crimes are also circular, as in a school the author once attended where all required textbooks were rented for the year to the students. If a student lost a book, he would steal it from another. This would set off a sequence of thefts, of which the initial perpetrator was sometimes also a victim.

We now broach the concept of "centralization" in networks of informational interactions characterized by full reciprocity. These networks may be described by ordinary, instead of by directed, graphs because the direction of each interaction is immaterial to this analysis.

We shall call a network V of interactions for a reciprocal relation r, with the property that every chain in V contains the decision-making entity h, *centralized on h* provided that h is the only member of S with this property. When furthermore, every pair in the graph just defined contains h, the network is *directly centralized on h*. A hierarchy, as we shall see in chapter 10, is centralized, although in most instances not directly.

"Redistributive systems," where the custody for given goods or assets is transferred according to certain rules, customs, or traditions from an initial custodian directly to an individual h, generally function as centralized networks. In the United States the Internal Revenue Service is directly centralized. A system in which the collection of taxes is "farmed out" to designated individuals is centralized but not directly.

Special interest attaches to the pair of relations "i pays taxes to j" and "j provides a service for i." These relations may be but are not necessarily reciprocal. Yet, from the viewpoint of the equity desideratum, it may make a good deal of difference whether a centralized redistributive network involves each interacting individual in a circular interdependency. If individual k only turns over goods and assets to other individuals and gets nothing in return from any other individual in the network, he is clearly being mulcted by the system. If the goods and services he draws in return have the character of public goods, the question arises as to the extent they may compensate him

11. For a good summary description, see Cyril S. Belshaw, *Traditional Exchange and Modern Markets* (Englewood Cliffs, N.J.: Prentice-Hall, 1965), pp. 12–20.

for his loss of the goods he produces or of his time and effort if he performs services for i or his "agents." One may wonder, for example, how much aesthetic satisfaction Egyptian peasants derived from viewing the pyramids in pharaonic days or how much security serfs received as compensation for their labors from their lords in the late Middle Ages.[12] On the other hand, redistribution from the "rich" to the "poor" may be considered equitable by some observers assigning a positive weight to this outcome in their norm function.

To get a first, coarse measure of the degree of redistribution in a system of the general type just described, one might wish to compare the number of individuals paying taxes or tribute to h with the number of individuals receiving goods or services from h, either directly or through a chain. (If the system were directly centralized, this would amount to a comparison of the sum of the entries in the hth column of the adjacent matrix for the tax-paying relations with the sum of entries in the hth row for the service-providing relation.) A more satisfactory measure consists of a pair of indicators, the first giving a summary measure of the degree of inequality in tax- or tribute-paying and the second the degree of inequality in the provision of services by h (e.g., a pair of Gini coefficients derived from the Lorenz curves calculated for tax paying and service receiving).

Less extreme forms of centralization in networks are easily conceived. One such notion is that of "polycentralization." If members of subset s of S are *centralizers* in the sense that every chain between any pair of members k and l of S must go through at least one member of s, the network may be said to be *polycentralized on s*. Whether, and if so how, the members of s interact will be a crucial trait of a polycentralized network. For example, a polycentralized network might be represented by the interaction graph of a set of independent "hierarchies" whose heads all belonged to s. (By "independent," we mean that no member of hierarchy h could communicate with a member of h' except through their respective heads.) This schema might be used to represent the network of interactions among the economic administrations of the member states of the Council for Mutual Economic Assistance (COMECON), insofar as the officials of each national hierarchy interacted with officials of other national hierarchies only through their representatives on the executive committees and joint commissions of COMECON. However, the model would be unrealistic to the extent that subordinate members of each national hierarchy communicated with each other directly rather than through their head.[13]

Special interest attaches to "centralization" and "decentralization"

---

12. See K. Polanyi, C. Arensberg, and H. W. Pearson, eds., *Trade and Market in the Early Empires* (New York: Free Press, 1957), p. 30.
13. On the concept of a hierarchy and of a "head," see below, sec. 10.3.

in the structure of informational networks. Marschak and Radner focus their analysis on the following class of situations. Suppose the environments of all m members of a network at any one time can be described as a vector e in m-dimensional space. The vector e is an element of E, the set of all such possible m-dimensional vectors. The environment e_i of i is then the ith coordinate of e. The question here is whether individual i observes only his own environment e_i. Let $e_i \cap e_{i'}$, the intersection of the environments of distinct members i and i', be empty. Each member i is then a *specialist* in the information relating to e_i. No one else can have information about it except by communicating with i.

Marschak and Radner call an informational network with these properties *decentralized* if each individual observes his own environment but transmits information about it to no one.[14] In such a network any information held by i and useful to another member of the group is *impacted*.[15] *Centralized complete information* characterizes networks where each individual observes his own environment and communicates information about it to all other individuals in the network. If the collection of information by i about his own environment is considered a message from i to himself, this network may be represented by an adjacent matrix in which every cell is filled with a number equal to unity.[16] Finally, if some of the individuals in the network observe their environment while others do not, but everyone in the first group sends information about his environment to everyone in the second, the network is characterized by *polycentralized incomplete information*.

The theory of directed graphs as we have presented it so far is founded entirely on the presence or absence of a specific *type* of interaction between pairs of individuals or persons in a finite set. Nothing was said about the intensity, importance, or cost of this interaction. The concept of directed graphs can be extended, however, by grafting onto each arc v_{ij} in V of a graph G some measure of the intensity or importance, cost or frequency of the informational or effective action initiated by i and affecting j. A convenient way to do this is to enter this measure (instead of 1 or 0) in the cell corresponding to the ith row and jth column of $A(G)$. Constraints may then be imposed on the row sums and the column sums of the matrix. Given an objective function (such as "minimize $\sum_{i=1}^{m} \sum_{j=1}^{n} \pi_{ij} w_{ij}$," where π_{ij} is the cost of the inter-

14. Jacob Marschak and Roy Radner, *Economic Theory of Teams* (New Haven: Yale University Press, 1972), p. 132. Decentralization in this case is almost identical to Hurwicz's concept of "privacy" (defined above, chap. 8, n. 4). "Almost" because privacy allows an individual not to communicate information about his own environment, but it does not require him to collect information about it in the first place.

15. "Information impactedness," a term coined by Oliver Williamson, was introduced as a primitive in chap. 2 (p. 16).

16. This network would be polycentralized on the entire set of m members in terms of our earlier classification of interaction graphs.

action with intensity measure w_{ij}), it is easy to see that such a problem may be solved by linear programming techniques of the type now routinely used for the solution of transportation tasks. Furthermore, by comparing the solution to the problem networks involving the same personnel but different networks of interactions (i.e., for the distinct graphs (S, V_1), (S, V_2), ...), we may hope to learn about the optimal network for carrying out certain tasks or functions. These and similar methods have long been in use in organization theory.[17] Thus far they have had little or no application to the study of economy-wide systems.

8.4 INFORMATIONAL AND EFFECTIVE ACTIONS

We now resume our exercise in classifying interactions. In this section we shall focus on the relation between informational actions and the effective actions they are intended to touch off or impel.

Of importance for the study of systems is the distinction between *tâtonnement* and *non-tâtonnement* processes. In a tâtonnement process, a sequence of informational actions (exchanges of messages) occurs before any effective action takes place. This preliminary exchange of messages may help two or more individuals discover the mutually advantageous effective actions they might undertake without exposing themselves to the risks and liabilities that a series of inferior effective actions might cause them to incur. As we shall now see, tâtonnement processes are also inherent in "planning."

A *plan for period* T *to* T + τ may be defined as a set of outcomes ("targets") for each time period from T to $T + \tau$ that the planners specify as desirable and feasible, together with a more or less detailed "strategy" for achieving these goals. A *strategy* in turn is defined as a set of decisions for each period contingent on the observation of a particular environment for the system. Most national economic plans specify a single set of decisions for each period on the implicit or explicit assumption that the environment of the economy can be predicted with sufficient accuracy in each period to dispense with contingent alternatives.[18] A planning process is a set of informational actions, simultaneous, sequential, or both, designed to supply the individuals in charge of setting the targets and devising the strategy to achieve them with

17. For a very instructive comparison of the "informational values" of centralized, decentralized, and centralized incomplete information systems in a two-member organization confronted with uncertain environments e_1 and e_2, see Marschak and Radner, op. cit., pp. 130–43. Incidentally, the "value" of an informational network is the difference between the value of a team's maximum expected payoff using this network minus the value of the maximum expected payoff in the absence of any information.

18. In the planning systems of East the idea that future environments cannot be predicted with complete accuracy is implicitly recognized in the setting of (relatively small) "reserves" of unallocated resources that are meant to be parceled out in the course of realizing the plan. This of course is not equivalent to stipulating alternative decisions contingent on the observation of various possible environments.

the most precise information possible for so doing. If the planning process for elaborating the plan for period T to $T + \tau$ ends before period T it may strictly be described as a tâtonnement process.

An example of a non-tâtonnement process in centralized decision making[19] would be a dispatcher system for the operational management of a railroad. In such a system an individual (or team of individuals) called "central dispatcher" receives messages about the location or the direction and velocity of trains in every part of the network. Every message emitted by the dispatcher is an order to carry out an effective action ("sidetrack train A," "keep train B at station S another five minutes," and so on). It may be objected that there is a tâtonnement element in a dispatcher system because messages to the dispatcher do not touch off effective actions but other informational actions (orders). A centralized warehousing operation where every message to the head of the warehouse causes some good to be shipped out and every message to a unit in the field consists of an order to the individual in charge of the unit to transfer some good from one location to another is a more precise (but perhaps less realistic) example of a non-tâtonnement process in a centralized network.

Until we have considered more closely the possible relations that may link superiors to their subordinates in a hierarchic organization, it would be premature to discuss the "operationality" of the plan, the degree to which the plan influences the decisions taken during the plan period by the various members of the organization. Suffice it to say at this juncture that, when this operationality is very weak, as in the hectic years of the first Soviet Five-Year Plan (1928–32), the dispatcher system may provide a better model of the way the organization actually functions than the paradigm of "planning."[20]

Up to this point in the present chapter, the only reference that has been made to the utility of an interacting individual in a system has been in relation to his preferences for or against specific partners with whom he might engage in an interaction. We now advert to his preferences with regard to the nature of the interaction itself, leaving aside for the moment the characteristics of possible partners.

A basic criterion for a classification of effective actions is the presence or absence of mutuality in the interaction of which these actions are a part. *Complete mutuality* requires that the action be utility maximizing for all parties participating in the interaction, subject only to the rules issued by ruling

19. "Centralized" in the sense of the interaction network described in the previous section.

20. It is interesting to note in this connection that the dispatcher system of U.S. railroads was frequently discussed in Soviet economic literature of the late 1920s and early 1930s and apparently influenced management practices on the gigantic state farms that were set up about this time. It is not known whether the influence of this "model" extended to the management of the entire economy. (Cf. various articles on the dispatcher system published in *Sovkhoz* and *Na agrarnom fronte* in the period 1929–31.)

organizations to govern such actions (e.g., a sale prepared by an exchange of messages or by a jointly issued message known as a contract). The rules may limit the range of voluntary actions from which a utility-maximizing individual would choose, but they must not be so restrictive as to compel an individual to engage in a certain action or sequence of actions. Thus, a government organ may issue rules on the conduct of business, which may still be carried on the basis of complete mutuality. But if it forces an individual to engage in a particular occupation or activity (draft or mobilization, *corvée*) or levies taxes on him, the interaction between that individual and the ruling organization involved is no longer "completely mutual." More generally, if the consent of one or more of the participants is not freely given—because a threat or order has been conveyed to him by another participant—then, even though he may maximize his utility subject to this constraint, complete mutuality cannot be said to characterize this interaction.

If a participant incurs a temporary disutility in the expectation of being compensated by another participant at a later time, the interaction will not have been based on complete mutuality, unless, in case the compensation fails to materialize, the adversely affected participant can publicly complain, bring suit, or otherwise apply pressure to "get his due." Thus if someone invites an acquaintance to dinner in the expectation that the invitation will be returned at a later time, complete mutuality is absent unless there is a prior understanding about the return of the invitation or a generally observed social rule that the acceptance of an invitation is tantamount to an obligation to return it within a reasonable delay. A sequence of illegal actions spread over a significant period is rarely based on complete mutuality. A bribe to a judge to adjudicate in one's favor can assure a favorable outcome only if the *threat* of violence or public disclosure in case of noncompliance coaxes out the desired action.

In all the instances mentioned in the above paragraphs where the conditions for complete mutuality are not met, *partial mutuality* may be said to prevail. More generally, there is said to be partial mutuality in an interaction when an individual undertaking an effective action incurs some, possibly temporary, disutility in order to forestall an action by one or more participants that would inflict on him an even greater loss in utility, to accumulate credits for future benefits, or in recognition of the legitimacy of certain claims. The interacting participants are then involved in an ongoing relation that they consider to be acceptable if not actually desirable (e.g., taxpayers with the Internal Revenue Service).

In all remaining interactions, there is *no mutuality* among the interacting participants (theft, pollution without compensation, and so on). In his recent book on the economics of blood transfusion, Richard Titmuss classifies individuals, usually but often inaccurately called "blood donors," into a number of groups differing in several respects including the degree of mutuality characterizing their interaction with the receivers of their "gift" (or with the intermediaries in the transaction).[21] These are: (1) paid donors,[22] (2) "responsibility-fee" donors, (3) "family-credit" donors, (4) "captive voluntary" donors, and (5) "voluntary community" donors. It follows from our definitions that paid donors and "voluntary community donors" (individuals giving away their blood neither for money nor for any fringe benefits and who are under no obligation or pressure to do so) are involved in completely mutual interactions. So are "family-credit" donors, who donate blood in anticipation that they or their family might need a transfusion in the future, provided their participation in such a cooperative scheme is voluntary and their claim on future withdrawals from the blood bank in case of need rests on contractual or other assured grounds. Responsibility-fee donors, however, who must repay a hospital in blood for the transfusion they or their family have been given, may be involved in only partially mutual interactions, especially if they were unaware before the operation that they would incur this obligation. Captive voluntary donors will be in the same (partially mutual) situation if they are put under moral pressure or threatened by penalties on the part of the institution (in case of noncompliance) to which they belong (prison, armed forces) to "give" their blood or if they fear losing their job or some privilege or advantage for failing to do so. Titmuss, who was clearly a very civilized person, did not even consider the possibility of nonvoluntary captive donors who would be bled willy-nilly (nonmutual interaction), even though this sort of compulsory giving must surely occur in some places.

For Titmuss what really matters is whether a donation is paid or unpaid. We shall come back to this distinction later on[23] in connection with our discussion of externalities. For our present purpose we note that blood may be given away for the most altruistic sort of motive or sold for the crassest reasons —and the interaction between donor and receiver will still be completely mutual in character in both cases.

The same initiating action may belong simultaneously to a sequence of actions characterized by complete mutuality for some participants and to another interaction characterized by partial or no mutuality for others. Thus the owner of a landsite near a highway, an advertising agency, and an outdoor display company may all agree to put up a billboard, the sight of which may be offensive to motorists traveling along that highway.[24]

We have seen that informational actions played a key role in the definitions

21. *The Gift Relationship: From Human Blood to Social Policy* (New York: Random House, 1971), pp. 75–89.

22. They are grouped into four main types ("the paid donor," the "professional donor," the "paid-induced professional donor," and the "fringe-benefit voluntary donor") whose characteristic differences are not essential to our present purpose.

23. Chapter 9, pp. 122–23.

24. Koopmans and Montias, op. cit., pp. 57–58.

of anonymity and competition. It remains for us to observe that there is also frequently a link between informational actions and the degree of mutuality of the transaction that ensues from these actions. A number of instances of such associations are tabulated below.

The reader's attention is drawn to the first two rows of table 8.1. For our immediate purpose, the main distinction between a proposal and a communication is that only the latter contains information specific to an

Table 8.1. Mutuality Basis of Some Interactions Touched off by Various Initiating Actions

Initiating action(s)	Mutuality characterizing interaction		
	Mutual agreement	Partial mutuality based on legitimacy of claim or punitive sanction	No mutuality
Proposal	Sale of a good	Enterprise undertakes to fulfill the output targets set for it in an indicative plan	—
Communication	Sale of a patent	Setting of output target by planning authority	Unauthorized adoption of a process described in patent
Rule or order calling for effective action	Payment of check by bank	Subordinate's compliance to an order in a hierarchy	Conscription of individual for military service
Threat or other message aimed at exerting influence	—	Wage settlement on threat of strike	Performing forced labor for another individual on threat of death
Implicit message conveyed via effective action	Gift of blood to Red Cross	Giving of present or favor in expectation of reciprocity	Sabotage; purchase and use of drum set in retaliation against neighbor's piano playing
Unilateral action unheralded by message	—	Traveling in a crowded subway	River pollution, theft

organization, such as the technological processes it uses, its rate of output, or the level of its inventories. L. Hurwicz calls a tâtonnement process *operational* if every message among the "units" participating in this process is either a proposal or an order.[25] In such a process the "units" enjoy *privacy* in the sense that they have no need to communicate any information to other units about their internal operations, technology, preferences, or about any other components of their own environment.[26] The "units" are individuals or organizations of individuals with a common payoff. Privacy is a necessary but not a sufficient condition for what Hurwicz calls an "informationally decentralized adjustment process." If this condition is fulfilled, the process will be informationally decentralized provided every message is also anonymous, as this word was already defined.

According to these definitions, a message from an organization transmitting information about the volume of its output or the state of its output or of its inventories to a ruling organization, which will then aggregate the information and use it in formulating its monetary or fiscal policy, cannot be part of an informationally decentralized process. On the other hand, a message referring to the aggregate demand for (or supply of) a commodity does not violate the privacy condition and may be part of such a process.[27]

In the modern industrial world the ideal type of Hurwicz's decentralization process is rarely encountered. Both in economies of East and West, firms obtain a good deal of "internal information" about one another, which is used in the selection of technological processes and in arriving at output and sales decisions. In the case of the sale and purchase of technologically advanced products such as computers, one may even question how some of the messages required to bring off a transaction can possibly exclude internal information: the seller of a computerized "informational system" has to know something about the internal operations of the buyer to suggest the right combination of hard- and soft-ware the client "really needs."

Nevertheless, Hurwicz's definitions serve the worthwhile purpose of orienting the analyst toward asking a number of critical questions relevant to "decentralization" and of offering the comparer some criteria that may be useful for describing and comparing systems along important dimensions. By "important" we mean of course that the principles of classification we adopt

---

25. Hurwicz includes orders in his definition of proposals.

26. For a formalization of this concept, see Hurwicz, op. cit., p. 93.

27. Ibid., p. 169. A message referring to the aggregate demand or supply for a good may be concocted by an organization that centralizes the offers and acceptances for this good. If the process is to be operational, this organization cannot collect information on the inventories of the good held by the units in the system. However, any attempt by this organization to set prices "on the basis of supply and demand" would be rendered far more difficult by the absence of inventory data.

must have something to do with the observed outcomes and with the norms of the systems compared. The anonymity of effective interactions clearly has a bearing on the welfare function or norm wherewith we evaluate systems. If barbers discriminate against Negroes, for instance, this will reduce welfare, as long at least as equity with respect to all races of individuals is positively valued in the relevant norm. Whether or not a process is informationally decentralized and "competitive" in a given environment will presumably help to determine the efficiency of the resulting allocation. (We shall return to this question in chapter 10.)

We should be careful, nevertheless, in moving from these principles of classification to the system traits we are ultimately interested in, not to rush to conclusions. The relative significance, for example, of the differing degrees of mutuality and conflict underlying effective actions differs widely from system to system with putative, but not always ascertainable, consequences for the relative efficiency in production and distribution and for the equity of the systems compared. The sale of a "monopolized" good to a customer may be made with the free consent of both buyer and seller, and it may be utility maximizing for both, given the information at their disposal. Yet, even though complete mutuality may prevail, the transaction does not lead to a state of Pareto optimality for both participants, since there may be some income transfer from buyer to seller, accompanied by a reduction in price and adjustment in the monopolist's output and supply, that would make both better off. Neither can one reason mechanically that actions based on informational anonymity and complete mutuality entail smaller social costs than those based on centralized information processes and partial mutuality (orders or threats). While it is true that the former saves on the resources needed to collect data centrally and to inspect and control the effective actions resulting from the orders and threats issued, the latter may incur significantly higher costs in making personal contact and in the negotiations and persuasion required to achieve mutuality.[28]

From the study of the degree of mutuality of interactions we are led to the consideration of "externalities," many of which are associated with interactions characterized by incomplete mutuality. The analysis of externalities, however, requires a prior understanding of ownership rights that form the subject of the next chapter. This analysis is therefore postponed to section 9.3.

28. Koopmans and Montias, op. cit., pp. 59–60.

9

Ownership and Custody:
Implications for Efficiency and Equity

9.1 PRICES AND PROFITS

In classifying interactions in the last chapter, we have been more or less obliged to employ such terms as "prices" and "ownership" that had not yet been defined. We now remedy these omissions and build up on these terms to restate familiar propositions on the relation of ownership or "property rights" to efficiency.

We first introduce the concept of *legal tender*. Suppose that entity A (an individual or an organization) participating in an interaction involving partial or complete mutuality incurs an obligation to deliver certain quantities of goods to entity B. This obligation may be written up in the form of a promissory note that can then be submitted by B to a third entity C as compensation for a claim that C may have on B for goods or services. C will accept the note if he expects that the bundle of goods promised by A would actually be delivered on demand and would be at least of the same utility to him as the bundle owned by B, or if he expects that he can get equivalent "value" or satisfaction from another entity willing to deliver goods or services in exchange for the note. The note thus passed on from one individual to the other extinguishes claims without necessitating the physical transfer of custody of A's goods. Indeed, if every entity in the interacting subset *believes* that another entity will deliver the desired equivalent in value upon demand, entity A need never deliver the goods at all (and may not even possess them to begin with). If the entity circulating the note is a ruling organization or if the note is circulated by an organization ("bank") under guarantee of a ruling organization, it is called a *fiduciary issue*. If, in addition, a ruling organization requires all entities in the system to accept such notes as compensation for claims, these notes qualify as *legal tender*. All circulating notes, whether issued by a ruling organization, a bank, or even a goldsmith, are considered to be *money*.

In modern systems, either exchange prices or transfer prices are an integral part of virtually all contracts. The *exchange price* offer for a good or service may be defined as an option for transferring to a separate entity custody and/or other property rights of one unit of a good or service against payment of a certain number of units of legal tender at a certain time. A *transfer* price differs from an exchange price only in that the option refers to a transfer between budget organizations that are component parts of the same organization rather than between financially autonomous entities[1] and in that actual payment may not be required (e.g., "bookkeeping transactions").

We shall also have occasion to refer to a third category of prices, called *aggregation prices*, which are not normally involved in transfers of custody but serve as weights to combine quantities of goods into a single aggregate. These weights reflect more or less faithfully the relative importance of the various goods combined. In the Soviet Union, aggregation prices, called "fixed" or "plan prices," remained on the level of the current prices in effect in 1926–27 until the mid-1950s, by which time they diverged considerably from these prices. Prices, in any of these three categories, are said to be *efficient* when they "correspond" to or are capable of "supporting" an efficient allocation.[2]

A message containing a price offer for a particular good expressed in monetary units will not generally call forth an acceptance by another entity unless the characteristics of the good have become part of the potential buyer's information set either through direct inspection or because its standardization has led him to expect predictable characteristics. The standardization of commodities effectively widens the intersection (the common subset) of the information sets of potential sellers and buyers and makes it possible for effective interaction to take place with significantly less prior transfer of information.[3] Standardization thus economizes on information costs and facilitates the transfer of goods, irrespective of other rules and patterns of interaction prevailing in a modern system.

Consent is of course a necessary but not a sufficient condition that has to be met if a message is to trigger an effective response, especially one consistent with the intent of the sender.[4] For instance, even though the legitimacy of a tax law may be recognized, the actual payment may fall short and be substantially inferior to the amount actually due because of concealment of

1. For a definition of "budget organizations" and "financially autonomous entities," see below, p. 115.

2. Efficiency in production was defined in sec. 4.1. A vector of prices "corresponds" to or is capable of "supporting" an efficient allocation when it is the solution to the dual of the maximization problem generating an efficient allocation.

3. In the case of nonstandardized goods, price catalogues containing detailed information are normally circulated by potential suppliers. This routine, which presupposes experience leading to stable expectations on the part of potential buyers with respect to the accuracy of the information contained in these complex messages, also economizes on the costs of inspection and contact.

4. Note, however, that under the hypothesis of "perfect competition" in a market economy, the entity quoting the price is assumed to be agreeable to any response or lack of response. Hence "intent" may not be strictly relevant in this limiting case.

sources of income. A ministerial order to an enterprise in a centrally directed economy may not be carried out despite possible sanctions. Likewise, a contract between two firms in a market economy may not be respected if its fulfillment turns out to run contrary to the essential interests of at least one of the parties. The precise response of a decision maker to an informational action will thus be conditioned by his *motivation*, which we define as a function that associates each course of action with the utility of the outcome, or probability mixture of outcomes, that he expects from that course of action.

To discuss one broad basis of motivation in organizations we shall need the term *profits*. This term applies when the inputs to an entity's activities are transferred from, and the outputs transferred to, the custody of other entities (for the set of activities under consideration). The profits of an entity per period are then reckoned as the algebraic sum of the (negative) value of inputs and the (positive) value of outputs, both valued at transfer or exchange prices, depending on whether the organization is a "budget" or a "financially autonomous" organization.

A *budget* is a schedule of receipts and expenditures intended for a given period. If the total receipts or the total expenditures in the budget of an organization appear as items in the budget of some other organization, the first organization is said to be *on the budget account* of the second. It is then one of its *budget organizations*. Both the receipts and expenditures of ministries and hospitals in the Soviet Union and in Poland are on the budget account of the central government.[5] Plants are budget organizations of the enterprise of which they are a part. On the other hand, if an organization only "settles" with other organizations on the basis of the difference between its receipts and its expenditures or of a fixed part of either its receipts or its expenditures (i.e., via taxes, subsidies, or profit levies), it is said to be on cost accounting or *financially autonomous*.[6] In the United States most churches and hospitals, as well as all foundations and corporations, are financially autonomous. Within this class of organizations, we shall call *enterprises* all financially autonomous organizations that are permitted by the rules of ruling organizations to earn profits for the organization as at least one of their goals (though possibly a subsidiary one). A division of an American corporation *may* be an enterprise; a Soviet firm (*predpriiatie*) meets the criteria for an enterprise, as does the East German association of nationalized enterprises (*Vereinigung Volkseigene Betriebe*).

On the basis of rather casual observation or theoretical reasoning[7] economic theorists in West have posited that decision makers—especially managers of enterprises—acted in such a way as to maximize the value of some goal

---

5. This terminology happens to coincide with that in official use.

6. A term equivalent to "on cost accounting" is the Soviet *khozrashchet*.

7. See sec. 10.4 below for a discussion of the maximizing or satisficing behavior of enterprise managers compatible with survival under competition.

function or payoff, such as profits in market economies and the income from bonuses for fulfillment and overfulfillment of plan targets in the centrally directed economies. We shall come back to this question in chapters 10 and 16.

Suffice it to mention for the time being that the rules governing the use and disposition of an economy's productive assets or "means of production" (objects of a certain durability that are capable of being used in a productive activity) usually place constraints on managers' actions and influence the objectives they pursue. Whether a manager of an enterprise maximizes short-run profits or the discounted sum of future profits may depend, for instance, on whether he "owns" part of the enterprise's means of production (on his "equity" in the enterprise) or at least on whether his income hinges in some way on their efficient utilization or disposition.

9.2 DEFINITION AND CLASSIFICATION OF OWNERSHIP RIGHTS

The word *ownership* refers to an amalgam of rights that individuals may have over objects or claims on objects or services. These rights may affect an object's disposition or its utilization. If the object has any degree of permanence and can be used to produce other objects or claims, special ownership rights may adhere to the products of this asset. We shall distinguish among these three rights—"ownership-disposition," "ownership-utilization," and "ownership-over-an-asset's-products"—which will now be defined.

When a right of custody over an object or a claim over objects or services is sanctioned by ruling organizations in the sense that an individual endowed with this right may dispose of the object or claim by transferring it to other individuals or persons subject to the rules of this ruling organization, whether or not they belong to any other organization to which he happens to belong, he may be said to have a right of ownership-disposition over this object. Whereas rights of custody may restrict permissible transfers to individuals belonging to the same (nonruling) organization, *ownership-disposition*, according to this definition, vests the owner with rights of transfer to a wider group of individuals.

When an individual has legally sanctioned rights to use an object or claim as he pleases, he has a right of *ownership-utilization* over it (*jus utendi* in Roman law). When he is permitted by the laws of the ruling organization to dispose of or consume its products, he has a right of *ownership-over-the-asset's-products*, or *jus fruendi*.

An individual or an organization (the *borrower*) may be given temporary custody over an object or a claim, which it must later return to the person exercising disposition rights over it (the *lender*). The borrower is thereby given temporary utilization rights, as well normally as jus fruendi, over the asset (example: a farmer renting land from a landlord may work the land as he sees fit—jus utendi—and reap the benefits from its utilization—*jus fruendi*;

however, both rights may in some particulars be restricted by the provisions of his contract). As we have already seen, the borrower does not necessarily have to return the same pieces of metal or paper that were entrusted to him. The object lent out is symbolic rather than tangible: it represents any other object or claim that will afford the same utility to the lender upon its return. The price that the borrower must generally pay for the temporary use of the asset is called *interest*. *Banks* are organizations specialized in borrowing and lending money or other claims. In both East and West, households, enterprises, and ruling organizations both lend to and borrow from banks.

The interesting cases, from a comparative point of view, are those where the various types of ownership are *not* vested in the same individual for important categories of objects or claims. Individuals may be deprived of both rights of disposition and utilization over assets if they are legally considered insane, senile, or otherwise incapable, but they may still be able to enjoy some of their fruits (e.g., the interest and dividends on a trust fund).[8] In West the delegation of disposition and utilization rights by the stockholders of a corporation to its managers may at times be irreversible, especially if the latter also own stock in it.

In recent years the notion of "ownership rights" has been stretched by the courts and by jurists, especially in the United States, to include claims on legally sanctioned benefits distributed by ruling organizations to individuals. Many individuals in the United States believe that if they are legally entitled to a government pension or state welfare payments, their legal right is tantamount to a property claim. (In former times, by contrast, the conferral of these benefits was treated by the public custodians as a "privilege" for the benefittees that could be revoked at their discretion.) According to this modern point of view, if claimants are denied their legal rights to such benefits, they are deprived of their property and should be compensated for their virtual loss.[9] These "new property" claims are not necessarily limited to jus fruendi. To the extent that welfare-rights organizations or similar interest groups wish to have a say in the distribution of government benefits, the claimants are involved, at least collectively, in the disposition of the assets defined. Finally, if the individuals claiming the benefits can influence the way the funds earmarked for eventual distribution are invested (e.g., in the case of the Swedish Pension Fund), they are directly or indirectly exercising a right of jus utendi.

These fairly extreme claims—extreme in the sense that they are, at least currently, made only by a small, chiefly disaffected part of the population

---

8. However, a judge may have rights of disposition over a child and be obligated by law to delegate custody for the child to a guardian.

9. Charles Reich, "The New Property," *Yale Law Journal* 73, no. 5 (Apr. 1974): 740–46.

in West—have an interesting counterpart in the criticism of "the system" among dissidents in East. In a recent *samizdat* pamphlet two Soviet citizens asserted that the job security of Soviet bureaucrats, sanctioned in the Soviet equivalent of civil service lists (*nomenklatura*), gave them a form of property rights over these jobs "as inalienable as capital in bourgeois society. [The nomenklatura] serves as a legal basis for our system much in the manner as the law of private property under capitalism."[10] There is some exaggeration in this claim. Soviet bureaucrats after all do not have rights of disposition over their offices; they cannot, at least legally, give or sell their place on retirement to their friends or relatives. The sale of offices, on the other hand, was fairly widespread in premodern societies. In France under l'ancien régime, for example, the practice was so deeply rooted that when Chancellor Maupéou attempted to abolish it in 1771, he met determined opposition, led by nobles who invoked "the natural rights of man, freedom of the individual and political liberty" in defense of this hallowed tradition.[11]

To resume, both welfare recipients and present-day bureaucrats have claims to certain payments by virtue of their *status* (as indigents or as qualified and loyal public servants), which cannot be transferred to others. Rights of ownership-disposition, in contrast, are essential to systems based on *contractual* relations among their participants.

Copyright and patent laws in all modern economies protect an individual's jus fruendi over his ideas in the form of books, articles, and inventions even though he may have alienated his rights of disposition over the objects in which these ideas were incorporated (e.g., the sale of a machine embodying a patented innovation). In most countries, including the United States, these rights are limited to a claim on the profits and gains that can be earned from the dissemination of the ideas through reproduction (the reprint of a book or the manufacture of machines incorporated in a prototype). French law since 1920 has extended the notion of ownership rights on the product of an artist's creation by allowing him and his heir to lay claim to a percentage of the sales price of an object he originally produced (and disposed of) each time it is resold at a public auction. An American jurist recently commented that, as a result of this *droit de suite*, "exclusive and total ownership, other than by the creator himself, is no longer possible in France, for some of the creator's interests subsist despite the alienation of the work."[12]

10. Cited in Walter D. Connor, "Dissent in a Complex Society: The Soviet Case," *Problems of Communism* 22 (March–Apr. 1973): 45.

11. Barrington Moore Jr., *Social Origins of Dictatorship and Democracy: Lord and Peasant in the Making of the Modern World* (Boston: Beacon Press, 1966), pp. 60–61.

12. Rita E. Hansen, "The French Droit de Suite," in *Copyright Law Symposium*, no. 11 (New York: Columbia University Press, 1962), p. 15.

9.3 Some Implications of Ownership and Custody for System Outcomes

Who-owns-what has a number of implications for the desiderata of equity and efficiency. The rights of enjoyment by a privileged few of the products of "owned assets" are considered so detrimental to equity in polities ruled by representatives of Communist parties that they are drastically restricted. Few participants in these systems are allowed to collect such "unearned income." The odium attaching to these gains is of course far greater for the earnings from productive assets *strictu sensu* than from the enjoyment of durable consumer goods capable of generating utility for prolonged periods. Thus, although in the aftermath of a Communist-led revolution private factories are almost always confiscated by the state and "nationalized," it is generally permissible for the former owners to keep or to sell off their jewelry and works of art, at least within domestic territory.[13] "Unearned income on owned assets," incidentally, does not encompass the higher salaries that an individual can get in these polities by taking advantage of the "human capital" he accumulated through education.

For basic equity reasons, ownership rights over *other* individuals (slavery), as well as rights of utilization over the labor of others extending over a prolonged period of time (*indentures*), are prohibited by law in all contemporary systems (in parts of the Arabic peninsula only since the early 1960s). Significant exceptions in premodern societies include the exploitation of endebted farmers forced to work for landlords until they pay off their debts and the de jure or de facto rights vested in husbands to use their wife or wives for productive purposes and in parents to put their children to work.[14] (Prohibitions on ownership are usually bound up with, but should be kept distinct from, restraints on the sale or purchase of assets, which will be discussed in the next chapter.)

In modern societies, slavery or any other coercion of labor except for military purposes violates most individuals' sense of equity. Many people

13. On restrictions on the disposition of ownership rights, see chapter 10, pp. 152–54.

14. In many parts of rural West Africa, where hired farm labor is scarce or nonexistent, a man will buy one or more wives to work his farm. The greater the number of his wives, the more land he will be able to "husband." In the nineteenth century in the many parts of Africa where the "peculiar institution" prevailed, slavery and "wifery" were virtually the only statuses a woman could assume. Sir Samuel Baker, a British traveler who explored the sources of the Nile in the 1860s, relates the case of an Abyssinian woman whom he had bought in the market place and then emancipated. He explained to her that she was now "free" and would henceforth be paid wages. The woman, overjoyed, embraced him under the delusion she had become one of his wives. As a later commentator put it, "She could only understand freedom as a European name for marriage" (Hugh Craig, *Great African Travellers* [New York: George Rutledge and Sons, 1890], p. 58).

consider slavery inefficient as well as repugnant. Human beings, it is often argued, will not put forth their best effort and initiative under threat of violence. Free labor by virtue of its higher productivity will outcompete forced labor even though the coerced workers may cost their owners less in upkeep than the wages that would have to be paid to hired hands. These commonly accepted notions may have to be reconsidered in view of the new light shed on Negro slavery in the United States in Fogel and Engerman's *Time on the Cross*.[15] Their findings strongly suggest that, at least on the large well-run plantations of the American South, a judicious mixture of threats of violence and incentives coaxed out more strenuous effort on the part of slaves than free men would willingly have exerted in exchange for money wages.[16] A man's preferences over various combinations of leisure, income, and pain (or fear of being whipped) would not have to be very odd to account for his behavior as a hard-working slave if he were threatened with violence and as an indolent "target worker" who would never labor for more than a short number of hours a day no matter what wage he was offered as a free individual.

On the pre-Civil War plantation the economies of scale arising from the strenuous exertions of slaves, together with the specialization and perfection of frequently repeated tasks in closely supervised labor gangs, are said to account for the relatively great efficiency—measured in terms of productivity per unit of combined labor and capital—of slave labor.[17] Needless to say though, the higher degree of exertion of the slave under the threat of the whip should be viewed as a contribution to greater efficiency only if the disutility that the slave attached to the status of slavery and to his suffering in the process of being coerced is totally disregarded in the observer's norm function.

The investigation of slavery by Fogel and Engerman was limited to the American South except for a few observations on the "peculiar institution" in the West Indies. A comparison of the effects of labor coercion on efficiency and economic growth in the United States and in Russia, where serfdom was only terminated by decision of the czar shortly before slaves were emancipated in the States, might reveal whether or not the Fogel–Engerman findings were valid only for the United States or had more general implications. Marxist economists have always been inclined to stress the inefficiencies of the serf labor system, both in agriculture and in industry. They have pointed to the much faster growth of industries in which free labor prevailed (cotton spinning and weaving) than of industries operated with serf labor (pig iron, woolens)

15. Robert W. Fogel and S. L. Engerman, *Time on the Cross: The Economics of American Negro Slavery* (Boston: Little, Brown, 1974).

16. Ibid., pp. 234–40.

17. Ibid., pp. 203–04, 234.

as evidence in support of this verdict.[18] If nothing else, Fogel and Engerman will have taught us to question the superficial examination of the statistics on which such judgments are based.[19] The Marxist view may well be right, but only a more rigorous examination of the data will now vindicate their conclusions.

9.4 OWNERSHIP RIGHTS AND EXTERNALITIES

It is evident that the efficiency of resource allocation in any system depends to a crucial extent on both the content of messages (e.g., in a market economy on whether prices reflect relative scarcities or in a centrally directed economy on whether orders correspond to efficient input allotments and output targets) and on the responses of the makers of economic decisions to these messages (maximizing behavior in a market economy, compliance with orders implementing the principal production and allocation decisions in a centralized economy).[20] In a "competitive market economy" in particular, efficiency cannot be attained unless all resources and means of production are in the exclusive custody of *some participant* or group of participants acting as a single person and are "managed" by these participants in such a way as to maximize the discounted stream of their future rents, corresponding to nondiscriminating rentals based on efficiency prices.[21] In the case of a productive activity, perfect efficiency requires that (1) the product be in the custody of the producer in the sense that he has some control over how much of each good or bad he produces and how he will dispose of it to the next custodian (which may be the city dump) and that (2) any individual or organization that may be adversely affected by the product(s) of the activity have custody over the channels through which the harm may be inflicted (e.g., have legally enforceable ownership rights over the air, land, water, or other elements in his or its immediate environment that, if desired, provide protection from such exposure).

18. P. I. Lyashchenko, *History of the National Economy of Russia to the 1917 Revolution* (New York: Macmillan Co., 1949), pp. 337–38.

19. Lyashchenko, a promoter of the orthodox Marxist view, claims that the Russian sugar-beet industry before 1861 "was chiefly maintained by, and flourished with, the aid of serf labor, cheap raw material resources, and high, nearly prohibitive duties on imported sugar." The "cheap raw material" was also produced on the estates with the aid of serf labor (ibid., p. 336). One important difference between the American South and preemancipation Russia was that Russian serf-owners could bring their influence to bear on the state to protect the system via high tariffs and subsidies for serf-operated industries, whereas American planters by and large could not.

20. We shall dwell in some detail on the matter of compliance to orders in sec. 13.3.

21. For further discussion of the role of pricing in attaining efficient allocation, see Koopmans, *Three Essays on the State of Economic Science* (New York: McGraw-Hill, 1957), essay I. On competition and competitive processes, see chapter 10.

Externalities occur whenever one or the other, or most frequently both, of these conditions are violated. *Negative externalities*, where the outcome of an activity in which one or more individuals engage reduces the utility of other individuals or the payoff of other organizations without their uncoerced consent, usually violate both conditions.[22] Malevolent individuals who are capable of controlling their harmful activities may surely inflict disutility on other individuals "for the fun of it," but in most instances the perpetrator of an externality cannot or is unwilling to pay the cost of eliminating the harmful side-effects of an otherwise profitable (and beneficial) activity.

Positive externalities expose individuals or organizations to effects that raise their utility or payoff without requiring them to compensate the producer of these effects in any way, even though the latter had no intention or desire to confer this benefit on the entities affected. Positive externalities thus violate the first condition (although not the second): for if the producer of the externality could control the outcome of his activities at no extra cost he would wish to dispose of them at a positive price to all those that would be willing to pay for them. The failure of a producer to control the output of benefits he confers on others introduces an element of inefficiency in resource allocation because it rules out the mutually satisfactory negotiation of the volume of this output between the producer and the benefittees willing to compensate him *pro rata* for it.

The direct contact and negotiation between producers of externalities and the entities affected are often so costly that they cannot be profitably undertaken to eliminate or even to mitigate their impact. The existence of these transaction costs must be allowed for in determining any suspected lapse from full efficiency ostensibly caused by externalities.

Negative externalities occur in all systems, but they are endemic in systems where the rules, customs, and traditions defining ownership rights do not securely assign custody for all valued assets to designated individuals. Access to resources held in common and not subject to such custody and management (pastures, forests, and even arable land in certain developing economies, crowded highways and city streets in developed economies, fishing grounds, especially in international waters) is often not sufficiently restricted for their efficient utilization under a market system without the intervention of ruling organizations. For under such conditions, pastures tend to be overgrazed, timber overcut, land overworked, roads excessively congested, and species of fish threatened with extinction. In the absence of custodial entities restricting access to these resources or man-made facilities directly or by an efficient rental charge, potential users are guided by the average costs they must bear

22. A number of instances of negative externalities are listed in table 8.1.

(e.g., the average congestion delay on a road), which do not take into account the total additional costs imposed on other users by their decision to share in its common use.

Certain types of positive externalities may also be explained by traits of the system structure. In all systems where laws ban slavery and indenture, an individual, beyond the duration of his work contract (if he is bound by any), may dispose of his skills and his human capital as he pleases. This freedom may inhibit employers concerned with the payoff of their enterprise rather than with that of the system as a whole from incurring expenses to train or educate their employees. (The positive externality in this case is due to the inability of the employer to control the eventual use of the assets he has built up.)

Recent theoretical speculation on externalities has shown that the assignment of ownership rights is in and of itself crucial to allocative efficiency, but to whom or to what entity these rights have been assigned—whether to the perpetrator or to his victim in the absence of such assignment—should have no effect in the absence of transaction costs, either in the short or in the long run, on the allocation of resources.[23] The implications for equity are undoubtedly momentous: compare a law that gives the tenant of an apartment the right to make any noise he pleases and forces his neighbors to pay him for abatement with a law that guarantees all tenants the right to silence, which will force the noisemaker to pay his neighbors for the right to pollute their silent air. In most systems, laws protect potential victims rather than the perpetrators. But there are some exceptions. Property owners may have to yield rights of way on paths crossing their land to passersby, show their art collections to the public, or allow poor people to collect firewood in "their" forests. Ruling organizations can draft individuals to serve in the armed forces against their will, quarter soldiers even on recalcitrant households, and so on.

The imposition of property rights on resources that were hitherto freely accessible is also likely to have equity effects. For example, Martin Weitzman has shown,[24] under certain simplifying assumptions,[25] that the competitive

23. See G. Warren Nutter, "The Coase Theorem on Social Cost: A Footnote," *Journal of Law and Economics* 11 (Oct. 1968): 503–07 and the literature cited therein.

24. "Alternative Management of Common Property Resources Under Free Access and Private Ownership," Cowles Foundation Discussion Paper No. 323, Nov. 10, 1971.

25. The principal assumptions are: (a) the production function for every property exhibits diminishing returns to the variable factor for any increment of output; (b) the production function is the same after the impositions of ownership rights as before; (c) an increase in the return to the variable factor will call forth an aggregate supply of the factor that will be at least as great as that which the previous return called forth.

return to the variable factor (wage of farm laborers, benefits to motorists or fishermen) after the imposition of property rights cannot be higher than what it was under free access.

It is interesting to speculate under what conditions the return to the variable factor will be equal to what it was before and under what conditions it will be smaller. The following example suggests the answer.

Consider two pieces of agricultural land on which a fixed number $\bar{x}$ of individuals earn their livelihood. One piece, called property F, is of superior quality to the other, called property G. The production function on F exhibits decreasing returns to labor, the variable input, for all levels of this input. The production function on G exhibits constant returns for all levels of the variable input. G may be called the *extensive margin*. The average and marginal productivity schedules[26] on F and G are shown in diagram 9.1.

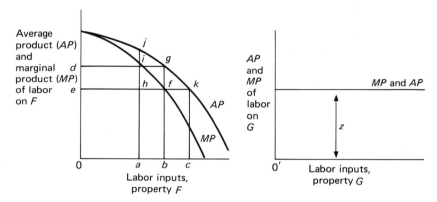

Diagram 9.1

In the absence of any restrictions on access to F and G, no individual would cultivate G unless $\bar{x}$ were greater than Oc, since up to Oc the average product of F is larger than the constant average product of G. If $\bar{x}$ were actually greater than Oc, precisely Oc individuals would cultivate F and the rest, or $(\bar{x} - Oc)$, would cultivate G, thus equalizing average product on the two properties.

If F is now placed under ownership-custody, how much rent will the owner be able to collect? He cannot pay his laborers less than z, the average product that they could earn on G. He will maximize his rents by hiring Ob laborers because their marginal product at Ob would amount to bf, which is equal

---

26. If the products of F and G are sold under "perfectly competitive conditions" (cf. chap. 10), the schedules representing the average and marginal *value* products of F and G for a variable labor input will be identical to those shown in the diagram, except for a common scale factor.

to z.[27] The rest of the laborers, or $\bar{x} - Ob$, will establish themselves on G. Rents will be equal to *defg*, and laborers will be neither better nor worse off than they were prior to the enclosure.

On the other hand, if $\bar{x}$ had been smaller than Oc, average product before the enclosure would have exceeded z, and laborers would clearly have been made worse off by the enclosure. (With $\bar{x}$ equal to Oa, for example, the wage after the enclosure could be anywhere between *ah* and *ai*, depending on the bargaining power of landlord and laborers; it would be lower in any case than the average product *aj*, which these laborers earned before enclosure.)

The analysis assumes of course that laborers, for any given level of income, are indifferent between working for themselves and hiring themselves out. More seriously, it ignores any improvement in cultivation that the enclosure might make possible. Such an improvement might leave laborers better off than they had been on their own before the enclosure, provided they were not numerous enough to cause wages to remain at z.

In the more general case of more than two properties with varying characteristics, Weitzman's results can be used to show that the income to the variable factor will be undiminished after the imposition of rents if there exists some property yielding no rent (the "extensive margin") that at least one individual would wish to cultivate both before and after the imposition of rents.

The conflict between efficiency and equity may arise when there is no mechanism to redistribute incomes in such a way as to compensate individuals who have been made worse off as a result of an efficiency-promoting measure. This may be the case in a situation where enclosures are put into effect under a law promulgated by a legislative body that represents mainly the interests of the prospective landowners. Where the ruling organization owns all basic productive assets, the equity case against their efficient management is much weaker, or nonexistent.

The "three-fix" campaign of the early 1960s in communist China provides an instructive example of the relation of custody and rights of utilization to efficiency in such an economy. Prior to this campaign the authorities of the "commune," which embraced tens of villages and averaged a population of 25,000 inhabitants, had been empowered to mobilize manpower, cattle, and

---

27. Let the production function on F be $f(x)$, where $f'(x) \geqslant 0$ and $f''(x) \leqslant 0$. Given an input $\bar{x}$, the maximum rent per unit of input that the owner will be able to collect will be $f(\bar{x})/\bar{x} - z$, where z is the constant product on G, because, if the rent were any higher, it would pay the marginal laborer to work on G, which yields no rents. Hence T = total rents = $[f(x)/x - z]x = f(x) - zx$.
To maximize T with respect to x:

$$\frac{dT}{dx} = f'(x) - z = 0.$$

Hence $f'(x)$ must equal z. At this point $x = 0b$ and the per laborer rent equals *fg*.

implements to carry out tasks wherever they might be needed on the massive landholdings of the commune.[28] This policy led to a decline in the interest and responsibility of commune members for the proper utilization of the lands that had formerly "belonged" to them or to the cooperative of which they had been members (before cooperatives had been amalgamated into communes). The decision to adscript ("fix") manpower, implements, and land to production teams, which cultivated approximately the same lands that were formerly owned by the team members' village, was meant to remedy this situation and to take advantage of the members' closer acquaintance with and greater "feeling" for the lands belonging to their village. This profound operational reform, however, did not undermine the principle of communal ownership, which was upheld as vigorously as ever in the official ideology.[29] The Nadudvar system on Hungarian and the *zveno* system on Soviet collective farms go even further in the same direction of granting small groups of individuals at least temporary ownership rights over patches of collectively owned property. These experimental modifications of the *kolkhoz* system give each designated group of members not only custody over the fields assigned to the groups but also a partial jus fruendi over the fields' produce in the form of a share of the crop.

We may also look at system-structure traits as the product of the long-term adaptation of the system to the environment. In successfully developing economies, rules from time to time have been adopted that increased the efficiency or the stability of the system. Granted that externalities are in one way or another inefficient and that this inefficiency was perceived, one is led to ask what steps were taken to curb externalities as development proceeded in Western Europe, North America, or Japan. In this spirit, Lance Davis and Douglass North have recently argued that "economic institutions are innovated and property rights are revised because it appears desirable for

---

28. T. J. Hughes and D. E. T. Luard, *The Economic Development of Communist China 1949–1958* (New York: Oxford University Press, 1959).

29. In 1932–33, when the gigantic Soviet state grain farms (*zernosovkhozy*) had become too large to manage as one unit, they were broken down into operationally autonomous entities called *usad'by*. For two or three years after this reform, giant-scale farming was still the officially approved norm. Then "gigantomania" was officially condemned and many of the *usad'by* became state farms in their own right. In Bulgaria, about 170 "agro-industrial complexes" organized between 1969 and 1971 encompassed about 95 percent of the arable land of the country as of early 1972. At the highest levels of the government–party hierarchy, there was talk about further amalgamation of these complexes, which might eventually be made to coincide with the 28 districts into which the country is divided. However, a Western analyst speculated that such units would become too large to manage and control effectively and that the collective and state farms that were merged to create the complexes might therefore regain some of the operational custodial powers they had held prior to 1970.

individuals or groups to undertake the costs of such changes."[30] They cite numerous instances in American economic development when externalities were "internalized" (within private or public organizations) because it was advantageous for "society" to do so.[31] Comparable development is taking place in parts of Africa where increasing population density is generating land scarcity and potential rents that are gradually being captured by the traditional custodians of these lands. It is worth noticing, though, that communal (tribal or village) ownership over land still prevails in most of these areas (e.g., in the Lakié region of Cameroon and in the parts of Chad where well water and grazing lands have become scarce), private ownership being so far more or less restricted to real estate in the more modern urban settlements.

Although the Davis–North conjecture has much to recommend it, one should keep in mind that the system structure did not always evolve in the direction of making individuals bear responsibility for the consequences of their economic decisions. On the contrary, another trend in economic legislation in Western development liberated individuals from their responsibility for certain extreme consequences of their decisions. If these decisions were made by individuals acting as members of organizations, their personal responsibility for the damages or losses incurred by the organization was restricted by laws of "limited liability." Bankruptcy laws, briefly discussed in chapter 10, also reduced the burden on individuals of assuming the risks of extremely adverse circumstances. By allowing bankrupts to escape in part or in whole the adverse consequences of their acts under these conditions, ruling organizations in effect created externalities. Limited-liability and bankruptcy laws were presumably motivated at least in part by the growth desideratum (since they might be calculated to encourage timid investors), but they also showed evidence of the legislator's concern for the plight of the individual investor, even at the expense of efficiency understood in the narrow sense.

9.5 PUBLIC VERSUS PRIVATE OWNERSHIP

Without going back on my promise that this book on the structure of economic systems would not turn on the issue of "socialism or capitalism" or of "public versus private ownership," I still feel that it is legitimate to devote at least a section of a chapter to the issue. Even though one cannot jump from the nature of the ownership prevailing in a system to any judgment on its

30. Lance E. Davis and Douglass C. North, *Institutional Change and American Economic Growth* (Cambridge, England: Cambridge University Press, 1971), p. 10.

31. For a similar, historically oriented viewpoint, see Harold Demsetz, "Toward a Theory of Property Rights," *American Economic Review* 57 (May 1967): 347–59.

efficiency, its stability, or its equity, this does not mean, as we have already seen in the last section, that there are no efficiency, stability, and equity aspects to ownership, and it may not be immaterial whether management or allocation decisions are made by public or by private authorities.

If publicly owned enterprises pursued precisely the same objective as privately owned enterprises—if, for instance, both types of decision-making units maximized the expected value of the sum of their future-profits stream—then it would be only a matter of equity whether an organization engaging in economic activities was privately or publicly owned. This is of course unlikely to be the case even if, by the rules of the system structure, all public organizations engaging in economic activities were declared autonomous and were instructed to "maximize profits." As long as the managers of these "public enterprises" were appointed by ruling organizations, they might be expected to take the chances of the renewal of their contract into consideration in making profit-oriented decisions that were contrary to the interests of the appointing bodies. Managers without an assured participation in both the present and the future profits of a public firm might also behave differently from managers of private firms with a stake in future profits. On the other hand, giving managers of public firms an "equity in the business" could be said to controvert the principle of public ownership.

The comparative study of public and private economic organizations revolves partly around differences in the objectives and interests of the decision makers in these two types of enterprises and partly on their interaction in "mixed economies." Only differences in interests will be dwelt on in this section; the interaction problem will be discussed in chapter 17.

Very few studies of decision making in private and public enterprises operating in a similar environment have been carried out. One of these, and a most imaginative one to boot, is that of Sam Peltzman, who has compared the prices of electric power and the mix of services of power producers under private and public ownership in the United States.[32] Peltzman conjectures that "the willingness of the government enterprise management to trade profits for political support will lead mangers to use the pricing system as a mechanism for redistributing wealth within the political constituency."[33] This leads him to various hypotheses about the level of prices, their changeability, their differentiation according to consumer groups, and so forth. He then compares these prices and services with those generated by *regulated* privately owned companies, on the assumption that regulation leaves these companies enough scope to manifest their "privateness."[34] The empirical results are

32. "Pricing in Public and Private Enterprises: Electric Utilities in the United States," *Journal of Law and Economics* 14 (Apr. 1971): 109–47.
33. Ibid., p. 112.
34. Ibid., p. 122.

ambiguous on the level of prices: they do not prove conclusively that publicly owned utility prices are manipulated "to create a group of benefitted customers, who will support the government firm."[35] Public enterprises were not found to discriminate systematically in favor of the more numerous consumer groups in order to marshall their support.[36] However, the extent of price differentiation among groups and the resulting output patterns turned out to be in accord with propositions derived from the basic conjectures. Finally, also in agreement with the conjecture was the finding that changeability of prices in response to cost fluctuations was greater in private than in public enterprises even though the former were regulated and the latter, for the most part, were not. Although Peltzman's results are not so conclusive as one might wish, his study provides a useful framework for making similar comparisons in other countries where private and public enterprises coexist.

Another recent study, by Marc J. Roberts, compares the behavior of three private and three public enterprises in the United States and Canada that produce electric power and related utilities.[37] On the basis of extensive interviews with senior executives of all six enterprises, he finds the distinction between private and public yields "little predictive information about behavioral differences."[38] Cost consciousness and concern for externalities, for example, do not seem to differ very significantly between the types. A public enterprise such as the Tennessee Valley Authority, which finances its budget from retained earnings and revenue bonds, may be as cost conscious and insensitive to the pressures of the press and public as a private enterprise, while another such as Ontario Hydro of Canada, whose budget must be reviewed by the Government of Ontario Province, may have to worry more about its political image than about costs and profits. The mode of control by public authorities seems to be more critical in explaining observed differences in the behavior of these enterprises than the legal rights of ownership.

The remaining speculations on the subject of the interests of managers of publicly and privately owned enterprises have only the barest empirical content and chiefly reflect my own interests—which may well differ from those of the reader.

Although the custodian of a public asset generally has no *legal* right to its

35. Ibid., p. 145.
36. In a supplementary study of liquor prices in states where liquor is retailed through state-owned stores and in states where it is retailed through private firms, Peltzman found some statistical support for his conjecture on prices since the cheaper brands, presumably consumed by broader consumer groups, were relatively less expensive in publicly owned than in privately owned outlets (ibid., pp. 143–45).
37. "An Evolutionary and Institutional View of the Behavior of Public and Private Companies," *American Economic Review* 65, no. 2 (May 1975): 4.
38. Ibid., p. 423.

usufruct, he often enjoys this right de facto by virtue of his special position. The custodian of a museum's collection of prints and drawings, for example, may enjoy the fruits of ownership (jus fruendi) of the collection perhaps as much as if the prints and drawings were "his." As custodian he uses the collection as he sees fit in cataloguing, framing, or exhibiting items (jus utendi). Finally, he normally has a wide range of discretion to buy, within the limits of his institution's budget, and even to augment the funds at his disposal by selling duplicates or less desirable items. In what sense then does he not "own" the collection? Ultimately because the rights of disposition are only delegated to him and subject to serious restrictions: he may buy and sell solely *for* the museum; he may not deal with items in the collection on his own account. He cannot pass on the collection to a member of his family or to a friend after he retires or dies. Neither can the staff of the museum, acting as a collective, decide to sell some of the drawings and distribute the proceeds among themselves or even turn them over to a fund for building a day-care center. Ownership of the drawings and prints is neither private nor collective but manifestly public.

If one considers, however, that a private collector of the same age as a chief custodian (say, 45 years old) can hope to enjoy his collection for only 25 or 30 years, depending on his life expectancy, and will then have to bequeath it to heirs who may have no interest in art and whose future utility from the collection may be very heavily discounted by the legator, the present and discounted benefits enjoyed by this full-fledged owner of art works may not be much less (given the same preferences in jus fruendi) than that which the public custodian of the same or comparable works would get out of it. It may be noted in passing that, in contrast to managers of privately owned enterprises, custodians of public property frequently lack a clear, precise, and quantifiable objective function, the value of which they might be expected to maximize. Their success or failure in managing the resources in their custody is particularly difficult to evaluate when the services of these resources are gratuitously distributed (as in free-admission museums). We should not be surprised, therefore, if custodians of publicly owned art works at times practice an inventory policy that would eventually bankrupt most private enterprises —buying or accepting as gifts paintings, drawings, prints, and sculptures that they then proceed to hoard in their vast "reserves" at an appreciable cost in insurance and in space occupied. Many of these works will never again be viewed by members of the public at large.[39]

Ruling organizations are in effect dispensing assets whenever they permit

---

39. Custodians of public collections of drawings and prints are usually satisfied that their treasures are "available to the public" as long as "bona fide" students of art can obtain permission to see them upon special request.

the exercise of profitable or otherwise beneficial activities to certain individuals or organizations and not to others. Taxi medallions distributed in tightly restricted numbers by city governments are a case in point, as are broadcasting licenses for television or radio broadcasting. A primary trait of the system structure is the extent to which these assets may be transferable by the licensee to other persons either temporarily (when the taxi is rented) or permanently (after the retirement or death of the licensee), and if they are transferable whether against payment or only gratuitously (e.g., to the licensee's heirs). Much has been written on ethical aspects of this question.[40] From a comparative angle we should be interested in the effect on certain system outcomes of allowing or disallowing such transfers. I would conjecture in the case of taxi medallions, for example, that the effect of denying transfer of licenses either temporarily or permanently, other things equal, would (1) increase the age of retirement of individual licensees driving their own taxis and (2) reduce the proportion of cabs individually operated by their owners to cabs operated by hired drivers in large, corporately owned fleets. The first conjecture follows from the assumption that a cab driver will retire sooner or take up a less strenuous occupation if he can sell his medallion for a large sum (the price of transferable medallions runs from $5,000 to $25,000 in large American cities)[41] than if this option is foreclosed. The second rests on the argument that a fleet owner endowed with medallions for a large number of cabs can hire drivers of all ages and is not so constrained by a rule prohibiting transfers as an individual licensee driving his own cab would be.

9.6 Collective Ownership

When an asset is "owned by a collective organization," the members of this organization may enjoy any of the three basic rights of ownership defined earlier. For example, they may decide upon the utilization or disposition of the asset by a majority vote or by some other procedure approved by the rules of the organization. Every individual in the collective normally has a claim to some of the asset's usufruct or yield. In many instances, especially including pension funds, rights of utilization are delegated to a separate organization, which may be private (the TIAA managing pension funds for university professors) or public (U.S. social security, the pension scheme managed by the Swedish government). A few examples of collective or semipublic forms of ownership will give some idea of the wealth of variations that can be played on this theme.

The Soviet collective farm (*kolkhoz*) cultivates land that technically belongs

40. See, e.g., Reich, op. cit., pp. 746–64, 742.
41. Edmund W. Kitch, Marc Isaacson, and Daniel Kasper, "The Regulation of Taxicabs," *Journal of Law and Economics* 14 (Oct. 1971): 294 and 346, no. 245.

to the whole nation and is accordingly termed "national property." On the other hand, accordingly to the Model Charter adopted by the Soviet government and the Central Committee of the Communist Party of the USSR in 1935, a kolkhoz holds the land it occupies "in perpetuity, that is, forever."[42] This right was confirmed by the Soviet Constitution of 1936. Since the management of the kolkhoz is, in principle at least, elected by the membership and the net income (receipts minus nonlabor expenditures) of the farm is distributed to the members in proportion to the labor they supplied during the year, one might be tempted to argue, given the legal status of its property rights, that it was indeed a collective enterprise. The trouble is that the ownership provisions of the Model Charter of 1935 and of the Constitution of 1936 were at times violated by the central government to promote efficiency, as the Soviet leaders perceived it. In the late 1950s, for example, many "weak" collectives were merged or amalgamated with state farms with or without the consent of their members. In any event the collective had limited rights of disposition because the members could not turn over kolkhoz lands back to their own private use. Neither could they sell them to other individuals or even to other organizations without special dispensation, although a kolkhoz was permitted to *acquire* private or public lands.[43] All in all, the kolkhoz may be said to be a semipermanent custodian of public property rather than a collective in the sense of our definition of the word.

In Romania a collective farm is the legal owner of the land its members cultivate. This legal bind has not prevented the central government, whenever it desired to do so, from consolidating or amalgamating weak collectives. A legal right, at bottom, is no stronger than the procedures sanctioned in the system structure for defending them (e.g., courts presided over by judges independent of ruling organizations). Legal controversy in recent years has turned on the "ownership rights" of the collective-farm members over the plots assigned to them for their private use by the collectives. The assignment beginning in 1971 was to an individual rather than to a family, as had been the case previously.[44] The distinction is crucial since the plot may be withdrawn or curtailed in size if its custodian has not contributed a minimum number of days' work to the collective. Thus if the individual rather than the family is assigned, and is responsible for, the plot, he cannot be deprived of the privilege because his wife or niece did not work a sufficient number of days on the collective.[45]

---

42. Cited in Lazar Volin, *A Century of Russian Agriculture: From Alexander II to Khrushchev* (Cambridge, Mass.: Harvard University Press, 1970), pp. 244–45.

43. Volin, ibid.

44. A. Stirbu in *Revista Romana de drept*, no. 2, 1972, quoted in Radio Free Europe Research, Rumanian Press Survey, no. 920 (May 19, 1972): 1.

45. Joint responsibility for taxes and other obligations on the part of all the members of the extended family was one of the basic features of the pre-Stolypin system of Russian agriculture.

There are severe limitations also on the ownership of the assets of enterprises by their collectives in Yugoslavia, although the collectives' rights of utilization and disposition are far greater than in any other economy where most of the means of production have been taken out of private hands. According to the basic law of December 26, 1953, the "right of use" over the fixed assets of an enterprise are vested in the Workers' Council, an elected body of representatives of its collective. The Workers' Council may sell its fixed capital to another enterprise or to a cooperative but not to a private individual or group of individuals. The government must be compensated for any loss caused by damage to the enterprise's fixed assets. The enterprise must also pay the government depreciation and interest on the book value of "its" fixed capital.[46] Finally, the termination of enterprises may be "ordered by the Government" for economic reasons.[47]

9.7 CONCLUSIONS

The trichotomy of ownership—private, collective, public—useful as it may be as an initial principle of classification, oversimplifies the complex rules governing utilization and disposition. Even by legal standards, assets cannot always be clearly classified as private, collective, or public. When one considers in addition that the ruling organization does not always abide by its own rules—as in the case of the Soviet government and the Soviet Constitution—the differences in the character of ownership that can be discerned from system to system become even more numerous and subtle.

As Dahl and Lindblom so persuasively argued in their pioneering work on *Politics, Economics and Welfare*, there is no necessary relation between public ownership of an enterprise and the "control" of its policies and decisions by a ruling (governmental) organization.[48] Some publicly owned enterprises are virtually free of detailed government controls (e.g., the British Broadcasting Corporation). Some privately owned enterprises are subject to detailed government controls (lease and contract by the Atomic Energy Commission).[49]

In chapter 15 we pursue further the relation between forms of ownership and outcomes. At that juncture, however, we shall shun description and aim for schematic simplification of decision makers' behavior to see whether we can predict how typical outcomes might differ under diverging assumptions

---

46. Svetozar Pejovich, *The Market-Planned Economy of Yugoslavia* (Minneapolis: University of Minnesota Press, 1966), p. 29. Pejovich devotes a whole chapter to the legal structure of the Yugoslav economy.

47. Ibid., p. 33.

48. "Controls" and "autonomy" (in the paragraph that follows) will be defined precisely in chaps. 13 and 14.

49. Robert A. Dahl and Charles E. Lindblom, *Politics, Economics and Welfare: Planning and Politico-Economic Systems Resolved Into Basic Social Processes* (New York: Harper Torchbooks, 1963), pp. 10–11.

about the goals pursued by decision makers when these goals or objective functions are themselves derived from the rules or traditions to which these decision makers may be subject under various ownership systems.

10

Competitive Processes

10.1 Homogeneous Goods

Competition and markets are terms that frequently differ in meaning according to the system in which they are employed. "Darkness and folly" will be our lot if we cannot build up these complex terms with sufficient precision to extricate them from the systems in which they are embedded.

To describe a competitive process, we require the concept of a *homogeneous good*. Consider a list of objects defined so precisely that no two objects existing in an economy at time t may be classified under the same item in the list. This list is then said to correspond to the *finest partition* of the objects existing in the economy.[1] We now coarsen the partition in such a way that *for a given set of participants in the system*, every element in the new list will consist of a set of objects (a sublist of the original partition) among which each of these participants is indifferent.[2] If all these objects are goods in the sense of our earlier definition of this word,[3] the element in the new list to which the objects belong may be termed a *homogeneous good for this set of participants*.

We shall assume a homogeneous good to be divisible into very small units—smaller, say, than any individual's power of discrimination. The concept of a homogeneous good can also be widened to include objects existing at different times. If every individual in the set of participants in question were indifferent between one object existing at time t and a second object existing at time $t + \tau$ in the sense that the first object, having survived until $t + \tau$, could be substituted for the second and leave the individual neither better nor worse off than if he had consumed this second object, both objects would be elements of the same homogeneous good.

1. For formal details, see Appendix.
2. This does not mean of course that if jumbo sized eggs no more than a week old and quarter pound sticks of wrapped butter are homogeneous goods for this set of participants, every individual in the set is indifferent between one dozen eggs or two or one pound of butter or two. It means that, given any distribution of x eggs and y sticks of butter for individual i, the substitution of another egg or stick of butter meeting the above specifications for any egg or stick in the original distribution will leave him indifferent.
3. This definition rules our satiety for any of the participants in the set because the object would not be a good for individual i if, when it was added to an initial distribution for i, it left him no better off than before.

10.2 COMPETITIVE PROCESSES BASED ON PRICE ADJUSTMENTS

In the following description of a competitive process, the price of a homogeneous good is a condition imposed by the seller for *an immediate transfer of ownership* ("spot price"). When a price offer is accepted and the transfer is actually effected, the interaction between buyer and seller is called a *transaction*.

Let a homogeneous good k in period t be defined for a set S of participants who are all "potential sellers" or "potential buyers" of this good, or both. Thus every individual in the set, either representing himself or some organization, would be willing to sell or to buy a positive quantity of k at some price in period t. It is supposed that all interactions among these participants are based on complete mutuality.

A sequence of interactions subject to well-defined constraints on the decision or strategy space of the interacting individuals is called a *process*. To describe a "competitive process limited to price adjustments," we shall make the basic assumption that there are no system-structure restraints of any kind on the prices at which homogeneous good k may be traded for money. However, we shall restrict the individual's decision and strategy space to two dimensions: (1) making or accepting a price offer and (2) buying or selling nonnegative amounts of k.

Initially, every member i of S has an "endowment" consisting of nonnegative amounts of k and of money, denoted x_{ik} and M_i. The costs (inventory or interest charges) of holding k and M are assumed to be zero.

We begin the process in period t with a single price p_k^t carried over from the previous period $t-1$. This price is supposed to be known to all the members of S, who expect it to remain constant for an indefinite period. For some reason we need not go into, the sum of the quantities that sellers of k would like to trade for money at price p_k^t (the total *supply* of k at p_k^t) exceeds the sum of the quantities that buyers would wish to acquire in exchange of money at that price (the total *demand* at p_k^t).

Let i be a member of S who would be willing to supply more k at p_k^t than potential buyers are willing to buy from him at this price. If i now makes an offer of a price below p_k^t, if in the time span required for one or more potential buyers to react to this offer at least one member accepts his offer, and if the difference between the total quantity of k supplied and the total quantity demanded is thereby reduced, this interaction may be said to represent a *stage* in a *price-competitive process among sellers*.[4] Similarly, if, starting from a situation

---

4. If between the time when the offer was made and the time it was accepted, the preferences or endowments of one or more members have changed, there may be a problem in ascertaining whether the lower price would have reduced the excess supply if "other things" had remained the same. It is taken that this inference can be made on the basis of statistical analysis or of other evidence.

where the total demand for k exceeds the total supply at price p_k^t, at least one buyer offers a higher price to a seller who accepts the offer and if as a result excess demand is reduced, the interaction is said to represent a stage in a *price-competitive process among buyers*. For the sake of variety, and without pretending to make any subtle distinctions, I shall use from time to time the term *price competition* to signify a price-competitive process either among sellers or among buyers.

If after a sequence of offers and acceptances at prices lower than p_k^t (in case of an initial excess supply of k) or higher than p_k^t (in case of an initial excess demand for k), the excess supply or demand has been eliminated, the competitive process has been *terminated* (for the initial preferences and supply conditions that were postulated). Upon termination of a competitive process, no potential seller has *uncommitted* supplies that he wishes to sell at the price or prices he is offered in excess of the quantities that were spoken for at that price or at these prices, and no buyer wishes to buy more k at the price or prices he is offered than the amounts supplied at these prices.

Given fairly rapid changes in the preferences of individuals in S for k and M (or for k and the other goods that M can buy), there is no presumption that the termination of a competitive process based on price adjustments will actually be observed. Neither should it be presumed, if it is so observed, that all offers that were accepted and led to a transaction were made at identical prices. Finally, the reader will have noted that coalitions of subsets of members of S aimed at maintaining high prices or at preventing prices from rising more than they would have in the absence of such a coalition are not ruled out under the terms of our definition. The only coalition that *is* ruled out is one that, starting from an initial situation of excess supply or demand, would bar any and all price concessions by sellers seeking buyers at a price lower than p_k^t (in the case of excess supply) or any and all price offers higher than p_k^t by buyers in search of supplies (in the case of excess demand).

For a competitive process operating through price adjustments to converge to a single price $\bar{p}_k$ at which all transactions are effected or would have been effected if the environment of the members of S had remained the same throughout the period of adjustment, certain fairly specific conditions must be satisfied. (1) Every price offer must be communicated within the period of adjustment and made available to all members of S (this condition rules out the possibility that transactions might be made at prices other than $\bar{p}_k$ due to ignorance or to discrimination). (2) Every member of the interacting set S must be willing to sell at least as large a quantity of k at a price higher than the last offer he received as he was at the lower price and willing to buy at least as large a quantity as before at a price lower than the last offer he received. Moreover, at least one member of S must be willing to sell a greater quantity *or* be willing to buy a smaller quantity upon receipt of a higher price offer

compared to the quantities he offered to sell or to buy at the lower price.[5]
(3) The costs of transactions carried out at prices other than $\bar{p}_k$ must be
negligible, either because acceptances of offers at these prices are only tentative
(tâtonnement process) or because the buyer or seller of a lot at a price differing
from $\bar{p}_k$ can sell off his surplus or buy the additional quantities he requires at
each new price he is offered without incurring any transaction costs. (4) Every
member of S consults only his own preferences and his own holdings of k and
M at t in issuing or accepting price offers (if this condition is not satisfied,
certain limits must be placed on the extent of admissible "speculation" about
aggregate supply and demand at time t and in all subsequent periods). (5) The
price and quantity adjustments by each member of S can be represented in
the aggregate by a single difference equation whose dependent variable p_k^t
converges to a price $\bar{p}_k$, called equilibrium price.[6]

Under "nonstationary conditions," where the period of adjustment to price
offers is long enough to allow significant changes in preferences to take place,
we can only conjecture that the price of k will at any time "tend toward
equilibrium," in the sense that on the basis of statistical evidence we are led
to believe that excess demand at the old price would have been reduced if
expectations and supply and demand conditions had remained the same.

The process generating $\bar{p}_k$ may be called a *convergent price-competitive process*.
It is difficult to state with precision what is meant by a "perfectly competitive
process." A necessary condition for such a process to occur must surely be that
no subset of the members of S should be allowed to collude to secure a higher
or a lower price than the one each member of the subset could obtain if he
"acted on his own." This requirement implies that every participant in the
competitive process make his price and quantity offers independently of any

---

5. This assumption is significantly weaker than the commonly accepted one that every
member of S should be "profit or utility maximizing" (cf. K. Arrow, "Toward a Theory of Price
Adjustment," in *The Allocation of Economic Resources: Essays in Honor of Bernard Haley* [Stanford,
Calif.: Stanford University Press, 1959], p. 46).

6. For each member let S_i^t and D_i^t be the quantities he would be willing to supply or to demand
at price p_k^t. Such a difference equation might be

$$\frac{p_k^t}{p_k^{t-1}} = h \left[\sum_{i=1}^{m_s} S_i^{t-1} - \sum_{i=1}^{m_s} D_i^{t-1} \right],$$

where $h' < 0$, $h(0) = 0$, and m_s is the number of individuals in S. (This equation is adapted from
Arrow, ibid., p. 43.)

This formulation is still excessively aggregative in that it ignores the fact, pointed out by Arrow
himself, that in the process of adjustment each member of S is likely to have some "monopoly
power" (he cannot buy or sell as much as he would like to at the price he finds it most advantageous
to offer). A full-fledged theory of price adjustment would have to start from the behavior functions
(price setting, acceptances) of each member of S.

information he might have about the price and quantity offers that any other member of S *might* make. Another necessary condition is that at the termination of the convergent competitive process, at which point aggregate supply equals demand at some price $\bar{p}_k$, no member be able to exert a "significant influence" on the price of k by supplying or demanding a quantity of k different from that which he would find most advantageous to buy or sell if this price were imposed by an outside force. It is clear that the number of interacting participants in S must be fairly large for this condition to be satisfied. How large will depend of course on the operational meaning we wish to attach to the words "significant influence."[7]

We shall call the ensemble of all mutually acceptable transactions in good k effected by the members of S in period t the *market* for good k and set S in this period. Suppose that a different ensemble of transactions among another set of individuals in the system occurs or is expected to occur at $t + 1$, another at $t + 2, \ldots, T$. Let ζ be the set of individuals or organizations in the system who engage in a transaction involving k at least once in the period 1 to T. *The market for k* is then a sequence of markets for k for subsets of individuals in ζ and for $t = 1, \ldots, T$. The reader will note that, because k has been defined as a homogeneous good, an ensemble of transactions cannot include objects that are widely separated in space unless, for technical reasons, they are perfectly substitutable for all the individuals in S (e.g., shares in a given common stock on the U.S. market).

A market as defined encompasses only interactions involving complete mutuality. It rules out transactions ordered from above by common superiors of the transacting parties, a situation that often occurs in the centrally directed economies.[8] The attributes "anonymous," "completely mutual," "competitive," "convergent competitive," and "perfectly competitive" may then be tacked on to the word "market" to refer to ensembles of transactions endowed with these characteristics.

The description of competitive processes so far has been restricted to the simplest possible conditions where the total amounts of k and M in the system were held constant, no charges were imposed for carrying inventories or holding money, and every price was expected to remain constant. I see no

7. On the relation between informational decentralization (defined above, p. 105) and perfectly competitive processes, see L. Hurwicz, "Centralization and Decentralization in Economic Processes," in Eckstein, op. cit., pp. 86–100.

8. Nevertheless, many seller–purchaser interactions in the Soviet Union and in the Eastern European states that are members of the Council for Mutual Economic Assistance are sufficiently free of controls (as to who will sell to whom) to qualify as market transactions. This is especially true since the inception of reforms in these economies that have gone far to loosen the control of common superiors over seller–buyer relations. Complete mutuality, incidentally, is compatible with transactions effected at prices fixed by higher authorities.

essential difficulty in relaxing the restriction on the decision space of members of S that kept them (if they found it profitable or otherwise advantageous) from transforming purchased inputs into good k according to some known technology, although the introduction of these activities would of course account for new lags in the reactions of suppliers to price offers due to the variable gestation period necessary to carry out the activity in question. A competitive process that would have been convergent, if the total amounts of M and k had remained constant, might not be convergent upon the introduction of manufacturing activities. It may also be more difficult to infer the effects of price changes on excess supply and demand since production costs as well as preferences may vary before a competitive process is terminated. Finally, "indivisibilities" and "economies of scale" in the production of k or of other goods may preclude "perfect competition." An environment where the known technology is free of indivisibilities and where increasing returns to scale are not sufficiently strong to "deconvexify the production set" of any producer is said to be *compatible* with a perfectly competitive process.[9]

The introduction of carrying charges on inventories and money and of speculation, while it would complicate the operation of a price-competitive process, should be fairly easy to incorporate into the model of such a process. One would expect, for example, that if the carrying charges on money were negative (i.e., if interest were paid on deposits) and if the carrying charges on k were large relative to its price, the convergence process might be more rapid than otherwise (viz., the formation of market prices for perishable goods, which sellers can hold back from the market only by incurring high refrigerating or other storage charges).

So far we have focused our attention on a good k and money. Sellers of other homogeneous goods also may be competing with one another for the money of potential buyers. If a seller of k reduces his price and an individual i responds by reducing his intended purchases of good l, then k and l are substitutes for i. If the effect of reducing the price of k is for i to increase his purchases of both k and l, they are complements for i, at least for the range of prices of k considered. If a lower price of k, other things equal, causes an increase in the excess supply or a reduction in the excess demand for l in a system consisting of m_s individuals, k and l may be said to be substitutes in this system (even though they may be complements for some members of S). Thus price competition

9. The production set of producer j is the set of all "productions" that are possible for j in the sense that they are producible according to a technology known to him. A production in turn is defined as a vector of specified quantities of inputs (negative elements) and of outputs (positive elements). The production set of j is convex if every combination of productions with weights between zero and unity also belongs to the set. On increasing and decreasing returns, see n. 6 of chap. 17 and Gerard Debreu, *Theory of Value: An Axiomatic Analysis of Economic Equilibrium* (New York: Wiley, 1959), pp. 40–41.

may encompass any number of goods that are substitutes for the system under observation.

A new problem arises once the decision space of individuals in S has been freed of all restraints. First, why should k rather than some other good be produced? A self-evident answer is that, given the ith member's preferences, including his proclivity or aversion for risk, he or the organization that he is qualified to represent will produce good k (or, leastways, plan to produce k) only if k appears to be at least as likely to raise i's utility or to increase the payoff of the organization that i represents as any other good he or his organization might be able to produce *at a mutually acceptable price*.

A sequence in a competitive process for good k may be interrupted or even be blocked at the very outset by a shift in supply from k to another good capable of being substituted for k in a buyer's consumption or in a seller's production process where such a shift appears advantageous to at least one potential seller. Thus if, at the initial price p_k^i, aggregate supply exceeds aggregate demand, some seller may offer good k', a "higher-quality" variant of k, at the same price p_k^i and sell a larger quantity than he would have sold of k at this price, thus reducing excess supply. This action too should be considered as a stage in a competitive process among sellers but this time one based on quality rather than on price adjustments. Indeed, the definition of a stage in a competitive process can be broadened to include any action, other than a price adjustment, on the part of a seller desirous of increasing his sales or of a buyer desirous of increasing his purchases, that has the effect of reducing the excess supply or excess demand generated by the last price or prices offered for a given set of well-defined homogeneous goods. Competitive actions of this type, including quality changes "to meet the competition," belong to the class of *nonprice competitive processes*.

Under what circumstances will competitive processes be based on price adjustments and under what circumstances on quality changes or on adjustments along other dimensions of the individual's decision space?

The following conjecture applies to an environment for producers compatible with a perfectly competitive process and to a situation in which there are no system-structure restraints whatever on the prices of any goods or on their production, purchase, or sale. For the purpose of this conjecture we also assume that every producer maximizes profits and every consumer maximizes his utility.

Conceive an initial "equilibrium" for all goods under a given price system $\bar{p}$. By the system being in equilibrium, I mean that every producer maximizes his profits at prices $\bar{p}$ for the productions he is supplying on the market in the period t (during which conditions are assumed to remain unchanged), every consumer is maximizing his utility at these same prices for the consumption bundles he is buying on the market in period t, and aggregate supply equals aggregate demand for every good. Now a change of preferences occurs in period $t + 1$ such that good k is more desired than before by some consumers and good k', a close substitute or quality variant of k, is less desired by these consumers. There will now be an excess demand for k and an excess supply of k' at prices $\bar{p}$.

The conjecture states that conditions of equilibrium cannot be restored through a perfectly competitive process by adjustments in production alone. In other words if $\bar{p}$ sustains an equilibrium for the old set of consumers' preferences, it cannot sustain it for the new. Conversely, it is conjectured that if only quantity adjustments are observed to restore equilibrium in a given situation, at least one of the assumptions made above is not being satisfied. In particular, if the environment is otherwise compatible with perfect competition, some restrictions of the system structure on prices or on the purchase and sale of certain goods must be present.

These conjectures may throw light on a system-structure phenomenon. It has frequently been observed that in periods of rapid increases in the average level of prices ("inflation"), the quality of goods and the services that accompany their sales or delivery declines. Generally, consumers are not offered a choice between paying a premium price for the old, higher quality but are forced to accept the new, lower quality if they wish to acquire the good at all. This phenomenon has been observed even in the case of goods produced and distributed under what are thought to be perfectly competitive conditions, such as food products produced by family farms (e.g., sales by peasant farmers of their products to city dwellers under wartime conditions, when both quality and service deteriorated). Barring changes in the relative production costs of better and inferior goods and services, the second conjecture suggests that prices are not fully "equilibrating," perhaps by reason of government-imposed price controls, of the fear on the part of producers that such controls might be imposed, or possibly of the producers' reluctance (a system value!) to raise prices to the level that "the traffic might bear."[10]

Nonprice competition is less commonly encountered where the environment is compatible with perfectly competitive processes based on price adjustments than under conditions where the sellers or buyers of a product are few. When increasing returns to scale are conducive to the large size of the few enterprises supplying the market, enterprises are generally structured as multitiered hierarchic organizations of the kind that will be formally described in the next chapter. Such organizations often have internal reasons for maintaining stable prices of their products. Control upon the efficiency of operations in lower tiers is often implemented through budgets and through the analysis of profits per unit of production. For purposes of intertemporal comparability,

10. Cf. Janos Kornai, *Anti-Equilibrium* (Amsterdam: North–Holland, 1971), pp. 240–48.

these controls require that prices be fixed or changed only at infrequent intervals. The responsible decision makers in these large enterprises frequently favor nonprice competition through advertising, quality improvement, or product differentiation to engaging in competitive processes based on price adjustments.

10.3 System-Structure Restrictions on Competitive Processes

This brings us to formal restrictions imposed by the rules of ruling or non-ruling organizations on the price-setting dimensions of individuals' decision spaces. These restrictions, called *price controls*, may be on the maximum level of prices, their minimum level, or on both, when prices are actually set by an organization other than that making the detailed production, purchase, or sales decisions.[11]

The "language" or degree of aggregation in which the restrictions are expressed is critical for the type of producer's quality adjustment that will be typically observed. It is virtually impossible for any organization to set, monitor, and maintain surveillance over the prices of objects defined so minutely that they can just be distinguished in the preferences of consumers.[12] In terms of the vocabulary developed at the beginning of this chapter, the partitioning of the objects controlled is necessarily coarser than the partitioning of objects generating a list of homogeneous goods (for all possible buyers of these goods). Suppose homogeneous goods k and k', which are close substitutes but not interchangeable objects for at least one potential buyer, are assigned the same price $p_{kk'}$ in the controlled list. Suppose further that the output of k can be segregated from the output of k' and that the "marginal costs" of the two goods, as perceived by at least one producer, are significantly different. Then if aggregate supply exceeds aggregate demand for both k and k', producers vying for customers in a nonprice competive process will produce the more desirable of the two goods, as long as price $p_{kk'}$ remains above the marginal cost of production of this preferred good or at least, if producers are not strictly profit maximizing, as long as it seems "advantageous," given their goal function, for them to increase the relative output of this good. If, *per contra*, there is an excess demand for both k and k', producers will be induced to concentrate output on the cheaper of the two. This latter alternative is depicted in diagram 10.1.

In diagram 10.1 the production-possibilities frontier, whose perceived

11. For this purpose we may stipulate that two organizations are different from each other if they do not share the same payoff according to some set rules.

12. When potential competitors collude, overtly or tacitly, to maintain prices, they may resort to nonprice competition to keep up or increase their share of total market demand, if for no other reason but that it is generally more difficult to monitor and control competitive moves of this kind than derogations to an agreement on prices.

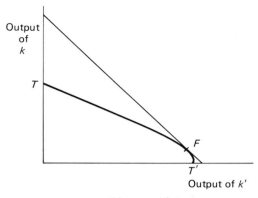

Diagram 10.1

existence is assumed here for the purpose of discussion, is represented by the curve TT'. It is evident that for most output mixes, the marginal cost of k' is smaller than that of k. Since the prices of k and k' have in effect been set equal, the maximand for this profit-maximizing producer may, in the space of outputs, be represented by a series of straight lines with a slope equal to minus unity. The tangency of the production-possibilities frontier with the line corresponding to the highest attainable value of the combined outputs of k and k' at the common price $p_{kk'}$ is shown at F. The hypothetical producer whose choices are depicted in the diagram will produce mainly but not exclusively k'. (He would produce nothing but k' if he had not incurred an increasing marginal cost of producing k' as he moved toward a mix that contained more k' and less k.) If, as is likely, k' is inferior to k in buyers' preferences, quality deterioration will have occurred as a consequence of (imperfectly detailed) price controls.

The phenomenon of a "sellers' market" characterized by chronic excess demand can easily be analyzed with the elementary conceptual apparatus set forth in this section. In a sellers' market, not all the nonprice adjustments are on the seller's side. Buyers may seek to compete for insufficient supplies at existing prices in a number of ways. The most obvious is for a customer to approach a seller with an offer to buy at the legal price before his supply is exhausted (e.g., by queuing up early). Another is to offer the seller various possible advantages in lieu of a higher price: a promise of a political favor or priority access to another good also in short supply may do the trick. This sort of competition among buyers for scarce resources (investment funds, critical materials, and so forth) is quite commonly observed in the centrally directed economies of East.

As we saw in chapter 8, partial mutuality of transactions characterizes situations where sellers are prevented by rules from demanding what they consider to be a fully satisfactory monetary equivalent for the goods at their disposal. It is also interesting to note that the beneficiaries of the special advantages conferred by buyers on sellers are often not the owners of the good (the state, the stockholders of a corporation, or the owner of a firm) but those of its custodians who are authorized to transfer ownership at established prices (sales clerks, ticket controllers, operators of foreign-exchange booths, officials in charge of distributing or rationing out goods in short supply). Even though a buyer may offer a monetary inducement ("bribe") to acquire a certain quantity of a good, this does not raise the sales price from the owner's point of view, because the advantage accrues not to the owner (at least directly)[13] but to the immediate custodian.

Many observers have noted that certain system structures are associated with a sellers' market and others with a buyers' market. The former, for example, is said to be typical of all centrally directed systems in East and the latter of highly developed market economies in West, at least during periods of recession or depression.[14] Is a sellers' market a system characteristic of the Soviet or Polish economy? Or is it the consequence of a particular policy under a given system structure? Unfortunately, policies and system structures are so closely bound up with each other it is hard to disentangle them. Centrally directed economies where most capital goods are publicly owned, as in the Soviet Union or Poland, are directed or "managed" by individuals pursuing goals of rapid industrialization achieved through high levels of investment concentrated on producer goods' and armaments' sectors and through plentiful short-term credits to publicly owned enterprises. If these policies tend to create situations of excess demand for most goods (at least under the system rules of centralized price setting), is the fault in the system or in the policies pursued? It may be worthwhile to observe in this connection that the Hungarian economic reforms, which have gone a considerable way toward decentralizing production decisions, are said to be stymied, or at least impaired, by the persistence of a sellers' market for most basic goods. Producers, despite their greater autonomy and the stronger incentives they have to produce for the market, still do not find themselves constrained by the necessity of meeting a limited buyers' demand that would require a sensitive adaptation of output to their desires. Even the most vigorous monetary and fiscal policy aimed at balancing aggregate supply and aggregate demand will fail if buyers

13. Just as waiters are sometimes paid less when tips are expected to be plentiful, so the supply price of custodians may be lowered if they "normally" receive favors or bribes. In this case the owners of the organization indirectly benefit from the nonprice competition.

14. In the next few paragraphs, a number of terms taken from the standard vocabulary used in West for describing macroeconomic problems (inflation, monetary policy, and so on) are used without prior definition for the sake of illustration and without any claim to descriptive accuracy.

expect excess demand to return and systematically try to buy more than they "need" for their present level of operation. Individuals' expectations often change more slowly than system rules. This is one of the many "legacies" a centrally managed system may leave in its track that will tend to weaken the effectiveness of the more decentralized system that replaces it.[15]

To end this discussion of restrictions on competitive processes, we suggest that the notion of price controls may be stretched to apply to services legally rendered free of charge by a ruling organization. Payment for the service to the individual rendering the service or to one of his superiors is of course legally punishable as *bribery*. In the U.S. construction industry this violation of price controls (to coin a euphemistic phrase) is so widespread that competition among would-be purchasers and sellers of these services may produce more or less standard "competitive rates" for their performance.[16] Price competition in this instance has much the same efficiency-making properties as elsewhere: services are better coordinated in time and place and get performed more promptly and willingly. Payment to city inspectors, however, usually secures their implicit or explicit willingness to tolerate minor, and sometimes major, violations of the building code. Whether or not these violations jeopardize efficiency in the long run (through the added risks of accidents and mishaps), it is certain that equity and other noneconomic desiderata of social morality are sacrificed when the officials of a ruling organization are sucked into the vortex of market relations.

10.4 IMPLICATIONS OF PRICE AND NONPRICE COMPETITION FOR RESOURCE ALLOCATION

When an enterprise reduces the price of one of its products or incurs an expense to increase its sales through a nonprice action, its profits must diminish *if it was profit maximizing to begin with.* (If not, in an environment where the seller was able to affect significantly the quantity of the product sold through his own price adjustments, it is conceivable that the price prior to the reduction might have been too high or the former quality of service rendered too low to maximize profits, so that the new lower price or higher quality could actually increase profits). If the new lower price may be expected to continue to prevail and if prices of all inputs are unaffected, the enterprise will lose some of its variable inputs to competing uses if they were formerly getting just the price

15. See Egon Neuberger, "The Legacies of Central Planning," Memorandum RM-5530-PR (Santa Monica, Calif.: Rand Corporation, June 1968).

16. "Study Finds $25-million Yearly in Bribes Paid by City Construction Industry," *New York Times*, June 26, 1972, and its sequel on June 27 and 28. In Imperial Russia, tips to officials for services rendered were called "sinless revenues." D. Mackenzie Wallace, an acute observer of the system, witnessed the case of an official who, upon receiving a sum larger than his due, "handed back the change" (*Russia* [New York: Henry Holt, 1877], p. 204).

COMPETITIVE PROCESSES   147

needed to keep them engaged in the enterprise and if this former price was approximately equal to the value of their marginal product as perceived by the manager or by his subordinates. The enterprise may also find it more difficult to obtain loans from banks or to attract purchasers for its bonds or "equities."

Eventually competitive pressures may become so severe that an enterprise cannot meet its current obligations (on loans, taxes, and so on); it is then said to be *insolvent*. At this point, in market economies where means of production are privately owned, a ruling organization—federal, state, or other—usually steps in to protect the rights of creditors and, in many instances, to grant relief to the debtor if he has reached the state of insolvency without egregious violation of existing laws. The ruling organization then designates particular individuals ("receivers," "trustees") to manage the property pending a final settlement. An insolvent person declared *bankrupt* by judicial process is subject to certain laws and procedures for the final disposition of his remaining assets.[17] In many countries a debtor may petition for bankruptcy to obtain relief from his current debts. In the United States, according to the Bankruptcy Act of 1898, "municipal railroad, insurance or banking corporations" could not become voluntary bankrupts, "such business having sufficient social significance to warrant a reorganization instead of complete dissolution or liquidation."[18] The tendency in West in recent years is for the central government to bail out important enterprises in a state of insolvency or near insolvency by granting them subsidies, tax relief, or other means (e.g., the rescue of Lockheed Corporation by the U.S. government in 1971). This is sometimes done to prevent foreigners from acquiring domestic assets (e.g., the famous Compagnie Bulle case in France).

In East, enterprises are never wound up merely because they could not meet their debts. If their activity is considered socially useful, they are subsidized by one ruling organization or another (through the central or through a local budget). In Yugoslavia's self-management system many enterprises are also subsidized, especially in heavy industry, but liquidation through bankruptcy is not uncommon (124 forced liquidations in 1968).[19]

The rules, customs, and policies regulating the fate of insolvent organi-

17. In France and Germany, "commercial failure" is distinguished from "bankruptcy," which in addition to insolvency implies some "indiscretion" or violation on the part of the debtor. Bankruptcy is treated more severely by the courts than commercial failure. We note in passing that one of the indiscretions that an insolvent German businessman could be declared bankrupt for, according to the law of 1898, was dealing in "futures" (*Encyclopedia Britannica*, 14th ed., vol. 3, p. 64).

18. Ibid., p. 66.

19. Joel B. Dirlam and James L. Plummer, *An Introduction to the Yugoslav Economy* (Columbus, Ohio: Merrill, 1973), p. 50.

zations are system traits that may have a decisive influence on system outcomes. According to traditional Western economic theory, for instance, an enterprise that has become insolvent because it could not pay the market price of the resources in its employ should be induced to release these resources so that they may be more profitably engaged elsewhere. This redeployment is essential to Schumpeter's theory of "creative destruction," according to which progressive enterprises are able to forge ahead by competing away resources from less innovative organizations—which are destroyed in the process. This cannibalization of the assets in the custody of enterprises unable to compete successfully may be an efficient way of resolving the problem, but it is perhaps too painful for those individuals whose interests are directly affected to be allowed to take place without mitigation in most modern systems.[20]

Only recently has theory begun to assimilate the critical traits of competitive processes, including the expansion of successful and the contraction of unsuccessful firms. Sidney Winter, Jr., in a pioneering article written in 1969,[21] has shown that the assumption of profit-maximizing behavior on the part of enterprise managers was not essential to models of price competition that capture the basic features observed in the actual operation of price-competitive processes. The critical behavioral assumption that *is* needed to simulate such processes is that both enterprises suffering losses with their ongoing technology and enterprises with no plants in operation (potential entrants) search for profitable techniques at going competitive prices. (In Winter's model, enterprises with profitable or break-even technological processes do not search; whether they expand or not, they replicate the same successful processes.) Enterprises operating profitable processes have a positive probability of expanding; enterprises operating unprofitable processes have a positive probability of contracting; break-even enterprises stay put. With a linear technology and a finite number of technological processes available to every enterprise (no technical change), the Markov process defined by the probabilities of expansion and contraction from any state can be shown to lead to a "closed" or equilibrium state where each enterprise remaining in the industry is exclusively operating break-even processes.[22] As a result of this competitive survival process, enterprises end up profit-maximizing; if they

20. However vital the subject might be, I know of no comparative study of the treatment of insolvency in different systems geared to direct or indirect system outcomes (rates of enterprise liquidation, reorganizations, receiverships, and so forth).

21. The original paper by Winter was entitled "Satisficing, Selection and the Saving Remnant," Institute of Policy Studies, University of Michigan, Ann Arbor, Jan. 1969.

22. This powerful result requires some additional assumptions about the size of the industry and the effect of industry output on prices. In particular, Winter introduces the plausible assumption that a process breaking even at an equilibrium price would yield a profit if industry output were smaller than its equilibrium value.

did not, given the nature of the technology, they would suffer losses and contract. Thus the enterprise rule postulated by most economists (and in chap. 15 below) becomes a resultant, which we may expect to hold when equilibrium prevails, of the competitive environment in which the enterprise operates. Extensions of the Winter model incorporating successively available blocks of possible techniques (with each block representing a particular level of technical progress) appear to lead to similar results.

What happens to "successful" and "unsuccessful" competitors in a competitive process that is not based on price adjustments? This long-ignored subject is now at least receiving some attention from economists concerned with education, medicine, defense, and other services whose expansion and contraction are generally not governed, even in "capitalist" economies, by the typical market processes we have just sketched.

Some of the questions that might be addressed to the available evidence include these. Can organizations deemed successful in their performance according to well-defined criteria of success bid away resources from other not-so-successful organizations? What pressures or inducements are there for less successful organizations to disgorge resources? Are the least successful organizations ever wound up or reorganized by order of some other hierarchically superior organization?

We have already seen that in centrally directed economies, enterprises compete on a nonprice basis for resources in deficit supply. Their managers may also vie with one another in their output performance to win distinctions, commendations, promotions, or other preferments from their hierarchic superiors. However, the link between successful performance on the output side and the ability to secure additional resources is most tenuous. Marketing organizations that supervise the rationing of producer goods tend to "protect" weaker enterprises by ensuring them their "fair share" of scarce inputs.[23] The process of "creative destruction" works slowly if it works at all in such economies. Innovating enterprises, at least in the short run, cannot get the resources necessary for their rapid expansion if this must be done at the cost of competitors whose output has been in the plan and cannot be curtailed.[24]

Richard R. Nelson, who has studied the behavior of sectors competing on a nonprice basis in an environment in which most other sectors were price competitors, conjectures that "sectors in which individual organizations are bounded geographically are less able to expand when they hold a [nonprice] competitive advantage than organizations that are not so closely bounded." Schools may be a case in point: their greater success in inculcating reading

23. These remarks are based on interviews with directors of marketing organizations in Poland in the late 1950s.

24. It is even more difficult for innovative *individuals* to create enterprises or to obtain managerial posts in existing enterprises if they wish to exploit their ideas.

or other skills to their pupils, thanks perhaps to innovations in teaching, is unlikely to help them grow at the expense of schools that are lagging in this regard inasmuch as they serve one neighborhood exclusively and are not in a position to bid either pupils or teachers away from their "competitors."[25]

Competition for scarce resources is one thing; nonmarket pressures to release resources from those that already have them in custody for the benefit of individuals or organizations that can make more productive use of them (from the viewpoint of the organization to which they also belong) is another. Since there is little or no incentive for them to disgorge resources, their custodians will not advertise the fact that they have on hand manpower or other resources that could be employed elsewhere more effectively. It is then up to the organizations that really need them (or to their common superiors) to locate these resources and make out a case for their transfer. Individuals whose services are hoarded may of course be aware of the superior opportunities waiting for them elsewhere, but their supervisors in the unit or the enterprise may prevent their transfer. (The author was once in an outfit of the U.S. Army where a conscript holding a Ph.D. in nuclear physics served several months doing menial work while he was waiting for permission to transfer to another branch, where he was to be employed directly on a nuclear-research project. The commander was unwilling to agree to the transfer because he was "short of personnel.")

The general principle underlying these various examples of competitive processes based on adjustments other than prices is that, in the absence of some mechanism whereby successful organizations can attract additional resources *and* expand their volume of activity, such processes will be haphazard or ineffectual—a poor substitute at best for the "invisible hand" of the market. This criticism naturally does not prejudge the issue as to whether central coordination *cum* nonprice competitive processes will do better or worse, in a given technological environment and for given preferences, than price competition operating in a market system. It is also possible, if not likely, that nonprice competition provides an important element of flexibility in centrally coordinated hierarchically organized systems.[26]

To conclude my discussion of this central topic in the traditional analysis of "comparative systems," I should like to comment on a recent work that

25. Richard R. Nelson, "Issues and Suggestions for the Study of Industrial Organizations in a Regime of Rapid Technical Change," Economic Growth Center, Yale University, Center Discussion Paper No. 103, Jan. 1971, p. 22.

26. This element of flexibility has been emphasized in the writings of Paul Craig Roberts, *Alienation and the Soviet Economy* (Albuquerque: University of New Mexico Press, 1971), Edwin Dolan, "The Evolution of the Soviet Planning System" (Ph.D. diss., Yale University, 1969), and Raymond P. Powell, "Plan Execution and the Workability of Soviet Planning" (unpublished manuscript).

does attempt, admittedly in a narrow sphere, to compare empirically market and nonmarket processes. This is the book already referred to on blood transfusion, Richard Titmuss's *The Gift Relationship*. Titmuss compares countries where blood for transfusion is predominantly bought from "donors" (i.e., United States, Sweden, the German Democratic Republic, and Romania) and countries where blood is voluntarily given, presumably for altruistic reasons (i.e., the United Kingdom, France, and, to a lesser extent, Czechoslovakia). From these examples it appears that the comparison cuts across the great dividing line between East and West.[27] Titmuss's essential argument is that price competition for blood is not only immoral but also inefficient in meeting the demand and potentially harmful for the recipients in increasing the danger of infection through serum hepatitis. The British system relies on moral appeals to individuals' sense of social solidarity. It is said to elicit blood in response to the demand and to allocate it to the patients who need it without placing significant reliance on the price system as a distributive mechanism. The analysis unfortunately is marred by both superficial reasoning and the lack of meaningful quantitative comparisons. The problem must be disembedded from the environment in which the entire system operates. There is a great deal more narcotic addiction in the United States than in England for instance, but this has nothing to do with social arrangements for blood transfusion. Hence if more infection through transfusion—a negative externality—occurs in the United States than in the United Kingdom, this may be due more to environment than to system structure. The most one can infer is that in the U.S. environment a system where blood is bought primarily from low-income individuals, many of whom are unemployed Blacks, may risk more infections than one where all blood is voluntarily donated. The results do not imply that paying for blood in England, where the danger of infection is less, would not produce more blood and be more efficient.[28] Furthermore, the fact that British nationals can be coaxed into giving their blood free—a matter of values—does not mean that this could be done on as wide a scale in South Korea (where 50 percent of transfused blood is actually bought). The ultimate argument—that a generalized system of price competition for blood subverts basic societal values—is plausible but nowhere demonstrated. This externality, if it exists, is a slender thread on which to hang a normative comparison.

In short, Titmuss has set up a vital problem in the comparison of systems; he has singled out some of the elements that bear on the theoretical comparison of relative efficiencies of price and nonprice adjustment processes in a restricted domain; and he has collected scattered information pertinent to

27. Curiously enough, both in the Soviet Union and in the United States approximately half the blood "donated" is bought (Titmuss, op. cit., pp. 174–75).

28. There are occasional shortages of blood even in the United Kingdom.

the subject. But a good deal remains to be done, both in elucidating the logic of the problem and in hypothesis testing, before conclusions can be reached on the relative merits of the alternative arrangements for securing blood for transfusions in each given environment.

10.5 OTHER SYSTEM-STRUCTURE RESTRICTIONS ON MARKET TRANSACTIONS

Controls on prices, which we briefly studied in section 10.2, are by no means the only restrictions imposed by a system structure on market transactions. No existing system allows all goods to be bought or sold, and most systems place restraints on who may sell or buy certain types of goods. Labor services, land, and works of art are affected by such rules in most countries.

In the last chapter we briefly alluded to the legal prohibitions on slavery. Laws on "indentures" (contractual obligations incurred by individuals on their custodians to serve for a long period of time under the untrammeled authority of a master), prostitution, and child labor restrict the purchase and sale of individuals' services in almost every modern economy. Professional sports both in the United States and in Europe exhibit the most flagrant exceptions to the almost universal system rule that permits individuals to sell the use of their services to other individuals or organizations for a period of time but that enjoins them from alienating their rights of disposal thereto.[29]

In less developed nations (both in historical and contemporary instances) all sorts of restrictions on transfers of ownership rights on land are imposed by ruling organizations, both secular and religious. Various rules or laws limit transfer of land to the descendant of the owner ("entails") or to religious organizations (Moslem wakf or vakuf). Fifty years after the freeing of the serf in Russia, purchases and sales of land obtained as allotments (*nadely*) by emancipated serfs were still severely restricted. In the United States American Indians in the late nineteenth century were also given (or given back) lands by the federal government, which they were not allowed to sell.

In the rich suburbs of a highly developed country such as the United States

---

29. "Assignment clauses" in professional contracts in a number of U.S. and Canadian sports specify that players have no control over where and for whom they may have to play. In Italian soccer, similarly, clubs have absolute control over the transfer of athletes (although no transfer fees are paid). In the Soviet Union soccer players must play for the team that trained them; coaches of competitive teams are not permitted to poach on other teams' preserves. In English soccer until 1963, the "retain and transfer" system, characteristically referred to as the "soccer slave system," gave clubs virtually unlimited power over the use of members' services and over their transfer, which was usually effected for a fee collected by the transferring club. Since 1963, players must give their assent to transfers and are entitled to 5 percent of the transfer fee. (The above information, culled from the *New York Times*, the *London Times*, and Robert Daley's *The Bizarre World of European Sports* [New York: William Morrow, 1963], was gathered for me by Henry Hu.)

restrictions on the minimum acreage of plots of landed property that can be put on sale are imposed by the ruling organization of the community or region (whose officials are normally elected from local residents) to keep out undesirables, maintain racial purity, save the environment, or for other worthy motives.

Medieval and modern curbs on the alienation of land have this in common, that they tend to keep the ownership of desirable land in the hands of a minority of the system participants, along with their heirs and their friends, with fairly clear implications for the equity of the system where such rules are encouraged or tolerated.

Restrictions on the disposition of land may, nevertheless, have the proper aim of promoting efficiency (even though at the expense of equity). Laws on *primogeniture*, for example, by vesting in the first-born child exclusive rights of inheriting his father's property, may help to prevent or delay the breakup of landholdings into small scattered strips that can be farmed only with a loss of efficiency compared to the undivided estate.

Most countries—the United States is a signal exception—have laws preventing the sale of important art works for export. In Hungary, works that are over a hundred years old are sold in state consignment shops only to Hungarian nationals (for fear they might be exported).

In centrally directed economies, basic producer goods are not only strictly rationed (distributed in limited quantities to authorized enterprises), but also the marketing organization is enpowered to "link up" sellers with buyers, thus limiting the set of authorized buyers to one.

When transfers of ownership prescribe what particular individual or enterprise is authorized to purchase a particular batch or quantity of a good, we may call this method of distribution *strictly ascriptive*. Otherwise, as in most of the examples cited above, access to a good is limited to a designated subset of participants, who may still compete for them through price offers or by other means. These methods of distribution may be termed *partly ascriptive*.

Many economists and sociologists claim that economic development cannot take place without the replacement of ascriptive methods of distribution by some sort of competitive process whereby all individuals may be given the opportunity of acquiring a good.[30] This view has much to recommend it, but we must keep in mind that nonprice competitive processes may be not only wasteful of resources but also occasionally just as iniquitous as traditional

30. "The gradual 'freeing up' of the factors of production from 'embeddedness' in a diffuse, ascriptive nexus and the mobilization of these resources through the mechanism of the market (or its analogue in 'centrally planned economies') are said to be essential features of economic development (R. V. Marsh and H. Mannari, "Lifetime Commitments in Japan," *American Journal of Sociology* 76 [March 1971]: p. 795).

ascription. In New York subways, for instance, the aged and the infirm have the same chance to compete for a seat as all other citizens, whereas in Paris they are assigned seats in priority status.[31]

---

31. Ernest Renan, a French philosopher who had known a society that was still largely ascriptive in his youth, found it hard, in his old age, to adapt to the competitive world of France in the 1880s. For example, because he thought that it was the greatest impoliteness and vulgarity to quicken one's step to get ahead of other passengers on a railroad platform so as to secure a good seat on a train, he was sure, barring the intervention of the stationmaster, to get the worst possible seat or no seat at all. "I was made," he wrote, "for a society founded on respect, where one is greeted, classified, and ranked according to one's clothing, where one does not have to protect oneself" (*Oeuvres Complètes de Ernest Renan* [Paris: Calmann–Levy, 1948], vol. 2, p. 899).

Part 4
Organizations

11

Who Belongs to What Organization

In this chapter we shall take a broad view of the various ways the participants in a system may sort themselves out among organizations. This will bring us to a first consideration of some intersystem problems in "industrial organization."

According to our original definition in chapter 2, an organization consists of a set of participants (members) regularly interacting in the process of carrying on one or more activities from a specific list. The unfortunate implication of this definition is that if in the period of interaction considered, the initial set of participants expanded or contracted or if an activity were added to the "specific list," the participants active in both periods could no longer be said to form an organization. This definition hardly conforms to common usage. The Ford Foundation remains *an* organization—indeed, *the same* organization—in the accepted ambit of the word even when some of its personnel are replaced and new programs are initiated. Clearly, some continuity is required for an interacting set of individuals to make up an organization. This requirement may be met in a variety of ways: by the constancy of the goals of the members making basic decisions for the organization, by the legal framework that sets limits to its activities (business license, incorporation, laws and regulations concerning the activities of foundations, and so on), by the identity of some of the chief decision makers in the set of participants, or by a combination of all three. To fix the minimum degree of continuity necessary for an interacting set to form an organization would be an arbitrary exercise in refining concepts. We plan therefore to modify the original definition only in allowing an organization (1) to have *some* turnover in its membership, and (2) to introduce changes in the sets of activities pursued (possibly due to a shift in preferences of some of its members), provided that a "reasonable degree of continuity" is preserved. In most cases this rather loose definition will tell us which interacting sets of participants constitute an organization and which do not. A gang formed ad hoc to steal the Hope diamond, for example, is obviously not an organization, but the Mafia or at least any of the more or less permanently established "hierarchies" of lawbreakers that belong to it, qualifies as such even if from time to time members happen to get arrested or executed.

"A market for commodity k" was defined in chapter 10 as a recurring ensemble of interactions (instead of as a set of interacting individuals). The set of participants involved in the interactions in a market in period t may have no member in common with the set in period $t + 1$. This is often the case, both on the selling and on the buying side, in certain highly specialized markets such as the market for Rembrandt paintings. Our criterion of reasonable continuity would surely demand that an organization have *some* members in common in each pair of consecutive periods. We conclude that the set of participants in a market may but does not necessarily make up an organization. (The set of regular traders on the New York Stock Exchange, for example, would qualify as an organization.)

In every economy each individual belongs to at least one organization (family, enterprise, consumers' cooperative, school, and so on).[1] In modern economies the great majority of individuals belong to several. They may participate voluntarily (e.g., join a chess club) or involuntarily (membership in a family, compulsory attendance in a local school, military conscription). It is useful to treat each partition of the set of individuals separately (family appurtenance, participation in an enterprise, membership in a labor union, and so forth) and eventually to consider the consequences for efficiency of simultaneous membership in several coalitions, which we shall do at the end of section 11.2.

Leon Hurwicz[2] draws attention to the efficiency aspects of the partitioning of the participants in a system according to individuals' membership in organizations with a common payoff (firms, households), which he calls "units." His concern is with the optimal size of the units into which the economy is partitioned, from the viewpoint of efficiency in production: how large production units, or firms, should be to take advantage of economies of scale and to "internalize" the consequences of their actions; how small they may have to be to meet the conditions essential to achieve an efficient allocation of resources in case communication between units were limited to price messages (offers and bids). The answers to these questions, as we already pointed out in chapter 10, depend on the environment, especially on the technology in use. Significant economies of scale, for example, are likely to "deconvexify" the aggregate production set and make it impossible, at least under decentralized decision making, to find any fully efficient partitioning of the set. Technical difficulties in restricting access to certain resources (clean water or air) may bias the solution toward units large enough to bring into the same organization both the individuals perpetrating the externality and

1. This discussion of the partitioning of the individuals belonging to an economy is adapted from Montias and Sturm, op. cit., pp. 13–17.

2. Leon Hurwicz, "Conditions for Economic Efficiency of Centralized and Decentralized Structures," in Gregory Grossman, ed., *Value and Plan: Economic Calculation and Organization in Eastern Europe* (Berkeley: University of California Press, 1960), pp. 166–71.

those affected by its consequences (thereby making it possible to achieve optimality through redistribution of joint payoffs).

The Hurwicz approach, enlightening as it is, represents an extreme simplification of the way organizations operate internally and in relation to one another. It is as though the transmittal of information inside the organization were costless while it was so costly between organizations that price offers and acceptances were the only messages that could be efficiently exchanged. Yet if we are to describe and compare the behavior of organizations across systems, we are compelled to recognize that informational interactions between pairs of individuals differ only in intensity according to whether they belong to the same or to different organizations. The decline in intensity of informational interaction between different suborganizations (departments or divisions) of the same organization may be nearly as important as the discontinuity that occurs when individuals interact across rather than within the complete organizations.

Such a flexible approach to the description of information flows immediately suggests why the Hurwicz solution of internalizing externalities through mergers is likely to prove unrealistic (and has so proved in the practice of the centrally managed economies). When we look more closely at the structure of organizations we find that the internalization of an externality through a compulsory merger may not be a realistic solution to the problem because the agglomerated organization may be too large and its structure too complex to permit the intensive exchange of precise information needed to reconcile the diverging interests of the formerly independent parties for the sake of the overarching goals of the integrated organization. The creation of centrally planned hierarchies in East has by no means guaranteed that the negative externalities perpetrated by some of their subordinated production units at the expense of others, would be tolerated only up to "socially permissible levels," if they were not eliminated altogether. These speculations will be given more precise theoretical content in section 12.4.

Where the rules of the system allow organizations to exchange goods and to contract for services through market transactions, the question arises whether their goals can best be achieved by arranging a transfer or an activity within the organization or by effecting one or the other through price offers and contracts with individuals or organizations external to it. In general, the costs of transacting across organizations must be set against the losses in communicating information internally that were just referred to. Some of these transaction costs are bound up in the information required to consummate deals (sec. 8.4), some in the bounded rationality of individuals who are unable to stipulate all the contingencies that a contract for goods or services should contain in order to provide adequate security to each of the contracting parties against fraud or deception by the others. Individuals often join an organization as members or paid employees because they cannot advantageously supply their services ad hoc to many different organizations within the time constraints to which they are subject. The (impacted) information they possess may also be of special value to the organization of which they are members—positive if the information is used within the organization, negative if it is disclosed to others.[3] Whether the individuals in an economy are partitioned into many small or a few large decision-making units may be determined by the net impact of these factors as well as by the scale effects and the potential externalities stressed by Hurwicz.

"Industrial organization" is the densely foliated branch of economics that deals mainly with the size of enterprises in relation to the total demand for their products (or in relation to the total supply of their inputs). It is essentially concerned with the inefficiencies in production and distribution caused by the preponderance of a few buyers or sellers in the market for one or more interdependent consumer or producer goods or services. Obstacles to entry, whether raised by ruling organizations in the form of government monopolies, licenses, or incorporation laws, by the environment ("natural monopolies"), or by the anticompetitive actions of the enterprises already in business, make it possible for these enterprises to charge prices appreciably higher than marginal costs, thus violating the efficiency rule which requires that marginal cost equal marginal benefit, where marginal benefit is here expressed by the price actually charged.

A tool frequently employed in the description of imperfectly competitive markets is their "degree of concentration," usually measured as the share of employment or sales represented by the n largest enterprises in the industry (where n may be any number, depending on the availability of the data or the purpose of the comparison, but often turns out to be 4). In principle the higher the degree of concentration, the greater the "market power" of the largest enterprises. The possession of "market power" does not necessarily mean that the deviation between the marginal cost of production of the largest enterprises and the price they charge will actually be wider than it would be if the degree of concentration were smaller, since they may wish to keep the price low to inhibit the entry of potential competitors into the industry. It does imply that if any of these large enterprises were to try to find an outlet for a larger volume of its output without altering the physical characteristics of the product or the information about it available to consumers (through advertising or "sales effort") it would have to lower the price of the product in question. The more market power an enterprise happens to wield, the greater the price reduction it would have to concede to sell a given increment in the quantity of its output.

3. These arguments are developed in Oliver E. Williamson's *Markets and Hierarchies: Analysis and Antitrust Implications* (New York: The Free Press, 1975). On the special properties of the hierarchic form of organization, see below, sec. 12.1.

In the opinion of this observer, intercountry comparisons of the degree of concentration have provided remarkably little insight into "imperfect competition" and its effects on consumption, growth, and equity.[4] These comparisons, if they are to acquire explanatory power, must be combined with a study of "the behavior of groups of economic agents whose modes of action and response, in the social organization and technological environment of the society studied, are the ultimate determinants of the levels of economic variables as well as their fluctuations."[5] Two countries may have a similar degree of concentration in one or more industries but one may be characterized by aggressive price competition and the other by the most egregious output-restricting practices, depending on the behavior of decision makers in the two economies: the propensity or reluctance of enterprise leaders to enter into collusive agreements (such as cartels for price maintenance), and the measures taken by ruling organizations to prohibit price agreements, discrimination, and other noncompetitive practices. The examples of postwar Germany and Japan suggest that the presence or absence of price-competitive behavior may depend more on the structure of ownership across as well as within industries and on the extent to which price agreements can be enforced through coercive action than on the measured degree of concentration in one or more markets.[6]

We shall accordingly continue to concentrate on the study of individual interactions within and across organizations in the hope of gaining some understanding of the exercise of "market power" in the process. In this spirit we shall examine briefly the size of establishments in relation to the structure of hierarchies (sec. 12.4), the relative importance of cartels and mergers (sec. 11.2), and collusions and their ability to enforce price agreements (sec. 12.6).

11.2 MEMBERSHIP IN ORGANIZATIONS

What holds an organization together? What makes for its continuity? It is easy to say that the members of an ongoing organization must consider themselves better off by adhering to their membership in the organization than by joining another organization or acting alone. But to be sensitive to

---

4. Little more has been found than that smaller countries have a higher degree of concentration. But since these smaller countries tend generally to engage more intensively in international trade, this tells us very little about their market power or the extent to which they use it. (For statistical information on this subject, see Joe P. Bain, *International Differences in Industrial Structure: Eight Nations in the 1950's* [New Haven: Yale University Press, 1966], pp. 67–122, and Frederic L. Pryor, *Property and Industrial Organization in Communist and Capitalist Nations* [Bloomington: Indiana University Press, 1973], pp. 197–209.)

5. T. C. Koopmans, "Measurement Without Theory," *Review of Economic Statistics* 29 (1947) reprinted in *Scientific Papers of Tjalling C. Koopmans* (Berlin: Springer-Verlag, 1970), p. 118.

6. See below, sec. 12.6.

systemic differences in organizational patterns, we must look more closely at this generalization.

By a member being "better off" we mean of course that he will prefer this outcome over some alternative.[7] This preference will have something to do with the payoffs he associates with each option. Such a payoff may be his share of the (pooled) benefits accruing to the organization (market receipts, subsidies from other organizations, tips in a restaurant where they are pooled, pride in a trophy received by the member's team) or the benefits directly accruing to him (moral satisfaction of working for a charitable organization, advantage derived from selling personally owned goods on a market, medals received for special distinction). The member may also take into consideration the expectation of future payoffs (from shared or directly accruing benefits). If he has the choice, he will surely weigh in his decision to stick to an organization all the actual and potential disadvantages of membership (the disutility of work, the liability he might incur if the organization were suddenly dissoved or "declared bankrupt," and so on). Finally, he may have a special preference for or aversion to membership in the organization in and of itself, irrespective of the net current and future benefits that he may expect from it. In this case, membership in the organization may be regarded as an argument in his utility function. (Two examples are a preference for working in a larger corporation because of the greater prestige it confers, given equivalent benefits in smaller corporations; and an aversion to taking a job in a South African concern because of the racial discrimination practiced by its management.)

In forming his expectations about future payoffs or costs, the member of an organization will recall his experience up to the present time (promotions, bonuses, grievances). He may also reckon his chances of improving his lot from the career patterns of other members.

It is not easy to disentangle a member's "pure preference" for an enterprise from his conscious or unconscious evaluation of his chances of future payoffs. One attempt to do so (based on a study of employees in a large Japanese plant carried out in 1969–70) is illuminating for both its method-

---

7. In chap. 2 we considered models of individual decision making by postulating, alternatively, the maximization of expected utility and "satisficing." The discussion that follows in the text is couched in terms of utility maximization but could easily be accommodated to satisficing behavior. A person may behave as if his loyalty to an organization were guaranteed in all but exceptional circumstances. The more or less conscious process of reckoning the expected utility of alternative courses of actions would then be triggered only once he became aware that compliance to orders or, more generally, normal comportment in accord with the demands of loyalty would be likely to yield him a level of utility below some threshold level. If we wish to explain why individuals join and quit organizations, however, we are impelled to study their behavior under exceptional circumstances that, by their very nature, preclude satisficing.

ological and its comparative aspects.[8] In their study Marsh and Mannari investigated the extent to which "reciprocal rights and obligations between [Japanese] employer and employee" were "institutionalized in the lifetime commitment system."[9] The hypothesis of the "lifetime commitment system" was developed by James Abegglen in his book *The Japanese Factory* (1958). On the basis of this study of large Japanese factories (with more than 1,000 employees), Abegglen argued that workers, whether laborers or managers, were committed for life to an enterprise because "loyalty to the group and an interchange of responsibilities—a system of shared obligation—take the place of the economic basis of employment of workers by the firm."[10] The statistical evidence at least supports the contention that the turnover of employees is a good deal smaller in Japan than in a country where the "basis of employment" is believed to be overwhelmingly "economic."[11] The question raised by Marsh and Mannari was whether relatively low turnover should be attributed to employees' "moral loyalty to the firm" or to their expectations that if they held onto their jobs long enough, their "loyalty" would be rewarded by the company over the years by an accumulation of pay increases, bonus and fringe benefits, paid vacations, and in general by a steadily advancing status in the company.[12] They sought an answer to this question by analyzing the attitudes of employees in large plants belonging to the company. Their conclusions, based on a detailed questionnaire administered to all employees, was that only a minority of the respondents were motivated by "moral loyalty." Out of 939 individuals questioned as to how they felt "about an employee who voluntarily seeks a position in another company," for example, only 2 percent answered that his behavior was "not Japanese," 11 percent replied that he was disloyal, and 10 percent that he was an unscrupulous opportunist. Two employees out of three answered that they could "understand his behavior."[13]

8. R. M. Marsh and H. Mannari, "Life-time Commitments in Japan," *American Journal of Sociology* 76 (March 1971): 796–808. I am beholden to Hugh Patrick for drawing my attention to this article.

9. Ibid., p. 796.

10. Cited in ibid., p. 797.

11. Average monthly separation rates for wage and salary employees in the manufacturing sector were roughly twice as high in the United States as in Japan from 1959 to 1969, with a small year-to-year variance in the ratio (ibid., p. 798). Because small enterprises are covered in these statistics, the difference, which is thought to be greater for larger firms, may be understated from the viewpoint of Abegglen's hypothesis. One may also note that the ratio of American males changing jobs per year was more than twice as high as in Japan (Robert E. Cole, "Permanent Employment in Japan: Facts and Fantasies," paper presented at the Annual Meeting of the Association of Asian Studies, Washington, D.C. March 1971, p. 17). Cole points out that U.S. labor mobility may be abnormally high by international standards.

12. Marsh and Mannari, op. cit., pp. 800–01.

13. Ibid., p. 806.

It turned out nevertheless that a majority of employees were committed, and thought their fellow employees were committed, to a lifetime employment for the company although this commitment, according to the authors, was based primarily on status enhancement not on "moral loyalty."[14] In other words, employees maintained or expected to maintain their membership in the organization mainly by reason of the net benefits they counted on drawing from the association rather than by reason of any special preference for serving the organization or its management throughout their career.

Two remarks on these results are in order. The first is that the Marsh–Mannari data do show that "moral loyalty" may have counted for something in the motivation of about a quarter of the respondents. A survey taken thirty or forty years earlier (in 1939 or 1929), when Japan's "feudal" traditions were presumably stronger,[15] might have revealed that this motive played a greater role than at present. Preferences for or against working in an organization regardless of the balance of tangible benefits and disadvantages cannot be ignored, particularly in systems where traditional ties of kinship or fealty are, or recently were, strong. Second, one must ask oneself *why* employees harbored the belief that loyalty to the company would pay off in terms of advancement and other benefits. The answer seems to lie in the reciprocal obligation or loyalty of management to employees. By and large, status, salary, and other privileges do increase steadily with age and years of continuous employment in the Japanese enterprise. Moreover, employees feel secure and their expectations of future benefits are strengthened because "the firm commits itself not to lay off a regular worker, even in recessions."[16] The conclusion is still inescapable that the values of the participants in the Japanese system make for stronger bonds among the members of a Japanese enterprise than one would expect to find in the United States. As we shall see in chapter 15, this difference in degree of intraorganizational cohesion may have significant consequences for production decisions and for other outcomes in the two systems.

In the introductory section to this chapter we briefly alluded to the fact that most participants in observed systems belonged to more than one organization simultaneously. In modern systems they will be members of a family and employees of an enterprise, a cooperative, or a ruling organization; many of them will belong to a labor union. In more traditional systems individuals will be members of their village group, their tribe, or some other overarching organization to which they owe a measure of their loyalty.

14. Ibid., pp. 807–08.
15. Abegglen traces the pattern of lifetime commitment, in part at least, to Japan's "traditional, feudal structure" (cited in ibid., p. 797).
16. Hugh Patrick, "What Makes Japanese Capitalism Tick?" unpublished paper, New Haven, 1972.

Divided loyalties breed conflicts in individuals' motivation that have been virtually ignored in the literature on comparative economics,[17] even though they may be helpful in explaining certain commonly encountered phenomena that are generally thought to be of interest. Take, for example, allegiance to the family and the pursuit of profits. In systems where the loyalty of enterprise managers to the family is deeply rooted, it may cause them to make decisions with a probable adverse effect on profits, provided they can afford the expected shortfall. A recent study of U.S. savings associations contrasted mutual savings and loan associations, which tend to have a self-perpetuating management due to the diffusion of ownership of shares (fifty being the legal maximum on shares owned), with stock associations, where voting power is generally more concentrated and inefficient management can be voted out by an insurgent group of shareowners (since there is no maximum on the number of shares owned). The author of the study found that there was a marked difference between the extent of "nepotism"—defined as a family relationship between the chief executive officer and other officers in any association—in mutual and in stock associations.[18] Top officers of mutual associations were secure enough in their posts to appoint relatives to major executive posts, whereas officers of stock associations were usually so pressed to show a profit record sufficiently impressive to maintain themselves in power that they could not afford to make inefficient personnel appointments for the sake of the "nonpecuniary reward" of family indulgence.

The relative attractiveness to owners of family businesses of drawing income or capital gains from selling (or merging) their business or of retaining it in the family at some sacrifice is undoubtedly a key factor in explaining the importance of mergers in different economies. In France, where family loyalty has traditionally been very high, mergers until quite recently were not popular. Such mergers as took place have tended to be between larger enterprises, where ownership was severed from family domination.[19] (Family loyalty is of course only one factor. Another principal consideration is the strength of rules prohibiting cartels and other agreements in restraint of trade. Other things equal, the stronger these rules, the more attractive enterprises will find it to merge in order to acquire "market power.")[20]

17. Egon Neuberger and William Duffy in their book on the comparison of systems advert to, and recognize, the importance of simultaneous membership for the analysis of comparative organization (*Comparative Economic Systems: A Decision-making Approach* [Boston: Allyn & Bacon, 1976], p. 37).

18. Alfred Nicols, "Stock versus Mutual Savings and Loan Associations: Some Evidence of Differences in Behavior," *American Economic Review* 57 (May 1967): 345.

19. Cf. Testimony of Jacques Houssiaux in U. S., Congress, Senate, *Economic Concentration: Hearings Before the Subcommittee on Antitrust and Monopoly of the Committee on the Judiciary*, 19th Cong., 2d sess., 1968, pt. 7: 3586–90.

20. Testimony of Egon Sohmen in ibid., p. 3453.

The success of "pariah entrepreneurs"—businessmen belonging to minority ethnic groups who are treated with contumely by members of the majority—may be explained in terms of comparative loyalty to the extended family, village group, tribe, or other ethnic class to which the majority owes allegiance but of which the pariah minority is free. The Lebanese and Syrians installed in Liberia, where they have met with extraordinary success since the 1950s, need not extend interest-free loans, price concessions, or other favors to anyone outside their immediate families, whereas the African entrepreneur is pressed to oblige his fellow tribesmen or villagers, to the detriment of his business. This situation is not confined to Liberia. In all the parts of West Africa I have visited, I have observed that the tradesman may come from the Middle East, Europe, or Africa itself, but he almost never belongs to the village in which he has established himself. Being alien and "hard nosed," it seems, has considerable survival value in the competitive game.[21]

21. Kinship ties in the extended family, on the other hand, may be turned to account in countries where agreements and contracts are poorly enforced. Since members of the family can more readily be trusted than others, they may be appointed to confidential positions without loss of competitive advantage (cf. the history of the Rothschild family in the nineteenth and early twentieth centuries).

12

Hierarchies and Associations

12.1 HIERARCHIES

The structure of an organization is normally codified in written or unwritten rules, which, if they change at all over time, change slowly. Some of these rules may stipulate who in the organization may order whom to do what, who can commit the organization to a decision or sequence of decisions, who can wind up the organization, and who decides how any pooled payoff of the organization will be distributed among its members. The "who" in question is usually not an individual named X but the individual(s) responsible for certain activities in the organization (the president, the board of trustees, a committee, the foreman in shop A, and so on). Wherever the responsible entity consists of several individuals, the rules of the organization determine how they will resolve differences among themselves to act "as one man" (e.g., voting procedures, appointment of a chairman and his prerogatives). The members of an organization normally comply with the rules and order of persons authorized to issue them because they realize that if they openly flaunt or ignore them, they may have to give up their membership in the organization. Their motivation for abiding by the rules is essentially the same as that for adhering to the organization. They may or may not comply with the orders of members entitled by the rules of the organization to issue such orders, but if they do not, they will normally attempt to conceal their noncompliance or justify it, at least to the extent that they consider the orders legitimate.

This explanation still begs a deeper question: Why do people band together in organizations where some individuals can issue commands to others and why are such organizations so much more commonly encountered than communes and other free associations where no member can order any one else around? One answer to both these questions has recently been put forward by A. A. Alchian and H. Demsetz.[1] Their basic argument is that hierarchic forms of organization are superior under the following environmental conditions. (1) The technology used in the activities in which the

---

1. "Production, Information Costs, and Economic Organization," *American Economic Review* 62 (Dec. 1972): 777–95.

organization is engaged requires members to work together in teams[2] to which they contribute their complementary inputs.[3] (2) The individual contribution to the output of the team's activities cannot be exactly controlled or measured although some idea of it can be had by surveilling his inputs (time spent on the job, apparent degree of activity, and so on). (3) If any one member of the team slackens his effort, the reduction in his reward from the common payoff, in the absence of direct supervision over his inputs, will be less than the true reduction in his contribution to the joint payoff. In these circumstances it will pay any one member, if he can escape detection by his fellow team members, to "shirk," that is, to substitute leisure for productive effort to a point where the marginal rate of substitution between his income from work on the team and leisure will diverge from the marginal rate of transformation between his marginal contribution to the team's payoff and leisure. But if everyone on the team were to act in this way, the joint payoff would be so reduced that every member would suffer. From this reasoning, Alchian and Demsetz conclude that when a team member puts in an optimal amount of effort into this team job—optimal, that is, from the viewpoint of the joint payoff—he is generating a positive externality; his effort will only turn out to be optimal for him if every one else "does his best." To ensure that every other member will make his optimal contribution, each member is likely to accept supervision provided other members are also supervised.[4]

Whether or not this conjecture is convincing as an explanation of the entire phenomenon of supervision in organizations, it may throw light on a situation related to that described by Alchian and Demsetz that recently came to my attention. In the Central African Republic, diamond prospecting is completely free of all government controls for African citizens. Traditional techniques of prospecting in alluvial deposits call for a minute amount of capital and no training. Team work raises average per-prospector productivity substantially. The advantage of team work is offset in part by the great temptation each member has of concealing any diamonds he may find in the specialized operations he is responsible for. Clearly, though, if each member sifting through a pail takes his pick of any diamonds that it may contain, there will not be anything left to compensate the members whose job does not give them direct access to the diamonds (filling the pails with alluvial sand, for instance). The team will then fall apart. Such teams, I was informed,[5] fre-

---

2. A team in this context is a group of individuals working together. It should not be confused with a team in the Marschak–Radner sense, which consists of a set of interacting individuals with the same objectives.

3. When product y is produced with input x_i of the ith member and input x_j of the jth member, $\partial^2 y / \partial x_i \partial x_j > 0$, if i and j are complementary inputs.

4. Alchian and Demsetz, op. cit., pp. 778–81.

5. By the Director General of the Mining Industry of the Central African Republic.

quently choose a supervisor from among themselves who makes sure that none of the members stashes away any diamonds in sifting through the sand-filled pails. Supervision eliminates or at least reduces the negative externality due to dissimulation as it does the shirking of effort in the Alchian–Demsetz theory.

The example is interesting because alternative explanations are hard to find. There is no obstacle whatsoever to prospectors' working by themselves (and many do). No one need accept supervision if he does not feel he is better off than if he worked independently. So little capital equipment is required, one cannot object that supervision is exercised by those who can finance the investment. Nor are there differences in status, education, and training among these former peasants that would justify the selection of superior individuals as team leaders for reasons other than those suggested by Alchian and Demsetz.

This digression illustrates the possibility already mentioned in chapter 3 that organizational rules (components of the system structure) may be determined by a system's environment. As Oliver E. Williamson points out, the Alchian–Demsetz argument for the superior efficiency of hierarchic organization rests on a special case of impacted information: each member of the organization knows how much work he is capable of putting out, but it is to his advantage to conceal this information. A supervisor, by observing the supervisee's productivity or by checking on his record before he is admitted to the group, centralizes at least some elements of this useful information. Similarly, the organizing principle of hierarchy may solve the communication problem inherent in reaching a complicated joint decision by members of a group who would otherwise have an equal voice in the decision-making process.[6]

Finally, we may (gingerly) invoke Arrow's possibility theorem as a rationale for hierarchy in cases where no amount of communication among members of a group would allow them to reach a decision, by majority rule or otherwise, that could not be overturned by a coalition of dissatisfied members. If the members believe the advantage of regularly and rapidly reaching *some* decision is preferable to paralysis of the decision-making process, they may acquiesce in the naming of one member as a supervisor ("dictator") empowered to overrule individual preferences.[7] This rationale, however, begs the

6. "Markets and Hierarchies: Some Elementary Considerations," *American Economic Review* 63 (May 1973): 321–22.

7. Kenneth J. Arrow, *Social Choice and Individual Values* (New York: Wiley 1951). The "possibility theorem" states that "if we exclude the possibility of interpersonal comparisons of utility, then the only method of passing from individual tastes to social preferences which will be satisfactory and which will be defined for a wide range of sets of individual orderings are either imposed or dictatorial" (p. 59).

question as to why an individual should accept a ruler instead of a rule for reaching a collective decision in a limited number of interactions (e.g., votes) among members. Most people after all would rather be overruled *some* of the time, or perhaps even most of the time, by a majority than be subject to the whims and volitions of a dictator.

In the last analysis the hierarchic structure adopted in any existing organization cannot be fully explained without reference to the history of the power relations among members of the group and to their backgrounds and educations. Who owns the productive assets with which the members of the organization will operate? How dependent on the owners or custodians of the assets are those individuals seeking to associate themselves with the organization? Have they been schooled, trained, or otherwise indoctrinated to accept the orders of superiors? Systems differ significantly in the ways people are prepared to play a role in hierarchies (or in associations). If nothing else, this conditioning tends to reinforce hierarchic (or nonhierarchic) forms of organization, whatever may be their ostensible efficiency (or lack of it).[8]

Before proceeding to the formal description of a hierarchy, we may observe that the formal rules of an organization do not necessarily allow an observer to predict how an organization will behave—the activities in which its members will engage, the decisions they will make, the policies to which they will commit the organization. For this reason I have avoided speaking of the "functions of an organization," a term to which it is difficult to apply a precise meaning, unless the organization acts as if it were governed by a single individual's preferences. Certain large organizations run by formal rules, known as "bureaucracies,"[9] may be used by their members to promote objectives that are quite at variance with the ostensible purpose for which they were established. Government agencies in the United States that are nominally in the business of "regulating" the conduct of important industries for the welfare of the public are sometimes said to be run by individuals intent on perpetuating their own power or bent on regulating for the sake of regulation.[10] The description of a hierarchic structure that follows makes no attempt to distinguish legitimate activities from those that are inconsistent with the rules or ostensible goals of the organization.

Suppose that by the rules of an organization a member i is entitled to issue orders directly to another member j with reference to one or more activities

8. For an excellent discussion of this subject, see Benjamin Ward's description of "The Command Society," *The Socialist Economy: A Study of Organizational Alternatives* (Berkeley: University of California Press, 1967), pp. 102–28.

9. See below, section 12.5.

10. James Q. Wilson, "The Dead Hand of Regulation," *The Public Interest* 25 (Fall 1971): 39–58.

in which the organization is engaged or could engage. Then i is said to *supervise j.*[11] If j in turn supervises member k and so on, i is said to be *superordinate* (or *superior*) to j, k, ... Conversely, j, k, ..., are subordinate to i. (For this relation to hold, member i does not need to supervise k, ...) By this definition, a member may be superior to another for one activity and subordinate or neither superior nor subordinate for another.

An *association* for an activity or a set of activities is an organization none of whose individual members is superior to another member in carrying out any of these activities. The New York Stock Exchange is an association for stock-buying and -selling activities. It may not be an association *strictu sensu* for defining or interpreting the rules of the organization, for exerting influence on Congress, or for other activities.

The supervision relation will now be used to describe the formal properties of a hierarchy in terms of the graph-theoretic concepts developed in chapter 8.

Consider a finite set of persons S (individuals or groups of individuals acting according to a decision rule) and a supervision relation on S for an activity a. The set S and the set V containing every arbitrary pair (i, j) of distinct persons in $S \times S$ such that i supervises j for a form the graph (S, V) for a. We now define a hierarchy for a as a subgraph (S_a, V_a) of (S, V), where V_a and the set S_a of distinct persons related in V_a have the following properties:

1. For each pair (k, l) in S_a, *either* k is subordinate to l or l is subordinate to k (for activity a) *or* both are subordinate to some third person h in S_a.

2. If one person in S_a is subordinate to another for a, there is a unique chain of successive supervisors for a connecting the two.

The set S_a is called the *personnel* of the hierarchy for a, denoted H_a. From this definition it may be inferred that hierarchy H_a has a unique head b and that every other member of S_a is supervised by precisely one member.[12]

---

11. In Koopmans and Montias, if member i, instead of issuing orders to member j, exercised "significant influence" on j's actions, he could also be said to supervise j (p. 23). The advantage of the present definition is that it appeals only to the rules of the organization and does not require any explanation as to why i can significantly influence j (see also n. 16 below).

12. To be precise we should speak of "the head of the personnel of a hierarchy" (since a hierarchy is made up of pairs and cannot have a head). But no confusion should arise from the use of this shorthand.

To prove that the personnel of a hierarchy for an activity a must have a head, we trace for any member of S_a the chain of its successive supervisors to an ultimate superior. That such an ultimate superior must exist if the organization is a true hierarchy is shown by contradiction. If it did not exist, we should eventually have to list the same element of S_a twice in the chain of supervisors (because S_a is a finite set). The presence of this loop from, say, element h to the same element h, contradicts the condition that there can be only a single chain of supervision in a hierarchy between a superior h and a subordinate i (an alternative path from h to i must exist, if only one going around the loop two or more times). Let the ultimate superior of i be denoted b. Consider a distinct element i' and his ultimate superior b'. Clearly, b and b' must be identical, lest the first

In the set of persons S, there may be more than one subset satisfying the definition of a hierarchy for a. This will be the case, for instance, if S is the set of persons engaged in producing a particular good in a nonmonopolized industry in the United States. The graph of the union of disjoint hierarchies is sometimes called a *directed forest*, the *trees* of which are the individual hierarchies.

There may also exist in the set S an individual to whom the head b of S_a is subordinate. If we include in the personnel of the hierarchy H_a (b^*) headed by b^* all the persons to whom b is subordinate in S for activity a and all the persons subordinate to b^* for a, this larger hierarchy will be the *complete hierarchy for a*.

Consider now the set A of all the activities in which any person in S may be engaged. We can extend the notion of a bigraph—defined in chapter 8 as the union of two graphs for two distinct relations r and r'—to a multigraph, the union of several graphs, one for each relation corresponding to a distinct activity for which any person i in S may supervise another person j also in S.

Thus a multigraph may be used to describe a hierarchy $H_A(b)$ for a set A of activities consisting of the union of all the hierarchies for the activities in A headed by b.[13] The hierarchy $H_A(b^*)$ *for activities in A* is complete if every component hierarchy $H_a(b^*)$, for any activity a in A, is complete. It may happen that b^* is the head of hierarchies spanning more activities than those contained in set A. The hierarchy $H(b^*)$ is *complete* if it is the union of all hierarchies for individual activities of which b^* is the head. It has been proved (by T. C. Koopmans) that in any set S of persons, every ordered pair (i, j) defined for a supervision relation regarding an arbitrary activity a belongs to one and only one complete hierarchy $H(b^*)$.[14]

To fix these ideas, it may be pointed out that if the personnel of a hierarchy for an activity headed by member b is not subordinate *for that activity* to b^*, then that hierarchy will not belong to $H(b^*)$. Thus the private medical

condition defining a hierarchy be violated (b cannot be superior or subordinate to b' if both b and b' are the ultimate superiors of i and i', respectively; for the same reason, neither can they be subordinate to an element b''). Thus b is the unique head of S_a.

That i cannot be supervised by two distinct members h and h' is also proved by contradiction. If either h is superior to h' or h' superior to h, there must be two alternative chains of successive supervision between either h or h' and i, one from h (resp. h') through h' (resp. h) to i and the other directly from h (resp. h') to i, bypassing the intermediate node in the chain. On the other hand, if both h and h' are subordinate to a third member k, the path from k to i must go through either h or h', in either case violating the unique-chain condition.

For a more fully worked out variant of this formal model, see T. C. Koopmans, "Note on a Social System Composed of Hierarchies with Overlapping Personnel," *Orbis Economicus* 13, no. 3–4 (July 1969): 2–11.

13. Ibid., p. 9.
14. Ibid., pp. 9–10.

practice of a physician employed by a company headed by a president $b*$ will not be a part of the company's complete hierarchy headed by $b*$. On the other hand, if the president heads a boy scout troupe on his free time, this troupe will belong to the complete hierarchy.[15] To circumvent this difficulty, the set of activities A in which $b*$ is assumed to engage may be restricted to those affecting the organization's payoff.

For the entire organization with membership S and a range of activities A to qualify as a hierarchy for one or more activities in A, the entire graph (S, V_a) must have the properties of a hierarchy for at least one activity a in A. An organization is a *quasi-hierarchy* for activity α in A if V_α is not empty—if at least one member of S is supervised for activity α by another member of S and yet (S, V_α) does not qualify as a proper hierarchy. In this third, residual category of organizations, members need not be related to one another by a single chain of supervision, more than one member may "head" the organization, or both. (The modern nuclear family consisting of father, mother, and children is an example of such a quasi-hierarchy.) A hierarchy or quasi-hierarchy may itself be a member of an association, or vice versa, if all the members of the member organization act according to or abide by the decision procedures of that organization.

We now introduce the concept of a *line hierarchy*. Consider hierarchy H_A for set A of activities, where $b*$ is the head of the complete hierarchy $H_a(b*)$ for activity a in A. If H_A is a line hierarchy, then $H(b*)$, the complete hierarchy headed by $b*$, must be identical with $H_a(b*)$. In other words in a line hierarchy if i supervises j for an activity a, then i supervises j for every activity in which the head $b*$ is engaged. An example of a line hierarchy is a regiment of the U.S. Army. The members who form the chain of supervisors are called *line personnel*.

In most line hierarchies, a supervisor situated in a higher tier has one or more individuals attached to him who help him make his decisions and formulate his policies but who have no authority to issue orders to individuals in the chain of supervision below him. These supervisees, who themselves may be organized as a hierarchy for the activity in which they specialize, constitute the supervisor's *staff*.[16]

12.2 HIERARCHIES IN SOME CONTEMPORARY ECONOMIES

Delicate problems of classification arise as soon as we try to apply the

15. Ibid. p. 11.
16. If the supervision relation were extended to encompass the "significant influence of i on the actions of j," then in many instances staff members would supervise members of the line hierarchy. For the organization to remain a hierarchy, such "significant influence" would have to be exerted on actions that were component parts of activities differing in a significant way from those supervised along the hierarchic "chain of command."

concepts defined in the preceding section to ongoing organizations. Is the Soviet economy managed by one gigantic hierarchy? If so, who or what stands at its head? Does the board of directors of a Japanese or U.S. enterprise organized as a hierarchy head the organization or does its president?

A substantial part of the present-day administration of state-owned enterprises in the Soviet Union is clearly hierarchically structured and may even be described as a line hierarchy. The personnel of this hierarchy is headed by the Council of Ministers of the USSR acting as a person. Below them are the all-union ministers. The hierarchic chain in each ministry then passes through the directors of "chief administrations" (*glavki*), or of "associations" (as the case may be), the directors of enterprises, the directors of plants, the heads of shops or sections, all the way down to the individual worker. Within this hierarchy, one-man leadership (*edinonachalie*) is uncontested. Staff members of ministers or of other line officials have no power to issue orders to personnel lower on the main chain.

Take the steel-making activity. Is the hierarchy just described complete for that activity? It is certainly complete in the sense that "the tree has been traced down to the last participant supervised" in that activity. But do not secretaries of the Central Committee of the Communist Party have the power to impose their rules and orders on the Council of Ministers? Is not the Politbureau, which normally includes in its membership most of these secretaries, the ultimate head of the complete hierarchy? If so, there is no great problem in enlarging the hierarchy to embrace the secretary or secretaries responsible for industrial sectors and the Politbureau itself at the very top of the pyramid. But what if the party secretary responsible for industry were known to issue orders to the Ministry for the Chemical Industry? Or if the secretary of an *oblast* (province) had the effective power to enjoin the behavior of the director of an enterprise? If the activities to which any of these orders apply are the same activities as those supervised in the governmental hierarchy initially described, we must conclude that this hierarchy is embedded in a larger quasi-hierarchy, some members of which may be supervised for the same activity by more than one supervisor. On the other hand, if activities supervised by the party can be regarded as being different in some significant way from those supervised by the personnel of the government hierarchy, then, as long as the Politbureau heads both the party and the government hierarchies, all the personnel in both hierarchies may be said to belong to the same complete hierarchy.

In actuality, some effort is made to demarcate party-supervised activities from the regular activities of the government administration. Party organs function mainly as controllers and coordinators of economic activities normally supervised by members of the government hierarchy. But double supervision for identical activities occurs not infrequently and, to the extent that it does, the hierarchic principle is violated.[17] Nevertheless, the fit may be close enough to warrant a discussion of the Soviet state-owned economy in terms of a complete hierarchy and its component hierarchies.

In Japan and the United States the stockholders of a corporation are not usually members of the organization of which the corporation is a component part, because they do not "regularly interact with each other" in pursuance of any activities. The board of directors in Japan is composed almost exclusively of officials of the company, such as the president, vice-president, managers of divisions, and so forth. Since "the members of the board have little to do that they are not already doing in their line positions in the company,"[18] it would be unrealistic to place the board at the head of the complete hierarchy for the activities in which the corporation is engaged. The situation in the United States and in most West European countries is more complicated. Outsiders are often members of the board, which in most companies does seem to have policy-making functions that go beyond the normal competence of the president and his subordinates. In this case the board may properly be viewed as the head of the complete hierarchy. The fact that the board handles certain broad policy questions (possible mergers, spinoffs, and so on) that are beyond the competence of the president operating by himself does not undermine the hierarchic principle, because the complete hierarchies for each of these policy-making activities (the personnel of which may be limited to the board itself acting as a single person according to a decision-making rule) are joined at the very apex of the organization with the hierarchy headed by the president.

The trickiest case to analyze in this framework is that of the self-managed Yugoslav enterprise, at least before the 1969 reform, which virtually abolished the participation of local government organs in appointing the enterprise's director. In each enterprise the workers' council, consisting of anywhere from 15 to 120 members depending on the size of the enterprise, is elected annually by the employees. The director of the enterprise is selected by a committee made up of enterprise members, but the committee's choice must be ratified by the workers' council.[19] The workers' council may propose at any time that

17. For an excellent description of the supervisory activites of party functionaries at the *oblast* level, see Jerry Hough, *The Soviet Prefects* (Cambridge, Mass.: Harvard University Press, 1969), esp. chap. 8 ("Types of [Party] Intervention in Production, Technical, and Planning Decisions").

18. Herbert Glazer, "The Japanese Executive," in R. Ballon, ed., *The Japanese Employee* (Rutland, Vt.: Tuttle, 1969), p. 82.

19. Until 1968, three out of six members of the committee were representatives of the local commune (*opshtina*). The 1968 constitution eliminated the participation of local government except in newspapers, banks, and insurance companies (Joel B. Dirlam and James L. Plummer, *An Introduction to the Yugoslav Economy*, [Columbus, Ohio: Merrill, 1973], p. 26).

the director be fired; however, until 1969 his actual dismissal had to be approved by the commune.[20] In principle the workers' council, like the board of directors of an American corporation, establishes the main policy lines of the enterprise, while the director "manages" the enterprise and executes the policies of the council.

Now if we assume that the Yugoslav enterprise was (and still is) organized as a hierarchy, the hierarchy before 1969 surely could not have been headed by the commune, whose only power of supervision rested on its representation in the commission for choosing the director. On the other hand the powers of the workers' council over the director were limited by the fact that the latter could not be dismissed without the approval of the commune. Except in cases where the double supervision of the director by the council and the commune was unambiguously resolved (possibly because one had greater informal power than the other), the Yugoslav enterprise was not strictly speaking organized as a complete hierarchy. Since 1969 a better case can be made for qualifying the Yugoslav enterprise as a hierarchy headed by its workers' council.

Interesting differences among systems in the structures of their organizations also show up in the character of their typical hierarchies. In some hierarchies staff personnel play such a vital role in regulating the activities in their sphere of responsibility all the way "down the line" that members in lower tiers can be said to be subordinate to them *for these activities* (examples: a chief accountant of a large corporation attached to the vice-president for financial affairs issuing directives to accounting departments of the various divisions of the corporation; a chief physician ordering the inoculation of all employees in a plant). In other systems, which are organized as true line hierarchies, all orders flow down the main chain of command. This was the case, at least until very recently, for most Japanese corporations, which were distinguished by the almost total absence of staff personnel at any level.[21] Unlike in the United States, "bright young men" in the typical Japanese corporations are not attached to the staff of senior line executives. They are positioned lower on the line, at that level of the hierarchy to which their age entitles them. And they will rise in the hierarchy through time only at the same pace as their age cohorts, most probably until they reach their fifties. How can such a "vertically structured society" (*tateshakai* in Japanese) cope with the technical problems

---

20. Svetozar Pejovich, *The Market-Planned Economy of Yugoslavia* (Minneapolis: University of Minnesota Press, 1966), p. 93. The executive board that is elected from among the members of the workers' council and that includes the director, whether or not he is a member of the council, seems, like the Japanese board of directors, to exert no more power than its members possess independently of their membership on this board (i.e., as directors or as members of the workers' council).

21. Glazer, op. cit., p. 84.

of a complex modern environment? The answer may lie in the *ringi* system of management,[22] where staff work is done by the bright young men in the middle echelons of the hierarchy. According to Kazuo Noda, "the ringi system allows the middle management levels to perform the detailed planning, programming, and execution of almost all management actions. Top management's authority is similar to that of a rubber-stamp general who delegates it formally to his subordinate officers."[23]

The notion of describing a hierarchy for a set of activities as the union of the hierarchies defined for each individual activity may give an illusion of organizational neatness that is not always warranted when the activities in question are interdependent. For example, in Czechoslovakia in the early 1960s certain ministries and, at the next lower tier, certain chief administrations were named "gestors"—agents responsible for the nationwide planning and distribution of designated products regardless of whether these products were produced by plants subordinated to these or to some other ministries and central administrations. Thus the Ministry for Building Materials was named gestor for cement although a substantial part of output originated as a side-product in plants subordinate to the Ministry of Metallurgy. Strictly speaking, gestors were not supposed to issue orders to producers of "their" products but were expected to come to an agreement with these producers and, if necessary, with their supervisors concerning their output and its disposition. It was soon discovered that gestors with powerful leverage in the administration were able to exercise power over plants belonging to other lines of command and that, when they did so, their counsels, advice, and virtual orders tended to undermine the objectives set for these plants by their superior authorities in the direct line of command. Gestors who were normally indifferent to the financial performance of their wards induced them to make decisions that lowered their profits or forced them to incur losses. On the other hand, when the gestors were less powerful in the administration, their counsels were generally ignored by plants that were not in their direct line of command.[24] Some of these examples suggest that the "power structure" of an organization may be far from congruent with its formal hierarchic chart.

12.3 COORDINATION

The elements of information theory developed in the Appendix may be applied to the study of the informational aspects of the "coordination problem." A coordinator h in an organization receives information from a subset O_s of its members and issues orders or makes suggestions to a distinct subset O_g

22. The *ringi* system is described in ibid. pp. 88–90.

23. Cited in ibid. p. 89.

24. For details, see J. M. Montias, "The Evolution of the Czech Economic Model 1949–1961," mimeographed (New Haven, Sept. 1962), pp. 53–54 and 100–01.

of members of S engaged in interdependent activities (where O_s and O_g may have one or more members in common). Given the possible states of the environments of h, O_s, and O_g, we may say that h *coordinates* the activities of the agents in O_s and O_g if the expected payoff of the organization is higher than it would be had he not issued these orders or made these suggestions. The coordinating orders may help the members of O_g to meet a joint physical or financial constraint, to balance the output mix produced by some of its members against anticipated consumption, or otherwise to increase the expected payoff by an improved ordering or sequencing of the interdependent activities in question. Coordination by h of the members of O_g may complement or be an alternative to payoff-enhancing interactions among the members themselves.

The information drawn by superiors in a hierarchy from the information sets of subordinates and/or from their own environment depends on the activities that have been assigned to them ("control,"[25] resolution of disputes within the hierarchy, coordination of interdependent activities, and so forth). To be carried out efficiently, the coordination of a sequence of interdependent activities (the activity of superiors we shall now focus on) requires detailed knowledge of each of the procurement, production, transportation, and transfer activities in the sequence as well as of the possibilities of substituting other activities for some of them whenever this may be efficient. To acquire such detailed knowledge himself, a superior might have to extract from his subordinates virtually their entire information sets. However, there are limits to this information-collecting process: information is expensive to collect; the capacity of superiors to process, store, and retrieve information is limited; and information that is not immediately communicated becomes obsolete as the participants' environment changes. With improvements in the technology and equipment for information handling, these constraints have become less stringent. Nevertheless, whether information has been obtained from samples or aggregated from exhaustive reports, in transferring it from each tier to the next losses and distortions in content and delays remain unavoidable.

A superior in a higher tier desiring to avoid such losses of information may send inspectors to the field (e.g., to the lowest tier) or try "to see for himself." Inspection, however, whether carried out by the highly placed member himself or by other members of his hierarchy, is expensive in terms of alternative uses of the personnel involved.[26] The interdependency among activities may depend on the circumstances of a given moment, so that a particular the face of this complexity, superordinates may not perceive the best opportunities for sequencing activities in a concrete situation.

To put the question formally, if coordinator h has a choice in the matter,

<hr />

25. On control, see sec. 13.2.
26. On inspection, see also sec. 14.4.

how fine or coarse should the information he obtains from O_s be to maximize the net expected payoff of the organization, defined as the gross payoff minus information costs?

It may safely be assumed that the finer the partitioning of the information conveyed by O_s to h, the more expensive it will be to collect and process. Therefore, he must not elicit information too fine for his information structure (as would be the case if his objective function induced him to issue the same set of orders to the members of O_s with the same expected payoff whether he received message m or message m', where m' was derived from a finer partition of the set of states in the environment of the members of O_s than m). On the other hand, if a complex of messages sent by O_s contained information that was *too coarse* for h, he would issue a set of orders and suggestions to O_g that might result in one payoff or another, depending on the actual finer information relating to the states of the environments of O_s that was aggregated in these messages. Similar considerations affect h's choice of "channels" for transmitting orders or suggestions to the members of O_g.[27]

So far information theory has not come up with theorems on the efficient choice of channels that will hold true under any probability distribution of the states of any objective function. However, we can state some conjectures that I think will stand up under a wide range of such conditions.

Suppose, to be specific, that h draws information from the set E of the environments (productive capacities, ambient temperatures, state of machines, and so on) of the members of O_g in period t and then issues a set of production plans to the same K members of O_g in period $t + \tau$. (This set τ of orders constitutes h's action at $t + \tau$.) The payoff of h is some function of the K output vectors.

There are three partitions to be considered: (1) the partition of E into events, denoted ζ; (2) the partition of E induced by the information function, denoted η; and (3) the partition of the set A of h's possible actions, denoted $\mathscr{A}$.

For a given payoff function ω, suppose that the partitions ζ and $\mathscr{A}$ are payoff-relevant: they are neither unnecessarily fine nor too coarse in the sense that distinct states belonging to the same event in z, an element of ζ, or distinct actions in an element a of $\mathscr{A}$ would generate different payoffs. Let h choose an information structure η—a description of the set of the states of the environ-

27. Jacob Marschak has demonstrated that there will be only one partitioning of the states of an agent's environment paired with one partitioning of the states of possible actions that the agent can undertake that will be "neither too coarse nor too fine," given the payoffs associated with each "state description" and each "description of the activities" that can be undertaken by this agent. In this statement a "state description" is an element of a given partitioning of the possible states of the agent's environment and a "description of the actions" of this agent is an element of a given partitioning of his possible actions. See Marschak, "The Payoff-relevant Description of States and Acts," *Econometrica* 31, no. 4 (Oct. 1963): 722–23, as well as the less formal and more accessible discussion in his "Problems in Information Economics," in *Management Controls: New Directions in Basic Research* (New York: McGraw-Hill, 1964), pp. 41–42.

ment of O_g—that maximizes his net expected payoff (i.e., his gross expected payoff minus expected information-gathering costs). Now suppose that h adopts a new payoff function ω', which induces a new payoff-relevant pair of partitions ζ' and $\mathscr{A}'$, where $\mathscr{A}'$ is coarser than $\mathscr{A}$ and ζ' is at least as coarse as ζ. The conjecture is that the information structure that will maximize h's net expected payoff will induce a partition η' of E that will be coarser than η for a wide class of a priori probability distributions of the states in E.

Suppose, for example, that h's payoff ω consisted of the K output vectors themselves in period $t + \tau$, that ω' consisted of their weighted vector sum, and that, as a result of the change in the payoff function, h's efficient set of actions were now limited to issuing the same average plan for all K supervisees (instead of a detailed plan for each). The conjecture states that it would pay h to reduce the degree of detail of the information collected at t. The conjecture also suggests that if h satisfices instead of maximizing his expected payoff, he will generally require less detailed information. Furthermore, if for one reason or another, the payoff based on the outcomes of his supervisors' actions is submitted to h in aggregated form and if as a result it pays him to issue less detailed orders, the information he will wish to collect about the states of his supervisees' environment will also be less detailed.[28]

Because supervisors do tend to satisfice in situations where they are highly uncertain about their supervisees' environments[29] and because their choice of actions capable of producing distinct outcomes under given states of their supervisees' environments is frequently quite restricted, the above speculations on the information structures of the members of an organization suggest, first, that in a line hierarchy where every supervisor is charged with coordinating the activities of his subordinates, the information communicated by a member to his supervisor in a given tier will generally be coarser than that available to him and, second, that it will suffer a "loss of detail" in every tier as it is transmitted from tier to tier all the way to the coordinators at the apex of the hierarchy.[30] Given the costs of collecting, communicating, and processing more finely partitioned information, such losses may be quite consistent with the efficient management of the organization.

28. What about the fact that the information h is drawing upon refers to states of the environment at t rather than to the true states that will affect the payoff at $t + \tau$? Does the introduction of this noise affect the choice of the information structure maximizing h's net expected payoff? Should this incorrect information—incorrect at least if the probability distribution of the states at t and $t + \tau$ happen to differ—be more or less detailed than if the information had been collected at $t + \tau$? As far as I know, answers to these questions have neither been posed nor answered, even for relatively simplified examples.

29. See sec. 13.2.

30. A similar idea was expressed by Pavel Pelikan in "Language as a Hidden Parameter: Some Notes on the Problem of Centralization vs. Decentralization," Occasional Paper, Carnegie-Mellon University, Graduate School of Industrial Administration, Pittsburgh, Sept. 1968.

12.4 Two Conjectures on the Coordination of Goods and Bads in Hierarchies[31]

First we define more precisely than we have hitherto some key attributes of hierarchies to be used in the conjectures. The *length* of any chain between two members i and j of the hierarchy is the number of members in the chain, including i and j. A *tier* is the set of all persons related to the head of the hierarchy by chains of the same length (the head being the first tier).

Let us make the extreme assumption, which will later be relaxed, that two members of a given hierarchy not in the same chain of supervision and responsible for different but interdependent activities cannot engage in informational interaction with each other. Coordination is thus effected exclusively through common superiors in the hierarchy. Suppose further that we take as given the quality of supervising personnel, the amount and accuracy of the information required by superiors to make effective coordination decisions, and all other variables affecting the efficiency of such decisions.

One would then seek to assign activities in a hierarchy in such a way that the most highly interdependent activities would be assigned to members with a common supervisor. When this assignment exceeded a supervisor's efficient span of control, it would become necessary to assign some still strongly interdependent activities to members whose nearest common superior was two (or more) tiers up the "chain of command." Our presumption is that the number and degrees of interdependency of activities in a modern economy are such, relative to the efficient span of control of supervisors, that even the best feasible assignment of activities from the point of view of efficient coordination through superiors would still leave pairs of activities of substantial interdependence to be coordinated by a nearest common superior many tiers up the chain. (One example is weaving fabrics for the upholstery of automobiles and making automobile bodies in the Soviet ministerial hierarchy.)

Consider two hierarchies H and H', say two plants initially engaged in disjoint sets of activities A and A' that have substantial interdependence between activities a and a' of the two sets, respectively. We conjecture that the longer the chains between the two heads of H and H' and their nearest common superior, the more likely it is that each of the two plants will initiate activities already belonging to the set of the other. Each will do so, we reason, because it will wish to ensure better coordination of some of the activities initially carried on in the other plant with its own activities. Furthermore, its incentive for this expansion will be the stronger, the more inefficient the coordination by the common superior in the initial situation. This inefficiency will be greater the longer the chains separating the common superior from the heads of the two plants. How many common activities both plants will

31. This section is in major part based on Koopmans and Montias, op. cit., pp. 71–75.

ultimately undertake will depend on variables other than the economies of information, such as the availability of equipment and other factors affecting costs of production (if costs matter).

Suppose that in the initial situation the two plants had been permitted and encouraged to interact directly, that is, to exchange information and to co-ordinate their own activities within limits set by their superiors. The incentive for "plant autarky" (the phenomenon we have just described) would have been weaker.

The first conjecture is that if complete mutuality were permitted, including the setting of mutually acceptable prices, specialization between any two hierarchies in the system would be carried further than under a more restrictive arrangement.

In the centrally directed economies of the Soviet Union and Eastern Europe, evidence has frequently been cited of enterprises engaging in a very wide gamut of ancillary activities—such as maintaining inventories, facilities for producing crucial inputs, personnel engaged in procuring inputs, repair facilities for machinery, design departments, R & D facilities—the apparent or sometimes explicit aim being that of protecting themselves from the vagaries of an undependable centrally supervised distribution system or of the inefficiencies of centralized research.[32] A verifiable implication of the first conjecture is that plants belonging to different ministries would be more likely to take over one other's activities than those belonging to the same ministry because their lowest common superior would be further up the hierarchy and there would presumably be less direct interaction between (or among) them.

The proliferation of activities in subhierarchies in the situation described has parallels in "market economies" not only because producers belonging to multiplant hierarchies may be insecure in their supplies but also because they may face an uncertain demand for their products. To hedge against the risk of wide swings in prices or of catastrophic declines in demand at existing prices, enterprises tend to produce a broader gamut of products than they would otherwise.[33] Similarly, developing countries may diversify their exports in order to avoid excessive dependence on a few markets.

In sum, uncertainties in demand and uncertainties in supply appear to have the common effect of inducing excessive duplication in the production programs of industrial enterprises, at least compared to a situation where these risks would be absent or less acute.

---

32. See, e.g., D. W. Conklin, "Barriers to Technological Change in the USSR: A Study of Chemical Fertilizers," *Soviet Studies* 20 (Jan. 1969): 357–65.

33. Note, however, that the *size of enterprises*, which may or may not be correlated with the number of activities in which they may be engaged, may either decline or increase with the degree of uncertainty. Smaller size will enable an enterprise to adapt more flexibly to variations in demand, whereas larger size will enable it to pool specific risks (by widening its product mix or otherwise).

An implication of our conjecture as it applies to uncertainties in supply is that, other things equal, industrial "establishments," which may be defined as ensembles of plant and equipment operating in a specific physical location and managed as a single organization, will be larger, according to any reasonable measure of size, the larger the hierarchic distance of the chain between their heads and the head of the complete hierarchy of which they are a part. (This corollary conjecture assumes that the head of the complete hierarchy exercises a significant influence on subordinates' procurement of inputs.) Again, we reason that the manager of a producing plant will try to lessen his dependency on supplies originating outside his subhierarchy as long as a superior organ is responsible for deciding what inputs he should get and when he should receive them. The greater his hierarchic distance from his ultimate boss, the greater will be his interest in pursuing self-sufficiency. We also surmise that more self-sufficient establishments need more personnel than those relying on outsiders for components or other inputs.[34]

Since size happens to vary significantly according to the technological characteristics of industries in all countries for which data are available,[35] "other things equal" means that we must control for industry effects. We may compare, for example, the size of establishments in the same industry for three types of hierarchic arrangements: (1) establishments operating as individual enterprises (chain of unit length[36]); (2) establishments subordinate to a multiestablishment enterprise (chain of length two); (3) establishments subordinate to enterprises that are themselves components of a larger hierarchy (chains of length three or more).

The data collected by Frederic Pryor are at least consistent with the conjecture. Among industrialized Western nations, establishments belonging to multiestablishment enterprises appear to be significantly larger in each industry than establishments run as independent enterprises. Establishments in Poland and in prereform Hungary, which of course were embedded in multitiered hierarchies, were appreciably larger on average, after controlling for differences in their gross domestic product (a proxy for market size), than establishments in Western industrialized economies.[37]

34. For a caveat, see n. 33.

35. Frederic L. Pryor, *Property and Industrial Organization in Communist and Capitalist Nations* (Bloomington: Indiana University Press, 1973), pp. 136–38.

36. Since the length of a chain between i and j, according to these definitions above, includes both i and j, the chain between i and itself is of unit length.

37. Pryor, op. cit., pp. 162, 165, 180. The data for Poland and Hungary were not standardized for differences in industrial structure (compared with the sample of Western countries). However, because the indicators of average relative size were three to four times larger than the size that would have been expected (given the GNP attained by these countries) if they had behaved like the Western sample, I have confidence that the conclusion would still hold after controlling for differences in industrial structure. The average size of establishments in Yugoslavia also appears to have been larger in 1963 than expected (it was almost as large in fact as Poland and Hungary).

We cannot claim that the data "confirm" the conjecture. Alternative competing (or overlapping) hypotheses can be adduced that would also be consistent with the data.[38] We should also be suspicious of the fact that our conjecture says something about the eventual size of an establishment after it has latched onto ancillary activities, but it has no predictive value for determining the size of establishments at the time they were created (unless the individuals responsible for their creation decided to set up larger units in anticipation of supply difficulties). What it does suggest, at least, is that hierarchic distance may be an important factor in determining the size of establishments and should be incorporated in any multivariate analysis purporting to explain differences in average size among countries.

A related conjecture is now set forth that involves the conflicting interests of two hierarchies engaged in production activities that possess heads who are in the same tier of their complete hierarchy (if one exists). We assume that both hierarchies have custody of their means of production and that the remuneration of at least some members with decision-making power in either organization depends on the outcomes of the activities of their respective organizations (volume of output, costs, proceeds, profits, and so on).

Suppose now that some members of one of the two hierarchies, in the pursuit of its objectives and without prior agreement with the other, undertake an activity that adversely affects outcomes of the other. Suppose also that the decision makers in the latter cannot or may not obtain compensation through mutual agreement for this bad fully equivalent in their preferences to its adverse effect. The action has thus given rise to an external diseconomy.

If the heads of the two hierarchies involved are supervised by the same member of a complete hierarchy, the conflict of interests will normally come to his attention. The common superior may or may not order that compensation be made, possibly depending on the effect of such action on the interests of the lowest component hierarchy of which both contesting heads are members (strictly speaking, depending on the superior's interpretation of these interests). He will also have to decide whether a repetition of the action

---

Pryor argues (p. 163) that this may be a legacy of the centralized system of the early 1950s, when many of these establishments were built. But it may also be a reflection of the fact that, in 1963 at least, enterprises were still subject to controls by all sorts of local, republican, and federal authorities.

38. Pryor, in particular, cites Walter Eucken's conjecture to the effect that "in planned economies production units are generally larger because of simplicity of administration and lower costs of coordination" (Pryor, op. cit., p. 143). This conjecture could also be applied to multi-establishment enterprises operating in a competitive market environment. The Eucken conjecture would be more relevant to the size of establishments at the time they were created (see text below), than when they were actually observed. With sufficiently detailed data on the age and size of establishments, the effects of the two conjectures on the size of establishments might be disentangled.

should or should not be prevented by a restraining order. If, however, the nearest common superior is several tiers up, the matter will be more difficult to resolve to the satisfaction of either organization because the common superior will have less accurate information about the interests affected than a supervisor.

The second conjecture is that, for given preferences of decision makers among goods and bads in every tier, there will be less likelihood of an efficient resolution of a conflict of this type the longer the chain separating the parties in the dispute from their nearest common superior.[39]

The conjectures on the efficient coordination of interdependent activities and on the efficient resolution of conflicts involving external diseconomies are clearly two facets of the same general problem of optimizing the interaction between two entities in a complete hierarchy where a mutually satisfactory cooperation is precluded by the rules and orders of superiors, by high transaction costs, or by the inability to reconcile the interests of the parties without such rules and orders (e.g., through mutuality).

Indeed, in a market system there will generally be no incentive for an entity inflicting damage on another to compensate the latter for its losses or even to abstain from inflicting further damage as long as transaction costs are significant. Ruling organizations, through the issuance of rules restraining the behavior of private organizations, through nationalization orders followed by such restraints, or, as Hurwicz suggests, through the compulsory merger of the conflicting entities, may be in a position to salvage some measure of efficiency in these situations. However, the serious pollution of the air over such cities as Chicago, Los Angeles, and Budapest suggests that those problems cannot easily be solved in either market or centrally coordinated systems.[40]

12.5 Bureaucratic versus ad hoc Decision Making

Consider these alternative modes of making decisions in a hierarchy. In the first, a subordinate observes a state of the organization's environment and then makes a decision in conformance with the rule or complex of rules that he thinks ought to apply in this particular case. In the second, the rules of the

39. Consider, for instance, how much easier it is to resolve scheduling conflicts in a university when courses are given in the same department than when they are given in different departments and the conflict must be resolved either through prolonged negotiation between department chairmen or in the dean's office.

40. It has been argued that, in the case of most actually observed externalities, mutually advantageous transactions are possible provided that all parties affected may freely interact and transaction costs are low. Restrictions on interaction may have complicated the Lake Baikal dispute in the USSR between paper mills polluting the water and the fisheries. There are also frequent cases where negotiations cannot take place because the perpetrator cannot readily communicate with the entities he adversely affects. How can people who would like to swim in a river, *if* it were not polluted, be compensated?

organization designate who will be responsible for making a decision upon the occurrence of a state of the environment belonging to a particular class of states, but the actual decision is left up to the responsible individual, who is instructed only to make the best possible decision in the light of the objectives of the organization, subject to any prior rules restricting his initiative. The first ideal type of decision making may be termed *bureaucratic*, the second *ad hoc*.

A typical example of bureaucratic decision making in West is the formal rationing of scarce consumer goods to households during wartime. Each category of consumers (from "males engaged in heavy physical work" to "children of one year or less") is entitled to prescribed quantities of carefully defined goods. Only a very small percentage of cases cannot be handled by a low-tier bureaucrat armed with a set of instructions. When such a case does occur (e.g., when an individual has lost his rationing book under moot circumstances), it may be adjudicated by a superordinate either ad hoc or in conformance with a higher rule, such as a pertinent court decision.

In the hierarchically structured economic administrations of East, the ad hoc mode of decision making is generally preferred to the bureaucratic, although the initiative of subordinates is often so hemmed in by a multiplicity of rules that they cannot help behaving bureaucratically. In a recent article in the Romanian newspaper *Scinteia*, for example, an authoritative commentator complained that the associations, which we have already mentioned as an intervening link between ministries and enterprises, were running their enterprises bureaucratically. He cited the case of one central that had issued 2,282 "instructions and circulars" to its enterprises in a short period, instead of managing them "operationally."[41]

Under what conditions should we expect bureaucratic and under what conditions ad hoc management? Three factors are likely to play a critical role in the relative efficiency of the two modes with respect to the attainment of the goals pursued by the organization: (1) how difficult it may be to devise and codify decision rules corresponding to each of the many possible states of the environment that may appreciably affect the organization's payoff, (2) how precisely the goals of the organization may be conveyed to all decision-making members of the hierarchy, and (3) how strongly these members may be motivated to strive for these goals as they understand them, and not to yield to pressures from below.

1. The bureaucratic mode cannot be efficacious if each member of the hierarchy has to be equipped with a different rule book with thousands of rules corresponding to all the circumstances he may encounter. This is especially so when these rules have to be altered each time the goals and policies of the organization undergo a change. Another obstacle to the use of this mode may be the difficulty of defining simply, clearly, and precisely all

41. *Scinteia*, June 4, 1974, p. 1.

the possible cases a subordinate may chance to meet in such a way that, even with very little education, he can be sure to come up with the right decision in most instances that matter.

2. If subordinates are to be freed of the restraints of excessively detailed rules, they must know what objectives to strive for. When the objectives are formulated by members of the hierarchy who are separated by a long chain of command from the "cadres" in the field and can be conveyed to them only in the most general terms, these lower hierarchs may have trouble figuring out what to do in complex situations.

3. Even when decision makers in lower tiers know what the higher members expect of them, they will not follow their "organizational conscience" unless they are motivated to do so.

Intense indoctrination of the members of the hierarchy may be the answer to problems 2 and 3. Ideological training is calculated to impress "cadres" with the goals of the organization and to induce them to do what's right once they understand it. This, in any event, has been the strategy pursued by Chinese communists, who have ostensibly rejected the bureaucratic mode symbolized in the official ideology by Liu Shao-Ch'i, the former chairman of the People's Republic of China.[42]

Nonetheless, in the economies of East, including China, the two modes of management continue to coexist. Rules must be invoked when lower-tier hierarchs, even properly motivated, cannot be expected to make the right decision or when the temptation to do wrong may be too strong and the consequences of a wrong decision too costly for the organization to take chances. (The extraordinary bureaucratic precautions taken in the handling of convertible foreign currencies in East are a case in point.) On the other hand, the ad hoc mode is still pushed vigorously in areas where bureaucratic decision making would be too slow and cumbersome, as in the making of many production and investment decisions.

The notion of autonomy, used imprecisely in this chapter, will be formalized in chapter 13, where it will be analyzed in the context of aggregated and disaggregated controls. We shall not reconsider the bureaucratic and ad hoc modes of decision making in our model although we suspect there may be some possibilities of formalizing these concepts within that framework.

12.6 ASSOCIATIONS

An association for an activity, as we saw earlier in this chapter, is an organization such that no one member supervises any other member for that activity. Interactions among members are based on complete or partial mutuality. An association may be embedded within a hierarchy in the form

42. For details, see Franz Schurmann, *Ideology and Organization in Communist China* (Berkeley: University of California Press, 1971).

of a coordinating committee, the members of which will have equal rights for the purpose of coordination. An association may also, as we already mentioned, be placed at the head of a complete hierarchy, as a board of directors or a politbureau. Individuals regularly interacting across enterprises (or other organizations with a common payoff), such as the salesmen of one firm and the purchasing agents of another or the directors of a number of enterprises in the same industry gathering together to discuss "common problems," may be viewed as forming an association. In the absence of any rules regulating the behavior of members, associations may be termed *informal*. The members of an association are usually bound by rules—"voting procedures"—that determine how differences in opinions will be resolved in order to reach a common decision.

An organization may be structured as an association for reaching decisions and as a hierarchy for carrying them out. This distinction in procedure is at the basis of Lenin's principle of "democratic centralism" (which, in actual Soviet practice, is more frequently adhered to in the implementation than in the decision phase). In the absence of a hierarchic structure for implementing agreements among members of an association with diverging preferences, rules are often needed to coerce members who find it disadvantageous to do their part. These rules may not be very effective unless they are enforced by an external agent such as a ruling organization.

The postwar history of the Japanese holding companies known as *zaibatsus* affords an instructive illustration of these elementary principles. When the American occupation broke up these holding companies soon after World War II, it looked as if the member companies could easily regroup as an informal association and carry on much in the old way. But this did not come to pass. As Eleanor Hadley testified in the congressional hearings on antitrust and monopoly in 1968:

> The presidents of companies which were, for the most part, formerly the designated subsidiaries of their respective combines, meet together once or twice monthly to discuss points of common interest. But while there is much "old school tie" about presidents' clubs and one can see evidences of joint activity with respect to new projects, there is clearly not the tight control of yesteryear. Presidents' clubs possess no power to compel. They can only argue and persuade.[43]

Eleanor Hadley then goes on to tell about the diverging goals and policies of the presidents represented in this informal association and the difficulty of reconciling them.

43. Eleanor Hadley, testimony, in U.S., Congress, Senate, op. cit., p. 3518. The "loose associations" described by Ms. Hadley are known as *keiretsu*. On these *keiretsu*, see also sec. 16.4.

The words "diverging of goals and policies" ought perhaps to be made more precise here since the expression may cover two situations that should be kept distinct. Goals may differ but be independent in the sense that the pursuit of goal A by individual i has no perceptible influence on the expected realization of goal B by j; or they may be in conflict, as when the pursuit of A by i lowers the expected realization of B by j. In an association where the members represent geographic regions or other nonoverlapping constituencies, as in the U.S. Congress or the British Parliament, there will be many projects submitted for approval that will be of positive value for one member without adverse effect on any other member's. In such instances members may form coalitions where i supports j's project and j supports i's. This cooperative behavior, called *log rolling*, occurs more rarely in associations of individuals with common economic interests because most economic activities are interdependent. Although in a cartel it may be to the advantage of any one member to grant price concessions, solidarity will be of benefit to all. There is usually nothing to be gained by a coalition of any subset of the members, because a price concession by any such group will normally have an adverse effect on all members' markets.

The German experience with cartels illustrates the importance of external enforcement in making price-maintenance agreements stick. In the pre-World War II period in Germany, as well as in most countries of Central Europe, the national government gave legal sanction and support to cartels. Germany was then known as a "cartel paradise."[44] After the war, the Allied occupation powers broke up these cartels and "deconcentrated" industry. Tacit agreements may here and there have taken the place of the old cartels. But until the mid-1960s, when the Federal Republic's "anti-cartel statute" of 1957 began to be interpreted in a more permissive way and certain cartelization agreements received *de facto* government support, this sort of informal collusion was not particularly effective. As Egon Sohmen explained in his testimony in the Senate hearings on concentration, German businessmen are given to spell out their contracts in the most minute detail. An informal agreement unsupported by a legally enforceable contract prescribing what each party to the agreement must do under every foreseeable contingency can, and generally will, be interpreted to each member's advantage, at the expense of the common interests of the entire group.[45]

44. Egon Sohmen's statement in ibid., p. 3449.
45. Ibid., pp. 3449–50. This comment on the difficulty of implementing tacit agreements in Germany should not be interpreted too broadly. Sohmen also testified that informal price-maintenance agreements in the U.S. steel industry were fairly effective because in this case "a tradition of loyalty to the industry as a whole . . . seems to be particularly pronounced" (p. 3444). This is one more instance when we must appeal to differences in the (initial) environment to explain why the behavior of decision makers differs among the countries we wish to compare.

In Yugoslavia, associations of enterprises in the same industry (*udruženja*) have no power over their subordinates (in contrast even to the postreform East European economies, where they generally do, *de facto* or *de jure*). Enterprises in the industry need not even be members. According to Dirlam and Plummer, the association of railway equipment manufacturers had among its tasks the streamlining of the production programs of its constituent members, the coordination of purchases of capital goods, the acquisition of patents and licenses, and the provision of facilities for joint marketing of members' products. According to a contemporary report, when the association met in November 1967 their competitive interests were so divergent that they could reach no agreement on "either specialization of output or price policy."[46]

When each member of the association heads or represents a large, multi-tiered hierarchy and must depend on information collected by individuals situated in lower tiers, the difficulties of reaching agreement on a joint program to which each participant can first subscribe and later abide are compounded. The Council for Mutual Economic Assistance of the Soviet bloc provides many illustrations of this point. The specialization agreements the council has sponsored have reaped only the most superficial and salient advantages that a more decentralized cooperation—through lateral contacts or through market pressures—might bring about.

To conclude this chapter on a broad generalization, I would argue that the *hierarchic principle* and *externally enforced rules* are alternative ways of realizing a "public good" for an organized subset of the members of a system in situations where it is to the private advantage of each member of the organization to act to the detriment of the common interest of the group. Interactions based on mutuality, furthermore, are not generally so apt to achieve an overarching goal, especially when the group is large and/or communication among members is impeded.[47] In the absence of hierarchic structure and external rules, *all* the participants must hold fast to strong values, the public expression of which, through scorn, derision, or other signs of disapproval, will discourage behavior destructive of the common good. Such is the effective use of social disapproval in certain African tribes that can shame a man or a woman into behaving properly—for instance not to violate conventional ceilings on prices. But then the distinction between formal rules and the expression of commonly held values through manifestations of approval or disapproval becomes too blurred to be meaningfully maintained.

46. Dirlam and Plummer, op. cit., p. 84.

47. The classical case where the "common good" may not be realized, even in a group limited to two individuals, is the "prisoners' dilemma." The prisoners have a common advantage in remaining silent about the crime they jointly committed. But each separately can do better by confessing than by remaining silent as long as he thinks the other prisoner is likely to confess, and implicate him, with aggravated effect if he has not already confessed.

13

Incentives and Power in Organizations

13.1 AN INTRODUCTION TO INCENTIVES

We have seen that an organization may have a pooled payoff, part or all of which may be distributed to the members, who may also derive direct benefits (e.g. "psychic income") from the activities they are engaged in. A superior in a hierarchy who is empowered to decide on the remuneration that a subordinate will obtain from the pooled payoff may establish a link between the subordinate's remuneration and the outcomes of his activities, or *performance*. If such a link is designed to steer a subordinate's efforts—the time and the mental and physical resources he brings to his work—toward the attainment of goals set by a superior, it is called a *material-incentive scheme*. Suppose the performance of subordinate i can be described by vectors y (in an appropriately defined space). Formally, we define a *material-incentive scheme* for subordinate i as a function r with a domain set R, with the property $r(y) > 0$ for all y in R and $r(y) = 0$ for all y not in R. The set R is called the *reward set*. A material-incentive scheme is part of an organization's structure and hence is endowed with a certain degree of stability. However, a subordinate's direct supervisor may not be satisfied with the outcomes induced by the subordinate's material-incentive scheme. If i fails to comply with the orders, targets, or plans that have been handed down to him by his supervisor, he may be subject to penalties. These penalties, given their ad hoc character, are not a component part of the material-incentive scheme, as we define it here.

When a subordinate pursues the goals set by his supervisor because he considers them legitimate and desirable in and of themselves, we say that he is actuated by *moral incentives*. This latter type of motivation is obviously related to the "moral loyalty" discussed earlier in connection with Japanese organizations. A moral-incentive scheme aims at building up the subordinate's feeling of loyalty to the organization, his pride in his work, or both by offering him "moral rewards" (a write-up in the wall newspaper, an official commendation, a chance to shake Chairman Mao's hand) or by influencing his values through exhortation and propaganda.

Finally, a subordinate may be motivated by the desire to gain status and to rise in the organization because of the greater remuneration he expects from a higher position, because of the "power" and prestige he attaches to such a position, or because of both. We may call these *promotion incentives*.

Whereas material incentives are normally proffered by a superior to a subordinate, promotion incentives may be strictly "subjective"—based on neither an explicit nor an implicit commitment by a superior.

13.2 CONTROL IN ORGANIZATIONS

So far we have defined the supervision relation exclusively in terms of the nominal power given to a member by the rules of an organization to issue orders to another. What is the subordinate's motive for complying with his superior's orders? What is the real "power relation" between superiors and their subordinates? Obviously the material and promotion incentives that the superior can manipulate to ensure compliance or minimize the extent of noncompliance are essential to this power, at least as long as moral incentives are weak or inexistent.

Before delving into the subject of hierarchic power, we must get a handle on the supervisor's goals or, more precisely, on his expectations regarding the performance of his supervisees. Suppose, first, that a supervisor h has only a single supervisee i. Let i's performance be represented as an n-dimensional vector y constrained to lie in a set Y. The constraints determining Y are physical, not imposed by superiors. To fix the following ideas, the n elements of y will be assumed to be either outputs or inputs, not including i's own effort, but they might also be budget items, quotas for domestic consumption and for exports, or numbers of students in a school with varying levels of proficiency.

We now introduce the set G, consisting of all the outcome vectors y "acceptable" to i's supervisor h. Every outcome vector is *acceptable* to h that does not cause him to levy any sort of "moral" or material penalties on i. The set G is called the *acceptable set* (of h for i).[1] An interpretation of G is that it represents the supervisor's satisficing set. The lower bound of G is then the class of i's outcome vectors yielding a minimum acceptable level of utility for h.

In this section we shall assume that any rewards or penalties corresponding to an outcome y are automatically handed out as soon as the outcome occurs. When h determines G while higher officials set the conditions for the distribution of rewards and hence determine R, it frequently happens that G and R do not coincide. A vector Y belonging to R may not belong to G. It may then simultaneously be rewarded by the rules of the organization and penalized by h, if only in the sense that disregarding h's orders or instructions will diminish i's chances of promotion or "make things harder for him" in the future. These

1. The notion of a supervisor's acceptable set was first introduced by Janos Kornai (op. cit., pp. 95–97).

cases, however, are presumably rare in hierarchies because (direct) supervisors normally have a say, if not a decisive voice, in both the distribution of awards and the meting out of penalties.

In this chapter we assume that a supervisee knows his supervisor's acceptable set or at least that he can predict with fair accuracy whether the likely outcome(s) of any of the actions he is seriously contemplating will be acceptable. If i believes that certain actions that he might undertake, under certain states of his environment, would produce outcomes that would not be acceptable to h, the attractiveness of these alternatives will be diminished by the disutility he associates with the expected penalties.[2]

The utility expected by i from action a will then depend on the following factors: (a) the utility or disutility he attaches to performing a regardless of outcomes, (b) the rewards he is due to receive in case the outcome of a should be in both G and R, (c) the penalties he will incur if the outcome of a turned out to be unacceptable, and (d) the probabilities that i attaches to the possible states of his environment.

The notion of "control" may be adduced to describe the effect of the imposition of G on i's decisions. If i has no other option, owing to the "physical" constraints limiting his choice of actions, but to produce in G, it would be vacuous to say that h "controls" i. Neither would the notion of control make sense if i aimed to produce in G because actions with likely outcomes in G were more satisfying to him than actions with outcomes not in G, irrespective of possible penalties or material incentives. Finally, although one might wish to extend the concept of control to encompass situations where the material-incentive scheme induced i to decide upon a course of action likely to generate outcomes in G, without regard to the penalties he might incur for not satisfying those constraints, I think it may be more fruitful for the analysis of the supervision relation to restrict the meaning of the term to the following definition: h exercises *controls* on i if i is more likely to take actions resulting in outcomes in G than he would if he could totally disregard G and the penalties for not producing in that set. If we denote by $t(y)$ the penalty function for all y not in G, then h exercises *controls* on i provided i's choice of actions in A is sensitive to changes in t or in G, the complement of the function's domain.

The controls of h on i are *loosened* when h's acceptable set is expanded in such a way that the new set G' strictly includes the old or when the penalty for at least one outcome vector y not in G is reduced (without any concomitant increase in the penalty for any other transgression). Controls are said to be *aggregated* when the set G is transformed in the following manner. Let M be a mapping from n-dimensional into q-dimensional space, where q is a number

2. For the supervisee's behavior under uncertainty, see sec. 14.1.

smaller than n.[3] By this mapping, every n-element vector y, whether feasible or not, is mapped into a q-element vector. This may be represented as $z \equiv M(y)$, where z is the aggregated vector resulting from the mapping M of y, an arbitrary n-dimensional vector. Let G^A be the set of all vectors aggregated from vectors in G by the mapping M. Since M is a mapping of vectors into a space of smaller dimensions, there may be many distinct vectors such as y and y', not necessarily belonging to G, that will map into an arbitrary vector z in G^A.[4] The set A, called the *disaggregated acceptable set under aggregated controls*, consists of all outcome vectors y that are mapped by M into arbitrary vectors in G^A.[5]

An obvious consequence of this very general type of aggregation is that it represents an unambiguous loosening of controls for i.[6] Controls are then loosened when supervisors, instead of imposing their controls on a producer's detailed output mix, decide to monitor only the value of his output or profits, *provided* that the aggregated value of any mix that was acceptable beforehand remains acceptable after the change of rules. More generally, a supervisor loosens the controls on his supervisee when he draws information about the latter's performance according to a coarser partition of the set of possible outcomes than before.[7]

In most instances h will not be able to predict i's environment or potential with sufficient accuracy to demand that his supervisee fulfill his order(s) with 100 percent accuracy. If the supervision relation is an ongoing affair and the supervisee's constraints are determined by the states of his environment subject to an appreciable variance, h will expect i to "come close most of the time" to the targets set for him.[8] G will therefore normally consist of more than one acceptable vector. In this relation the set G will contain any "average performance" of i over a period T that would be acceptable to h.

---

3. M need not necessarily be linear. If it is linear it can be represented by a $q \times n$ matrix of aggregation weights.

4. One way to see this is to recall that if the mapping is linear, the aggregation matrix is noninvertible, i.e., more than one vector in the old space will map into the same vector in the new space.

5. In set-theoretic language:

$$A = \{y | M(y) = M(g), g \in G\}.$$

6. The new set A strictly includes G, since every vector g in G must belong to A because, trivially, $M(g) = M(g)$, and because there must exist some vectors in R^n, not in G, that can be mapped into q-dimensional vectors such as z.

7. Cf. Appendix.

8. The relation among targets or orders, positive incentives (bonuses), and the fulfillment of the targets or orders in an uncertain environment has been analyzed by Michael Keren in his article "On the Tautness of Plans," *Review of Economic Studies* 39, no. 4 (1972): 469–86. In Keren's model the supervisee produces a single output. His performance depends on his effort and on a random variable representing his unique resource constraint. He is rewarded with a bonus for

Most of our applications and illustrations of the above concepts will have to do with the positive (output) elements in performance vectors. Nevertheless, we should have in mind that the limitations of supervisors on negative or input elements can be encompassed by this approach. If material inputs, for example, are distributed to a supervisee in specified quantities, these limits on inputs may be thought of as a part of the acceptable set. The alternative is to treat these limits as constraints on Y. But the incorporation of the limits in G has the advantage, from the viewpoint of the analysis of autonomy, aggregation, and decentralization, that it permits us to study theoretically the impact on G and on the autonomy of supervisees, of changes in the distribution system that would have the effect of coarsening the partition of inputs (e.g., giving supervisees greater choice with respect to the detailed assortment of their rationed inputs, as in the case of a new rule that would enable a plant to buy 1,000 tons of any kind of steel it pleased instead of 500 tons of 5-millimiter plate carbon steel and 500 tons of 8-millimiter plate of vanadium alloy as formerly). In any event it must be clear to the reader that every representation of an acceptable set in output space assumes given levels of all inputs in vectors y acceptable to h.

An example of a reward set R and of an acceptable set G in output space is given in diagram 13.1. The diagram represents the opportunities open to a supervisee producing two goods, labeled 1 and 2. The production set is drawn for given levels of inputs, a given state of the environment, and an assumed constant level of effort on the part of the supervisee (and his subordinates if any).

In the diagram, G is the acceptable set in output space and P is a plan target, or order, handed down by h. The *autonomy space* of the supervisee, denoted E, contains all feasible vectors that are also acceptable. Thus E is the intersection of G and Y. If i is rewarded for exceeding the value at prices π of plan P, set R contains all the points of Y above the line drawn through P.

---

100 percent fulfillment of his target but receives nothing more for overshooting his mark. For a given bonus and level of his input constraint, his effort and his performance are shown to depend on the level of the target set for him to fulfill. (In the absence of uncertainty he will precisely fulfill the target as long as the utility to him of the bonus-cum-effort-necessary-to-fulfill-the-target is at least as great as the utility of no-bonus-cum-no-effort.) This interdependence between targets, orders, or plans, on the one hand, and production sets, on the other, is not explicitly recognized in the approach followed in this section. One may, however, interpret the constrained production set in diagram 13.1 as the set of attainable outputs corresponding to the supervisee's effort elicited by plan P. The approach in this chapter is perhaps more appropriate if the analyst's primary concern is with the mix of outputs as it relates to the problem of coordination. Keren's, however, is the more appropriate model if we wish to study the supervisee's absolute level of performance.

In any case it should be noted that most bonus schemes, both in East and West, do reward above-target performance, although not necessarily at the same rate as just fulfilling the target. For these schemes it may make sense to assume that the supervisee maximizes a linear function of his outputs.

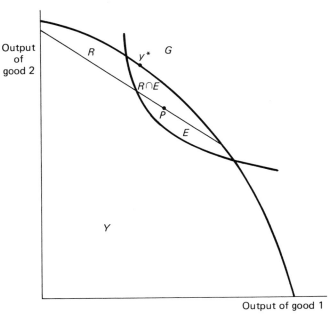

Diagram 13.1

The maximum attainable value of $r(y)$ at prices π occurs at y^*, a vector that happens in this case to be in G.[9]

13.3 Relative Powers of Supervisors and Supervisees

The *power* of h over i may be defined as the ability of h "to get i to do something that i would not otherwise do."[10] If incentives are set by one of h's superiors, we must conclude in the case illustrated in diagram 13.1 that h has no power over i, since the performance vector y^* maximizing i's objective function happens to lie in the acceptable set G and hence no power is required for h to get i to do what he would like him to. We shall suppose, in the following discussion of power relations, that i would *not* wish to "produce" in G in the absence of ad hoc penalties levied by h for noncompliance (in case y^* falls outside G).

We first define the *amount* of h's power over i as "the net increase in the

9. If h has more than one supervisee, say a number v_h of them, what he expects from i may depend on the performance of i's $(v_h - 1)$ cosupervisees. For details, see sec. 14.3.

10. Robert Dahl's definition cited in John Harsanyi, "Measurement of Social Power," in M. Shubik, ed., *Game Theory and Related Approaches to Social Behavior* (New York: Wiley, 1964), p. 184.

probability of i's actually performing some action a, as a result of h's using his means of power against i," where these *means of power* are the specific actions by which h can influence i's behavior.[11]

As John Harsanyi points out, however, h may incur costs in attempting to influence i (e.g., the rewards he must pay out if i submits to h's influence); also, i may have to consider the costs of refusing to do what h wants him to do. If the opportunity cost to h of using his power is low and the opportunity cost to i of not yielding to h's influence is high, the amount of h's power over i will be relatively great.[12]

Let us try to apply these definitions to describe the influence of a supervisor over a supervisee in an organization nominally structured as a hierarchy, in a situation where the supervisee would not "produce" in the supervisor's acceptable set if no means of power were applied to make him do so. If there is only one possible environment e in period t—if in other words i knows his environment with certainty—he will "comply" (i.e., produce a vector y in G) or not, depending on whether the utility of the reward for complying is greater than the disutility for not complying. If the environment is uncertain, he will seek to maximize his expected utility on the basis of the expected outcomes of his action(s). If the same order(s) were issued in a series of periods, the utility-maximizing behavior of i might lead to compliance in a proportion p of the periods and to noncompliance in a proportion $(1 - p)$.

There are some states of i's environment, as h perceives them, that justify noncompliance, whereas other states do not. Obviously i will enlarge his options and be potentially better off if he has some control over the information filtering to h, if for example he can supply h with information ("excuses") showing that his environment really did not allow him to comply (because his machinery had broken down or because he did not get the materials that he was supposed to buy from another member l). It is also evident that the coarser h's information structure happens to be, the easier it will be for i to find excuses or pretexts for his failure to fulfill h's orders. By controlling h's information, i has acquired some measure of power over h because, by varying the information transmitted to h, he can influence the rewards that h will deal out to him.

But, as long as h is strictly applying the rules of the incentive scheme, i has no *bargaining power* over him. For i to acquire this bargaining power, the rules must be relaxed to allow h to decide whether or not to reward or penalize i at his discretion. i can then point out to h the *costs* of his alternative actions. ("If you denounce me to the FBI for stealing government documents, I'll tell them you have been embezzling for years." "If you fire me for disobeying

---

11. Ibid.
12. Ibid., pp. 189–92.

your orders, you will have to find another qualified computer programmer, and you know how scarce *they* are!").

According to one model of such a *bilateral power* situation, which makes the heroic assumption that the utility of h may be compared with the utility of i, the amount of h's power over i with respect to an action (say, a recurring order $\bar{a}$ that must be fulfilled sufficiently well to land the performance vector in G) will be equal to the increase in probability that i will perform $\bar{a}$, compared to the situation where the rewards and penalties were absent. It is given by the formula

$$\Delta p = p_2 - p_1 = \tfrac{1}{2} \left(\frac{r + t}{x} - \frac{t^* - r^*}{x^*} \right)$$

subject to the condition

$$\Delta p \leqslant 1 - p_1.$$

In this formula, the probability of the supervisee's performing $\bar{a}$ is p_1 when rewards and penalties are absent and p_2 when they are present; x is the disutility to i of performing $\bar{a}$; r is the value to i in utility units of the reward he would get for performing $\bar{a}$; t is the disutility to i of the penalty he would incur for not performing $\bar{a}$; x^* is the utility to h of having i perform $\bar{a}$; t^* is the utility cost to h of imposing a penalty on i in case of nonperformance; and r^* is the utility loss to h of the reward proffered to i.

The first quotient in parentheses, $(r + t)/x$, represents the opportunity cost to i of noncompliance (lost reward plus penalty incurred) per unit of disutility of $\bar{a}$. The term $(t^* - r^*)/x^*$ is the opportunity cost to h of retaliation in case of noncompliance (utility costs of imposing the penalty minus the utility of the reward economized) per unit of utility to h of having $\bar{a}$ performed. The solution of the formula is then a halfway compromise between the most disadvantageous outcomes ("concession points") for h and i.[13]

A self-evident implication of the model is that if the utility cost to h of imposing a penalty for noncompliance is very high (e.g., if h fires i, he will be denounced for embezzlement or he will not be able to find a suitable replacement), the amount of his power will be low. A curious and rather counterintuitive inference is that the higher the utility cost to h of rewarding i for compliance, the greater will be the amount of his power over his supervisee.

An interesting point to observe in applying these notions empirically is that the bargaining between supervisors and supervisees in the centrally directed economies of the Soviet Union and Eastern Europe does not occur mainly *after* the orders (or plans) have been issued but before, when the plan is being worked up. This may be because, once the plan has been promulgated, it is to the advantage of supervisees to try to fulfill them, seeing that both the

---

13. The formula corresponds to a Zeuthen–Nash solution (Harsanyi, op. cit., pp. 201–02).

bonuses for fulfillment and the penalties for nonfulfillment (possible demotion, loss of political power, and so on) are relatively high.[14] Bargaining goes on in the process of setting the plan because the opportunity costs to a supervisee, such as the manager of an enterprise, of not complying with his supervisor's orders ("Set as challenging and 'mobilizing' a plan as you can, making explicit all the 'reserves' you can exploit during the year") are very small. And a principal reason for the weakness of h's power over i in this instance is that i holds the information trump card: h simply cannot tell—his information structure is too coarse and he is too dependent on i for conveying detailed information to him—whether the plan figures he proposes to i are really as difficult to fulfill as i claims. He will be too uncertain of i's real potentialities to punish him by imposing "discontinuous penalties" such as dismissal or demotion. Moreover, in most of these economies he has no rewards to proffer to i for submitting a challenging "counterplan."[15]

If the entire planning process is considered, the task of actually measuring the amount of power of a supervisor over his supervisees would seem to be insuperable. Nevertheless, the concepts and ideas that have been developed in the foregoing pages can pinpoint the critical elements in a bilateral-power situation and suggest how the power relation would be modified if one of these elements changed in an ascertainable manner. This may already be an important step forward in the analysis of the real power structure of organizations.

An element that was present in all our discussions of the power of supervisors over their supervisees was the information available to both. John Kenneth Galbraith in his book *The New Industrial State* develops at great length a particular aspect of the relation of information to power. He argues essentially that, as a result of the technological revolution of recent years, the employees of large corporations in West who possess the scientific and technical knowledge that is essential to the progress of their enterprise are at the power nub of their organization. The "techno-structure" as Galbraith calls it is virtually beyond the control of its nominal superiors.[16]

A remarkable illustration of Galbraith's conjecture is offered by large

14. See the discussion of Keren's model in n. 8.

15. An interesting feature of the Czechoslovak economic reform of 1958–59 was that it attempted to make it more advantageous to the management of an enterprise to overfulfill "mobilizing" than soft plans. The idea was that if an enterprise in its finally approved plan raised the profit targets that it had been asked to attain in the initial version of the plan ("control figures"), it was allowed to keep a larger percentage of these profits for its own use than if it had accepted the earlier version without "raising the ante." One effect of the reform was to shift the object of bargaining to the "norm" determining the percentages of planned profits retained by the enterprise out of the initial and augmented targets. This is also a feature of the most recent Soviet incentive reform. For a formalization of this feature, see M. Weitzman, "The New Soviet Incentive Model," Working Paper No. 141, MIT, Department of Economics, Oct. 1974.

16. See esp. chap. 8 of Galbraith's *The New Industrial State* (New York: Houghton Mifflin, 1967).

modern Japanese corporations where the growing real power of technicians and scientists has begun to force the breakdown of the ringi system described in the last chapter. Gradually the technostructure is acquiring a rank and status that correspond to the real power of its members in the corporation, irrespective of their seniority.

In the Soviet economic administration and in the American corporation, officials in a supervisory position by and large have sufficient means of power to channel the behavior of their subordinates in desired directions. Plans and budgets in both types of organizations seriously influence the current decisions that will be taken in the period to which these forecasts apply because each individual in the hierarchy is made responsible for fulfilling a specific part of the plan or budget. Thus, in the Soviet Union every part of the plan is said to be "addressed" to a certain individual responsible for its implementation. In many developing countries in contrast, national economic plans "hang in the air": there is no one-to-one relation between the plans' component parts and the members of the government's hierarchy. Or, if plans are "addressed," the supervisors responsible for a component part do not have sufficient power over their supervisees in the governmental hierarchy to compel them to work toward their fulfillment: the system makes no provision for material rewards, and penalties cannot be invoked, for fear of transgressing civil-service regulations. At times also, the fulfillment of the plans depends on the good will of provincial authorities, over whom for constitutional reasons the federal authorities have little or no power.

13.4 Incentives Once Again

Plant superintendents in many large corporations in the United States receive bonuses for reducing expenditure below "standard costs." Managers of enterprises in the Soviet Union in the early 1960s were rewarded for fulfilling and overfulfilling their gross-value-of-output plans. In the Cuba of Fidel Castro and the China of Mao Tse-tung, moral incentives are said to play vital role. Can these different ways of stimulating the most responsible members of subordinate hierarchies be traced to "ideological preconceptions"? Or are there also environmental differences among these economies that might help to account for these disparate systems?

As we have already seen, in Cuba and China, where the official ideology is all embracing and intrusive, ideology not only influences the choice of system characteristics but also reinforces them once they are instituted as a result of the inculcation of "proper attitudes" and values in the minds of participants via education, the press, and all other communication media. Thanks to these value-molding campaigns, moral incentives are turned into more powerful stimulants of proper behavior than if people had been left to themselves. Leaving aside for the moment these ideological considerations, we now list the conditions that are necessary for a system of material incentives to goad individuals with decision-making powers to exert their utmost efforts in the pursuit of outcomes desired by their superiors.

1. The individual subject to an incentive system must have a significant impact on the outcomes that are rewarded or penalized. If his environment is not predictable with certainty, this condition implies that his decisions and his efforts must be capable of raising significantly the probability of occurrence of the desired outcomes.

2. The superior in charge of meting out the rewards and penalties to his subordinate in question must be capable of monitoring the outcomes accurately. Under conditions of uncertainty he should, in making his awards and imposing his penalties, be able to discriminate to some extent at least between the contribution of the subordinate and the chance factors affecting his performance. Otherwise, the individual who is being "stimulated" will suffer fluctuations in his income (or other payoff) that he will not know how to relate to his effort or to the wisdom of his decisions. If he is averse to risk, as we would expect him to be in many situations, he will be worse off than if his income had been steady, and his efforts are likely to slacken.[17] In Soviet parlance a poorly functioning incentive system that did not fulfill this condition would be "demobilizing."

3. To be a decisive factor in his motivation, the rewards and penalties offered to an individual to prod him toward desirable outcomes must have a utility or disutility to him sufficiently different from the utility or disutility of the payoff he would expect to receive irrespective of his performance.

Whether or not these conditions can be fulfilled and, if they can be, by what sort of material-incentive system, may help to explain observed differences in the systems, or at least those differences that should not be attributed to ideological factors.

The decision space of the individual subject to incentives frequently offers the single best explanation for the type of material-incentive system with the greatest currency in an economic system. A plant superintendent in an American multiplant corporation can exert himself to reduce unit costs, but the other key variables influencing profits are not under his control. For the most part his fixed technology determines the quality of his product(s); his output is closely correlated with sales, which in turn are affected by advertising and marketing efforts that lie beyond the sphere of his responsibilities. As was mentioned, his incentives often depend on his ability to reduce unit costs. On the other hand, bonuses for promoting sales, increasing profits, or both are commonly given to officials at division headquarters who do have influence on these variables.[18]

17. The effect of greater uncertainty in his constraints is to cause a supervisee to slacken his effort, as Keren shows under the simplified assumptions of his model (op. cit., p. 21).

18. Information obtained from employees of several multiplant corporations in the United States.

In the prereform Soviet economy, where the centralized distribution of material inputs was fairly comprehensive and enterprise managers could do little else than assemble the inputs at their disposal to produce as much of the products desired by their superiors as possible, it made good sense to tie incentives to the volume of output and its composition (the "assortment plan"). By the same token the shift in incentives in the direction of sales and profits has its parallel, at least in the East European economies where reforms have proceeded further than in the Soviet Union, in a gradual loosening of the system for distributing materials and equipment to enterprises.

In contemporary Cuba the primary reliance on moral incentives cannot wholly be explained by the aversion of pure revolutionaries to "materialism." This explanation might have been valid in the first two or three years after the revolution, but by 1963–64 there were definite signs that Cuba was moving toward the adoption of a classical Soviet-type system with centrally co-ordinated yearly plans governing "basic" production decisions and material incentives geared to the fulfillment of these plans. About 1965, however, at the time Castro and Che Guevara opted for a new economic policy focusing on agricultural development, serious efforts to coordinate plans *ex ante* seem to have been abandoned along with the system of material incentives that was meant to bolster the execution of these plans. Management of the economy "por la libre"—that is, in a freewheeling manner with central decisions responding to the pressures of the moment—appeared to hold sway again in 1967–68, much as it had at the beginning of the decade.[19] In a dispatcher-like system of ad hoc management of the economy, where the yearly plans have little or no operational significance, the environment of enterprise managers is likely to be extremely uncertain.[20] From day to day a manager may not know what his production tasks will be and with what materials he will carry them out. To make his income dependent on the volume of output in the annual plan, prior to the revisions that it will most probably go through during the course of the year, would be at cross-purposes with the realization of the latest directives. To tie incentives to each new set of tasks may well be impractical. Given the state of extreme uncertainty under which managers must operate, it is highly improbable that their superiors in the ministry would have the information in fine enough detail to judge whether gains in output, productivity, or profits resulted from the efforts and judicious decisions of managers or from favorable factors in their environment. Material incentives, under these circumstances, could only be "demobilizing." They would be more likely to discourage subordinates than to prod them on to greater effort.

---

19. For details see A. Lataste Hoffer, *Cuba: Hacia una nueva economia politica del socialismo?* (Santiago, Chile: Editorial Universitaria 1968), pp. 50–51.

20. On the dispatcher system, see chap. 8, p. 107.

Moral (or promotion) incentives offer the advantage of goading subordinates to the pursuit of their superiors' goals, at least as they are able to see them. The success of these incentives does not depend as much as does a material-incentive system on the ability of superiors to send their subordinates accurate signals for the goals they pursue in the form of success criteria that the subordinates can then latch onto in applying their own efforts, come what may. A manager sensitive to moral incentives follows the "spirit" of his superiors' decisions rather than their "letter." That the arbitrariness of these decisions and their possible inconsistency may eventually demobilize the best-intentioned and most zealous managers is another matter.

In fulfilling the third condition for a successful material-incentive system—the availability of rewards that will offer subordinates sufficient motivation—both the Chinese and Cuban economies would have problems. In these two countries the equity desideratum militates against excessive differentiation of incomes, including bonuses from incentive funds. On the other hand, because rationed consumer goods, obtained at a relatively small monetary cost, form a substantial part of citizens' real incomes in Cuba and in China, only relatively *large* money bonuses (or penalties) will normally have a strong impact on individuals' motivation. In China, moreover, resources are so limited that giving out large bonuses to reward superior performance might jeopardize the distribution of goods required to sustain the minimum rations or living standards of other employees.

Although these considerations only go partway toward explaining the adoption of one or another of the possible incentive schemes that might be devised to get subordinates to do what their superiors want them to do, they may point to questions worth raising and they suggest hypotheses that might be tested in trying to account for these different systems.

14

Autonomy of Subordinates, Aggregation of Controls, and Decentralization of Organizations

14.1 AUTONOMY OF SUPERVISEES UNDER UNCERTAINTY

In this chapter we continue our formal analysis of supervisor–supervisee relations under somewhat restrictive assumptions. The reader will judge whether the gain in analytical precision is worth the loss in generality due to the choice of simplifying assumptions.

In the previous chapter we described the behavior of a supervisee faced with his supervisor's demands as if he knew with certainty not only the outcomes of his own actions but whether or not a given outcome would be acceptable to his supervisor. In other words we reasoned as if both the attainable set Y and the acceptable set G were known to the supervisee with certainty. In typical situations, however, the supervisee will be uncertain about the outcomes he can "get away with" without suffering a penalty (or at least disapproval), just as the supervisor will be uncertain about the attainable outcomes of his supervisee's actions. (It may not be too unrealistic to assume that a supervisee will know his own attainable set.) If supervisee i is uncertain about G, he will not necessarily always act in such a way as to produce an acceptable performance vector y. We must therefore explicitly introduce a penalty that will be levied if y does not happen to be in the true acceptable set G, denoted $\bar{G}$. To simplify our exposition we assume that the penalty, denoted t, is the same for any unacceptable performance and that the reward set R is known to i and contains $\bar{G}$.

If $r(y)$ and t are taken to be positive and negative amounts of money, respectively, the utility of i, given outcome y, may be written $u[\omega(y, \bar{G})]$, where $\omega(y,\bar{G}) = r(y) > 0$, for all y in $\bar{G}$, and $\omega(y,\bar{G}) = t$, for any y not in $\bar{G}$.

The *autonomy space* of i is defined, under uncertainty, as the set of attainable vectors y in the true acceptable set $\bar{G}$. This set, the intersection (if it exists) of $\bar{G}$ and Y, is denoted $\bar{E}$.

The only information i is supposed to have about $\bar{G}$ is y^p, a plan, an n-dimensional vector with positive elements for output targets and negative elements for input quotas.[1] If we let G stand for the set of all G that i believes may have some probability of being the true acceptable set of h, then, for any y^P he will maximize his expected utility by choosing a decision rule $\alpha(y^P)$ for which the following expression attains a maximum:

$$\sum_{G \in G} u(\omega[G, \alpha(y^P)]) \phi (G|y^P),$$

where $\phi (G|y^P)$ is i's (subjective) conditional probability, given y^P, that the true acceptable set is a particular G in G.

The program $y^E[\equiv \alpha(y^P)]$ is then a vector in Y maximizing the above conditional expected payoff for a given y^P.[2] The expected utility of i, upon the choice of y^E, may then be written $E(u[\omega(G, y^E)])$, where it is understood that this expected value depends on the conditional probabilities $\phi(G|y^P)$ for all G in G.

Consider now the utility of i's payoff in the absence of *all* constraints on acceptability. This utility will equal $u[r(y^*)]$, where y^* is the attainable program in R for which the reward $r(y^*)$ has at least as great a utility to i as any other program in Y. (There is no need to introduce an expectation operator in this case, since by assumption there is no uncertainty about either Y or R.)

A plausible measure of the *relative autonomy of a supervisee* is given by the ratio

$$\frac{E \, u[\omega(G, y^E)]}{u[r(y^*)]}.$$

This is the ratio of the expected utility of i under controls by h to his utility in the absence of such controls. It should be observed that the autonomy space of i may become larger when h loosens his controls on i without increasing the latter's relative autonomy, if, given y^P, it happens that the loosened controls do not allow him to choose a program with higher expected utility.

1. Note that y^P may be only a set of output orders (in which case all input elements are zero) or only a set of allotments or limits on consumption of inputs (in which all output elements are zero).

2. Suppose there were also uncertainty about i's production set in the sense that various states in i's environment might occur that would generate different attainable sets. Let e be a state in E, some elements of which are taken to be constraints on acceptability (i.e., constraints generating a particular G in G), others constraints on the attainable set. Then, on receipt of y^P, i may maximize:

$$\sum_{e \in E} u(\omega[e, \alpha(y^P)] \phi (e|y^P).$$

To derive operational propositions, we must now specialize our reward function and make some further simplifying assumptions. Rewards will henceforth be proportional to the value of the outcome vector expressed in (nonnegative) "incentive prices" π_1 to π_n. Thus, if we let π stand for a vector of these prices, the reward for an outcome vector y in R will be $w\pi y$, where w is a number between 0 and 1.[3] This specialization of the reward function still allows us to deal with incentive schemes that proffer a given reward for just fulfilling the plan y^P or otherwise satisfying h and then provide supplementary benefits to i in proportion to the value of the outcome vector at incentive prices. (Note that if incentive prices for inputs are set at zero, the scheme rewards only output gains; on the other hand if the incentive prices of the outputs are zero, we have a cost-reduction reward scheme. When both input and output prices are positive, the supervisee is rewarded for earning profits, provided prices π are also the prices at which the products are sold and variable inputs are bought.)

The simplifying assumptions are: (1) The effort exerted by i is the same for any action maximizing expected utility (whether constrained by acceptability conditions or not). (2) The utility of i is strictly proportional to the expected *net reward* (the gross expected reward minus any expected value of penalties).

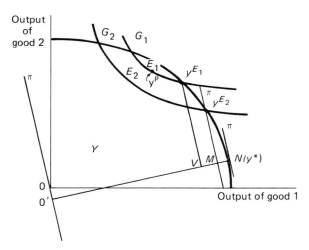

Diagram 14.1

3. The transpose sign transforming the row vector y into the column vector y^T is omitted throughout this and the following chapters. Thus πy means

$$\sum_{j=1}^{n} \pi_j y_j,$$

where j is the jth element of both π and y.

In view of the last assumption, if i maximizes his expected net reward, he will also be maximizing his expected utility.

An example limited to two goods is illustrated in output space in diagram 14.1 (for fixed levels of all inputs). Parallel lines, with a slope equal to the ratio of π_2 to π_1, have been drawn through the origin, y^{E_1}, and y^{E_2}, and the tangent to Y at N. In the absence of all restrictions on acceptability, i would produce y^* at N. There are only two possible states of G in $\overset{\frown}{G}$: If h is "tough," he will impose penalties on all y not in G_1; if he is "soft," he will be content with any y in G_2.[4] Under certainty, y^{E_1} maximizes πy on Y under the acceptability constraints set by G_1, and y^{E_2} maximizes πy on Y under constraints set by G_2. Suppose i, aiming to maximize his conditional expected utility, given y^P, chooses y^{E_1}. He will obtain the same payoff $w\pi y^{E_1}$, regardless of whether G_1 or G_2 is the true acceptability set $\bar{G}$. If he chooses y^{E_2} he will receive $w\pi y^{E_2}$ if G_2 is the true $\bar{G}$, and he will be penalized by having to pay the sum t if it is not. Which of the choices is better will depend on

$$w\pi y^{E_1} \gtrless (w\pi y^{E_2})\phi(G_2) + t\phi(G_1), \qquad (14.1)$$

where $\phi(G_2)$ and $\phi(G_1)$ are the probabilities that i attaches to G_2 and G_1 being the true states of $\overset{\frown}{G}$, respectively.[5] We observe that the ratio of the rewards under certainty for y^{E_1} and y^{E_2} equals $\pi y^{E_1}/\pi y^{E_2}$, which in turn is expressed by the ratio $0'V/0'M$ in the diagram. If we set $t = 0$ in equation 14.1, we see that y^{E_2} will not maximize i's expected net reward unless the probability of G_2 is *at least* equal to $0'V/0'M$. If t is not insignificant and the probability of G_1 is substantial, it will pay i to play safe and choose y^{E_1}.[6] Since his expected payoff will be $w\pi y^{E_1}$, his relative autonomy will be $w\pi y^{E_1}/w\pi y^* = 0'V/0'N$ (assuming πy^* differs from zero).

14.2 RELATIVE AUTONOMY AND AGGREGATION OF CONTROLS

In this section we ignore the supervisee's uncertainty about his supervisor's acceptable set. This does not seriously undermine the realism (or such realism as we can still lay claim to) of the analysis, since we can define y^E as the program maximizing the expected net reward over all G in $\overset{\frown}{G}$ and then draw

---

4. G_2 of course includes G_1.

5. To simplify the notation, y^P, the condition on which the probabilities of G_1 and G_2 depend, has been omitted from the expressions for these probabilities. It is assumed that $t \leqslant 0$. The formula implies that when $t = 0$, i gets his reward when he produces y^{E_2} and the only acceptable set is G_1.

6. It should be evident that no performance vector other than y^{E_1} or y^{E_2} will come under consideration to maximize i's expected reward. Any y on the arc between y^{E_1} and y^{E_2}, for instance, will have the same (negative) payoff t if G_1 is the true $\bar{G}$ and a smaller expected net reward than y^{E_2} if G_2 is correct. This line of argument suggests that there will always be a certainty equivalent to the choice of y^E. That is, there will be a particular G^* in $\overset{\frown}{G}$ such that the program $\bar{y}^E$ maximizing the expected net reward on Y will also maximize πy for all y belonging simultaneously to Y and G^*.

the acceptable set *G for which* y^E *is a maximizer for* π *on* Y.[7] It will then follow that any increase in net reward above πy^E due to the aggregation of controls from G to a larger acceptable set A will also increase the expected net reward under uncertainty.

In the last chapter we defined the aggregation of controls in terms of a mapping from n- unto q-dimensional space, where q was a smaller number than n. We now investigate the effects of the aggregation of controls on a supervisee's relative autonomy under the assumption that the mappings are linear.

Consider again supervisee i reporting his daily performance y to his supervisor in terms of an n-dimensional nomenclature, where the n elements may comprise such factors as the production of goods or the performance of certain activities. Suppose the rules of the organization are now changed to permit i to submit his reports less frequently, to average them over a longer period, or to consolidate the n elements of y into a smaller vector of, say, q elements (where $q < n$). These changes in the monitoring system will have the effect of loosening the controls on i, provided (1) h's acceptable set in the original nomenclature remains the same and (2) h is willing to accept any performance vector, expressed in the new nomenclature or averaged over several periods, that is "equivalent" to a vector that would have been acceptable in the old reporting system. If, for example, y_t was in G before the change, any average $\bar{y}_T$ over the new reporting period T or any q-dimensional vector with the same "aggregate value" as y_t will be equivalent to this vector.[8]

Two vectors y_t and y_t' have the same aggregate value given aggregation weights λ (a vector of elements λ_1 to λ_n), if and only if $\Lambda y_t = \Lambda y_t'$ for some aggregation matrix Λ generated by the partition of λ. These vectors are then said to be *equivalent under aggregation*.

An example of matrix Λ generated from a partitioning of λ might be

$$
\begin{matrix}
\lambda_1^1 \ldots \lambda_{n_1}^1 & 0 \ldots 0 & \ldots 0 & \ldots 0 \\
0 \ldots 0 & \lambda_1^2 \ldots \lambda_{n_2}^2 & \ldots 0 & \ldots 0 \\
\vdots & \vdots & \ddots & \\
0 \ldots 0 & 0 \ldots 0 & \ldots \lambda_1^q & \ldots \lambda_{n_q}^q
\end{matrix}
$$

7. We know that such a G in $\mathbf{G}$ will exist by the argument on certainty equivalence of the preceding footnote.

8. This is a fairly strong assumption. If the supervisor's utility loss due to i's choosing a program y outside his actual acceptable set $\bar{G}$ were large enough, he might choose to tighten up his acceptability conditions under aggregated controls to the point of rejecting some programs that would have been acceptable under disaggregated controls. Whether or not he will do so may also depend on the disutility to h of imposing penalties on i (see sec. 13.3). My conjecture is that if, for a given set of aggregation prices λ, maximizers for π on A were worth more at these prices than y^E (we shall soon see under what conditions this will obtain), then the (tightened up) aggregation of controls that would be optimal from the point of view of h would still leave i better off than under disaggregated controls.

In the above matrix $\lambda_j^d (j = 1, \ldots, n_d)$ is the jth element of the dth subvector of λ $(d = 1, \ldots, q)$, and the q subvectors of λ are generated by the appropriate partition of the nomenclature of λ. There are of course many ways of partitioning a vector of n elements into q subvectors, and there will be a different aggregation matrix for each such partition.

The new acceptable set A may be defined, as in the more general case discussed in chapter 13, as the set of all y such that $\Lambda y = \Lambda g$, where g is any arbitrary vector in G. A maximizer for π on A is denoted y^A. Since all vectors in G satisfy the definition of A, it follows that G is included in A, and $\pi y^A \geqslant \pi y^E$. The relative autonomy of i cannot be less than what it was before. The interesting question is, Under what conditions will aggregation *increase* the supervisee's relative autonomy?

Before turning to this question, we note that the elements of the aggregation vector λ may be the prices of the corresponding goods (if the elements of y are inputs or outputs), but they may, and often will, be "quasi-prices" where aggregation is effected by adding the quantities or the numbers of different items produced or consumed, or where activities are summed as if they were identical (e.g., instead of reporting on his individual trips, the supervisee submits the number of miles he traveled for the organization, the number of customers he visited, or, even more simply, the number of his trips). It is easy to see that "averaging performance over a period T" may also be viewed as a form of aggregation—from a vector of Tn elements to one of n elements, where T is the number of reports that had to be made before averaging was allowed.[9]

We again assign a positive sign to an output element of y entering i's reward function with a positive weight and a negative element to inputs or other elements entering the function with a negative weight. As before, the set E, the intersection of G and Y, is assumed to be nonempty. A minimizer for λ on the set G is denoted y^m, (i.e., $\lambda y^m \leqslant \lambda y$ for all y in G).

It greatly facilitates the analysis if we can make the reasonable assumption that a performance vector y whose elements are all at least as great algebraically as those of another vector y' in G must also be in G. In other words, if other elements of y and y' are equal, h will never reject y because the absolute quantity of one of its outputs is too large or of one of its inputs too small relative to the corresponding elements of y'. We also assume, for use in the case of partial aggregation, that h's preferences are such that the acceptability conditions in each subspace d $(d = 1, \ldots, q)$ can be treated independently or, to be more specific, that G can be represented

---

9. A somewhat different situation arises when reports, instead of being averaged over a period, are requested at more distant intervals or when performance is sampled more or less at random by the supervisor. I have not analyzed these variants in detail but I conjecture that, properly interpreted in terms of probabilities and expectations, both these types of change in the reporting system would have the effect of loosening the controls on supervisees.

as the Cartesian product of the acceptable sets in each subspace $(G \equiv \prod_{d}^{q} G_d)$.

These assumptions allow us to prove the following propositions *under conditions where aggregation weights λ are identical with the price weights π in the supervisee's objective function.*

    1. When performance vectors are aggregated from n elements to one, every maximizer y^* for π on Y must be in A, which implies that $\pi y^A = \pi y^*$.

    2. When performance vectors are aggregated from n elements to q $(n > q > 1)$, either at least one maximizer y^* for π is in G and $\pi y^E = \pi y^A = \pi y^*$ or y^* is not in G and $\pi y^* \geqslant \pi y^A > \pi y^E$.[10]

We conclude from these propositions that, when incentive and aggregation prices are identical, the loosening of controls via the aggregation of reported outcomes necessarily permits supervisees to achieve greater relative autonomy, provided their relative autonomy was not complete to begin with.

So much for the case where incentive prices are identical to aggregation weights in the reporting system. In most organizations we would expect these two price systems to differ, if only because aggregation by tonnage or other quantity indicators is frequently used when the items to be aggregated have basic characteristics in common and/or are jointly produced (e.g., carbon

---

    10. In the case of aggregation from n to 1 we have: (1) y^m is a vector in G (since it is a minimizer for λ on E, a subset of G); (2) $\pi y^* \geqslant \pi y^m$ (by the definition of y^*); (3) $\lambda y^* \geqslant \lambda y^m$ (since, by assumption, $\pi = \lambda$); (4) by the monotonicity assumption, there must exist some vector $y^{\bar{m}}$ in G such that $y^{\bar{m}} \geqslant y^m$, with the property $\lambda y^* = \lambda y^{\bar{m}}$. Hence y^* must be in A (by the definition of that set).

    In the case of aggregation from n to q, it is assumed that no product in any subspace d is used as an input in the production of any product belonging to another subspace. Let f_d be an allocation to the dth group of products of the f exogenous factors available, and let $(f_1, \ldots, f_d, \ldots, f_q)$ be the efficient allocation of these factors generating y^E, a maximizer for π on E. In each subspace d, the allocation defines an attainable set $Y^d(f_d)$ $(d = 1, \ldots, q)$. Clearly, y^{dE}, the subvector of y^E in the dth subspace, must belong to $Y^d(f_d)$ and to G^d, and hence to $E^d \equiv Y^d \cap G^d$, where G^d has been assumed independent of $G^{d'}(d' \neq d; d' = 1, \ldots, q)$. Furthermore, y^{dE} maximizes $\pi^d y^d$ for all y^d in E^d. Let $\bar{y}^d$ maximize $\pi^d y^d$ for all y^d in $Y^d(f_d)$. Then $\pi^d \bar{y}^d \geqslant \pi^d y^{dE}$ since $E^d \subset Y^d(f_d)$.

    (§) Suppose $\pi^d \bar{y}^d > \pi^d y^{dE}$. Let y^{dm} minimize $\lambda^d y^d$ on G^d. We now define A^d as $\{y^d | \lambda^d y^d \geqslant \lambda^d y^{dm}\}$. By virtue of the assumed identity of π and λ and of the fact that y^{dE} belongs to G and hence to A^d, $\lambda^d \bar{y}^d > \lambda^d y^{dE} \geqslant \lambda^d y^{dm}$. This proves that $\bar{y}^d$ belongs to A^d. We now construct a vector $\bar{y}$ with $\bar{y}^d$ in the dth subspace and the elements of y^E in the remaining $q - 1$ subspaces. Since $\pi^d \bar{y}^d > \pi^d y^{dE}$, $\pi \bar{y} > \pi y^E$. But $\bar{y}$ also belongs to A because $\bar{y}^d$ is in A^d and every other subvector $y^{d'}$ is in $G^{d'}(d' \neq d; d' = 1, \ldots, q)$. We have then found a vector acceptable upon aggregation with a higher value at price π than y^E. Since $\pi y^* \geqslant \pi y^A \geqslant \pi \bar{y}$, we conclude for this case that $\pi y^* \geqslant \pi y^A > \pi y^E$.

    (§§). Suppose $\pi^d \bar{y}^d = \pi^d y^{dE}$ in every subspace d $(d = 1, \ldots, q)$. Hence, for every d, $\pi^d y^{dE} \geqslant \pi^d y^d$, for all y^d in $Y^d(f_d)$. The acceptability constraints G^d have no influence on the choice of a maximizer for π^d in any of the attainable sets for the q subspaces. If $(f_1, \ldots, f_q)$ was an efficient allocation for y^E, it must also be efficient for y^*, a maximizer for π on Y in the absence of these constraints. Then y^* is identical with a vector $\bar{\bar{y}}$ made up of $\bar{y}^d$ in subspace d and $\bar{y}^{d'}$ in every other subspace $(d' \neq d; d' = 1, \ldots, q)$. Thus $\pi y^* = \pi \bar{\bar{y}} = \pi y^E$, and y^* is in G.

steels of different shapes and flame coals of different sizes), even though they may have substantially different sales or transfer prices. This is often the observed case in the industrial sectors of centrally directed economies in East.

We shall focus on situations where the unconstrained maximizer y^* for incentive prices π is unacceptable, whether h collects information about i's performance in disaggregated or in aggregated terms. In symbolic terms, y^* is neither in G nor in A. We begin by considering aggregation of vectors from n elements to a scalar. We assume Y, the set of feasible vectors for i, to be convex.[11] It is easy to show under this condition that, if $\lambda y^E > \lambda y^m$, where, as before, y^E maximizes πy on E and y^m minimizes λy on E, then y^A, the vector maximizing πy on A, must be worth more at prices π than y^E. Hence i, as a result of this particular aggregation of controls, must enjoy some gain in autonomy. This proposition becomes self-evident if we have in mind that every convex combination of y^E and y^* with the weight on y^* greater than zero must be worth more at prices π than y^E. Since y^E, by assumption, must be an interior point of the half space defined by the hyperplane λy through y^m, there must be some convex combinations of y^E and y^* in the neighborhood of y^E that are worth more at prices π than y^E.[12]

A stronger proposition providing a measure of the minimum gain in autonomy can be constructed. The difference $(w\pi y^* - w\pi y^E)$ may be thought of as the amount of payoff forgone by i due to the imposition of G compared to the unconstrained situation. The difference $(w\pi y^A - w\pi y^E)$ is the increment in payoff due to the imposition of aggregated instead of disaggregated controls. The ratio $(\pi y^A - \pi y^E)/(\pi y^* - \pi y^E)$ is then clearly a measure of the *relative gain* in autonomy due to the aggregation of controls. Using information limited to y^*, y^m, and y^E, we can at least devise a (lower bound) approximation to this ratio. It is easily shown[13] that

11. If vectors y and y' are both in Y, then any vector y'' equal to $\alpha y + (1 - \alpha) y'$ will also be in Y provided that Y is convex (α is any number between 0 and 1).

12. For a formal proof, see J. M. Montias, "A Theoretical Framework for the Analysis of Reforms in Soviet-type Economies," in M. Bornstein, ed., *Plan and Market: Economic Reforms in Eastern Europe* (New Haven: Yale University Press, 1973), Appendix B.

13. Let y^0 be a convex combination of y^E and y^* such that $\lambda y^0 = \lambda y^m$. Then $y^0 = \alpha y^* + (1 - \alpha) y^E$ for some positive α (since, by assumption, $\pi y^* > \pi y^E$, y^* and y^E must be separated by the hyperplane λy through y^m). Clearly, $(\pi y^A - \pi y^E)/(\pi y^* - \pi y^E) \geqslant (\pi y^0 - \pi y^E)/(\pi y^* - \lambda y^E)$. The right-hand side, after substitution of $[\alpha y^* + (1 - \alpha) y^E]$ for y^0 turns out to be equal to α. If we substitute y^0 for y^m in the ratio $(\lambda y^E - \lambda y^m)/(\lambda y^E - \lambda y^*)$ and again expand, we find that this ratio is also equal to α. Thus:

$$\frac{\pi y^A - \pi y^E}{\pi y^* - \pi y^E} \geqslant \alpha = \frac{\lambda y^E - \lambda y^m}{\lambda y^E - \lambda y^*}.$$

Note that if λy^E equals λy^m, and y^E is therefore not an interior point of the half space defined by the hyperplane λy through y^m, then no gain in autonomy need occur from the aggregation of controls. This inference is of course in agreement with our earlier proposition.

$$\frac{\pi y^A - \pi y^E}{\pi y^* - \pi y^E} \geqslant \frac{\lambda y^E - \lambda y^m}{\lambda y^E - \lambda y^*}.$$

The following illustration may give the reader some "feeling" for how good or bad the above expression may be. Consider a supervisor issuing a disaggregated plan to his supervisee that he may exceed in any dimension but may not otherwise violate. In other words, h hands down to i an n-element vector y^P and confronts him with an acceptable set G consisting of all outcome vectors y such that $y \geqslant y^P$. If the jth element of y^P is an input, $y_j \geqslant y_j^P$ means that i must not consume more of the jth input than the set amount y_j^P. If j is an output, i must at least produce y_j^P. The reward set R contains all the outcome vectors y such that $y \geqslant y^P$. The actual reward depends monotonically on πy. Using the same notation as before, y^E and y^* maximize πy on E and Y, respectively.

We compare this situation, where i is constrained by G, with the situation where h exercises aggregated controls separately on outputs and on inputs. First we decompose every vector y into a vector of outputs y^+, equal to $\max(y, 0)$, and a vector of inputs y^-, equal to $\min(y, 0)$, where max and min are taken one element at a time. When aggregated controls on outputs and inputs are

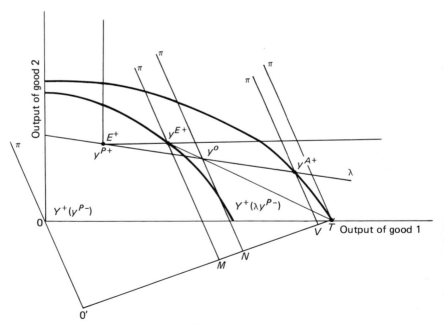

Diagram 14.2

exercised separately, the new acceptable set contains all vectors y, with output components y^+ and input components y^-, such that $\lambda y^+ \geqslant \lambda y^{P+}$ and $\lambda y^- \geqslant \lambda y^{P-}$.[14] The superscript $+$ attached to Y, E, or A signifies that Y^+, E^+, or A^+ is the projection of Y, E, or A on the positive orthant (i.e., on the n-dimensional space of nonnegative real numbers). *Mutatis mutandis*, the same applies to the superscript and the negative orthant.

The two situations are compared in diagram 14.2 for outcomes consisting of two outputs (shown in 14.2) and $(n - 2)$ inputs that determine the production possibilities for these two outputs. Two production sets have been drawn in the diagram, the first, denoted $Y^+(y^{P-})$, corresponding to the subvector y^{P-} of maximum levels of inputs in y^P and the second, denoted $Y^+(\lambda y^{P-})$, to λy^{P-}, the maximum *value* at prices λ of the inputs i is allowed to consume after the aggregation of controls on allocated inputs. This greater freedom of choice on the input side allows i to expand his production set to the outer boundary in the diagram.

All points marked in the diagram identify output subvectors, the remaining (input) elements of the vector being fixed at the level y^{P-} for the inner production set and λy^{P-} for the outer. y^{P+}, the output subvector in the plan, is identical to y^{m+}, the minimizer for λ on the set of acceptable outputs, on the assumption that both outputs have positive prices λ_1 and λ_2. The line with the slope $-\lambda_1/\lambda_2$ going through y^{P+} is the equivalent in two dimensions of the hyperplane λy through y^m. The point T corresponds to y^{*+}, the subvector of outputs maximizing πy^+ on $Y^+(\lambda y^{P-})$.[15] The value of y^{*+} at prices π is equal to $O'T$, of y^{A+} to $O'V$, of y^o to $O'N$, and of y^{E+} to $O'M$. The segment MT is a measure of the reward lost due to the constraint imposed by G. Almost all this loss is actually recovered if i can produce at y^{A+}, the maximizer for π on A^+. The ratio MN/MT in this case is a poor approximation to the ratio MV/MT, which measures the relative gain in autonomy as a result of the aggregation of controls. By drawing the appropriate lines in the diagram we can easily verify that the approximation would be much better if i's inputs remained fixed at their levels in y^{P-} and i were therefore confined to the production set with the inner boundary. This loosening of controls on the output side coupled with the maintenance of restraints on the input side is a feature of certain "economic reforms" in the centrally managed economies of East, where the allocation of inputs by the head of the complete hierarchy has not been abandoned (i.a., in the Soviet Union).

It may be remarked in passing that when G is defined as in this example (where h allows no trade-off between exceeding the plan in one dimension

14. The aggregation is then from n- to 2-dimensional space. But it is complete (from n to 1) for outputs and for inputs separately.

15. Note that there may exist a vector y^{**} distinct from y^* maximizing πy on Y subject to no constraint on inputs at all.

and underfulfilling it in another), there *must* be a gain in relative autonomy from aggregation, whether from n to 1 or from n to q ($q > 1$), provided that all price weights in λ are positive.

Generally, if we interpret the lower bound of G (in output space) as the locus of the minimum acceptable combinations of outputs 1 and 2 (the lowest "indifference curve"), the critical difference $\lambda y^E - \lambda y^m$ will be seen to depend on the elasticity of substitution of goods 1 and 2 along this curve: the lower the elasticity, the greater will be our critical difference. This observation reflects the crucial fact that whenever linear aggregation takes place, elements that were not perfectly substitutable in consumption or as inputs in production (at least as far as the supervisor saw them) acquire the apparent property of perfect substitutability. *Aggregation of controls complicates the coordination problem by signaling to the supervisee that his outputs or his inputs are perfect substitutes when in fact they are not.*[16]

The propositions that we have developed so far can be extended to the case where h has several supervisees. The analysis may then be recast in terms of the opportunities open to all supervisees simultaneously as a result of the aggregation of controls. How the spoils are divided turns out to depend on the rates of transformation of any goods j and j' on the efficiency frontier of $\bar{Y}$ at points such as $\bar{y}^E$, $\bar{y}^A$, and $\bar{y}^*$, where $\bar{Y}$ is now the sum of the production sets of all the supervisees, $\bar{G}$ is the acceptable set for joint outcomes by all supervisees, and the three vectors in question are defined on $\bar{Y}$ and $\bar{G}$ in the same way as y^E, y^A, and y^* were defined for the single supervisee i.[17]

Let us now define a *decentralizing rule with respect to tier* s *of a hierarchy* ($s = 1$, ..., S) as a new rule having the effect of increasing the relative autonomy of at least one supervisee in s and reducing it in none.

The testable hypothesis that we finally distill out of the preceding analyses is this: If, in the absence of any other change in incentives or prices, a modification occurs in the reporting system from supervisees in tier s to supervisors in the next higher tier of a hierarchy and if this modification increases the coarseness of the partition according to which activity vectors are reported, it acts as a decentralizing rule.[18]

It is important to specify the tier affected by the loosening of controls because a particular rule or set of rules may be decentralizing with respect to one tier and centralizing with respect to another. New rules introduced in

---

16. On this point, see also below, p. 218.

17. For details, see Montias, "The Aggregation of Controls and the Autonomy of Subordinates," Economic Growth Center, Yale University, Center Discussion Paper No. 157, sec. 2.

18. Unfortunately, the introduction of a new set of aggregation weights or incentive prices changes all the critical data of an autonomy-measurement problem. It may turn out that autonomy in terms of the old price systems will have increased as a result of the aggregation of controls but that it would have decreased in terms of the new.

Czechoslovakia in the early 1960s, to cite a classical example, tightened the controls on individual plants that were formerly called "enterprises" and loosened the controls on their supervisors in the next higher tier ("leading enterprises" and "associations of enterprises").[19]

As we have seen, a change in reporting rules may coarsen the partition of inputs as well as of outputs. A supervisee may have a greater choice of the inputs made available to him or may even be free to purchase any inputs subject to a limit on total expenditure. The "reforms" of system structures that have been promulgated in the last ten years or so in several East European countries have loosened controls on both inputs and outputs.[20]

14.3 ADVANTAGES AND DISADVANTAGES OF LOOSENING CONTROLS ON SUPERVISEES

Decentralizing measures are generally aimed at remedying two short-comings of an "overcentralized" system structure. (1) Superordinates are overburdened with responsibility for the detailed direction and coordination of their subordinates' activities. (2) This "petty tutelage" deprives subordinates of the opportunity to make decisions that might increase the payoff of the organization of which they are a part. Why then must the higher-ups in a hierarchy be swamped with coordinating tasks that they cannot really handle and the lower downs constrained by rules and orders that put a clamp on their initiative? Why not loosen controls on subordinates as soon as these shortcomings become apparent? One answer is that the cure may be worse than the ill. When controls are loosened, unless the incentive system is modified to bring about greater harmony between the goals of supervisors and supervisees, it may induce producers to shift their input and output mix in directions that are so unacceptable to their coordinating superiors as to vitiate any benefits that might be reaped by the organization as a whole from the exercise of greater initiative at lower tiers.

Consider a supervisor h with v_h subordinate enterprises subject to detailed controls. We shall use the subscript k to identify a subordinate enterprise (the subscript i in this book normally refers to an individual or to a consumer). The supervisor's experience tells him that if each of his v_h supervisees produces an outcome y_k in his acceptable set G_k, the joint production y ($\equiv \sum_{k=1}^{v_h} y_k$) will be acceptable to *his* supervisor. In other words production vectors in G may be construed as coordinated joint programs, in the sense that failure of the v_h enterprises to produce collectively in G will cause their joint program to be

19. See J. M. Montias, "The Evolution of the Czechoslovak Economic Model, 1945-1961," mimeographed (New Haven, 1962).

20. On the "detail of plan tasks" in the East German reform, see Michael Keren, "Concentration Amid Devolution in East German's Reforms," in Bornstein, ed., op. cit., pp. 148-50.

incompatible with the production programs of other subhierarchies, and the resulting program of net outputs for the system as a whole will be inferior (inefficient as well as less than optimally desirable).

Suppose now that h loosens controls by demanding less detailed reports on his supervisees. As a result, greater initiative is deployed and the production set of every enterprise expands. On the assumption of an unchanged environment and constant prices, the pre- and post-loosening situations for subordinate enterprise k are depicted in diagram 14.3 in the output space for two goods 1 and 2. In diagram 14.3 the subscript k and the superscript $+$ are

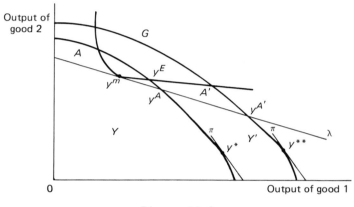

Diagram 14. 3

omitted from all the vectors and sets referring to k. The original production set for k is denoted Y, the expanded set Y' (the expansion being due to a loosening of the controls on the choice of its inputs). At incentive prices π, the entreprise would choose to produce at y^* in Y and at y^{**} in Y' if it were totally unconstrained. If it had to submit a production program in G with inputs constrained, it would be limited to set Y and would produce at y^E. In A', the new disaggregated acceptable set for aggregated controls generated from the initial set G by the aggregation prices λ, it will pick program $y^{A'}$, maximizing πy for prices π on this new set.

The boundary of G, as we have already argued, may be regarded as an indifference class yielding the supervisor a minimum level of utility. It is evident from diagram 14.3 that $y^{A'}$ cannot be in the set of output mixes generating this minimum level of utility unless goods 1 and 2 are related by an infinite elasticity of substitution between y^m and $y^{A'}$.[21]

The output program y^{**}, of course, need not fall outside A. If it does come

21. This is true for any pair of goods j and j' in the vector y $(j \neq j'; j, j' = 1, \ldots, n)$.

within A', what are the chances that it will also be in G? For the type of expansion of Y shown in the diagram or, for that matter, for any expansion that does not make it *relatively* easier to produce good 2 than good 1—or, more precisely, that does not reduce the marginal cost of good 2 more than that of good 1—it is easily seen that y^{**} cannot be in G.

When the production and the acceptable sets are summed over all v_h supervisees under a given supervisor h, a similar situation to that shown in diagram 14.3 emerges. Indeed, diagram 14.3, upon an appropriate reduction in scale, may be used to represent the aggregate production and acceptable sets for the v_h supervisees. In this case y^m is the sum of the minimizers for λ on the acceptable sets imposed on the individual enterprises. It must also be a minimizer for λ on the sum of the acceptable sets.[22]

We conjecture that for $y^{A'}$ (on the joint set Y') to be in the joint acceptable set G, the two goods must be related by an infinite elasticity of substitution in each of the acceptable sets imposed on individual enterprises. Barring an expansion of the aggregate set in the direction of good 2, which would bring y^{**} into G, it is most unlikely that the loosening of controls would lead to an acceptable joint program.[23]

This line of argument suggests that decentralization measures cannot be isolated from changes in the incentive system and in incentive prices (as well possibly as in the information-gathering process) that will counteract any adverse tendency that the loosening of controls might have on the coordination of production programs in the entire organization. The "unburdening" of the petty details of supervision for which supervisors were responsible prior to a decentralization measure must be accompanied by their increased responsibility for setting prices and for designing incentive systems that are apt to guide the enterprise more effectively. Otherwise the benefits to the organization as a whole expected from the conferral of greater autonomy on supervisees will not be captured.

14.4 EXAMPLES FROM EASTERN AND WESTERN INDUSTRIAL PRACTICE

American corporations are commonly said to be "decentralized" when their individual divisions or units are permitted to operate as profit-maxi-

22. Confer proposition 1.2 in T. C. Koopmans, *Three Essays on the State of Economic Science* (New York: McGraw-Hill, 1957), p. 12.

23. Note that the expansion of the joint production set is not guaranteed even if all the individual production sets undergo expansion. For if the various supervisees consume each other's products as inputs, it may happen that the loosening of controls on the output mix would induce a reduction in the output of certain intermediate goods that would show up as a contraction along these coordinates in the production set in output space. The situation will be aggravated if the enterprises consuming as inputs the goods whose output has been reduced cannot run down their inventories of such goods. For them the impact will not be limited to a reduction in the net output of goods in reduced supply but may have deep repercussions on the output programs of the consuming enterprises.

mizing entities, buying their inputs and selling their outputs in anonymous interaction with any client they please to deal with and reporting only their profits to headquarters.[24] Most of the so-called centralized corporations exercise more or less aggregated budget controls over their divisions that leave the heads of the latter with more autonomy than the extremely detailed controls on inputs and outputs that constrained the autonomy of plant managers in the Soviet Union and in Eastern Europe in the early 1950s. And even in these economies, which many observers claimed were "hyper-centralized," the nomenclature of controls was never sufficiently fine to stifle all initiative at any level. The limitations on the time and expense needed to collect and process detailed information, as we already argued in chapter 12, are such that the language of communication between supervisors and super-visees in a hierarchy must be coarsened from tier to tier and controls must thereby, to some extent at least, be loosened. Suffice it to mention that the number of distinct goods in modern economies has been estimated to run in the millions (where "distinctness" consists in a good having a separate price quotation), but no coordinating organization in an economy of East, such as the State Planning Commission, has ever been known to plan the output and allocation of more than 1,000–1,500 aggregated groups.[25]

Aggregation (whether it be of qualities of different goods produced, budget terms, or of profits) enables hierarchies to control a larger span of activities and individuals than they could otherwise. The *control span* of a supervisor—the number of supervisees whose activities he can effectively supervise—must be defined for a given degree of aggregation of controls. The failure to recognize this point weakens the analysis of economists who attempt to determine the "natural limits to the coordinating powers of a hierarchy."[26] The question, properly posed, is, "What is the loss in the organization's payoff, due to inferior coordination, when controls must be aggregated in order to make it possible to widen the span of control of supervisors?"

Another question is whether for a given price and incentive system, there

24. See Kenneth J. Arrow, "Control in Large Organizations," *Management Science* 10 (Apr. 1964): 401-11.

25. There were estimated to be 3 million distinct goods in Czechoslovakia. The number in the Soviet Union or in the United States is presumably larger. According to the Soviet economist I. Kalimin, Gosplan of the USSR prepared "material balances" for 274 products that had to be approved by the Council of Ministers; balances for 1,669 products were prepared and approved by Gosplan; balances for 17,484 products were prepared by Gosnab, a procurement organization subordinate to Gosplan; and balances for 40,000 products were prepared and approved by ministries (data cited in J. W. Gillula, "Industrial Interdependence and Production Planning in the Soviet Union," Duke University–University of North Carolina Occasional Papers on Input–Output Analysis in the USSR, Durham, N.C., Feb. 1974, p. 3).

26. Paul Craig Roberts, *Alienation and the Soviet Economy: Toward a General Theory of Marxian Alienation, Organization Principles and the Soviet Economy* (Albuquerque: University of New Mexico Press, 1971), p. 62.

may be a degree of aggregation beyond which controls become "ineffective." In this situation the head of the hierarchy cannot give effective direction to its personnel in pursuance of the goals it seeks to attain. The individuals in charge of subordinate hierarchies have sufficient autonomy to conduct their own policies, each pulling in the direction that his interests dictate. A nominally "centralized" economy that has reached this point has been termed "poly-centric."[27]

We have seen that any aggregation of controls, including the assignment of profit-maximization targets to supervisees, risks the danger that, as a result of the loosening of controls, pairs of goods related by a finite elasticity of substitution in consumption or in productive uses will be treated as perfect substitutes. How serious this problem is will normally depend on the environment in which the organization operates. When an organization is embedded in a competitive market, the products of many of its interdependent activities[28] can be traded with other organizations. When a good is produced in quantities superior to its expected consumption within the organization, it can be sold off; when an input is in deficit supply, it can normally be purchased. If there is a large number of sellers and buyers in each of these markets, the trade-offs may be fairly constant regardless of quantities bought or sold. The losses due to the assumption that goods are perfect substitutes when they are not so *within the organization* is then limited to the additional transportation, marketing, or purchasing expenses that must be borne by the organization when surpluses above internal consumption must be disposed of or deficits above production within the organization must be made good from outside. By contrast, the activities of enterprises in a centrally directed economy of the Soviet type are coordinated with one another mainly through controls exercised by superordinates in the complete hierarchy that administers them. The prices usually set by officials in the highest tiers of the complete hierarchy are built up from essentially arbitrary formulas (as an approximation to average unit costs in the "industry") and have no precise relation to marginal rates of substitution, opportunity trade-offs, or supply and demand equilibrium. Surpluses and deficits resulting from aggregated controls cannot be resolved through an anonymous market, at least domestically. And the expense of resolving them through foreign trade may be prohibitively high.[29]

27. See ibid., esp. chap. 3. My own impression is that the Soviet and East European economies were never in a state where the directives of the ruling party could not be implemented, at least in their broad features, because the hierarchies charged with fulfilling the plans were too large to permit effective control.

28. But not of all. See chap. 6 on the technological limitations to changes in custody outside transfer states.

29. In these economies all foreign-trade transactions must "go through" the Ministry of Foreign Trade. Transaction costs must be relatively high for small quantities of goods to be disposed of or acquired (not in terms of quantifiable expenditures but in terms of the outlays of "bureaucratic" labor that must be lavished to obtain approval). The situation is further aggra-

One important aspect of coordination in large organizations has been left out of the foregoing analysis. We have studied a hypothetical relation between supervisors and supervisees featuring a single-channel reporting system. When supervisees took advantage of the aggregation of controls to produce outputs or to consume inputs that would have been unacceptable if supervisors had been able to impose detailed controls and when these lower-tier decisions were likely to cause a deterioration in the coordination of interdependent activities, we implicitly assumed that the supervisors (and their superiors) stood by and accepted this state of affairs supinely. We thus ignored a key dimension in their strategy space: the right usually given them by the rules of the organization to *inspect*, that is, to collect information about the performance of their supervisees in more disaggregated form than in the routine reports they receive, and, if they deem the inspected outcomes unacceptable, to take punitive measures to induce supervisees to avoid such derogations in the future. The supervisor may be able to collect, process, and utilize information expressed in several degrees of coarseness, including highly aggregated routine reports, regular monthly inspection tours, and occasional "investigations" that will comb through the outcomes of supervisees' activities in the most minute detail. That supervisors have more than one arrow in their quiver does not mean that their supervisees will always "produce" in the acceptable set corresponding to the finest partition of outcome vectors. They know that inspection costs are appreciable, that penalties are limited by the bargaining power of supervisees, and that disruption of programmed activities can be expensive in terms of production or other output activities forgone. There is usually some autonomy that can be exploited from the aggregation of routine controls, though not as much as if inspection were ruled out.[30]

The possibility of inspection at various tiers in a hierarchy makes the comparison of organizations from the viewpoint of their relative degree of decentralization and of subordinates' autonomy that much more difficult. Even a comparison through time of the same organization undergoing a change in reporting-system rules may founder on this shoal. "Reforms" of the system structure in Eastern Europe have been decentralizing in the sense that we have used the word here, insofar as the number of compulsory directives has been reduced and many directives have been amalgamated. But the

vated by the difficulty of selling surpluses or buying deficit supplies on short notice or from fellow members of the Council for Economic Assistance (COMECON), which themselves are by and large centrally directed and are afflicted with similar organizational problems. Trade with Western countries on the other hand is limited by all sorts of inhibitions and prohibitions imposed by both "socialist" and "capitalist" ruling organizations.

30. The supervisor–supervisee relation in a situation where supervisors can either collect aggregated information or inspect may be modeled as a nonzero sum game (see Montias, "Aggregation of Controls," sec. 3).

powers of supervisors in ministries and associations to intervene when the output mix of enterprises was "distorted" or when expenditures on individual items such as labor were "excessive" were not effectively curbed by the new rules. When routine controls are aggregated, supervisors may have more time or processing facilities at their disposal to inspect more frequently or collect information more comprehensively. Whether the autonomy of managers of producing plants and of wholesale and retail distributing organizations is really increased as a result of the reforms cannot normally be ascertained from a superficial analysis of the new rules. Only the most detailed investigation by the comparer of the behavior of these managers can possibly yield the answer.[31] It is discouraging to observe that even those highly placed officials of organizations who decree structural reforms are not always able to assess the benefits and losses of the changes in rules they introduce. No wonder wide swings between "decentralizing" and "recentralizing" measures perenially occur in many large organizations, public and private.[32] These difficulties of evaluation are compounded when one tries to compare empirically the effects on outcomes of system rules that allow for different degrees of subordinate autonomy in organizations operating in diverse environments.

14.5 Relative Efficiency of Prices and Quantity Orders as Channels of Control

We now broach a new problem in supervisor–supervisee relations with weighty implications for the relative efficiencies of alternative system structures. Instead of concentrating, as we did previously, on the supervisee's strategy under uncertainty about his supervisor's acceptability conditions, we will look at controls from the supervisor's vantage point. The supervisor's problem is to set "optimal" quantity orders for the supervisee to fulfill or prices to guide his actions under conditions where he (the supervisor) is uncertain about his supervisee's capabilities. By "optimal," I mean that the prices or quantity orders supervisor h will set must maximize his expected utility, given the subjective probabilities he assigns to the various possible states in his or his supervisee's environment that may influence his performance or the benefits he expects therefrom.

·The situation we wish to model is one where supervisee i has sufficient autonomy on the side of his inputs to attain any quantity orders that h may

---

31. As we have already remarked, the comparison is also complicated, if not at times rendered totally impossible, by the changes in price and in incentive systems that often accompany such reforms.

32. On the centralization–decentralization issue in British nationalized industry, see Richard Pryke, *Public Enterprise in Practice: The British Experience of Nationalization Over Two Decades* (London: McGibbon and Kee, 1971), pp. 31, 443, 466-67.

assign him under any state of his (i's) environment.[33] The randomness of the states of i's environment will then work its impact through the costs of fulfilling a particular set of orders. Martin Weitzman, who devised the basic model for analyzing this problem,[34] also introduced randomness in the supervisor's payoff or benefits under various possible states of his environment.

In the Weitzman model the supervisee is subject to an incentive scheme that induces him to maximize profits. For the time being, we confine our analysis to the case of a single good whose level of output is written y. For any price p set by h, i will maximize profits on his production set (assumed to be convex)[35] by equating marginal cost to p.

As before, we let e_i stand for a state of i's environment in E_i and denote by e_h a state of the environment in E_h. The total cost associated with e_i and y is written $C(e_i, y)$ and the corresponding marginal cost $C'(e_i, y)$. Similarly, total and marginal benefits for e_h and y are $B(e_h, y)$ and $B'(e_h, y)$, respectively. Given a price p, the quantity $\tilde{y}$ is that for which marginal cost $C'(e_i, \tilde{y})$ is equal to p.

To maximize his expected utility so that costs properly reflect utility forgone, h must choose, alternatively, a price or a quantity order that will maximize the difference between expected benefits, given the probability distribution $\psi(e_h)$ over E_h, and expected costs, given the probability distribution $\phi(e_i)$ over E_i. The optimal price $\tilde{p}$ or quantity order $\hat{q}$ will clearly have the property of equating marginal expected benefit to marginal expected cost.

The simplifying assumption is now made that the states in E_i and E_h affect only the intercepts of the marginal-cost and marginal-benefit functions but not their slopes.[36] The supervisor's problem can then be analyzed graphically with the aid of diagram 14.4. In the diagram are shown two pairs of arbitrarily selected marginal-cost schedules and of marginal-benefit schedules that correspond to the pairs of states (e_i^1, e_i^2) and (e_h^1, e_h^2), respectively. The dotted marginal-

33. If this condition is not fulfilled, a set of rules must be devised to guide h and i under conditions where the quantity orders are not attainable. This sets in motion a more complicated process that probably cannot be handled with simple analytical techniques. Moreover, an efficient set of quantity orders that will be unattainable for the less probable states of i's environment will presumably also make it possible for i to overfulfill the orders under *some* more or less probable states. It is then necessary to specify the incentive–reward function and the prices that will govern his actions in that case. This leads us back to the problems discussed in the models of the previous section.

34. "Prices versus Quantities," Working Paper No. 106, MIT, Department of Economics, Apr. 1973.

35. Note that i's production set may be convex even in the absence of any exogenous constraint (such as a limit on an input), owing to the nature of his technology (constraint on diminishing returns).

36. Weitzman invokes as justification for his assumption Paul Samuelson's approximation theorem of portfolio analysis (*Review of Economic Studies* 37 [Oct. 1970]: 537-42).

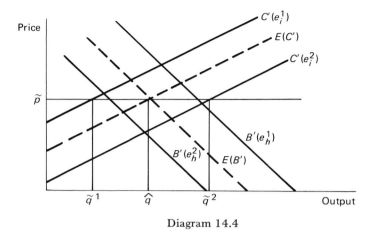

Diagram 14.4

cost and marginal-benefit lines are the expected schedules, given $\phi(e_i)$ and $\psi(e_h)$ and the effects of the states on the intercepts of these parallel schedules.

The price $\tilde{p}$ equating expected marginal cost and benefit is optimal under the "price mode of controls." $\hat{q}$, which also equates expected marginal cost and benefit, is optimal under the "quantity model of controls." Suppose $\tilde{p}$ were set under the price mode. Then i would maximize profits at $\tilde{q}^1$ when e_i^1 occurred and at $\tilde{q}^2$ when e_i^2 occurred. What will be the expected average of quantities produced, given the complete distribution of states $\phi(e_i)$ and $\psi(e_h)$? Under the assumption of a common slope, it is easy to see that $E(\tilde{q})$, the average quantity, must be equal to $\hat{q}$, which, in addition to being the optimal target under a quantity mode, is also the quantity that results when expected marginal cost equals price.

That the average quantity produced will be the same under the two modes does not imply that the two modes are equally efficient. A case will now be illustrated where the quantity mode is superior to the price mode. In diagram 14.5 I have drawn only two marginal-cost schedules C_1' and C_2', corresponding to states e_i^1 and e_i^2, respectively, and a single marginal-benefit schedule that happens to be identical to the expected marginal-benefit schedule. (This coincidence facilitates the exposition but in no way restricts the generality of the conclusion.) Once the optimal $\tilde{p}$ is set under the price mode, the profit-maximizing quantity $\tilde{q}_1$ is selected by i when C_1' occurs and $\tilde{q}_2$ when C_2' occurs. Now if h had known that C_1' was the true marginal cost (or the marginal cost that would occur), he would have set either $\bar{p}_1$ or $\bar{q}_1$ with the same optimal result. The total amount of net benefit forgone by setting $\tilde{p}$ instead of $\bar{p}_1$ for this state is the area ACZ shaded with positively sloped strokes (since the additional benefit of moving from $\tilde{q}_1$ to $\bar{q}_1$ is the integral of the area under the

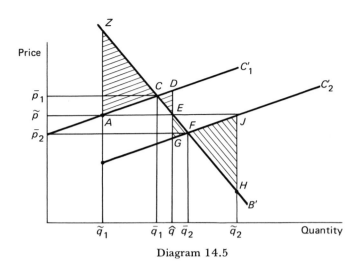

Diagram 14.5

line segment ZC, while the extra cost of so doing is the area under AC: the difference between additional benefits and additional costs, representing additional net benefits, is thus the area ACZ). The total amount of net benefit forgone by setting $\hat{q}$ under the quantity mode instead of $\bar{q}_1$, the optimal quantity order under certainty, is CDE (by a similar reasoning). Since ACZ is greater than CDE, the deviation from maximum expected net benefit is smaller for the quantity mode than for the price mode. A comparison of the triangles EFG (net benefit forgone under the quantity mode when marginal cost is C_2') and FJH (net benefit forgone under the price mode for the same C_2') confirms the above conclusion.[37] This conclusion will necessarily hold for any set of marginal-cost and -benefit schedules, provided the absolute value of the (common) slope of the former is smaller than that of the latter.

Per contra, the reader can easily verify that the net expected benefit forgone, compared to a situation under certainty where marginal cost and marginal benefit can be equated for any pair (e_i, e_h) in E_i and E_h, will be smaller for the price than for the quantity mode when the marginal-benefit schedules have a smaller absolute slope than the marginal-cost schedules.

This analysis brings us to the self-evident conclusion that quantity and price modes are equivalent whenever the common slope of the marginal-benefit schedules is equal (in absolute value) to the common slope of the marginal-cost schedules (as in diagram 14.4).

37. This is intuitively convincing: when all the marginal-cost schedules are relatively flat, the variance in quantities selected under a price mode will be large. For any given e_h, if marginal-benefit schedules are also steeply inclined, the expected total benefit will be appreciably smaller than the (certain) benefit generated by fixing a quantity at some optimal level.

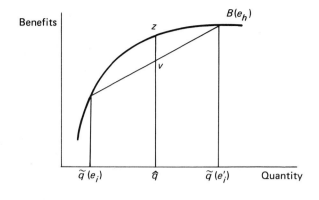

Diagram 14.6

Weitzman's algebraic formula for the net advantage, denoted Δ, of the price over the quantity mode is

$$\Delta = \frac{(C'' + B'')}{2C''^2}\, \sigma^2,$$

where C'' and B'' are the common slopes of the marginal-cost and marginal-benefit schedules, respectively, and σ is the variance of the vertical shifts in the marginal-cost schedules.[38]

The formula is of course consistent with our diagrams illustrating the workings of the model. C'' and B'' have opposite signs. When their absolute values are equal, they cancel each other out, and Δ reduces to zero. The larger σ, the variance around expected marginal cost, the greater will be the variance in quantities produced under the price mode. If the total-benefit function has a high degree of curvature (i.e., if B'' has a large absolute value), and the total-cost function has a low degree of curvature (i.e., C'' has a low value), then Δ will be negative and large—the quantity mode will be vastly more advantageous than the price mode.[39]

Diagram 14.6 may help the reader visualize what is going on under these assumed conditions. The diagram exhibits an arbitrary total-benefits curve (for state e_h). If the price mode were in effect, i would produce at $\tilde{q}(e_i)$ if state e_i occurred and at $\tilde{q}(e_i')$ if e_i' occurred. (We may think of e_i and e_i' as states of environment E_i associated with marginal-cost schedules one standard deviation removed from expected marginal cost.) It is evident that expected benefit under the price mode, represented by the line segment from $\hat{q}$ to v, is much lower than the length of the segment from $\hat{q}$ to z. In general, the greater the

38. Weitzman, op. cit., p. 16.
39. The low value of C''^2 in the denominator also tends to raise the absolute value of Δ.

curvature of the benefit curves, the larger will be the difference between the value of the abscissa on the curve and its value on the chord joining any two selected points on the curve, and hence, other things equal, the greater the relative advantage of the quantity mode.[40]

The comparison of the two modes where i is producing more than one good has been investigated by Gary Yohe as one of the problems in his dissertation on the general topic of "prices versus quantities." He finds that gross complementarity for any pair of goods in the supervisor's benefit function will, other things equal, shift the balance toward the quantity mode and gross substitutability toward the price mode. This conclusion is intuitively convincing. Heuristically speaking, when two goods are highly complementary, it will be advantageous to produce them more or less in proportion, irrespective of costs. The price mode has the same effect as the aggregation of controls studied in the last section: it may easily cause wide swings in the relative outputs of the two goods in response to changes in relative marginal costs. This of course will not happen under the quantity mode, the disadvantage of which, however, will lie in the failure to even approximate the equality of marginal costs for any state of i's environment with the ratio of marginal benefits of the two goods for the corresponding state of h's environment.

Weitzman draws far-reaching conclusions from his model. He points out for example that his model may be applied to economies that normally allocate resources through markets and price competition and that are restructured in wartime as command-ordered hierarchies. The rationale for this restructuring, as seen by Weitzman, is that the benefit curves are likely to have greater curvature in a wartime situation, where military goods are needed in certain quantities and proportions, and the economy cannot afford the wide swings in absolute and relative outputs in response to even moderate changes in relative costs that would result from price competition and market allocation.

The model suggests another conjecture in the theory of resource allocation by hierarchies. Consider two supervisor–supervisee relations, the first embedded in a two-tier hierarchy operating in a market environment (e.g., a competitive enterprise composed of an entrepreneur running several small plants), the second embedded in a multitier hierarchy where resources are transferred from one subhierarchy to the other by coordinators in a higher tier in isolation from any price-competitive markets. The conjecture is that, for

40. Any relative disadvantage of the quantity mode vis-à-vis the price mode would not show up in the diagram. This disadvantage resides in the failure to equate either marginal cost or marginal benefit to price for any states of i's or h's environment, except, trivially, those that would cause $\hat{q}$ to be produced under the price mode. Under the price mode, marginal cost, if not marginal benefit, is at least equated to price. If the marginal-benefit schedules are relatively flat, the loss in net benefit due to equating only marginal cost to price may be relatively small.

a given distribution of the states of the environments of supervisors and supervisees, the balance of advantages and disadvantages will incline toward the price mode in the first situation and toward the quantity mode in the second. This is because in the first situation the possibility of selling outputs at competitive prices reduces the curvature of the benefit curves compared to the second situation, where coordinators must make sure that outputs are more or less in desired proportions to satisfy the explicit demands of consumers in the hierarchy.[41] If this conjecture is valid, it may help explain why decentralizing reforms in Eastern Europe frequently run into opposition from production-minded officials in higher tiers in the hierarchies administering these economies. In the absence of price-competitive markets to smooth over producers' deviations from desired proportions, the substitution of the price for the quantity mode—or, for that matter, the aggregation of controls—can only lead to dis-coordination and perceived losses in planners' welfare. In my opinion, this is one of the principal reasons why successful reforms cannot be engineered without dismantling the entire economic hierarchy pari passu with the creation of price-competitive markets (as the Yugoslav political authorities did in the early 1950s).[42]

41. The more multiproduct plants are supervised by a single supervisor, however, the more possibilities there are for the supervisor of manipulating the aggregate product mix of the sub-hierarchy at small cost and hence presumably the smaller the curvature of the benefit function that any one plant will be facing. (In effect the deviations from optimal proportions of any one plant are at least partially canceled out by countervailing deviations by other plants.) These possibilities tend to reduce the contrast between the two situations.

42. Janos Kornai correctly emphasizes that a system may, for some time at least, dispense with hierarchic coordination as long as routine links between enterprises are maintained and allocation decisions follow routine patterns. When a new environment—or a new probability distribution of the states of the economy's environment—comes into existence, the welfare losses due to this "auto-coordination" may become substantial. On this point see Kornai, op. cit., pp. 176-89.

Part 5
Enterprise Goals and Their Implications for Efficiency

15

Goals of Enterprises in Different Systems

15.1 Theoretical Approaches

In the first chapter of this book I limned (or caricatured) three primitive approaches to the comparison of systems. There is a fourth, more sophisticated approach, which has attracted a number of excellent economists, perhaps in part because of the opportunities it provides for the display of their technical virtuosity. This approach consists in taking a basic decision-making unit common to the systems undergoing comparison, assigning to that "typical unit" a maximand (goal function) or some other behavior trait characteristic of its system, and then reasoning out what the decisions of this unit would be under alternative assumptions about its environment. If the unit is an enterprise, for example, the analyst may trace the repercussions of an increase in demand for one or more of its products or a reduction in the price of some of its inputs in each of the systems under ceteris paribus assumptions.

This goal function for the enterprise as a whole will determine its decisions and over a longer horizon its policies, which, given the environment in which the organization operates, will influence the outcomes of the system. Whether enterprise managers are taken to maximize profits or to satisfice, what choices they will make between the chance of earning greater profits or larger production bonuses and the option of achieving a greater security of their payoff, and what amount of effort they will exert to attain a larger payoff, all depend on the preferences of these deicision makers. As long as the period of observation or comparison is relatively short, these preferences may be considered stable, as if they were held over from the initial environment.

The prediction of outcomes with the aid of models that assume a "typical" mode of behavior will be illuminating to the extent that they reveal tendencies in the behavior of decision-making organizational units that were not self-evident to begin with. However, when the attempt is made to aggregate the logical decisions of these units to predict how the entire system would behave under alternative environments, it can lead to misleading results—to hypotheses that can be rejected on the basis of the most casual observation of the facts—if interactions with other decision makers in the economy are left out of account. To take only the most flagrant example, a model of the Soviet economy anchored to the behavior of bonus-maximizing enterprises will be of limited interest if it ignores the constraints on the output mix of enterprises imposed by their superiors in the ministries and in the party apparatus. The fallacy is not in the technique of analysis but in trying to squeeze more out of these models, predicated on the monistic behavior of the "basic decision makers" in each system, than these models can contribute. Nevertheless, we shall explore some examples of this approach in the present chapter, deferring to the next two chapters the study of the industry-wide and economy-wide effects of particular modes of managerial behavior.

15.2 How Goals Are Set

So far we have postulated that each individual in an organization had preferences that could be modeled with the aid of a utility function, but we have said little or nothing about the relation between these individual preferences and the goals pursued "by the organization." How are these preferences "integrated?" Does the aggregate function for an enterprise preserve the internal consistency that we generally impute to the individual functions?[1]

In the case of a hierarchy where the real power of superiors over their subordinates coincided with their nominal power, our first guess would be that the goals of their organization would be identical to or "governed by" the preferences of the head. But even in this hypersimplified situation, risk and uncertainty may drive a wedge between the preferences of the head concerning his personal consumption or that of his family and the goals he would wish to impose on "his" enterprise. For example, if the rules of the system provide for the "limited liability" of the owners of an incorporated enterprise, the head may be less risk averse in ordering an investment for the organization than he would be if he were to take the same chance on a personal investment and risk bankruptcy. From this point to arguing that the enterprise "maximizes profits" regardless of risk is a long step—although one that is often taken without sufficient safeguards by many economists.

It should be evident from the analysis of chapters 13 and 14 that situations of unilateral power are unlikely to occur in hierarchies. Unless the penalties that superiors are entitled to mete out are very severe and can be inflicted at little or no cost to the organization, the superior's will cannot be imposed on his subordinates without encountering resistance. And even if penalties are heavy and liberally applied, the finer information that is usually at the subordinate's disposal may give him *some* countervailing power. Although, for instance, the heads of subordinate departments of a corporation may

1. One frequently cited requirement of consistency of preferences is transitivity. See above chap. 2, n. 13.

quake at the thought of being dismissed, the chief of the sales department may still influence the goals set for the organization by the president or general manager, provided he is consulted at all on alternative policies. His influence springs from the fact that he has information about market prospects that is not normally available at higher levels. If he is consulted on the option of raising the general level of the firm's prices, he may by exaggerating the risks of a decline in demand effectively prod the corporation toward a policy of maintaining or increasing the volume of its sales, despite the adverse effect such a policy might have on profits.

In situations characterized by a measure of bilateral power, the tier of the hierarchy to which a responsible official is assigned may have much to do with the influence he wields on the formulation of the goals pursued by the organization. The rank in the hierarchy occupied by the official of an automobile company in charge of research on pollution control, for example, may determine the extent to which he will be able to bend the policies of the corporation to his own goals. In general we find that heads of financial departments rank near the very apex of the hierarchy in American corporations. Their "nearness to the throne" gives them an opportunity to stress their financial viewpoint—against the R & D or public relations departments—when the occasion arises. In Soviet ministries and enterprises the head of the financial department generally fulfills subordinate staff functions and has far less opportunity to press his case.

Nearness to the seat of power may be necessary for influence, but it is not sufficient. In large modern Japanese corporations, certain specialized staff functions, including long-range planning and operations research, are carried out in a department attached directly to the president of the company. (*Shachoshitsu*, the name of this system, means "president's room.") The long-range planning and operations research that go on in this department, however, are thought in many instances to have little influence on top-management decisions, apparently because these staff functions fit awkwardly into the traditional Japanese hierarchic scheme.[2]

These examples, as the reader may well have noticed, are ambiguous in one respect. If we do not take the structure of the hierarchy as exogenous but suppose rather that it can be flexibly adapted to the goals of the organization, the relative influence of officials derived from their position in the hierarchy is itself determined indirectly *by* these goals. The head of the department in charge of the antipollution program has little influence because he has a low rank in the hierarchy, and he has an inferior rank bacause the top decision

2. See Herbert Glazer, "The Japanese Executive," in R. Ballon, ed., *The Japanese Employee* (Rutland, Vt.: Tuttle, 1969), pp. 86-87.

makers in the corporation give pollution controls a low priority. The same consideration applies to the difference in status of finance departments in U.S. and Soviet organizations.

Be that as it may, hierarchic structures of organizations change slowly in response to shifts in the goals pursued by their leaders. In the short run at least, these structures can be taken as given, and the type of "interest aggregation" described above may have to be explicitly recognized by those who wish to construct realistic, predictive models of enterprise behavior in different systems.

In the neoclassical models of the behavior of enterprises operating in a market system, the principal—and sometimes the only—variables subject to decisions are the production program of the enterprise and, in situations where it has "market power," the prices of its products. When demand drops, the model predicts that some mixture of output contraction and price reduction will occur. Actually, as we have already seen, the level of inventories, the advertising budget, the sales force, R & D outlays, and many other competing terms of expenditure may be reduced or expanded under the impact of a perceived decline in demand. Which items are most affected will often depend not only on the actions and reactions of competitors but also on the place in the hierarchy of the departments involved and the extent to which responsibility is "delegated" by superiors in the hierarchy to these subordinates. In American enterprises, budgets and official price policy are generally the province of departments in upper tiers. Not unexpectedly, budgets and prices react sluggishly to changes in the enterprise's environment. Small improvements in the quality of or the delivery conditions for products, confidential price discounts, and increased sales efforts are often matters decided in lower tiers. And they are liable to be the variables that will be manipulated first in case of a sudden change in the enterprise's environment. If the change is temporary, the policies of higher-tier departments may remain unaffected.

In centrally directed economies price policy is also an upper-tier responsibility. Prices are set by a department usually attached to the highest tier of the administrative hierarchy (the council of ministers or the planning commission that the council directly supervises). Prices of producer goods are very infrequently revised, generally not more than every three to five years. One apparent difference between the operations of a complete hierarchy in East and a corporation in a market economy in West is that in the former, subordinate enterprises are not permitted to change the prices of most products in response to supply or demand conditions, whereas in the latter the prices actually charged by subordinate enterprises, plants, departments, and subsidiaries often diverge from the official lists; these divergent markups or discounts are tolerated if not wholly approved by officials in the higher tiers.

This system difference is obliterated when ruling organizations prohibit such informal rebates and markups through "fair pricing" and similar laws. However, in neither type of system can the rules prevent the subtle and easily concealable changes in product quality and in the provision of ancillary services that can be effected at lower tiers when demand exceeds supply or vice versa.

With regard to the study of the behavior of private enterprises in West, it has frequently been suggested of late that certain policies, called "rules of thumb,"[3] govern the choice of actions of decision makers at various levels of the hierarchy or quasi-hierarchy managing the organization and that these policies may be incompatible with the actions that would theoretically maximize profits for the enterprise. This is so at least if information and processing costs of improving on such policies are not so high as to completely offset any potential increment in profits that might result from a more systematic pursuit of that goal.[4] The question then is that of the long-run viability of rules of thumb such as "price charged should be full-cost plus ten percent" or "orders should be rejected if they fall below the break-even point"—or even "never introduce a new activity or process in place of an old one unless the enterprise is earning less than a normal rate of return." Can an enterprise in a competitive "industry" survive if it does not maximize profits? Provided that the enterprises in an industry conduct divergent policies, which may not be the case if all managers imbibed the same notions in their business-school courses, the competitive process, as we saw in chapter 10, *may* winnow out the enterprises that pursued the least efficient course and deviated most grossly from profit-maximizing activities. This line of reasoning suggests that the environment of the enterprise—including its initial endowment in physical and financial resources, the competitive moves of other producers, and the training and education of its managers—is likely to have some influence on the goals and policies pursued by a privately owned enterprise.

One last remark on the aggregation of divergent interests of the individuals in an enterprise is that the pursuit of profits as an overriding objective, which highly placed individuals in the organization are in a position to impose by dismissing recalcitrant subordinates, provides a relatively good criterion for resolving conflicts: of two contending courses of action the one more likely to increase discounted profits (the "net worth" of the enterprise) will be adopted, where "likelihood" will be determined by the superordinate in a

---

3. These policies should not be construed as rules in the sense in which this word has been used throughout the present work. They are not part of the bylaws of the organization and their violation will not normally draw sanctions on the transgressor.

4. It may also be pointed out that "rules of thumb" save on the costs of decision making in a complex hierarchy (in particular on the costs of communication between subhierarchies).

position to resolve the difference. When goals are more diffuse and lack a quantitative criterion ("serve the community," "improve the public image of the organization," "help minority businesses"), it is more difficult to cut the Gordian knot of internecine conflict without antagonizing the losers in the dispute. On the other hand, there are greater possibilities in this situation for individuals to grasp their own ends, to engross power, or perhaps merely to bring relatives and simpaticos into the enterprise—under the cover of serving the hard-to-define goals of the organization.

In the next section we shall for the most part ignore differences in the power of individuals in the organization and concentrate on the effects of particular goals on rules of behavior without concerning ourselves with the precise way they came to be established.

15.3 GOALS OF A COOPERATIVE ENTERPRISE

In recent years a number of economists, both within the field of "comparative systems" and without, have investigated the implications of goal functions other than the maximization of profits for the behavior of "typical" enterprises. We have already mentioned, in connection with our examination of ownership rights, the work of Sam Pelzman on the behavior of managers of public enterprises maximizing the support of the voters who ultimately determine their job tenure.[5] Mention may also be made of the work of Monsen, Chiu, and Cooley on the effects of separating ownership from "control" in the performance of large firms in a market economy,[6] of Henry G. Grabowski on growth-maximizing firms constrained by the necessity of earning sufficient profits to maintain the market value of stockholders' shares in order to prevent a takeover,[7] and of Harvey Averch and Leland Johnson on profit maximization by a regulated enterprise constrained by a limit on its ratio of return on capital investment.[8]

One of the first studies of alternative goal functions with important implications for the study of economy-wide systems was Benjamin Ward's classic investigation of the behavior of a cooperative enterprise maximizing

5. "Pricing in Public and Private Enterprises in Electric Utilities in the United States," *Journal of Law and Economics* 14 (Apr. 1971): 110-18.

6. R. J. Monsen, J. S. Chiu, and D. P. Cooley, "The Effect of Separation of Ownership and Control on the Performance of the Large Firm," *Quarterly Journal of Economics* 82 (Aug. 1968): 435-51.

7. "A Note on Stockholder Welfare Maximization Versus Growth Maximization," mimeographed (Yale University, 1970).

8. "Behavior of the Firm Under Regulatory Constraint," *American Economic Review* 52 (Dec. 1962): 1052-69. On this model, see below, chap. 18, p. 294. For an excellent summary and discussion of the literature on alternative goal functions of the enterprise, see Oliver E. Williamson, "Managerial Discretion and Business Behavior," *American Economic Review* 53 (Dec. 1963): 1032-57.

"net income" per member of its working collective, where net income is defined as sales minus charges on capital imposed by the government and payments for other factors of production exclusive of the members' labor.

In working out the implications of this goal for the behavior of an enterprise, Ward made the crucial assumption that the decision variables under the manager's control included the number of individuals in the collective itself as well as the level of all other inputs and outputs. This assumption is compatible with the principle of workers' representation in policy making, provided the majority of representatives in the workers' council were willing to delegate to the manager the right to reduce the size of the collective when he thought this might be necessary to maximize the average income of *remaining* members. Such a course of action, however, would be so divisive and so contrary to most members' sense of equity that one would hardly expect a manager to adopt it. In sum, it is hard to see how the goal function postulated by Ward could emerge as the result of free interaction among individuals in any real-life organization faced with demand conditions where maximization of net income per member would entail a curtailment of the membership. The goal of maximizing net income per member might he pursued in the long run when the enterprise was expanding under dynamic conditions, but it would stand to be modified in the short run, possibly by imposing a no-dismissals constraint on the manager's decisions.

Nevertheless, the Ward model is worth studying, if only to trace through the logical consequences of the postulated goal in situations where these consequences would violate another rule or principle of interaction among individuals belonging to an organization. In any event, the model offers illuminating insights into the behavior of one variant of "workers' self-management" and deserves at least a summary of its main features.[9]

Let the output y of a single-product firm be a function f of capital K and labor L exclusively. The amount of labor L represents the number of individuals working in the collective, not the number of hours they work or the effort they put out, on the assumption that working hours and effort per member are fixed. It is assumed that $\partial y/\partial K$ and $\partial y/\partial L \geq 0$.

The cost of capital is a fixed amount R, the rental charged on the given amount of capital invested in the firm, which must be paid out to the ruling organization providing the capital. The enterprise, assumed to be perfectly competitive, sells its product at the "market price" p. Its postulated goal is

9. Ward, "The Firm in Illyria: Market Syndicalism," *American Economic Review* 48 (1958): 566-89. This work has inspired a number of other economists (e.g., Evsey Domar, Eirik Furubotn, J. E. Meade, Svetozar Pejovich, Charles Rockwell, Stephen Sacks, and Jaroslav Vanek) who have added a good deal of flesh—along perhaps with some excess fat—to Ward's skeleton. The following summary is chiefly based on Ward, *The Socialist Economy: A Study of Organizational Alternatives* (Berkeley: University of California Press, 1967), p. 191.

to maximize net income per member of the collective, or $(py - R)/L$, in contrast to a profit-maximizing enterprise, which would maximize $py - R$.[10]

How large should the collective be in order to maximize net income per member when in the short run the capital stock is fixed at a level K_0? The optimum size of the collective can be calculated from the solution of the equation $dS/dL = 0$, where S stands for net income per member, or

$$\frac{dS}{dL} = \frac{p(L\frac{\partial y}{\partial L} - y) + R}{L^2} = 0,$$

whence

$$p\frac{\partial y}{\partial L} = \frac{py - R}{L*} \tag{15.1}$$

and

$$\frac{y}{L*} - \frac{\partial y}{\partial L} = \frac{R}{pL*}, \tag{15.2}$$

where $L*$ is the optimal size of the collective.

Equation 15.1 tells us that the marginal value product of labor must equal net income per member of the collective. We shall come back to this condition in connection with the long-run adjustment of the enterprise to price changes.

The left-hand side of equation 15.2 represents the difference between the average product and the marginal product of labor. This difference will be positive because the right-hand side is positive (provided $R > 0$). But as output expands beyond the point where marginal and average products are equal, the difference must increase since marginal product declines more rapidly than average product. Hence the larger R is, other things equal, the larger will be the difference between y/L and dy/dL and the greater will be the output-maximizing net income per member. On the other hand, the larger p is, the smaller will be the difference and hence the smaller the equilibrium output. In other words, raising the rental value on capital that the enterprise must pay to the state causes it to expand output, whereas an increase in demand, manifested in the form of a higher price for its output, causes it to retrench.

It is evident from the model that to every price p there corresponds one and only one optimum output y. The *supply schedule* of the enterprise is the graph of this relation. We conclude from this analysis that the short-run supply

---

10. The profit-maximizing enterprise would actually maximize its sales volume py since K and hence R are assumed to be constant.

schedule of the enterprise maximizing net income per member of the collective is negatively sloped (i.e., bends backward) within the range of output in which it will normally operate.

This is an extreme and rather unlikely result. When the supply of labor to the enterprise is less than perfectly elastic, when lower prices must be charged to sell larger outputs (under imperfectly competitive conditions), when more than one product is produced, and when other variable inputs besides labor have to be considered, the previous response of output to price increases is no longer a necessary consequence of the logic of maximizing net income per member.[11] Nevertheless, it remains generally true that the short-run supply of output produced by enterprises pursuing this objective will be less price elastic than what it would be if they were to maximize total profits under the same conditions.

Before analyzing the behavior of a cooperative enterprise in the long run when capital inputs can be varied and new enterprises may enter or leave the industry, it is essential to redefine the enterprise's goal *for the long run*.[12] For an enterprise maximizing profits in the short run, the sum of discounted profits over an infinite horizon is a plausible goal. In principle, as long as the "capitalist" may sell his shares he need not concern himself about any difference between his private rate of discount and the market rate for a given degree of risk. If he is impatient to obtain a quick return and his private discount rate is higher than the market rate, he should still choose the investment yielding the highest profit discounted at the market rate because his policy should enable him to sell his shares immediately at their highest value. If he wishes, he may then buy into another venture with a shorter maturity. But this conceptual neatness is beyond our reach when we treat the long run of the collective enterprise. How are we to compare an investment alternative yielding an expected yearly net income of 1,000 value units per member starting five years hence with another alternative yielding 850 value units per member per year starting two years hence? How should the alternative yields be discounted to the present? The rate of interest charged on the capital made available by the state to the enterprise—no matter how this rate is arrived at—bears no necessary relation to the discount rate that an individual member might like to apply in comparing these alternatives, since claims to future profits in a Yugoslav-type "self-managed" enterprise cannot be bought

11. In addition to Ward's book, readers interested in a detailed analysis of the behavior of the enterprise under these various conditions of supply and demand should consult Jaroslav Vanek, *The General Theory of Labor-Managed Economies* (Ithaca, N.Y.: Cornell University Press, 1972), esp. chap. 4–6.

12. Neither Benjamin Ward nor Jaroslav Vanek in their basic books on this type of enterprise are explicit on this point.

or sold.[13] Members' own rates of discount therefore do matter. A member about to retire from the enterprise will presumably discount profit opportunities at a very high rate because he will lose any claim to profits accruing after his retirement; on the other hand, a younger worker may favor long-range investments if they guarantee him a better prospect of future shares than investments maturing in a shorter period. The subjective probabilities attached by each member to the net income shares that might be expected from different investment opportunities will also affect their relative preferences over these opportunities, as will their attitude toward risk. These problems would arise—and indeed are said actually to arise in the Yugoslav system—with particular acuity in the apportionment of past profits between reinvestment in the enterprise and current dividends to members. Members with a short horizon want a greater share of profits distributed to the collective than do members who can afford, by reason of their youth or of their less immediate needs, to wait patiently for the fruits of past investments to reach their full maturity.

All this suggests that the manager's choice of investment projects in a collective enterprise would be as delicate and complex as the short-run decisions he might have to make regarding the size of the collective itself. In the case of either decision a consistent aggregation of divergent preferences would in all probability be impossible, and to get anything done, the manager might have to act as dictator.[14]

Leaving aside these problems, if for the sake of argument we may assume a given rate of discount of future net incomes per member, the long-term goal of the enterprise under certainty may be described as follows: the choice of a size of collective, of a capital stock, and of a level of material inputs per period that will maximize net income per member of the collective so defined, given a constant technology and prices for both inputs and outputs that are expected to remain fixed over an indefinite horizon.

The classical comparative-statics exercise consists in analyzing the effects on the levels of inputs and outputs of a change in the long-term price of the output. As it turns out, the results depend on the nature of the production

13. If claims *were* sellable, the goal of a manager would be even harder to define. Should he maximize net income per share, regardless of whether the share was held by a working member of the collective? The internal rules of the enterprise would also have to be modified to provide for the rights and the possible representation of shareholders who were not working members. These system rules would bring us too far from observable examples of collective enterprises to warrant pursuing their logical implications. On this and related points, see Svetozar Pejovich, "The Banking System and the Investment Behavior of the Yugoslav Firm," in M. Bornstein, ed., *Plan and Market* (New Haven: Yale University Press, 1973), pp. 294–301.

14. On the relevance of Arrow's possibility theorem to this point, see above p. 169, n. 7. For a recent discussion of organizational rules that may make it possible to get around this problem, see Donald J. Brown, "Aggregation of Preferences," *Quarterly Journal of Economics*, 89 (Aug. 1975): 456–69.

function assumed. In the case of a function exhibiting constant returns to scale, a rise in the long-term price leads to precisely the same result as a rise of the same magnitude in the short-run price. In contrast to a profit-maximizing enterprise, where the capital stock could be expected to expand after the short-run adjustment had been made to the rise in price, there is no incentive for the manager of the enterprise maximizing net income per member of the collective to alter the size of the enterprise's capital stock.[15] In other words, the long-run elasticity of supply of the enterprise is identical to the short-run elasticity, which, as we have already argued, will be smaller than that of its profit-maximizing counterpart.

If, on the other hand, the production function of the enterprise were such that increasing returns at small levels of output were eventually followed by constant and then by decreasing returns—the long-run average cost curve describing a ∪-shaped locus—the enterprise would always operate at points of maximum physical efficiency (i.e., at bottom of the ∪-shaped average-cost curve). A rise in price may or may not lead to an increase in output; it will "normally" be conducive to an increase in the capital/labor ratio.[16] In any event, long-run elasticity will be less than in a comparable profit-maximizing enterprise facing a price in excess of its minimum average cost.

Now when an enterprise with a ∪-shaped cost curve produces at minimum average cost, it is operating at constant returns to scale in the neighborhood of this minimum. Hence, whether the function is constant returns to scale at all levels of output or only at minimum average cost, the observed scale parameter of the function (provided net income per member is really being maximized) should be close to unity. One test of the theory of the labor-managed enterprise, referred to in the next chapter, rests on this conclusion.

As we saw earlier, the Illyrian enterprise, if it is to be considered a realistic analogue of the Yugoslav "labor-managed firm," must be governed by the rule that members have no rights of disposition over their claims to the future profits of the enterprise. This rule has far-reaching consequences for the behavior of managers representing their members' interests. We observed earlier that the rule would incline managers to distribute a larger share of total current net income to members—at the expense of investment—than would a profit-maximizing manager. Furthermore, as Furubotn and Pejovich

15. Vanek, op. cit., p. 47. The reason is essentially that, under conditions where constant returns to scale prevail, returns to the individual factors, once capital and labor are optimally adjusted, exhaust the value of the product. If for any short-run price p, the net income per member equals the marginal-value product of members' labor (equation 15.1), it follows from the first proposition that the returns to the existing capital stock must also be such as to equal the marginal-value product of capital to its price. This implies that there will be no incentive to alter the size of the capital stock in the long run (cf. Vanek, p. 32).

16. Ibid., pp. 48-49.

have argued, managers would be induced to finance the investments that they decided to make by using bank credits rather than by ploughing profits back into the enterprise.[17] As we shall see in the next chapter, the effects of this ownership rule on measurable outcomes have been easier to detect in Yugoslav financial statistics than the implications of the Ward–Vanek model.

15.4 GOALS OF AN ENTERPRISE SUBORDINATE TO AN ADMINISTRATIVE HIERARCHY

A good deal of theoretical work has been done on the behavior of enterprises subordinate to an administrative hierarchy, as in East, where the incentive system for managers is supposed to determine their input and output decisions. A very simple example will illustrate the type of inference that can be drawn from a modification in the incentive system reflected in a change in managerial goals. Suppose an enterprise manager receives bonuses, in the form of a percentage addition to his salary, for fulfilling and overfulfilling his output plan, which is initially defined as the total quantity (tonnage) produced of two items—"large nails" and "small nails"—in the enterprise's production plan. The *tonnage* of large nails produced is y_1 and of small nails y_2. The number of nails in a ton of large nails is z_1, in a ton of small nails z_2. The modification in the incentive system consists in redefining output as the total *number* of the two kinds of nails produced. The comparison is portrayed in diagram 15.1. The production set of the enterprise (lined area) is bounded by a straight line with a slope of $-\frac{1}{2}$, implying a constant rate of transformation of one ton of small nails for two tons of large. If the manager wishes to maximize the tonnage of output, or $y_1 + y_2$, he must give equal weight to a ton of large

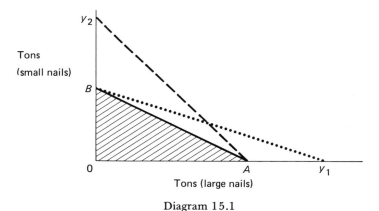

Diagram 15.1

17. Eirik Furubotn and Svetozar Pejovich, "Property Rights, Economic Decentralization, and the Evolution of the Yugoslav Firm, 1965–1972," *Journal of Law and Economics* 16 (Oct. 1973): 281.

and to a ton of small nails. We can imagine a whole family of lines with a slope of -1, each line representing a given level of aggregate output. Aggregate tonnage will be maximized at the point where the production set just touches the line corresponding to the highest aggregate output. This is point A in the diagram, the intersection of the upper boundary of the production set with the dashed line representing the highest aggregate tonnage attainable.

Now let there be three times as many nails in a ton of small nails as in a ton of large, so that $z_1/z_2 = \frac{1}{3}$. Then if the manager wishes to produce the largest possible number of nails, he must maximize $y_1 + 3y_2$. The highest attainable line with a slope of $-\frac{1}{3}$ is the dotted line touching the production set at B. As a result of the modification in the incentive system, the production program of the enterprise has flipped from all large nails to all small nails.[18]

Elaborating on this general line of reasoning, Aleksis Wakar and Janusz G. Zielinski, in an article written in 1962,[19] argued that the effect of a rise in the relative price of one of two products turned out by an enterprise subject to a value-of-output incentive scheme in a centrally directed economy could have the effect of increasing its relative demand. Let there be two enterprises A and B, where B's variable inputs include the products of A. The perverse effect on B's demand of a rise in price in one of A's products is liable to occur provided (1) both products are substitutable inputs in B's production function, (2) the two inputs are used in different proportions in making B's various products, and (3) the prices fixed for the products of B reflect their average costs of production (as is typically the case in the economies of East). Under these conditions, a price rise in one of A's products would trigger a relative increase in the cost of those of B's products that used this input intensively. Enterprise B would then find that the relative weights of these products in its maximand (the value of output at fixed prices) had increased. It would then be induced to tilt its output mix in the direction of these same products. This would in turn cause it to shift its input mix toward greater consumption of the input whose relative price had increased. Its demand for this input would expand at the expense of the other.

In the genre of analyses we have been considering, no more thorough or systematic contribution has been published than the book of Edward Ames on *Soviet Economic Processes*.[20] The enterprise goal he focuses on is the maximization of output, which he subjects to only one system-structure constraint,

18. A cartoon in the Soviet satirical weekly *Krokodil* a number of years ago showed a hoist loading an enormously large nail unto a truck. The implication was that the bonus system for the nail factory was now based on tonnage rather than number.

19. "Socialist Operational Price Systems," *American Economic Review* 53 (March 1963): 109-27. In a subsequent "Comment" (*American Economic Review*, 53 [Dec. 1963]: 1085-93) I attempted to make more precise, and to state the limitations of, the propositions in the Wakar and Zielinski article.

20. (Homewood, Ill., Richard D. Irwin, 1965).

the obligation of the enterprise to cover its costs from its sales receipts. Given a twice differentiable production function exhibiting constant or decreasing returns, fixed amounts of one or more of the inputs, and at least one continuously variable input, marginal costs must rise above average cost beyond a certain output. From this point on, average cost must also be rising. As Ames points out, the policy of maximizing output subject to the necessity of at least covering costs requires that the manager equate price to *average* cost (provided price exceeds minimum average cost), in contrast to a profit-maximizing enterprise, where price would be equated to marginal cost.[21]

Ames's most original contribution consists in his linkage of the enterprise's objective function to the input and output plans laid down for it by its hierarchical supervisor. He argues essentially that output targets and rationed levels of inputs can be incorporated as points of discontinuity in the enterprise's revenue and cost functions. On the input side, for instance, a ration v_0 of an input may be interpreted as the maximum amount that can be purchased by the enterprise at a price (or cost) of w per unit. If more of the input is demanded than v_0, a higher price will have to be paid or a higher cost incurred than w (the enterprise may obtain extra supplies by producing the item for its own use at a higher cost; alternatively, it may, at some cost to itself, try to secure a larger ration by "lobbying" at higher levels in the hierarchy or by directly putting pressure on a supplier).

On the output side, the enterprise may be able to sell above-target output at a higher price (as in the case of "decentralized" Soviet agricultural procurements). A feature of many systems in the centrally directed systems of East in the 1950s and 1960s was that enterprises were able to retain a larger fraction of profits from the sale of above-target output than from output below or on target. To the extent that retained profits were weighted more highly in the utility function of enterprise managers than profits turned over to the state budget, above-plan output could be said to be worth more than below- or on-plan output.[22] This again could be interpreted as a two-step price system.

Ames sets forth the conditions necessary for maximum output (in a one-product enterprise) subject to the no-loss constraint, using step (Stieltjes) integrals to describe the revenue and cost functions.[23] Finally, the expression

21. Ibid., p. 60.
22. Ibid., p. 88.
23. Let output be a function of consumed inputs $v_1, \ldots, v_j, \ldots, v_n$. The expression for total costs is

$$\sum_{j=1}^{n} \int_{z_j \leqslant v_j} dw_j(z_j),$$

where dw_j is a marginal increment in the jth input price, and z_j the actual consumption of j.

for the optimum may be differentiated with respect to the output target or to any of the input rations to predict the impact of small changes in targets or rations on the equilibrium condition.[24] As in the case of the comparative statics of the profit-maximizing enterprise, there is no simple general solution to the problem of tracing the complex ramifications of a disturbance in an initial equilibrium due to a small change in either the availability of an input or an input plan. In both cases the solution involves partial second derivatives of the output with respect to every pair of inputs j and k $(\partial^2 x/\partial v_j v_k)$. The difference is that for the constrained enterprise all such cross derivatives are multiplied by $(1 + p_1\lambda)$ or $(1 + p_2\lambda)$, where p_1 is the price obtained for quantities sold below target and p_2 for larger quantities, and λ is the shadow price associated with the constraint that obliges the enterprise to cover costs from receipts.[25]

Ames's formalization of the role of the plan in the determination of an output-maximizing enterprise's production program can at least in part be reconciled with our earlier approach, in which we conceived enterprises as being constrained by the acceptable conditions imposed on them by their supervisors. For below-plan output, we may think of the enterprise receiving a penalty or negative price. For output at or above target (i.e., in the acceptable set), price becomes positive. Similarly for inputs, quantities up to the sanctioned quotas are in the acceptable set (and are charged at a lower price) and above quotas are charged with a penalty price. Ames's approach is more flexible in that it allows the enterprise to generate a program, some of whose input or output elements will be in the acceptable set and some will not (at the cost of paying higher prices for above-quota inputs and getting lower— possibly negative—prices for below-target output). Its disadvantage is that it cannot cope with situations where the supervisor is willing to accept some

---

To simplify, suppose there are only two steps for each input price: the price w_{j1} obtains if $v_j \leqslant v_{j0}$ (a maximum ration of the jth input) and w_{j2} if $v_j > v_{j0}$:

$$\int_{z_j \leqslant v_j} dw_j(z_j) = \begin{cases} w_{j1}v_j & \text{if } v_j \leqslant v_{j0} \\ w_{j1}v_{j0} + w_{j2}v_j & \text{if } v_j > v_{j0}. \end{cases}$$

Total cost may then be obtained as the sum of all such two-valued expressions for the costs of separate inputs.

24. Ames, op. cit., pp. 90–91.
25. λ is the Lagrangian multiplier in the expression

$$G \equiv x - \lambda \left[\int_{z \leqslant x} dp(z) - \sum_{j=1}^{n} \int_{z_j \leqslant v_j} dw_j(z_j) \right],$$

where $x = x(v_1, \ldots, v_n)$. The maximization of G presupposes that the enterprise maximizes output x subject to the no-loss constraint in brackets.

trade-off between a larger output of some good and a lower output of another or between a larger input of one good and a smaller input of another. In effect the acceptable sets implicit in Ames's approach are bounded for any pair of goods by "corner indifference curves." Which model is more appropriate will of course depend on the particular problem at hand and on the possibilities of deriving interesting (preferably testable) inferences from the logic of either set of behavioral assumptions.

15.5 Alternative Goals Viewed as Systemic Constraints on the Behavior of Enterprises[26]

In this section we attempt to formalize a system trait introduced in chapter 11, where we alluded to the virtual security of employment in large Japanese enterprises. An injunction against firing employees can of course be regarded as a policy rather than as a system rule. The difference between a policy and a rule is that a policy may be violated under certain states of the environment —whenever its enforcement would lead to a serious loss—whereas a rule is most appropriately treated as a constraint on managerial decisions. In a linear-programming model of the enterprise the policy might be expressed in the objective function,[27] the rule in the set of constraints. For the sake of convenience rather than of principle, we will assume that the enterprise is strictly bound by a no-dismissals constraint.

In keeping with a time-hallowed precedent, we shall call the countries where our "representative enterprises" are supposed to operate not by the names of the countries they are meant to be typical of but by mythical names suggestive of the applications we have in mind. Thus Friedmania is the economy where enterprise managers feel no compunction about dismissing employees when demand for their products declines and Nipponia the economy where managers are bound by the no-dismissals constraint.[28]

---

26. The following analysis of a Japanese-type enterprise subject to a no-dismissals constraint has benefited from some of the ideas on this subject in Miss Amy Stevens's Yale College, senior essay, written at my suggestion and under my supervision (New Haven, May 1973). However, her model differs in some essential respects from the one outlined below.

27. Perhaps the easiest way to do this might be to assign a large negative weight in the objective function to the slack activity in the employment equation. For most other concatenations of constraints, activity coefficients, and weights in the objective function, this slack activity would be operated at zero level of intensity (i.e., it would not enter the optimal basis). For some extraordinary concatenations, however, it may be presumed that it would be operated at a positive level. It is of course conceivable that employees might be kept on the payroll even though they were redundant. We assume in this discussion that redunduncy implies dismissal.

28. The term "Nipponese" enterprise was already used to describe an enterprise subject to a "no-dismissals" constraint by E. Neuberger and Estelle James in their paper, "The Yugoslav Self-Managed Enterprise: A Systemic Approach," in Bornstein, ed., op. cit., p. 268.

We suppose that Friedmania (F) and Nipponia (N) have the same resource endowment, level of development, and "relative scarcities" (i.e., the same price ratios prevail in F and N for any pair of goods or services). The manager of the "representative enterprise" in F maximizes profits subject only to the constraints of his technology and his fixed capital investment. The manager of the representative enterprise in N also maximizes profits but must comply with the additional system-structure restraint that he cannot dismiss any of his enterprise employees. If employment in the enterprise in N rises from L_1 to L_2, then, by this ratchet principle, L_2 becomes the minimum level of employment henceforward.

Enterprises in F and N operate in a "perfectly competitive environment," by which we shall mean that they either have no influence on the prices they can get for their output and on the prices for which they can buy their inputs, or that they choose to ignore such market power as they may have and take "market prices" as given. The representative enterprises in F and N have the same technology, or production function, relating their outputs—a single commodity—to the inputs they consume. They both face fluctuations in the prices of their outputs relative to the prices of their inputs (more on this later). For the sake of simplicity we shall assume that the prices of the inputs remain the same throughout the period of analysis.

The common technology of the enterprise in F and N is described as follows. Output y is a function f, homogeneous in the first degree and twice differentiable with respect to its arguments. Its three arguments are capital goods K, labor L, and materials M:

$$y \equiv f(K, L, M),$$

where $\partial y/\partial K > 0$, $\partial y/\partial L > 0$, $\partial y/\partial M > 0$, $\partial^2 y/\partial K^2 \leqslant 0$, $\partial^2 y/\partial L^2 \leqslant 0$, $\partial^2 y/\partial M^2 \leqslant 0$ for all levels of output considered. Thus, marginal productivities are positive throughout, and the marginal productivity of capital, labor, or materials is either reduced or remains constant when an increment of any of these factors is added to the input mix. These assumptions imply that marginal-cost curves will be convex from below (but not necessarily strictly convex). For purposes of diagrammatic illustration, but without loss of analytical generality, I will also assume that L and M are complementary factors in production (i.e., $\partial^2 y/\partial L \partial M > 0$). In the following discussion we shall ignore fixed capital costs and call "profits" the difference between the value of output and the costs of labor and materials. As is well known, the behavior of an enterprise maximizing these quasi-rents should theoretically be identical to that of a comparable enterprise maximizing profits net of capital costs.

In diagram 15.2, when the stock of capital available to enterprises in F and N is fixed at K_0 but both L and M can be freely adjusted, the marginal cost

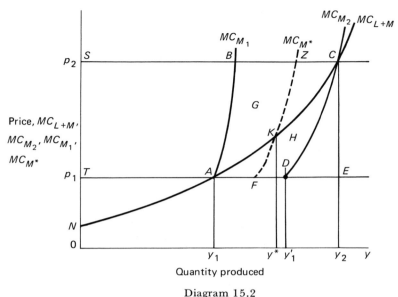

Diagram 15.2

of production traces out the curve MC_{L+M} as y is increased. We assume that only two prices can occur: a low price p_1 and a high price p_2. The incidence of these prices is random, the distribution being the same for both enterprises. Suppose that p_1 occurred in the first period. Both types of enterprises will maximize profits when price is p_1 at the output y_1 corresponding to the intersection (at point A) of MC_{L+M} and the p_1 price-level line. If the price were now to rise to p_2, the enterprise in F would maximize profits at an output y_2 corresponding to point C.

Curve MC_{M_1} in diagram 15.2 represents marginal cost when employment is fixed at the level that would maximize profits instantaneously for a price equal to p_1; similarly, MC_{M_2} is the marginal-cost curve when employment is fixed at the (instantaneous) profit-maximizing level corresponding to p_2. When output is expanded to y_2 upon the occurrence of p_2 and price in the next period falls to p_1, the (instantaneous) profit-maximizing output becomes y_1' (at the intersection D of MC_{M_2} with p_1).

Finally, the dashed curve labeled MC_{M*} is the marginal-cost curve obtained when employment is fixed at a level corresponding to an output between y_1 and y_2 that would maximize profits for a hypothetical price between p_1 p_2. Because MC_{M*} is associated with a fixed level of employment that is smaller than that corresponding to y_2 but larger than that corresponding to y_1, it must be steeper than MC_{M_2} but less steep than MC_{M_1} (since L and M are complementary factors in production).

We now return to the original situation, where price has risen from p_1 to p_2. What should the enterprise in N now do if it wishes to maximize expected profits over an indefinite horizon, but with a fixed capital stock still equal to K_0? If the choice of its outputs were limited to y_1 and y_2 and if the manager expected that p_1 and p_2 had about the same probability of occurrence, it would move to y_2. The reason for this is as follows. Whenever p_2 occurred after it had moved to y_2, the increment in profits over and above the profits earned if it had stayed at y_1 would be represented by the area bounded by the points A, B, and C (the area marked G). On the other hand, whenever p_1 occurred, the incremental loss would be ACD (the area marked H).[29] Since MC_{M_2} will be less steeply inclined than MC_{M_1} (because materials are combined with larger amounts of other inputs at y_2 than at y_1) and since $MC_{L + M}$ is convex, G must be larger than H. If p_1 and p_2 are equiprobable, it should therefore pay the enterprise in N to move to y_2.

Consider now the possibility of expanding employment and output to an in-between position such as that shown by point K. It is clear from the diagram that if employment is set at the level associated with y^*, the reduction in profit compared to the situation at y_2 (the area ZKC) is smaller than the reduction in labor costs that this contraction in employment will make it possible to economize (the area $CDFK$). Hence, if p_1 and p_2 are equally probable, it will be more profitable to set employment at the point corresponding to y^* than to the point corresponding to y_2.

If we are willing to make the simplifying assumption that all second and cross-partial derivatives with respect to L and M vanish, an assumption that may be justified as a linear approximation in the neighborhood of the long-run profit-maximizing output,[30] we can prove a stronger result, which will be stated below.

Diagram 15.2 is now redrawn as 15.3 with the linear marginal-cost curves implied by our new assumption. It should be evident from diagram 15.2 that there is no loss in generality in restricting our attention to the prices $p_1 = 0$ and $p_2 = 1$.[31]

In diagram 15.3, y^* identifies the cost-minimizing output at which employment L has been fixed. The output y^* would have been chosen by a profit-maximizing entrepreneur in the absence of any restrictions on the

---

29. For L fixed at the cost-minimizing level for output y_1, profits when p_2 occurs equal the area $NABS$; for L fixed at the level corresponding to y_2, profits when p_2 occurs equal the area bordered by MC_{L+M} from N to C or $NACS$. The increment in profits from p_1 to p_2 is therefore the area BAC, marked G.

30. For such a justification, see Martin Weitzman, "Prices vs. Quantities," MIT, Department of Economics, Working Paper 106, Apr. 1973, p. 14.

31. However, we must assume that when $p_1 = 0$, the enterprise in N will still produce a positive output corresponding to the point where its short-run marginal cost equals zero (y^1 in diagram 15.3). Our procedure is equivalent to a displacement of the origin of the coordinates in the northeast direction.

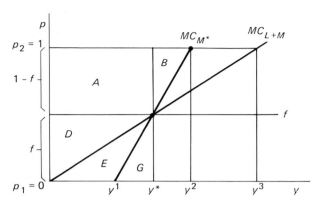

Diagram 15.3

dismissal of employees if the short-run price f had occurred (since the price line f intersects the marginal cost line MC_{L+M} at an output equal to y^*). Clearly $0 \leqslant f \leqslant 1$. Let ρ_1 be the probability of p_1 and ρ_2 the probability of p_2. The expected price $E(p)$ equals $\rho_1(0) + (1 - \rho_1)(1) = 1 - \rho_1$ (since $\rho_2 = 1 - \rho_1$).

It is easy to verify the following proposition: To maximize profits over an indefinite horizon (but with a fixed capital stock) when only prices $p_1 (= 0)$ and $p_2 (= 1)$ can occur, the enterprise should fix employment at a level L^* corresponding to the output, denoted y^*, that would be profit maximizing in the absence of any constraints on employment in both short and long run if the price $f = \rho_2 (\equiv 1 - \rho_1)$ were expected to prevail.[32] In other words the marginal cost for L^* should be set equal to expected price.

32. *Proof.* Let the constant slope of MC_{M^*} be denoted σ_{M^*} and the slope of MC_{L+M}, σ_{L+M}. Note that the line segment $0y^*$ is equal to f/σ_{L+M}, the segment y^1 to y^* to f/σ_{M^*}, and the segment y^* to y^2 is equal to $(1-f)/\sigma_{M^*}$. It is immediately verified that, when L is fixed at $L(y^*)$, profits, on the occurrence of $p_2 (= 1)$, will be equal to the sum of the areas $D + A + B$ or

$$\pi_2 = \frac{f^2}{2\sigma_{L+M}} + \frac{(1-f)f}{\sigma_{L+M}} + \frac{(1-f)^2}{2\sigma_{M^*}}.$$

On the occurrence of $p_1 (= 0)$, losses will be equal to area E, which is equal to $(E + G)$ minus G; hence

$$\pi_1 = \frac{-f^2}{2\sigma_{L+M}} + \frac{f^2}{2\sigma_{M^*}}.$$

Expected profits $E(\pi)$ are equal to $\rho_1\pi_1 + (1 - \rho_1)\pi_2$ or

$$E(\pi) = \frac{\rho_1 f}{\sigma_{M^*}} - \frac{f}{\sigma_{M^*}} + \frac{f^2}{2\sigma_{M^*}} + \frac{1}{2\sigma_{M^*}} - \frac{\rho_1}{2\sigma_{M^*}} - \frac{f^2}{2\sigma_{L+M}} + \frac{f}{\sigma_{L+M}} - \frac{\rho_1 f}{\sigma_{L+M}}.$$

We can also show that the expected profit in N will be equal to area $E + G/f$, whereas the expected profit in Friedmania will be $E/f + G/f$.[33] As long as $f < 1$, expected profit will be smaller in N than in F, the difference being inversely proportional to the probability of occurrence of the higher price. The difference in expected profit is also proportional to the area E, which in turn will vary positively with the difference between the slopes of MC_{M*} and MC_{L+M}.

There is no simple expression for the expected variance of profits in this model. But calculations based on a few examples show either that the expected variances are equal in N and F (in the case where $\rho_1 = \rho_2 = \frac{1}{2}$) or that it is actually greater in N than in F.

The conclusions we draw from our comparative analysis of the "typical enterprise" in N and F are these. (1) The *average* level of output and employment in N and F will be approximately the same (resp. identical under the simplifying assumption of vanishing second derivatives). (2) Output will rise less when the price is high and fall less when the price is low in N than in F (i.e., the expected variance in output will be less in N than in F). (3) Expected profits will be smaller in N than in F (the difference varying inversely with the probability of occurrence of the higher price). (4) There will be no compensation for the risk-neutral or -averse entrepreneur in N due to a smaller expected variance in profits than in F.

It is also easy to verify that if the capital stock of the enterprise in N is expanding while the probability distribution of prices remains the same, it will be profitable to expand employment to a level relatively closer to that which would be optimal if p_2 were known to occur in all periods than in the static case.

All these differences in outcomes in N and F will be the more pronounced, the greater the proportion of labor to material costs in both representative enterprises.

I will not burden the reader with a detailed comparative analysis of the

---

After taking the derivative of $E(\pi)$ with respect to f, setting the result equal to zero, and simplifying, we obtain

$$f^* \left(\frac{1}{\sigma_{M*}} - \frac{1}{\sigma_{L+M}}\right) = -(1 - \rho_1)\left(\frac{1}{\sigma_{L+M}} - \frac{1}{\sigma_{M*}}\right) \text{ or } f^* = 1 - \rho_1 = \rho_2.$$

33. This can be seen by replacing $(1 - \rho_1)$ by f in the expression for $E(\pi)$ in N in the preceding footnote. This yields after simplification

$$E(\pi) = \frac{f^2}{2\sigma_{L+M}} + \frac{f(1 - f)}{2\sigma_{M*}} = (E + G) - G + \frac{f}{2\sigma_{M*}} = E + \frac{G}{f},$$

where E and G denote the areas in diagram 15.3. In F, $E(\pi) = (1 - \rho_1)/2\sigma_{L+M} = f/2\sigma_{L+M} = (E + G)/f$.

behavior of a "monopolistic enterprise"[34] in N and in F. Suffice it to say that if both enterprises were faced with a random "demand"[35] in the form of parallel linear schedules D_1 and D_2 with equiprobable incidence, outputs in N would vary within a smaller compass than in F, whereas profit-maximizing prices—at the outputs where the appropriate marginal cost equals marginal revenue—would exhibit a wider range in N than in F.[36] My unproved conjecture, based on some illustrative examples, is that the level of profits in N will be lower than the one corresponding to the profit-maximizing output where expected marginal revenue equals MC_{L+M}. Given "bounded rationality" and limited information,[37] I should think an enterprise in N could not do better than follow the rule of thumb of setting employment at a level corresponding to the output generating a marginal cost equal to expected price.

So far we have proceeded on the assumption that the capital stock of the enterprise in N and F was at least initially fixed at the same given level. If we now eliminate this restraint, what can we predict about the long-run adjustment of the enterprise in the two hypothetical economies operating in an identical environment? Since the enterprise in N will face lower profit expectations than the one in F for a given capital stock, the entrepreneur in N will wish to invest less and build a smaller-size plant. However, he may design the plant for a smaller labor force—he may choose a higher capital/labor ratio—than he would if employees could be freely laid off when demand declined. He will be especially intent on reducing his employment relative to the size of his capital investment in a situation where his impacted labor force might be expected to outlast his equipment.[38]

34. For this purpose we may define a monopolistic enterprise as one that can sell larger quantities of its product at a lower price, where the schedule relating quantity sold to price is uniquely determined by the incomes and preferences of the individuals in the system. This definition is unsatisfactory, but it cannot be improved upon without an elaborate discussion of the price and quantity decisions open to producers of substitute products.

35. The "demand" for x is defined here as the quantity of the product that the enterprise is able to sell at every price. It is the image of the functional relation $D = D(p)$, where price is a nonnegative number. The usual assumption is made that the supply and demand schedules are independent.

36. The reader can easily verify this proposition with the aid of a diagram. In addition to D_1 and D_2 and their corresponding marginal-revenue lines MR_1 and MR_2, he will need to draw four marginal-cost curves corresponding to four different rules regarding the optimal level of employment: (1) MC_{L+M} (variable cost minimizing employment); (2) MC_{M_1} (employment set at the level of output where MR_1 intersects with MC_{L+M}); (3) MC_{M_2} (employment set at the level of output where MR_2 intersects MC_{L+M}); and (4) MC_{M*} (employment set at an in-between level that maximizes the sum of discounted profits for equiprobable D_1 and D_2). The precise location of this last marginal-cost schedule cannot easily be ascertained.

37. For these concepts, see chap. 2, p. 16.

38. I am indebted to Egon Neuberger for this point.

One would predict also that the management in F would choose machinery and equipment that was less complementary with labor and, generally speaking, that was less specialized than the management in N would opt for. Such a policy would provide more leeway for adjustment to fluctuations in demand in F via changes in capital intensity. There is nothing to be lost in N by designing a plant with extreme complementarity between labor and equipment as long as the proportions between the two factors cannot be altered.

It would be idle to pursue the logic of these special assumptions any further. The assumption of an identical environment, in particular, is untenable at least as long as the enterprises in N and F are really representative of the industry to which they belong and as long as the industry is large enough to have an impact on the total effective demand of the participants in the system. For under these conditions the environments in which the two contrasted enterprises operate are most unlikely to be identical. In particular, the fluctuations in demand in N may be less pronounced than in F. Owing to the smaller size that we have just predicted, enterprises in N might also face more competitive conditions than those in F. Finally, as we shall see in the next chapter, where the economics of the entire industry will be discussed, the no-dismissals rule can be modified in any number of ways to mitigate its depressing effect on profits. An enterprise may vary the labor input of its fixed working force by inducing them to work shorter or longer hours or by putting pressure on them to work more or less intensively. It may hire temporary workers with a status different from "permanent employees." And it may subcontract orders to smaller enterprises and let them take the brunt of adjustment to fluctuations in demand.

From this last proposition we infer that the efficient partitioning of an economy may also be influenced by the internal rules adopted by "production units."

A final remark concerns the relationship between the behavior of the enterprise with a goal of maximizing net income per member of the collective and the enterprise in N operating under a no-layoffs constraint. We have questioned, with regard to the former, whether the size of the collective was likely to be under the manager's control. If we suppose instead that the size of the collective could not be curtailed, would it behave identically with the enterprise in N, at least in the short run?[39] One crucial difference would remain. The profit-maximizing manager of an enterprise in N faced by a higher price *that he considered to be permanent* would wish to increase employment to the point where marginal cost equaled price. This would not be true of the

---

39. Neuberger and James, op. cit., pp. 266–67, argue that the collective enterprise is likely to behave as if it were subject to a no-dismissals constraint.

manager of the collective, because with a fixed capital stock he would generate the maximum net income per member with the existing size of the collective. The only short-run gain in output that could possibly result would be due to the longer hours the members might be willing to work or the greater effort they might put forth. But since the substitution effect of income for leisure that accompanies the rise in income shares could easily be swamped by the negative effect on work and effort of higher income, this result could not be expected with any degree of certainty. In the long run there would be an incentive for the collective enterprise with a ∪-shaped long-run average-cost curve to adjust its capital stock in such a way as to minimize long-run average costs at the new higher price,[40] but, whether it did so by expanding or by contracting the size of its capital stock, the comparable enterprise in N would exhibit a higher level of output and employment.

40. Vanek, op. cit., pp. 31–33.

16

Industry-wide Implications of
Various Enterprise Goals

16.1 SUPPLY SCHEDULE OF THE HOMOGENEOUS INDUSTRY AND ITS WELFARE IMPLICATIONS

An *industry*, the set of enterprises consisting of all the producers of a particular good, may be more or less homogeneous in the rules constraining managerial decisions or it may be heterogeneous. Homogeneity is more likely to be observed when the goals and constraints of enterprises are shaped by system-wide rules. Heterogeneity is more likely when the system structure is permissive in this respect *and* more than one internal rule is "viable," in the sense that any two randomly chosen enterprises in the system pursuing different goals and subject to different rules will both have an appreciable chance of survival over the period of observation or comparison. We shall first study the aggregate behavior of enterprises in a homogeneous industry and then move on to the consideration of "mixed systems."

The first question to be posed in an industry-wide context is whether a specific goal pursued by an enterprise in a competitive environment is necessary to its survival. In chapter 10 we argued, on the basis of Winter's model, that enterprises might be compelled to maximize profits under the pressure of competition. Could there be similar pressures on Illyrian enterprises to maximize the net income per member of the collective or on the Nipponian enterprise to maximize profits subject to a no-dismissals constraint? These pressures would have to come from the side of collective members in the first case and of employees in the second. For instance, one could imagine that a collective enterprise would not be able to retain a member unless his net-income share was at least equal to some parametric "competitive income" that he could earn elsewhere. In that case the maximization of net income per member would be tantamount to the maximization of profits.[1] However,

---

1. Suppose that each collective member's income w is competitively determined at the level w^*. The collective maximizes net income per member when $(py - R/L) \geqslant w^*$, where p denotes the competitive price of the unique good produced, y is the level of this good's output, R stands for the exogenously imposed capital charges, and L is the size of the collective. This is equivalent to the maximand, $py - R - w^*L$, of a profit-maximizing enterprise, provided the effort put forth and the number of hours worked per member of the collective were fixed.

there is no mechanism in a workers' management system for ensuring the equality of incomes for equivalent skills across enterprises. (There is no incentive for an enterprise pursuing the maximization of net income *per member* to hire an additional member simply because he would be willing to accept a lower expected income than the average level in that enterprise.) Similarly, in the case of "Nippon," an employee might refuse to work for an enterprise unless he were given assurances that he would never be dismissed, but for this behavior to put effective pressure on the prospective employer, the attitude of employees on the subject of life tenure would have to be homogeneous throughout the economy. Otherwise, employers would be able to make up their labor force exclusively of individuals who did not have a strong preference for security.

Since it is unlikely that the hypothetical goals of the enterprise in Illyria and in Nippon would be reinforced by competitive pressures, we are all the more obliged to question whether the behavioral assumptions we speculated on in the last chapter are compatible with the way in which organizations made up of people with differing preferences might reasonably be expected to behave. I have already expressed my doubts in the last chapter with regard to the decision-making process for determining the size of the collective of an Illyrian enterprise under effective workers' control. The no-layoffs rule, on the other hand, does not seem to contradict any principle of organization and should stand a good chance of survival in a competitive process, provided that all other managers were also bound by the rule. In a mixed system, however, enterprises subject to the no-layoffs rule would have to have some competitive advantage, due to technology, size, special ability to recruit skilled personnel, or other factors, that would offset its lower expected profitability.

When in the last chapter we compared the classical profit-maximizing competitive "Friedmanian" enterprise unconstrained by system rules with the "Illyrian" enterprise maximizing net income per member of the collective and with the "Nipponian" enterprise maximizing profits subject to a no-dismissals constraint, we found that the increase in output of a good induced by an increase in its competitive price was likely to be smaller for the Illyrian or the Nipponian enterprise than for the unconstrained profit-maximizing enterprise operating in the same environment. What are the consequences of this smaller supply elasticity for the industry as a whole? Clearly, if the enterprises composing the industry are otherwise identical[2] in all three systems, the supply schedule of the industry for this good should be more steeply inclined "in the short run" in Illyria and Nipponia than in Fried-

---

2. By "otherwise identical," I mean that they have the same capital stock and technology and are directed by individuals possessing the same managerial skills.

mania. (The *short run* is here defined as a period that is not protracted enough either to allow existing producers to alter substantially the size of their plant or to permit entry into the industry of new producers attracted by higher prices within the range that we wish to study.)

Consider the solution or solutions of the equation $D_1(p) = S_1(p)$, where $D_1(p)$ is the aggregate demand function and $S_1(p)$ the short-run aggregate supply function for good X and where S_1 and D_1 are assumed to be independent. A *partial equilibrium price* p^* is defined here as a "locally stable" non-negative solution of the above equation.[3] Suppose now that, owing to a relative increase in consumers' preferences for X, demand shifts to $D_2(p)$, where $D_2(p) > D_1(p)$ for all positive p. The smaller elasticity of supply at all levels of aggregate output in N and in Illyria implies that the rise in the partial-equilibrium price from p^* to p^{**} as a result of the demand shift will be steeper in N and in Illyria than in a system where all enterprises maximize profits without any system-structure restraint on managers' decisions.

In the analysis of the typical enterprise in F and N in the last chapter input prices were assumed to stay unchanged as output prices varied. If we relax this assumption for the industry as a whole, we reason that the disparity in outcomes in N and F, for a given variance in output prices, will be reduced, provided wages are flexible downward in F. This is so because profit-maximizing entrepreneurs in F will be induced, when demand slackens and a part of the work force is laid off, to retain a greater number of employees at lower wages than they would if input prices were fixed. The more inelastic the labor supply facing the industry in F, under conditions where wages are flexible downward, the smaller will be the effect on output of a change in output price, and hence the smaller the difference in output between N and F. Conversely, minimum wage laws and strong unions capable to preventing a decline in wages in F will tend to accentuate the disparity in the response of N and F enterprises to changes in output prices. (I presume of course that the labor unions in F are not powerful enough to block layoffs when demand is down.)

Even after taking account of changes in the prices of the inputs utilized by

3. Let η and ε be two arbitrary small positive numbers such that $\eta > \varepsilon$. The solution p^* of the equation is *locally stable* if

$$S_1(p^* + \eta) - D_1(p^* + \eta) > S_1(p^* + \varepsilon) - D_1(p^* + \varepsilon) > 0 \quad \text{and}$$
$$D_1(p^* - \eta) - S_1(p^* - \eta) > D_1(p^* - \varepsilon) - D_1(p^* - \varepsilon) > 0$$

for any η and ε such that $\eta > \varepsilon > 0$. Benjamin Ward points out, in the case of the enterprise maximizing net income per member of the collective, that there will be no locally stable equilibrium—indeed no equilibrium at all—if both $D(p)$ and $S(p)$ are linear and $S(p)$ is negatively sloped unless the slope of $S(p)$ is algebraically smaller than that of $D(p)$ (*The Socialist Economy* [Berkeley: University of California Press, 1967], p. 192).

the industry and of the possibilities of subcontracting, we may expect greater fluctuations in prices for comparable short-run shifts in demand in an N-type than in an F-type economy. When demand slackens, owing for example to a drop in aggregate income, prices will go down more in N than in F. In an international market where N-type and F-type enterprises located in the same or in different countries are competing, the former will tend to gain sales at the expense of the latter. In the 1974–75 recession, for example, Japanese manufacturing enterprises were said to be reducing their prices faster than their competitors in the United States and Western Europe. Their share of the international market for their exports would have increased even faster if the overall strength of demand for Japanese products had not propped the exchange value of the yen and moderated the decline in prices expressed in other currencies.[4]

Adaptation to changing demand conditions, as evidence culled from the Japanese economy suggests, will also come from subcontracting, overtime hours, and the hiring or firing of "temporary workers." Empirical evidence on these points, however, requires at least a brief discussion of Japan's "mixed system", which will be considered in sec. 16.3.

To return now to the balance of advantages and disadvantages of the Illyrian economy, the basic issue is the freedom *and* speed of entry of new enterprises in the industry when prices are high and of the exit of the less efficiently managed or less well situated enterprises when they are low. Now the creation of a new enterprise, even when entry is encouraged by national or by local ruling organizations, is not a simple matter. If employment is reasonably full, the new coalition must to formed by bringing together individuals with certain skills and talents who belong to existing organizations. At the very least it takes time to find such people and to allow them to wind up their current affairs. If their net incomes are presently low but their expectations are higher because their enterprise has invested heavily, they will have a stake in future profits that may prevent them from quitting despite immediately superior prospects in another enterprise. (Of course, mobility would be enhanced if the stakes in future profits were transferable, perhaps in the form of equity shares or bonds, but the conspicuous absence of a mechanism for transfer in any of the six republics of Yugoslavia suggests that one ought not to place too much weight on this alternative at the present time.) Finally, the ruling organization dispensing capital to new enterprises will have to investigate the prospects of the potential entrant, which also may take fairly long.[5]

4. I am indebted to Richard N. Cooper for this point.

5. For an exhaustive analysis of the entry problem in a labor-managed economy, see Stephen R. Sacks, *Entry of New Competitors in Yugoslav Market Socialism*, Research Series No. 19, Institute of International Studies, University of California, Berkeley, 1973.

In sum, I should think it would be highly optimistic to expect that entry and exit would eliminate, or come close to eliminating, the swings in prices that the analysis of the short-run leads us to anticipate. What is worse, lags in the positive response of supply to an outward shift in demand that does not happen to be permanent may delay the expansion of supply until demand has shifted downward again. Supply may increase when demand is slack and contract when it is buoyant. This cobweb-type phenomenon is familiar to students of agriculture in situations where supply cannot respond until the planted seeds come to maturity or until newborn hogs grow to an age at which they can be advantageously marketed.

If these speculations are to yield any judgments on the relative merits of system rules, they must be accompanied by an evaluation of the probable outcomes in terms of some norm—be it only the norm favored by the com- parer. Price swings will cause roughly proportional fluctuations in the income shares of members of collectives. To the extent they are risk averse, as we should expect most individuals to be at relatively low levels of income, these fluctuations will give rise to an odiosum or, obversely, will have an adverse effect on the achievement of the stability desideratum. This is surely a count against any system whose rules would inhibit supply response in this way. However, by itself it would not be enough to condemn such systems, because the odiosum involved must be compared with the hardship inflicted on dis- missed employees of profit-maximizing enterprises when demand flags. To reach a judgment about the merits of two such contrasting systems operating under hypothetically identical environments, one would have to examine other elements of the system structure, including unemployment insurance schemes in "capitalist" economies and the opportunities open to individuals in collective economies for mitigating the effects of fluctuations in their net- income shares by borrowing on their expected earnings in times of slack demand.

The analysis of the system becomes more complicated if we allow for the pressure of enterprises on ruling organizations to modify system rules in their interest. The most likely move in this direction would be a request to allow collusion in order to dampen the wide swings in prices, and hence in net incomes per member, arising from competition. In view of the heavy weight placed on equity and stability by political leaders in collective economies, it would not be surprising if these pressures tended to throttle competition. Ruling organizations, alternatively, might on their own decide that price and income fluctuations were intolerable and clamp price controls on enterprises.

To confuse further the evaluation of the relative merits of the Illyrian system rule, a couple of hard-to-pin-down but potentially important points must be adduced. It has been argued that members of a collective would be apt to work harder and more efficiently for "their" enterprise than would a subordinate in a hierarchically organized profit-maximizing enterprise. One may even urge that, irrespective of any putative effect on labor productivity, the collective member's feeling that he is "his own boss" and that he is free of "alienation" ought to be given a substantial positive weight in the economy's norm function.[6] Unfortunately, the evidence from Yugoslavia does not give much support to far to either the claim that productivity is stimulated or the claim that members get substantial "psychic income" from collective owner-ship.[7]

16.2 EMPIRICAL EVIDENCE ON THE BEHAVIOR OF COLLECTIVELY MANAGED ENTERPRISES

With the exception of a couple of casual references to the Yugoslav experience, we have confined our exposition to a priori theorizing on the behavior of an enterprise maximizing net income per member of the collective and of an industry made up of such enterprises. A number of propositions emerge from this analysis with regard to (1) the supply inelasticity of industries, (2) the extent of fluctuations in prices and outputs, (3) lasting disparities in net-income dividends distributed per member in different enterprises, (4) the relatively high capital intensity of enterprises, and (5) the constancy of returns to scale in the neighborhood of production points. These propositions would appear to be testable, at least if the behavior of collective enterprises could be compared with profit-maximizing enterprises in market systems. To my knowledge, no fully satisfactory tests have been carried out for any of these hypotheses, owing in part to the paucity of available system-wide observations on the behavior of collective enterprises. Besides Yugoslavia, Peru and Bangladesh have experimented with "self-management" in publicly owned enterprises, but these experiments have not lasted long enough and have not generated sufficiently reliable data to include these two economies in a multicountry comparison, where the presence or absence of an Illyrian-type system could be expressed by a dummy variable.

In the fairly extensive quantitative work that has been done on the Yugoslav economy, there has been surprisingly little interest in testing hypotheses derived from system rules. Much effort has been devoted to the measurement of "technical progress" reflected in the portion of the growth in outputs that cannot be explained by increases in measurable inputs. On the whole, these

6. For an eloquent statement of some of the more subtle advantages of the "labor-managed economy," see Jaroslav Vanek, *The General Theory of Labor-Managed Economies* (Ithaca, N.Y.: Cornell University Press, 1972), pp. 243–48 and chap. 13.

7. For a review of the fragmentary evidence on these points, see Egon Neuberger and Estelle James, "The Yugoslav Self-Managed Enterprise: A Systemic Approach," in M. Bornstein, ed., *Plan and Market.*

residuals have been high,[8] and a number of observers have succumbed to the temptation of attributing this apparently high level of "dynamic efficiency" to the superiority of Yugoslavia's system structure. Thus Trent J. Bertran concludes from his comparative study of changes in capital and labor productivity (with respect to GNP) in six East European and eight West European economies in the period 1951 to 1964 that "Yugoslavia's decentralized system with workers management progressively developing in the enterprises was more productive in the period than the more centralized economies of Eastern Europe and of comparable productivity to the economies of Western Europe."[9]

Charles Rockwell in his unpublished study of Yugoslav economic growth has attempted to break down the productivity residuals into three contributing factors: higher levels of education of the labor force, structural change (caused by the movements of factors from low to higher marginal and average productivity), and a "residual technical change." He finds that the rate of growth of "residual technical change" (i.e., the growth of total factor productivity purged of the contribution of higher education and structural change) declined from 3.7 percent per year in the period 1952–61 to 2.3 percent per year in the period 1961–66.[10] The observed increase in productivity per unit of combined capital and labor services from the first to the second period was due in large part to the higher education of the labor force. When this factor and the contribution of structural change were netted out, the contribution of net residual technical change turned out to have declined. Unfortunately, no such breakdown is available for the other countries in Bertran's sample.

Rockwell's results are disquieting: for if Yugoslavia's high rates of technical progress—whether measured by one method or another—have anything to do with its decentralized arrangements, we should expect that these rates would have risen in the period 1961–66, when enterprises were freed from a number of administrative controls, including restrictions on the right to divide net incomes between dividends to the collective and investment.[11] A decline in "system productivity" would be a surprising result of the govern-

8. The most elaborate study of technical progress so far published is Teodosija Vujković, *Kvantitativna analiza techničkog progresa*, Informator, Zagreb, 1972. For the period 1952–67, Vujković, after fitting available capital, labor, and output data to a constant-elasticity-of-substitution aggregate production function for Yugoslav industry, estimates an average rate of technical progress for the period of 3.7 percent per year (p. 91).

9. *The Macroeconomics of Workers Management: Theory and Practice*, Program on Comparative Economic Development, Cornell University, 1969, p. 156.

10. Unpublished manuscript on Yugoslav economic development, p. 16-A.

11. For the effects of the 1959 reform on the regulations for the distribution of dividends from net income, see L. Madžar, "Funkcionalna raspodela dohotka u jugoslovenskoj privredi," *Ekonomska Misao* 6, no. 3 (Sept. 1973): 14.

mental decision to grant enterprises autonomy with respect to the distribution of their net incomes.

There is some evidence supporting the hypothesis that disparities among enterprises in incomes paid out per member tend to persist, owing presumably to the absence of a competitive mechanism that would bring about their elimination. Studies of income differentials among industries show that the range of incomes per member and the coefficient of variation significantly increase after 1960, when, as we recall, enterprises first became free to decide on the proportions of net income distributed and reinvested.[12] A comparison of relative increases in average "personal incomes" per member for 20 industries with relative changes in labor productivity for these same branches from 1959 to 1969 shows a positive correlation (0.36), with a relatively small scatter of observations around the 20-industry average labor-productivity index and a large scatter around the index of average personal incomes per worker.[13] A similar comparison of increases in wages with increases in labor productivity in Great Britain from 1924 to 1950 shows a wide dispersion in the labor productivity indexes by branch of industry, a small dispersion of increases in wages, and no significant correlation between the two sets.[14] This last result is of course precisely what we should expect if competitive conditions prevailed in the labor market. That differential labor productivity gains are in part captured in the form of higher incomes by members of collectives in Yugoslavia suggests that "workers' management" may have had a significant impact on outcomes in this particular case. On the other hand, it may be argued that federal and republican controls on wages in the 1950s made for an artificial wage structure, which was gradually corrected in the 1960s as market forces began to work their impact on the supply and demand for labor of different skills in the various republics.[15]

Another piece of evidence turned up by Erik Furubotn and Svetozar Pejovich originates in the relation of the Yugoslav enterprise to the banking system. As we saw in the last chapter, the rule that members of the collective

12. In a comparison of "personal incomes" paid to members of collectives in socialized sectors in 1956 and 1966, Howard Wachtel found that the ratio of the highest average income paid in any branch to the lowest increased from 1.52 to 1.93 while the coefficient of variation rose from 11.8 to 21.6 (*Workers' Management and Workers' Wages in Yugoslavia: The Theory and Practice of Participatory Socialism* [Ithaca, N.Y.: Cornell University Press, 1973], p. 139).

13. Marijan Korošić, "Intenzitet kapitala i položaj industrijskih grana na tržištu," *Ekonomist* 24, no. 2 (1971): p. 219.

14. Ibid., p. 223. The study of British wages and labor productivity is by W. E. G. Salter.

15. Wachtel inclines to the belief that Yugoslav wage differentials in the mid-1960s were consistent with "neoclassical theory" under the assumption of profit maximization by enterprises (op. cit., p. 177). Wachtel's statistics are based on data aggregated by industry. Disaggregated data on net income per man-hour for 823 enterprises (in 54 industries) were studied by Thomas Marschak for 1959 and 1960, the last two years for which such detailed statistics were available

have no disposition rights over their share in the expected future profits of the enterprise implies that members will prefer borrowing investment funds from banks to reinvesting current profits. To the extent (1) that the Yugoslav enterprise is left free to decide on the proportions of net income reinvested and distributed as personal incomes to members, that (2) managers reflect the preferences of members, and that (3) banks are willing to extend long-term credits at a reasonable cost (compared to expected rates of return), we should expect a high proportion of investments to be financed by bank loans. A dramatic increase in the share of capital investments financed by banks did take place from 1963 to 1971—from 9 to 51 percent—but it was not accompanied by any significant change in the proportion of investments financed from the retained earnings of enterprises. The growth in the banks' share was mainly at the expense of various local, republican, and federal ruling organizations, which drastically curtailed their investments in "labor-managed" enterprises. In sum, the evidence provides only very tenuous support for the hypothesis.[16]

These and other scraps of evidence[17] are confined to the effects of Yugoslav system rules on the distribution of net incomes (along with its implications for the financing of investments). Charles Rockwell has made an ingenious attempt to test a direct implication of enterprises' goal functions from produc-

---

(as of 1968). Marschak tested the hypothesis, consistent with the maximization of net income per member, that differences in interenterprise profits per man-hour would be positively correlated with differences in the value of capital assets per enterprise. He failed to find a significant correlation between the two variables (T. A. Marschak, "Centralized versus Decentralized Resource Allocation: The Yugoslav Laboratory," *Quarterly Journal of Economics* 82 [Nov. 1968]: 581). It would be highly interesting to test this hypothesis on data for the mid-1960s once they become available.

16. For a more positive assessment, see Furubotn and Pejovich, "Property Rights, Economic Decentralization, and the Evolution of the Yugoslav Firm, 1965–1972," *Journal of Law and Economics* 16 (Oct. 1973): 280–81. Data showing the stability of the share of enterprises' reinvested profits in total investment in fixed assets are from Sacks, op. cit., p. 69.

17. Ljubomir Madžar's work on the distribution of "personal incomes" and enterprise liquidity should perhaps be mentioned in this connection, if only because it purports to offer a test of some of the implications of the Vanek model ("Raspodela dohotka i nelikvidnost," *Ekonomska analiza* 7, nos. 1, 2 [1973]: 19–35). Madžar argues from Vanek's model that "personal income per worker" should rise in periods of high demand for an enterprise's products and drop in a period of low demand, thus absorbing all the exogenous shocks of changes in its environment. Enterprises, it follows, should suffer no financial losses, even in depressed periods. But "actual developments in our economy were and still are in flagrant contradiction with [these] implications. Personal incomes not only did not serve as a variable, the flexible variation of which would avert the incurrence of losses, but, due to their excessive rise, directly contributed to the accumulation of losses in certain sectors of the economy. ... Increase in personal incomes *and* losses are by no means a rare event in our economy" (p. 2). The statistics he adduces and his regressions do seem to demonstrate what the author calls the "autonomous character" of incomes distributed, which are apparently frequently increased even at the expense of enterprise "liquidity" (pp. 20–24).

tion function data. We saw in the last chapter that enterprises maximizing net income per member of the collective should produce at points on their production function where every input including labor is earning its marginal-value product. At such points, the sum of imputed earnings must equal the total value of output, and the function is homogeneous of degree one; hence constant returns to scale prevail in the neighborhood of the enterprise's objective-function maximizing output. Thus, whether the function is constant returns to scale for all levels of output or whether, for any input combination, returns are at first increasing and then decreasing, only constant returns to scale should be observable. Rockwell, in his econometric study of 41 Yugoslav industries, assumed that output y_j in each industry j could be represented as a geometric average of its capital assets K and labor force L, with the specific form $y_j = A_j K_j^\alpha L_j^\beta$, where $\alpha + \beta \gtrless 1$. When data for the 41 industries were fitted to this Cobb–Douglas function, estimates of the sum of the parameters α and β were obtained. A sum significantly larger (resp. smaller) than unity was taken as evidence of increasing (decreasing) returns to scale. Rockwell found that for 30 out of 41 industries the hypothesis that the sum of the parameters was equal to unity could not be rejected.[18] This is a weak test, however, considering that we have no evidence of any kind to compare these results with the returns to scale that would be exhibited by profit-maximizing enterprises in a comparable sample of industries.

My sense of the matter is that we shall not reach even a tentative judgment about the effects of workers' management on the objectives pursued by enterprises and on their implications for static and dynamic efficiency until the data for Yugoslavia have been analyzed in a wider intersystem context. To get around the inescapable fact that a full-fledged labor-managed system exists at present in only one nation, it may be necessary to treat each of the six Yugoslav republics as a separate system and then to pool these six sets of data with comparable data culled from a large sample of market economies at various levels of development. In this way we may hope to purge observed differences in the observed outcomes of decision making in labor-managed and in privately owned enterprises from incidental factors properly belonging to their respective environments.[19]

16.3 INDUSTRIES WITH MIXED SYSTEM RULES

The coexistence of enterprises pursuing different goals has hardly been

18. "Factor Growth and Factor Inputs in Yugoslavia: Some Cross-Sectional Results," unpublished conference paper, Dečeni, July 1966. These results are discussed in Sacks, op. cit., pp. 34–35.

19. Cf. sec. 5.5.

studied at all by comparatists.[20] The few publications in this area have dealt with competition between state-owned and private enterprises.[21] A rare theoretical contribution in another direction is a paper by Yair Mundlak on the implications of maximization with several objective functions, which attempts to explain the low elasticity of supply of groups of farms pursuing divergent goals.[22]

To give the flavor of models of mixed government and private enterprise industries, I shall briefly summarize a paper by Joe Minarik written for a seminar in "comparative economics" at Yale.[23] The industry is composed of four enterprises. Three are systematically profit maximizing, and the fourth is either a government-owned enterprise aiming to maximize the output of the entire industry or, for the sake of comparison, an otherwise identical private profit-maximizing enterprise. The products made by the different enterprises are not perfect substitutes. Nevertheless, the government enterprise maximizes the unweighted sum of the outputs of all four enterprises. The quantity of output sold by each enterprise is negatively related to its own price and positively related to the prices of the other enterprises.[24] The government enterprise sets the prices of its output to achieve the goal of maximizing the industry's output, but in lowering its price below a profit-maximizing level it is constrained by the necessity of earning a minimum rate of return on its capital to pay bondholders. The interaction among all four organizations proceeds through time, the only change in the environment being a steady increase in the intercept of the linear demand schedule faced by each enter-

---

20. Lest I be thought inconsistent in my use of terms—substituting comparatist for comparer—I propose the following distinction. A comparatist, the broader of the terms, is an economist specialized in comparing economies or systems. A comparer makes ad hoc comparisons without necessarily having a specialized interest in the matter. An Indian doctor contemplating emigration to a country where his services will be better rewarded is undoubtedly a comparer but almost surely not a comparatist.

21. The pioneering article here is W. C. Merrill and N. Schneider, "Government Firms in Oligopoly Industries: A Short-Run Analysis," *Quarterly Journal of Economics* 80 (Aug. 1966): 400–12.

22. "On Some Implications of Maximization with Several Objective Functions," Working Paper No. 7006, The Center for Agricultural Economic Research, Rehovah, Israel, 1971.

23. "Public Enterprise and Monopoly," New Haven, Jan. 1973.

24. The demand function for enterprise i (private or government owned) is assumed to be the following:

$$Q_i = A_i - b_i p_i + \sum_{\substack{j \neq i \\ j=1}}^{4} C_{ji} p_j \quad (i = 1, \ldots, 4),$$

where Q_i is the quantity sold by enterprise i, A_i is a constant intercept, p_i is the price of i's product, p_j is the price charged by the jth enterprise, and C_{ji} and b_i are positive constants ($j \neq i$; $j = 1, \ldots, 4$).

prise.[25] On the assumption of quadratic cost functions with positive coefficients for all enterprises, a perfectly elastic supply of capital, and linear demand functions, it is possible to show that a price cut by the government enterprise will induce price cuts on the part of all private enterprises. However, the effect on total output becomes increasingly smaller as the cuts of the government enterprise become deeper. In effect then, the government enterprise acts as a price leader down to the lower bound set in each period by its minimum rate of return. Although it is manifest that total industry output will be greater than if all four enterprises behaved as profit maximizers, whether colluding to hold up prices or not, it is not evident at all that the output of each private enterprise will be greater than it would be under these alternative assumptions. Simulation of a fair number of numerical examples suggests, on the contrary, that the government enterprise would gradually capture the entire market and that the output of each private enterprise would contract, despite the postulated periodic increase of the demand intercept. The author of this study is now investigating the supply elasticity of the mixed industry compared to that of the four-member oligopoly of private enterprises.

In Israel the kibbutzim, collective enterprises that may be thought to maximize net income per head, compete in factor and product markets with privately owned farms and even with industrial enterprises presumably maximizing profits. Theoretical aspects of, and empirical evidence on, this competition have been studied in another seminar paper by Robert Z. Lawrence.[26]

A few words about the environment in which competition among organizations pursuing different goals takes place may be in order. In Yugoslavia the principal rules governing the behavior of enterprises apply to all enterprises in the "public domain." The individual who does not wish his take-home pay to hinge on the vagaries of his collective enterprise's net income per member has a very limited choice of options: he can work in the narrowly controlled, undercapitalized private sector—in agriculture if he is able to buy a farm—or he can work abroad, provided he can get permission to do so. (Certain highly skilled individuals are not authorized to become temporary migrants.) In Israel on the other hand, the kibbutz is a very special type of organization, membership in which does not at present exceed 3 percent of the Jewish population.[27] With few exceptions those who belong do so because they have a preference for the kibbutz "way of life," both in its collective-consumption

---

25. Thus the constant A_i in the demand function of industry i increases in each period at a constant rate.

26. "The Cooperative in a Capitalist Environment," New Haven, Dec. 1972.

27. The percentages of total population, as cited by Lawrence, are 7.9 percent in 1949, 4.8 percent in 1955, 3.6 percent in 1964, and 2.9 percent in 1969.

and production aspects. They have the kind of motivation that will make them bear sacrifices in material consumption for the sake of preserving their preferred mode of living. The education the children of kibbutz members receive is likely to reinforce their loyalty to collective organizations. New members recruited from outside presumably represent personality types and backgrounds that are not randomly selected from the population at large.[28] It is perfectly plausible under these conditions that their marginal productivity should be higher in a kibbutz than in a comparable profit-maximizing enterprise, whereas workers with a strong individualistic background may do better in a private enterprise. The long-run viability of the kibbutz as a special organizational form probably depends critically on the continued availability of individuals with the required kind of motivation. (The complex sociological reasons why the supply of such people has been dwindling in Isreal are beyond the scope of the present analysis.)

Interestingly enough, the "pure" collective kibbutz where the members furnish all the necessary labor is in a minority in Israel. More commonly, the kibbutzim hire laborers—usually Arabs, Middle Eastern Jews, and other Israeli citizens who are neither intent on becoming members nor are desired to be.[29] Since the number of these casual laborers can be increased or decreased at will, the mixed kibbutzim are likely to exhibit greater supply elasticity than one would expect from the pure collective, at least if the comparison is made on the plausible assumption that the membership of both types of kibbutz is fixed in the short run.

Granted this same assumption of fixed membership, it is easy to see that the "pure kibbutzim" should theoretically increase their share in the entire industry's output when prices go down and reduce it when they go up. If casual labor can be hired and fired, the relative shares in total output of all kibbutzim and private enterprises should not vary as much with changes in demand as when this possibility is ruled out, but some variation should persist. The fact that demand for products produced by both kibbutzim and private enterprises (both agricultural and industrial) has been rising rapidly and steadily may help explain why the kibbutzim's share of the market has been declining over time, the other explanation being of course that the total supply of potential members has not kept up with the expansion of the economy.

28. Lawrence points out, for instance, that almost all kibbutz members are of European origin, perhaps because the tradition of collectivism is stronger in Europe than in Asia or North Africa. In any event, wage earners "who come from Asia and North Africa view members [of kibbutzim] who work without pay or reward with mistrust and suspicion" (Lawrence, citing F. Zweig, *The Israeli Worker* [New York: Herzl, 1961]).

29. Lawrence shows that, in terms of its collective goal, it may pay to hire laborers even when the going wage exceeds the net income per head of the collective at the old labor-input level.

16.4 JAPAN'S MIXED SYSTEM

It may very well be that in Japan, as in Israel, the predominant type of enterprise is profit maximizing and is not bound by any constraint on the dismissal of its employees when demand is slack. "Small Japanese enterprises," which generally do not guarantee life-time employment, accounted for 54.4 percent of total employment in manufacturing in 1966, 77.6 percent in construction, and 60.8 percent in trade.[30] These small enterprises are of course by far the most numerous (over 93 percent of all enterprises). A great many are linked with large enterprises through intricate and far-reaching subcontracting arrangements. According to James Abegglen, "a feature which makes big companies more financially stable is their use of small companies as a buffer to business fluctuations."[31]

Each large corporation cooperates in a *keiretsu*, a loose amalgam of enterprises generally belonging to diverse industries and bound together by common banks and interlocking committees.[32] Each of the leading enterprises in the keiretsu "directs, organizes, and fosters a multitude of sub-constractors."[33] When we also consider that the large Japanese enterprise adapts to fluctuations in demand by varying the number of hours worked by its emloyees (stepping up or curtailing overtime)[34] and, much like many of the kibbutzim, by hiring temporary workers when demand is buoyant and laying them off when it is slack—a practice, incidentally, which is condoned by labor unions because it helps to secure the lifetime tenure of regular employees —we perceive why the no-dismissals rule might not have dramatic effects on industry output and prices.[35]

30. Information cited by Amy Stevens, Yale College senior essay (New Haven, May 1973). "Small" enterprises are those with less than 50 million yen capital (about $15 million) in manufacturing and construction and 10 million yen (about $3.3 million) in trade.

31. Cited by Amy Stevens.

32. The keiretsu is the postwar heir of the *zaibatsu*, discussed in sec. 11.6.

33. G. C. Allen, *Japan's Economic Expansion* (New York: Oxford University Press, 1965), p. 115.

34. In the Japanese iron and steel industry, for example, overtime ("nonscheduled") hours made up 16.7 percent of all hours worked in 1968, a year of high demand, and 10.6 percent of all hours in 1972, a year of relatively low demand. In the United States, overtime accounted on the average for a little more than 5 percent of total hours in this same industry, varying between 4.5 percent in 1967 and 7.2 percent in 1969. In nearly all Japanese industries, as one would expect, overtime's share of total hours worked was substantially greater than in the United States. (The data for Japan are taken from the Ministry of Labor, Statistics and Information Department, *Year Book of Labour Statistics 1972* [Tokyo, 1973], pp. 219–22; for the United States, from U.S. Department of Labor, Bureau of Labor Statistics, *Employment and Earnings, United States 1969–1972*, Bulletin 1312–9, p. 108.)

35. Temporary workers represent only about 10 percent of the Japanese labor force, but the majority (61 percent in 1961) were employed by large enterprises with more than 500 (temporary and permanent) workers (Kozo Yamamura, *Economic Policy in Postwar Japan* [Berkeley: University of California Press, 1967], p. 169, cited in Janis Potter's Yale senior essay, "Japan's Not So Dual System," 1973).

In point of fact, the tendencies on the part of large enterprises to subcontract and to hire temporary workers to avoid the adverse effects on profits of an impacted labor force when demand slackens are much easier to detect and to test for than are the direct implications on output and total employment of the no-dismissals constraint. The obvious reason for this is that Japan has experienced very rapid growth in all basic sectors of its economy for almost a generation. When business is bad, demand does not decline but ceases to grow or grows more slowly than it did before. Large modern enterprises are rarely faced with a situation where they would cut losses appreciably by dismissing a significant number of their employees. Their choice is usually between hiring and not hiring rather than between hiring and firing. By increasing overtime work, hiring temporary workers, and subcontracting when demand is up, they maintain the flexibility necessary to cope with moderate dips in demand. The recent recession, which was triggered by the sensational rise in the prices of imported oil of 1973–74, may be the first real test of Japan's security-of-tenure principle.[36]

In this chapter we have traced the industry-wide consequences of alternative goal functions for autonomous enterprises and brought together some of the available evidence that might be expected to confirm or impugn the hypotheses implied by alternative goals. Almost all the evidence cited has come from published and unpublished papers on Yugoslavia, Israel, and Japan, each of these countries serving as a "laboratory," to quote Thomas Marschak, for a particular type of enterprise behavior. The analogy with a scientific laboratory would be more appealing if the empirical studies cited had been more success-ful in controlling outcomes for differences in the environment. In the social sciences this can be done only by comparing the outcomes of alternative system rules in disparate environments, that is, in different countries or in different regions of individual countries representing a sufficient sample of the environ-mental features that might influence outcomes. Much more work along these lines will have to be done before we can determine whether organizations behave as the nominal rules constraining their behavior or fixing their objec-tives would lead us to expect.

---

36. It was reported in October 1974 that a number of large Japanese enterprises that normally gave their employees security of tenure were forced by the slump in demand for their products to lay off—or "give temporary home rest to"—many of their workers (*New York Times*, Oct. 24, 1974).

17

General Equilibrium Analysis

17.1 Producers and Consumers

We now plunge into a much more complex world where individuals' decisions are interdependent within and across *all* the organizations that can be distinguished in the entire economy. To begin to understand this world, one must first reduce these myriad organizations to a few categories. I propose to examine the compatibility of decisions in a highly simplified model limited, at first, to enterprises and "households" and then to introduce ruling organizations into this schema. Although this model probably distorts reality in the sense that the environment it assumes is unlikely to be typical for any contemporary system, it is sufficiently revealing of the conditions under which the compatibility of interdependent decisions will occur under alternative system rules to warrant extended discussion.[1]

Most individuals simultaneously belong to enterprises or ruling organizations and to households. Their activities (or "roles") in the different organizations to which they belong will be assumed to be fully separate and distinct. It will also be assumed, for the purpose of modeling complex interdependencies, that all the individuals in any of the three types of organizations act "as one person." In an enterprise this person is called a *producer*, in a ruling organization a *ruler*, in a family or household a *consumer*.

With each producer is associated a technology—a set of processes that he can operate with what will be assumed to be certain outcomes. A vector of outputs (positive elements) and inputs (negative elements) produced by enterprise k is denoted y_k. In the absence of any constraints on the enterprise's inputs or outputs, the feasible vectors y_k belong to a set Y_k. (So far the notation is the same as was used in the preceding chapters.) System differences are reflected in the objective function governing the choice of an optimal vector y_k in Y_k.

The technologies of producers are assumed independent. There are no public goods. Import and export transactions with individuals in other national economies are carried out through specialized import or export enterprises, also qualifying as "producers."

---

1. Janos Kornai in his book *Anti-Equilibrium*, overstresses, in my opinion, the lack of realism of general equilibrium analysis and underestimates its value as a heuristic instrument.

The vector sum of the v producers, or $\sum_{k=1}^{v} y_k$, is denoted y. This vector shows the net outputs available to consumers. y includes the net imports of goods bought by import enterprises but excludes the exports used to acquire these imports.

Consumers obtain outputs from producers; each furnishes what we shall take to be a single type of labor (which will presumably differ for different consumers). To describe i's labor supply we resort to a roundabout but convenient device. We imagine that consumer i can at most furnish $\bar{l}_i$ hours of labor per day. The lth element $\tilde{l}_i$ in the consumption vector x_i is defined as the number of hours of leisure (nonwork) per day that i reserves (or "buys back") for himself, where of course $\tilde{l}_i \leqslant \bar{l}_i$. The labor supplied by i, denoted l_i, is clearly equal to his available labor capacity minus leisure retained or repurchased, or $\bar{l}_i - \tilde{l}_i$. The labor l_{ik} supplied by i to enterprise k is a negative element (qua input) of y_k. This device enables us to assign positive signs to all the nonzero elements in any vector x_i and negative elements to all the inputs in y_k. There are m consumers in the economy.

To express the constraint imposed on a consumer by the limit on his labor capacity and by the fact that his consumption of goods and services may be insufficient to allow him to supply this maximum, we postulate that every feasible x_i must belong to a set X_i, called consumption set.[2] This consumption set is assumed to be convex and to have a lower bound (i.e., for every consumer i, there are numbers β_{ij}, for $j = 1, \ldots, n$, such that any x_i in X_i must satisfy $x_{ij} \geqslant \beta_{ij}$, where x_{ij} is the jth coordinate of x_i).

Every consumer i is assumed to have a complete, reflexive, and transitive preordering over all possible vectors x in X_i. A complete preordering means that, for any two vectors x_i and $x_i{}'$ in X_i, one and only one of the following alternatives holds for i: (1) x_i is preferred to $x_i{}'$; (2) $x_i{}'$ is indifferent to x_i; (3) $x_i{}'$ is preferred to x_i. The statement "$x_i{}'$ is not preferred to x_i" implies that either (1) or (2) holds—but not (3)—in the above trinity. In this case it may also be said that x_i is "at least as desired as $x_i{}'$." Reflexivity implies that x_i is at least as desired as itself, transitivity that if $x_i{}^1$ is at least as desired as $x_i{}^2$ and $x_i{}^2$ as $x_i{}^3$, then $x_i{}^1$ is at least as desired as $x_i{}^3$.

Our first system-structure assumption is that all consumers and producers may buy and sell goods and services, including labor, in unlimited amounts at nonnegative competitive prices. All goods are dated. Prices, including charges for holding goods in inventory, exist for all present and future goods. Consumers and producers choose a program of consumption or production, as the case may be, extending into the indefinite future.

2. If a consumer consists of a family, a household, or even a "commune" pooling incomes and available goods and services, the supply of labor of individual members may depend on how those goods and services are distributed among them. But the purposes of this very general model will not be served by delving into these complications.

The vector product px_i (a scalar) represents the value at prices p of a consumption–labor–supply bundle x_i. The vector product py_k represents the net value, or discounted sum of profits, associated with program y_k and prices p. The initial holdings by i of all goods including labor power are represented by a vector $\bar{x}_i$.[3]

A second system-structure assumption defining a "private ownership economy" is that any positive profits earned by producers are entirely distributed among consumers. The nonnegative numbers θ_{ik} ($i = 1, \ldots, m$; $k = 1, \ldots, v$) stand for the share of the profits of the kth producer accruing to the ith customer. Since all the profits of any producer are distributed, $\sum_i \theta_{ik} = 1$. Consumer i receives a total of $\sum_{k=1}^{v} \theta_{ik} (py_k)$ from all the producers in the system. His expenditures px_i cannot exceed his income or, more precisely, his wealth, because all goods and services are dated and he discounts their future prices to the present. This constraint is expressed by the following budget equation:[4]

$$px_i \leqslant p\bar{x}_i + \sum_k \theta_{ik} (py_k) \qquad (i = 1, \ldots, m).$$

We suppose that all resources available from nature, if they are scarce under any supply or demand conditions, belong to individuals as part of their initial endowments. The vector of resource endowments $\bar{x}$ is then simply the sum of the m individual endowments $\bar{x}_i$.

When we sum the budget equations over all the consumers, we obtain

$$px - p\bar{x} - py = p(x - \bar{x} - y) \leqslant 0,$$

where $(x - \bar{x} - y)$ is the vector of surplus demands at prices p. This equation, which when it is satisfied is known as Walras's law, signifies that the value at prices p of the economy-wide vector of surplus demands $(x - \bar{x} - y)$ must be equal to or smaller than zero. This inequality depends only on the satisfaction of consumers' budget constraints. It has nothing to do with the objective function of producers or even with the choice of a utility-maximizing bundle of consumer goods and services by each consumer.

Given a resource vector $\bar{x}_i$, let each consumer choose a consumption vector $x_i{}^*$ in X_i and each producer a production vector $y_k{}^*$ in Y_k. If the corresponding overall vectors $\bar{x}$, x^*, and y^* are such that all the elements of the surplus-demand vector $(x^* - \bar{x} - y^*)$ are negative or zero, we say that the decisions

---

3. These holdings are assumed to be sufficiently large to permit a consumer to survive in the absence of any market transactions. This strong and unrealistic assumption is required to ensure continuity of the demand correspondence.

4. Note that he sells all his available labor time at current wages and then buys back a certain number of hours of leisure at this price. The difference is the amount of income (or wealth) available for purchase of goods and services other than his own leisure.

of the m consumers and v producers are *compatible*.[5] The $(m + v)$-tuple of vectors $[(x_i{}^*), (y_k{}^*)]$ is then said to be an *attainable state*. If, furthermore, for every i, $x_i{}^*$ happens to maximize i's utility on the set of attainable consumptions (bounded by his budget constraint) and if, for every k, $y_k{}^*$ is also an extremal point maximizing the value of his objective function, then $[(x_i{}^*), (y_k{}^*)]$ is an *equilibrium*. Such an equilibrium has the well-known property that, barring a change in the environment (including the resource vector, the consumption sets and the preferences of consumers, and all v production sets), there would be no pressure to alter any of the $x_i{}^*$ or $y_k{}^*$.

Now let there be a function or correspondence,[6] as the case may be, between the prices in p on the one hand and the utility-maximizing (x_i) and the objective-function-maximizing (y_k) on the other. If p^* induces $(x_i{}^*)$ and $(y_k{}^*)$, then $[(x_i{}^*), (y_k{}^*)]$ is an *equilibrium for p^* in a private ownership economy characterized by the numbers θ_{ik}.*

What environmental conditions and what system rules are sufficient to ensure that there exists a price vector p^* capable of supporting an equilibrium? What are the "welfare properties" of this equilibrium if it exists?

It has been shown that if every producer in a private-ownership economy maximizes profits (py_k) on Y_k at prices p and every consumer maximizes his utility on X_i subject to his budget or wealth constraint, there will exist a price vector p^* generating a nonpositive vector of surplus demands, provided certain environmental conditions are satisfied. The most important from an economic point of view is that the sum of the production sets over all v producers should be convex. This excludes the possibility that any producer will choose a production vector y_k in the subset of his production set where increasing returns prevail.[7]

---

5. The reader will note that with no public goods or externalities, there should be no excess supply of produced goods. If the initial resources of any good are so abundant that the supply exceeds the demand at a given set of prices, the extra resources will not be utilized. This also should not give rise to a disposal problem. For these reasons we have assumed that decisions were compatible even though some surplus demands might be negative (i.e., even though there might be excess supplies of some goods).

6. A function f maps an element x in a set S (the range of the function) into a single element y in the set T (the domain of the function). A correspondence ζ maps the point x in S into a subset $\zeta(x)$ of T, which subset will normally consist of more than one element. When a production function for producer k exhibits constant returns to scale and all the inputs can be varied at will, the set of production vectors maximizing py_k for a given competitive p includes (1) the zero vector if $py_k < 0$ for all y_k in Y_k, (2) a vector of arbitrarily large inputs and outputs if $py_k > 0$, and (3) all the vectors of the form λy_k for $\lambda \geq 0$ where $py_k = 0$. Since the set of maximizers $\zeta(p)$ on Y_k contains an infinity of elements, $\zeta(p)$ is a correspondence rather than a function.

7. The other conditions include irreversibility of production processes, convexity of the set of consumption vectors preferred to any vector $\bar{x}_i$, and the assumption that not only the consumption set X_i but any set of vectors that i prefers or is indifferent to a vector $\bar{x}_i$ must be closed. Finally there exists a consumption vector x_i^0 in X_i all the elements of which are smaller

We now define a *Pareto-optimal state* for a system (a term formally used as a primitive) as an $(m + v)$-tuple of vectors $[(x_i'), (y_k')]$ such that, compared to any alternative attainable state $[(x_i), (y_k)]$, x_i' is at least as desired as x_i (for all i).

An equilibrium for a private-ownership economy characterized by the numbers θ_{ik} can be shown to be Pareto optimal. Indeed, optimality can be proved for a more general definition of equilibrium that does not depend on any specification of the distribution of profits. We need only specify that an equilibrium price vector p^* exists for an economy where the vector x_i^* chosen by i has the property that no other vector x_i in X_i costing at most as much as px_i^* is preferred to x_i^*. If, in addition, y_k^* maximizes py_k on Y_k and (x_i^*, y_k^*) is an attainable state, this equilibrium state for p^* can be proved to be Pareto optimal, provided only that, for any i, (1) X_i be convex, (2) the state of vectors strictly preferred to any vector $\bar{x}_i$ be convex, and (3) no satiation consumption exists for i.[8]

Also relevant to the analysis of systems is the converse theorem: "A Pareto-optimal state is an equilibrium relative to some price system." In other words, to any Pareto-optimal state there must correspond a price vector p such that every producer k maximizes profits on Y_k and every consumer i maximizes his utility on the subset of X_i bounded by his income (or wealth) constraint defined at the prices p. The only significant assumption required to prove this theorem—additional, that is, to the assumptions required to prove the Pareto optimality of an equilibrium—is that Y (the overall production set) should be convex.[9]

This last proposition strongly suggests that the *only* objective function that will sustain a Pareto optimum is a profit maximand. We shall look more closely at this conjecture in connection with an alternative objective function that we have already discussed in a partial equilibrium context, namely, the maximization of net income per member of the collective.

Consider first an enterprise k maximizing net income per member of the collective, or $\bar{p}u_k/L_k$, where u_k is an $(n - 1)$-dimensional vector of inputs, exclusive of labor, and outputs; $\bar{p}$ is a corresponding vector of prices; and L_k represents the number of individuals in the collective with identical skills and working an identical number of hours per period. The vector u_k then consists

---

than the corresponding elements of $\bar{x}_i$ (i.e., the individual can survive on his own resources without hiring himself out or trading his assets). The set of vectors strictly preferred by i to $\bar{x}_i$ is convex provided that any convex combination of $\bar{x}_i$ and of a vector x_i in this set be strictly preferred to $\bar{x}_i$. For a precise statement of these conditions and a proof of existence, see Gerard Debreu, *Theory of Value* (New York: Wiley, 1959), pp. 83-88.

    8. Ibid., pp. 93–96.

    9. The other "technical" assumption is that, for every i, and any x_i' in X_i, the set of consumption vectors x_i preferred or indifferent to x_i' should be closed in X_i, and that the set of vectors to which x_i' is preferred or indifferent should also be closed (ibid., p. 95).

of the first $(n - 1)$ elements of a vector y_k in n-dimensional space, the nth element of which will be represented by the total labor force L_k (the size of the collective). We posit that if any vector u_k contains a positive element, it requires some labor; hence $\bar{p}u_k/L_k$ is always defined. Call w_k the average net income per member of the collective. Given the price vector $\bar{p}$, suppose that the objective function attains its maximum at $\bar{p}u_k^*/L_k^*$. The value of this ratio at such a point equals w_k^*. This is the net income per member at an "equilibrium production" maximizing the value of the producer's objective function. Clearly, $\bar{p}u_k^* - w_k^*L_k^* = 0$. Maximization of net income per member of the collective is thus equivalent to the maximization of profits at prices $\bar{p}$ for the first $n - 1$ inputs and outputs and at wages w_k^* for labor.

Suppose that technological knowledge were freely available and that individuals could freely form new collectives whenever there were above-average net incomes per collective member in existing collectives that could be competed away. Faced with any price vector $\bar{p}$ for the $(n - 1)$ goods and services, each enterprise chooses a vector u_k^* and a size of collective L_k^* maximizing the ratio $\bar{p}u_k^*/L_k^*$. As a result of competitive pressures (among enterprises and among individuals forming new collectives), this maximum ratio turns out to be equal to a unique level of net income per capita w^* for all individuals (assuming again that individuals had identical skills).

Given the assumptions already made about consumers' preferences and the convexity of consumption sets, the additional assumption that all available technologies are constant returns to scale is sufficient to prove the existence of equilibrium prices in a collective economy by analogy with an otherwise identical private-ownership economy, as will now be shown.

The above assumption on available technologies ensures that all producers in the comparable private-ownership economy will make zero profits. (Since profit maximization implies that marginal cost must equal price and since marginal cost equals average cost when returns are constant returns to scale, maximum profits must be zero.) Thus $py_k \leqslant 0$ for an arbitrary price vector p, or $\bar{p}u_k - wL_i \leqslant 0$, where $(\bar{p}, w)$ is the vector disaggregated from p and (u_k, L_k) the vector disaggregated from y_k. The last inequality implies $\bar{p}u_k/L_k \leqslant w$. It is now evident that, for any y_k^* maximizing py_k, $py_k^* = 0$, $\bar{p}u_k^* - wL_k^* = 0$, and the ratio $\bar{p}u_k^*/L_k^*$ attains its maximum at w.

To underscore the point: given any private-ownership economy (with a constant-returns-to-scale technology) satisfying the necessary conditions for the existence of equilibrium, if p^* is a vector of equilibrium prices and (x_i^*, y_k^*) is an equilibrium attainable state for this economy, then p^* and (x_i^*, y_k^*) are equilibrium prices and an equilibrium state, respectively, for an otherwise identical collective economy where producers maximize net income per member. It is evident from the "converse theorem" cited above that (x_i^*, y_k^*) must also be a Pareto-optimal allocation for the collective economy.

If we now admit that available technologies may exhibit decreasing returns at least in certain ranges of input–output combinations, we have to figure out what to do with the profits that will be generated when $py_k > 0$ in these ranges. How will incomes per member be equalized among enterprises as a result of free entry and competition when some individuals will be working for enterprises making positive profits and others will not?

We pointed out in chapter 15[10] that the competitive enterprise maximizing net income per member will operate in the long run when capital inputs can be varied at will, at a scale of output where every input, including labor, will be earning its marginal-value product. In the immediate neighborhood of this point, returns must be constant returns to scale (and long-run average costs must be at a minimum). Given a fixed number of enterprises, there is no reason to believe that demand will always be satisfied, for any initial holdings of consumers, in the constant-return-to-scale range of the production function of those enterprises that happen to run into decreasing returns above certain levels of output. When demand increases for a product, new enterprises must instantaneously be formed that will operate at "maximum physical efficiency" (i.e., at the bottom of their average-cost curve). The smaller the output level at which decreasing returns set in, the more enterprises will have to be created to achieve equilibrium to meet a given increase in the demand for a particular good—and the more enterprises will have to be liquidated in other industries to transfer labor and other resources to the new enterprises. In long-run equilibrium, we conclude, resource allocation in the collective economy should be the same as in an otherwise identical private-ownership economy after profits had been wiped out by competition.

It remains unclear, however, by what process this equilibrium would be approached in the collective economy. One may easily imagine a situation where an increase in demand would touch off short-run decisions that would lead the economy away from equilibrium. Adjustment *toward* equilibrium, particularly in the short run, is the key problem of the theory of the Illyrian economy.

The analysis so far has been conducted in a "classical environment," where the technology available to individual producers in both hypothetical economies compared did not exhibit sufficient economies of scale to "deconvexify" the overall production set Y. Under somewhat restrictive conditions, equilibrium can be shown to exist in a collective economy where producers maximize net income per member even though the production sets are nonconvex. The model[11] postulates that each producer k has a "Leontief-type" (fixed coefficients) technology limited to one basic process a_k, with an output of product j of one unit and nonnegative inputs of all other goods and services.

10. Chap. 15, n. 15.
11. This model was suggested to me by Herbert Scarf.

The entire vector a_k, however, depends on a scale factor λ. The process vector for producing one unit of j when the scale of output is λ is denoted $a_k(\lambda)$. Economies of scale are then expressed by the following assumption: if $\lambda' > \lambda$, $a_k(\lambda') < a_k(\lambda)$. Suppose that all profits earned in enterprise k are distributed to the individuals who furnish the homogeneous labor inputs to this enterprise. Given a price system $\bar{p}$ (for all but labor inputs), the scale factor $\bar{\lambda}$ will determine an income $\bar{w}$ per individual in the collective left over after deducting the value of nonlabor inputs from the value of the output at prices $\bar{p}$. Now if we treat $\bar{w}$ as the (parametric) wage cost per worker (employee or member of the collective), profits π will be zero when the scale λ equals $\bar{\lambda}$. Profits will be positive when λ is larger than $\bar{\lambda}$ and negative when it is smaller. For given values of $\bar{\lambda}$ and $\bar{w}$, the graph of π as a function of λ is shown in diagram 17.1.

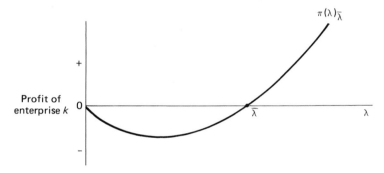

Diagram 17.1

There will of course be a different profit schedule $\pi(\lambda)$ for every scale $\bar{\lambda}$ determining wage costs $\bar{w}$. In the general equilibrium process the scale of operation $\bar{\lambda}$ will be determined, much as in the case of a constant-returns-to-scale economy, by the demand for j (as well possibly as by labor supply if it is fixed for the enterprise). We have here the basic elements of a competitive general equilibrium in a collective economy, despite the nonconvexity of the production sets, where this equilibrium could only be achieved in a private-ownership economy *if every producer obeyed the rule that he must not increase his scale of output beyond the point where his profits were equal to zero.*

Because we have postulated all along that goods and services were dated and that producers and consumers chose at any point of time programs extending into the indefinite future, we have glossed over differences in system outcomes that might arise from disparate ways of dealing with future prospects. Is it likely, for instance, that managers of collectives would discount future incomes per member in the same way as managers of private enterprises discount future profits? In general equilibrium analysis, the manager of a private enterprise is treated as a profit-maximizing automaton with no utility function of his own, no preferences between future and present incomes. The owners, whose shares of profits are specified in the analysis, are themselves only interested in the "net worth" of the enterprise, the value of discounted profits over an indefinite future (net of any obligations incurred in setting up the enterprise). These fictions can be maintained because the expectation of future profits is included in today's net worth and owners can sell their shares therein at any time.

In the course of this digression we have respected the basic assumption about the system structure of the hypothetical economies under discussion— that the only agents in the system were producers and consumers. We know from Yugoslav practice that ruling organizations—including the federal government, the governments of the constituent republics, and the communes —all have a say in the determination of the proportions of the current net income of enterprises that will be given over to members as distributed shares and that will be ploughed back for future investment. Our model of a collective economy remains remote from reality if it ignores the crucial role that ruling organizations are likely to play in such systems.

17.2 RULERS, PRODUCERS, AND CONSUMERS: DECENTRALIZED ALLOCATIONS

Interaction between rulers on the one hand and producers and consumers on the other will be limited in this section to transfers of income and wealth to and from rulers (in the form of "taxes" and "transfer payments"), to rulers' purchases of inputs from producers, and to the production of public goods by rulers.

Ruling organizations may derive their incomes from "direct taxes," "indirect taxes," or both. Direct taxes are preempted by system rules (as well sometimes as by special orders) from producers, in the form of a share in their profits, and from consumers, in the form of taxes on their wealth or their incomes. Indirect taxes are levied as a percentage of the prices paid by or to producers or of prices paid by consumers. Ruling organizations may buy goods supplied by producers and resell them, give them away, or transform them into other goods "private" or "public."

A public good, as we saw in chapter 6, is a good that can be "shared among any number of individuals without affecting the utility of any of them." One interpretation of the public character of a good is that the utility an individual derives from it depends only on its level of production, not on its distribution. The distribution of private goods, on the other hand, affects the utility of the individuals consuming them. In the case of private goods "the scarcity constraint has an additive form";[12] in the case of public goods it does not. If

12. Jean-Claude Milleron, "Theory of Value with Public Goods: A Survey Article," Technical Report No. 12, Center for Research in Management Science, University of California (Berkeley), Aug. 1971, p. 4.

x_{ij} is the consumption of good j by i, where $i = 1, \ldots, m$, and y is the production (or total availability) of j, then for a private good we have $\sum_{i=1}^{m} x_{ij} \leqslant y_i$, and for a public good $x_{ij} \leqslant y_j$. If the public good is restrictable (e.g., a television signal that can be switched off), x_{ij} may be smaller than y_j. Otherwise, for public goods that are sometimes called "environmental" (e.g., defense), x_{ij} necessarily equals y_j.

Since by definition the consumption of public good j by i has no effect on the consumption of j by any other consumer, i will have nothing to gain by restricting the consumption of j by anyone else. There can be no custody of a public good; neither therefore can these goods be traded or exchanged. It follows that their prices cannot be defined. "Personalized prices" of public goods j and j' for consumer i, equal to the marginal rate of substitution of j for j' in i's utility function when i's utility is maximized, are a convenient fiction for analyzing certain public-goods problems. However, because they do not convey any information about the terms of exchange available to i, they cannot qualify as prices as we have previously defined the term.[13] Better suited to comparative-systems analysis is the conceptual framework recently developed by Claude Fourgeaud,[14] which I shall now describe in broad outline.

As before, there are m consumers and v producers in the economy. There are n custodiable, or private, and l noncustodiable, or public, goods. Consumers maximize their utility subject to their income (or wealth) constraint. A consumption vector x_i is defined in the $(n + l)$-dimensional space of private and public goods consumed. The projection of x_i unto the n-dimensional space of private goods is denoted x_i^1.

Producers maximize profits on their production sets. The jth enterprise's production set Y in $(n + l)$-dimensional space is assumed to be convex and compact (closed and bounded). Its projection unto the n-dimensional space of private goods is denoted Y_k^1. The profits of j for a given price vector p in n-space is py_k^1, where y_k^1 belongs to Y_k^1.

There is now added a new agent—a ruling organization called the state—producing public goods.[15] The state's actions belong to a convex and compact set Z in the $(n + l)$-dimensional space of real numbers. A feasible program z is composed of two subvectors: z^1, representing purchases by the state of goods and services, and z^s, representing the production of l public goods. Call Z^s the

13. On Lindahl-Samuelson "personalized prices," see ibid., pp. 20–48 and literature cited therein.

14. "Contribution à l'Étude du rôle des administrations dans la théorie mathématique de l'équilibre et de l'optimum," *Econometrica* 37, no. 2 (1969): 307–23.

15. Fourgeaud refers to "administrations" in the plural, but he adduces a unique preference ordering for all these units. We may infer therefore that the administrations operate as a single entity.

projection of Z onto the l-dimensional space of public goods. It is assumed that the state has a complete preordering over all z^s in Z^s, which can be represented as a continuous utility function.[16] The "budget constraint" on the state is of the form $pz^1 \leqslant H$, where H equals the sum of direct and indirect taxes minus transfer payments to consumers.

Given the price vector p, the vector of prices net of indirect taxes equals Tp, where T is an $n \times n$ diagonal matrix. The jth element of Tp is $(1 - \alpha_j)$, where α_j is the indirect-tax rate on good j. The profits of enterprise k, net of indirect taxes, are distributed in the following way. There are numbers θ_{ik} and θ_{Ak}, all between 0 and 1, such that $\sum_{i=1}^{m} \theta_{ik} + \theta_{Ak} = 1$, where θ_{ik} is the ith consumer's share of the kth enterprise profit (as in the stateless model) and θ_{Ak} is the share of the state in these profits.

Each consumer pays to the state a fraction λ_i of his income net of transfer payments. The latter in turn are a proportion τ_i of the state's total revenue from direct and indirect taxes.

Each individual i has an initial endowment of private goods $\bar{x}_i$ including a fixed supply of available labor.[17] The value of these endowments at prices p is $Tp\bar{x}_i$, inasmuch as all the elements of his initial endowment including his available labor are subject to taxation.

The "organizational parameters" of the system, as Fourgeaud calls them, are (λ_i), (θ_{ik}), and (τ_i) for all i and k, and the matrix T. These parameters must satisfy certain conditions that, loosely speaking, ensure that for any price vector p, every consumer would be able to survive even in the absence of any public goods.[18]

Granted all these assumptions, Fourgeaud shows that there must exist a price vector p^* that will support an equilibrium with the usual property that the optimizing actions of all participants in the system will be compatible. This rather general statement requires a precise interpretation. Consider a vector (z^1, z^{s*}) of private goods consumed and public goods produced by the state such that z^{s*} maximizes the state's utility. Given p^*, each consumer chooses a preferred vector x_i^* on the set determined by his budget constraints and by z^{s*}. Each producer k chooses a vector y_k^* that maximizes his profits

16. That only Z^s is preordered and not Z or Y is a strongly restrictive assumption. It implies for instance that the state cannot choose among alternative industrialization policies. It is not clear to me whether this assumption could be relaxed at least to the extent of imposing the state's preordering on the entire set Z rather than just on Z^s.

17. This fixed-labor-supply assumption is more restrictive than the one made in sec. 17.1, which allowed consumers to consume more or less leisure (and hence supply more or less labor) in response to price and wage changes.

18. Fourgeaud, op. cit., pp. 313–14. This assumption is approximately equivalent to the one made in the previous section that required that every consumer could survive on his initial endowments in the absence of any market transactions.

given p^* and z^{s*} in a set $Y_k(z^{s*})$.[19] These decisions will be compatible if

$$\sum_i x_i^{1*} + z^1 \leqslant \sum_k y_k^{1*} + \sum \bar{x}_i.$$

The above is a system of n inequalities in the space of private goods (denoted by the superscript 1). It signifies that the aggregate consumer demand for any private good j plus the demand for this good by the state (as an input into z^{s*}) must not exceed the total of its output by producers plus any initial holdings of j by consumers ($j = 1, \ldots, n$).

Fourgeaud distinguishes what he calls a "private optimum" where every consumer is as well off as he can be, given a vector of public goods z^{s*}, from a general Pareto-optimum on all the attainable states of the economy where transfers τ_i can be adjusted to achieve such an optimum (while the taxation parameters remain fixed). He shows that an equilibrium $\hat{E} = (x_i^*), (y_k^*)$, (z^*) for a price vector p^* will be a private optimum if and only if the tax rates on the n goods and services are uniform. In order for such an equilibrium to be Pareto optimal (after suitable transfers) for a given set of taxation parameters, one more assumption is necessary. Consider any vector z^s of public goods produced that are at least as desirable to the state as z^{s*}. Then (1) (x_i^*, z^s) must be as desirable for every consumer as (x_i^*, z^{s*}) and (2) y_k^{1*} must be contained in $Y_k^1(z^s)$, the attainable set for k given z^s, for every k.

These relatively strong conditions do not imply that the state's preferences are identical to consumers'—only that (1) a consensus exists on the set of states preferred to the equilibrium and (2) none of the vectors of public goods preferred to z^{s*} would cause a deterioration in the production conditions for any producer k such that the profit-maximizing y_k^{1*} of the equilibrium set could no longer be produced.

This French contribution to general equilibrium theory has not received the public discussion it merits, in part because it is highly abstract and technical. No doubt also, the assumption Fourgeaud makes that the state is concerned only with public goods is unrealistic: the relative priorities of official decision makers for spending on ballet and missiles are likely to be different when the population has food to eat and when it does not. Finally many welfare economists in West may feel uncomfortable about the assignment of preferences to the state distinct from the preferences of consumers. They may not readily accept the argument that in a democratic polity the preferences of the state may diverge very seriously from those of consumers, because if this were the case, the holders of public office would presumably get turned out at the next elections.

19. The set $Y_k(z^s)$ is the feasible set of producer k, given his technology and the "environmental" vector of public goods z^s. On this and subsequent pages an asterisk after a superscript indicates that the vector with this superscript is a maximum or optimum vector in the appropriately defined set.

Whatever one's attitude might be to "planners' preferences" in a democracy, it should be recognized that Fourgeaud's paper goes a long way toward demonstrating how these preferences, in polities where they do hold sway, can be imposed through the price mechanism on a decentralized system structure within a fixed fiscal framework. His demonstration that an equilibrium cannot be a private optimum unless indirect taxation rates are uniform for all goods and services points to an important area of inefficiency in distribution in East, where a patchwork of differentiated "turnover taxes" on goods and services persists despite recent "reforms."[20] Fourgeaud's attempt to show under what conditions state preferences would be compatible with consumers' is also instructive.

The main reservation one might have to Fourgeaud's approach applies as well to almost all the work done so far in general equilibrium theory: that it assumes away economies of scale in production and is therefore incapable of dealing with nonconvex producers' sets that do not permit an efficient full-fledged decentralization. The modeling of situations where limited competition prevails for essentially the same reason lies beyond the scope of the theory.

Let us come back one more time to the collective economy in which producers maximize net income per member. The actions of a ruling organization maximizing its preferences over the vectors of public goods that it is capable of producing can be grafted onto the general equilibrium system with producing collectives and consumers outlined in the preceding section. We may conjecture that an equilibrium exists for such an economy when the ruling organization finances the production of public goods from the proceeds of taxes levied on individuals' total endowments. If we are to move a step or two closer to a realistic modeling of a Yugoslav-type economy, however, we should have to allow the state not only to produce public goods but also to act as an intermediary in the financing of investments.[21] My guess is that this additional function imputed to the state should not present much of a theoretical problem either in proving the existence of an equilibrium or in inferring a private or a Pareto optimum from the equilibrium provided it exists. In my opinion the really hard problems that will have to be looked into if we wish to understand how a competitive economy made up of collectives

20. Oskar Lange, at least in private conversation, urged that the rates of turnover taxes should be uniform in the Polish economy as early as 1956.

21. In an unpublished paper presented before the Northeast Meetings of the American Association for the Advancement of Slavic Studies, John Whalley pointed to an analogy between Yugoslavia and Sweden in the role of the state as a financial intermediary collecting a part of the net income of enterprises, including, in the case of Sweden, social security payments by employees, and using the proceeds as an investment fund. A crucial point of similarity in the system structures is that individuals have no right in either country of disposal over their claims to jointly held savings (in Yugoslavia to net-income shares, in Sweden to the jointly owned pension fund).

might really work lie in the potential for internal conflicts due to the divergent interests of members in different age groups and with different attitudes toward risk rather than in the relation of the collectives to the state.

17.3 MARKET-CLEARING PRICES FOR CONSUMER GOODS AND FOR LABOR SERVICES IN CENTRALLY DIRECTED ECONOMIES

In most economies in East—China being the most notable exception—the majority of individuals are free to decide for what state or collective enterprise or other organization they wish to work. An employee may quit the organization he works for if he is not pleased with his wages or his working conditions although he may suffer a loss in seniority, jeopardize his right to a full pension, or be subjected to psychological pressures by his superiors in the organization for so doing. Even in the highly centralized Soviet and East European regimes of the early 1950s, there was some competition by employers for workers, which if it did not take the form of bidding up wages—owing to the constraints on the enterprise imposed by its "wage fund" and by centrally set wage categories—could be effectively pursued by offering prospective employees faster promotion, better housing, or other perquisites. Thus labor was allocated to a significant extent through the wage–price system. Prices of consumer goods, except in time of war or of extreme stress when such goods were rationed to consumers, were set by various federal or regional ruling organizations with an eye to maintaining orderly market conditions—not so high that flagrantly excessive inventories would accumulate, not so low that consumers would regularly have to queue up to buy them or that they would be systematically preempted by "speculators" intent on reselling them at higher prices. No one would claim that the price-setting authorities fully succeeded in achieving these aims, but it would appear nevertheless that prices of most nondurable goods were not too far removed from the level that would have been necessary to equate existing supply with demand. Models based on the assumption that wages and consumer prices in these centrally directed economies equilibrate supply and demand in the labor and consumer goods markets may then be sufficiently realistic to warrant an investigation of their structural properties.[22]

The highly simplified description of a classic "Soviet-type" economy that follows is meant to capture some of the basic traits of these economies with special emphasis on the determination of prices for goods allotted to the consumer market and of wages. The description provides a framework in which equilibrium can be defined and the assumptions necessary to achieve it discussed. However, no proofs of equilibrium will be offered. It is by no

22. In the following delineation of the problem, I have profited from numerous discussions with Herbert Scarf and with Andrew Feltenstein (cf. the latter's Ph.D. dissertation, "General Equilibrium in a Model of an Economy of the Traditional Soviet Type" [Yale University, 1976]).

means evident that the rules stipulated below are consistent with the existence of equilibrium. Indeed, the examples that will be given following the description suggest that there will be an inconsistency in the model unless the incentive system for managers is calibrated in such a way as to maintain a macroeconomic balance for any set of market prices and wages.

1. Planners, possessing exact information on the technologies available to enterprises and the capacity constraints to which they are subject, first choose on the basis of their preferences a program of outputs $\hat{y}^+$ for the n goods produced in the system. From this program they devise a list of total allotments $\hat{y}^-$, equal to $A\hat{y}^+$, where A is an $n \times n$ technology matrix for currently produced goods. The program $\hat{y}^+$ is such that $B\hat{y}^+$ satisfies the capacity constraints b, where B is a rectangular matrix of input coefficients for the various types of capacities listed in the vector b.

2. Rulers set "producers' prices" for all currently produced goods in such a way that the producer's price π_j of each good j covers the direct and indirect labor costs incurred in producing it according to the information available to the center. Thus $\pi = u_0(I - A)^{-1}$, where $\pi \equiv (n_1, \ldots, n_n)$ and u_0 is a row vector of wages w per unit of output in each of the n sectors. Wages are determined in a free market by supply and demand.

3. Output targets $\hat{y}_k^+$ and input allotments, $\hat{y}_k^-$ (not including labor) summing respectively to $\hat{y}^+$ and $\hat{y}^-$, are distributed to all v enterprises in some "convenient manner." (Various rules for setting targets and allotments consistent with $\hat{y}^+$ and $\hat{y}^-$ may be considered.)

4. Each enterprise k is assigned an incentive function geared to the price system p_j as well as to the targets $\hat{y}^+$ and the allotments $\hat{y}^-$. Their objective is to maximize the value of their expected rewards on the basis of this function. An example of such an incentive system for the kth enterprise may be

$$R = \alpha \pi y_k - \beta \pi (y_k^+ - \hat{y}_k^+)^2, \qquad (17.1)$$

where R is the bonus to the enterprise's manager, α and β are constants, y_k is the enterprise's productive vector, and y_k^+ is a vector of its outputs (the positive elements in y_k).[23]

5. Consumers supply labor hours to enterprises at wages w and consume such goods as the rulers make available to them at market prices p (to be defined later).

6. Each enterprise chooses a reward-maximizing production program y_k^* in its production set Y_k, subject to the constraints set by its allotments of currently produced inputs and its available capacities. The program includes a demand for a certain number of labor hours to be supplied at market

---

23. If no penalty attaches to the failure to fulfill targets, β is in effect equal to zero, and the manager is rewarded in proportion to the value of his profits in terms of producers' prices, as in the models of chaps. 13 and 14.

wages w. Y_k is assumed to be invariant to the availability of public goods (of which more later).

7. When the enterprise-specific production programs y_k^* (with positive elements for outputs and negative elements for inputs) are summed over all v enterprises, they add up to a net-output vector y^*. It is assumed that the actual method used in setting output targets and input allotments is sufficiently accurate to guarantee that all elements of y^* are either positive or zero.

8. Rulers preempt nonnegative quantities of goods to be used for public purposes from each of the n outputs in y^*. After subtracting from y^* the vector of these state purchases, denoted y^I, any quantities left over are allotted to the consumers' market and sold at market-clearing prices p. This residual vector is denoted y^c. Goods preempted by the state in a vector y^I, unlike in Fourgeaud's model, are not transformed into public goods. They have no influence on consumption or on production sets.

9. Each consumer on the basis of his preferences for goods and leisure chooses a bundle of goods y_i^c and supplies a certain number of labor hours l_i. (As in the private-ownership model of sec. 17.1, l_i plus leisure consumer $\tilde{l}_1$ cannot exceed $\bar{l}_i$, the total number of hours available to the consumer in the "plan period.") He chooses y_i^c and l_i in such a way as to maximize his utility u_i subject to his budget constraint, $w\bar{l}_i + p\bar{x}_i$, where $\bar{x}_i$ denotes his bundle of initial holdings of the n goods evaluated at market prices p.

Consumers and the state cannot spend more than their receipts. The model assumes that no saving takes place. These two conditions imply that receipts equal expenditures in both sectors.

The state purchases y^I at prices π and pays out bonuses $\sum_{k=1}^{v} B_k$. It takes in the difference between the value of y^c at market and at producer prices, $(p - \pi)\, y^c$, plus profits at producer prices, $\pi y - \sum_i wl_i$, plus direct taxes T:

$$\pi y^I + \sum_{k=1}^{v} B_k = (p - \pi)y^c + \pi y - \sum_{i=1}^{m} wl_i + T,$$

which simplifies to

$$\sum_k B_k = py^c - \sum_i wl_i + T.$$

This last equality also holds for consumers, since $\sum_k B_k + \sum_i wl_i - T$, the sum of consumers' receipts from bonuses and wages minus taxes, must in the absence of saving match consumers' expenditures on available goods.

The sum of bonuses minus taxes, denoted H, is a balancing item,[24] which may be positive or negative depending on the relation of y^I to y^c. If H is

24. If bonuses are identical to transfer payments in Fourgeaud's model in sec. 17.2, H has the same significance as in the equation $pz^1 \leqslant H$ in that section (p. 280).

positive, then instead of levying taxes on consumers, the rulers distribute social dividends to the population.

Simple examples may be constructed to show that equilibrium in all markets can be achieved only in "degenerate cases" as long as consumers' incomes are not made dependent on the market prices of all goods produced.[25] In one elementary model for instance, equilibrium will not be attained unless the incomes of consumers are (1) augmented by the value of bonuses and (2) reduced by taxes equal to the value of y^l, the vector of goods preempted by the rulers, valued at market prices.[26] In more complicated models, how-

---

25. Consider for instance an economy made up of one producer and one consumer, who consumes the producer's entire output. The producer's technology consists of a single process for making the unique good, whose output is denoted y. A unit of y is produced with one unit of capacity and one unit of labor. Ten units of capacity are available to the producer. The consumer has 40 units of labor or leisure, $\bar{l}$, available. His utility function is $u = y^\alpha \tilde{l}^{1-\alpha}$, where $\tilde{l}$ denotes his consumption of leisure. His supply of labor equals $l \equiv \bar{l} - \tilde{l}$. To maximize his utility the consumer will spend a fraction $(1 - \alpha)$ of his total income on leisure. If his income is limited to the value of his labor holdings $40\,w$, the following equality must hold in the labor–leisure market:

$$\frac{(1 - \alpha)\,(40\,w)}{w} = 40\,(1 - \alpha) = 40 - l.$$

If the producer's incentive system causes him to maximize y, he will produce 10 units of this good and use up 10 units of labor. Thus, $l = 10$ and $40 - 40\alpha = 30$. This equality will be satisfied only if α is exactly $\frac{1}{4}$, the "degenerate case" referred to in the text. In all other cases there will be disequilibrium in the labor market. Note that in the market for y, $40\,\alpha = 10\,p$. For $\alpha\,\frac{1}{2}$, $p = 2$. But then $py^c = 2(10) > wl = 10$. The consumer's outlay exceeds his income, in contradiction to the assumption of equality of income and expenditure.

Suppose on the other hand that H, the value of bonuses net of taxes needed to balance incomes and expenditures, were included in the consumer's income. Then:

$$(1 - \alpha)\,(40 + H) = 30 \quad \text{(labor market)} \tag{17.1'}$$
$$\alpha\,(40 + H) = 10\,p \quad \text{(market for the good)}, \tag{17.2'}$$

where the second equation shows that the consumer's expenditures on the good must equal the value of the good's output (10) at the market price p.

From these equations it follows that $H = 10\,(p - 1)$ and $p = 3/(1 - \alpha)$. It is easily verified that for any value of α, $py^c = H + wl$. (For $\alpha = \frac{1}{2}$, $p = 6$, $py^c = 60$, $H = 50$, and $wl = 10$.)

Note also that the producer will break even when p equals $1(w) + 1(r)$, where r is the implicit price of capacity. Hence, since $w = 1$, $r = p - 1$, and H equals $10\,r$, the value of the capacity constraint at the price r. To achieve equilibrium, in other words, the implicit rents on capacity must be paid to the consumer in the form of bonuses.

26. In the example of the preceding footnote, y^l was equal to zero. If it were positive, equations 17.1' and 17.2' would have to be rewritten as follows:

$$(1 - \alpha)\,(40 + 10\,r - T) = 30 \tag{17.3'}$$
$$\alpha\,(40 + 10\,r - T) = (10 - y^l)\,p, \tag{17.4'}$$

where $10\,r$ is the value of implicit rents. As in the first example $r = p - 1$. Substituting this expression for r in the above equations and solving for T in terms of p and y^l yield $T = py^l$.

ever, no simplistic rules can be invoked that would allow the authorities to set the equilibrating value of taxes, except of course for the general principle stated earlier that, for any set of equilibrating prices and wages, bonuses net of taxes must equal the value of consumer goods at market prices minus total wages paid out by enterprises. The ad hoc level of bonuses cum taxes needed to balance macro-economic accounts would seem to be incompatible with stability either in the incentive system (needed to give producers a precise notion of the rewards they may expect of their efforts) or in the fiscal system (needed to allow consumers to make plans for the future). Given the absence of markets for monetary assets and of decentralized investment decisions, it is not surprising that the level of taxes required to maintain macro- and microeconomic equilibrium should be as difficult to predict ex ante as the effect on market prices of the state's investment decisions.

The main point of this discussion is that, in contrast to Fourgeaud's model, the existence of equilibrium prices cannot be guaranteed if the "organizational parameters" of the economy, such as tax rates and coefficients in the bonus function, are set before a decision has been made on the division of the economy's net output between private and public consumption.[27] Either taxes or bonuses must be adjusted ad hoc to maintain aggregate balance between the incomes and the expenditures of consumers and of the state.

Production targets play a subsidiary role in the examples constructed so far. More work is needed to explore the influence on market equilibrium of (1) the production targets selected, (2) the vectors of private and public consumption extracted from net output, and (3) consumers' preferences and their decisions on market purchases. For example, we should like to know whether in the framework of this general model a change in consumer preferences from one good to another will always increase the marketed supply of the first vis-à-vis the second and cause a corresponding shift in relative prices. It is surely plausible that a positive response of supply to increases in demand would hold for certain parameters of the incentive function and not for others. Constraints on the rulers' choice of y^l in y^* (or on their preferences themselves) may also have to be imposed to ensure this "normal behavior."

Even on the basis of these preliminary investigations regarding application of diverse system rules to general equilbrium models, I feel that the method brings to light problems of sufficient interest for understanding how the particles of a complex economic system interact to justify further work in this direction.

---

27. It should be recalled, however, that labor in Fourgeaud's model is in perfectly inelastic supply. It also appears that transfer payments may play a critical balancing role in his model.

Part 6
Conclusions

18

Lapses and Lacunae: Hints for Further Research

We started our inquiry by building up a pedantically precise vocabulary, where even words with as self-evident a meaning as "action" and "choice" were systematically derived from words already defined or from primitives. We ended it with cavalier references to enterprises behaving as utility-maximizing individuals and to equilibrium prices brought into existence without aid of man by the immaculate process known as competition. Somewhere along the way we relaxed our ideal of conceptual precision for the sake of getting at least a toehold on a more complex reality.

At least some readers may go along with the idea that certain problems of comparison require a highly detailed and accurate description of reality, whereas others turn on salient traits that can most fruitfully be analyzed by glossing over less important distinctions. To invoke once again the concept of information that I have used and abused in this book, the optimal degree of fineness of the information required to make a fruitful comparison depends on the nature of the outcomes of interest to the comparer. When, say, the equity of two systems is being compared, we do not wish to clutter up our description with traits that have little effect on income distribution or on other indicators of this desideratum or that have approximately the same expected effect (under ordinary states of the environment) on these indicators in both systems. The main thing to keep in mind, I feel, is that the comparer must make his classification of traits with purpose aforethought. He must aggregate system traits with a sense of their relative importance, that is, of their expected effect on outcomes weighted according to some specified norm.

Let me offer an example of a refinement in definition that I might have (but did not) introduce in connection with the notion of "supply" in competitive processes. In the chapter on that subject I concentrated on the general nature of competitive processes, which could take many forms besides the bidding up of prices by buyers under excess-demand conditions and their reduction when supply was in excess. Another aspect of a competitive process is the buyers' search for low-price suppliers and the sellers' search for buyers willing to pay the highest prices. For a buyer faced with several possible sources of supply quoting prices that may be treated as stochastically independent random variables with given distribution parameters, the problem is to find the source of supply quoting the minimum price; for a seller, a similar model of the search for the maximum price may be constructed.[1] System rules may be established or may develop spontaneously as a consequence of an adaptive process that will facilitate the sellers' search for buyers, and conversely. In chapter 6 we mentioned the standardization of the physical characteristics of goods as an aid in bringing buyers and sellers together where this standardization may be voluntary or compulsory. More important still are rules for creating or for facilitating the development of markets. These search-facilitating and expectation-stabilizing rules may stipulate where and when prospective buyers and sellers can meet, how they can exchange bids, and what dissatisfied transactors can do about their complaints of fraud or misrepresentation.

The rules that define the structure of a market identify, and impart specific meaning to, an ensemble of transactions. In the Soviet Union the market rules that govern transactions in private housing are extremely restrictive, permitting only advertisements on bulletin boards and in newspapers for local consumption (as alternatives to a highly inefficient search through personal contacts). In the United States, subject only to the registration of offers and to laws on misrepresentation, Florida real estate may be promoted on New York radio as well as through a host of other media. The facilities for exchanging commodity futures, insurance premiums, and commercial paper representing short- or long-term obligations vary significantly from country to country but, in general, tend to be far better developed in high-than in low-income countries.

A careful description of the search process for effecting transactions in different systems may then be productive of significant structural differences. Nevertheless, when information costs are moderate and the variance in suppliers' conditions is reasonably low, search may be ignored in a study of the chief forces making for the mutual adaptation of supply and demand in different systems (just as transportation costs are ignored in many basic models of international trade).

In attempting to survey the most important issues that merit consideration in the description and comparison of systems, I have been preoccupied with some aspects of the field at the expense of others. Perhaps the most gaping hole has been neglect of macroeconomic problems, except for a brief and tangential discussion of nationwide policies in chapter 5. The difficulty, I confess, is to integrate monetary and fiscal policy in the individual decision-making approach that I have pursued throughout the greater part of this

---

1. George J. Stigler, "The Economics of Information," *Journal of Political Economy* 69, no. 3 (June 1961): 213–25.

book. It is by no means clear whether the method of building up operational definitions that refer to observable objects and actions can be used in this domain. Take, for example, the notions of "full-employment income" or "full-capacity national product." Can we discover the things of which these are the names?[2] Or are these names to which no thing in particular corresponds? In systems where individuals do not have to work, where they are not allowed to work for less than some minimum legal wage, where they may collude to withdraw their labor to obtain higher wages, there is not likely to be any level of aggregate demand, regardless of prices, at which everyone would be employed. In systems where enterprises may restrict their output to obtain higher prices, it is just as unlikely that all capacities will be utilized. (I assume that some operational meaning can be given to the concept of full utilization of a given capacity.) As soon as we fall back on a concept of "reasonably full employment" based on a maximum tolerable fraction of the "labor force" that may be unemployed at any given time, we have left the realm of value-free system description. Individuals may disagree on the "tolerable fraction" in question, depending on the system-wide costs they may be willing to incur, in terms of changes in the level of prices and in the distribution of incomes that would ensue from the adoption of the monetary and fiscal measures needed to achieve the targeted reduction in unemployment.

More work remains to be done in the micromodeling of money and credit, in my opinion, before the broader questions of macroeconomic policy can be handled in our individual decision-making framework. Theorists have only recently begun to shed light on the public-good properties of money and credit. Ross Starr has explored the concrete advantages of introducing money in a barter economy.[3] Mordecai Kurz has attempted to model general equilibrium in an economy with money and transaction costs.[4] Lloyd Shapley and Martin Shubik have recently modeled a situation where the ability of traders to repay borrowed funds depends on the amount of money in the system at any given time.[5] In the framework of this model, any contraction in the money supply will force a certain number of traders, who had borrowed money in good faith, to default on their obligations. By lending money, banks make it possible, when the number of traders is small and each trader's

2. Y. T. D. Weldon, *The Vocabulary of Politics* (Baltimore, Md.: Penguin Books, 1960), p. 12.

3. Ross Starr, "Equilibrium and Demand for Media of Exchange in a Pure Exchange Economy with Transaction Costs," Cowles Foundation Discussion Paper No. 300, New Haven, Oct. 1, 1970.

4. "Equilibrium in a Finite Sequence of Markets with Transaction Cost," *Econometrica* 42 (Jan. 1974): 1–20.

5. "Trade Using One Commodity as Money," Cowles Foundation Paper CF 40138, New Haven, 1974.

expenditure has an appreciable influence on the prices of traded goods, to attain Pareto-optimal allocations that could not be otherwise achieved.[6]

The Shapley–Shubik model has the peculiarity that prices are formed spontaneously as a result of mutually independent traders' decisions on the amounts of money they wish to spend out of their own and out of borrowed funds.[7] I cannot see how it would be relevant to the analysis of an economy where prices were centrally fixed and discrepancies between supply and demand were resolved by allocation decisions made by hierarchic superiors. Credit and banks perform important functions in such economies that can hardly be accounted for in this framework.

Suggestive as the Shapley–Shubik model may be of the role money and credit can play in facilitating transactions among a small number of traders, it does not really get at the efficiency-in-production aspects of lending and borrowing. Credit makes it possible to transfer temporarily idle resources held by individuals or by enterprises to put them to productive use elsewhere. The discrepancies in the return to capital in different uses that credit tends to eliminate are inherent in the "diachronism"—the lack of simultaneity— between the schedules of incomes that individuals and enterprises expect to receive and the schedules of outlays they expect to make, or can be induced to make if they are paid to postpone them. The necessity for some sort of arrangements for borrowing and lending holds for a barter as for a monetary economy, for a competitive market economy as for a centrally directed economy cum fixed prices, if any of these systems are to achieve efficiency.

Mutual crediting by enterprises and individuals may go some way toward matching the supply and demand for temporarily idle resources, but specialized intermediaries such as banks are in a better position, given information and transaction costs, to bring together savers—individuals willing to postpone expenditures on goods and services—and investors—individuals wishing to anticipate such expenditures—than are most savers and investors when they have to search each other out. It is interesting to remark in this connection that central bank officials in the centrally directed economies of East have always tried to keep interenterprise crediting as small as possible. And this is so not only because such crediting may lead to an inefficient distribution of working capital but also for the simple practical reason that mutual obligations *among enterprises* are not symmetrical. Some enterprises have high wage

6. Ibid., p. 3.

7. The price of a commodity in this model equals the total amount traders wish to spend on it divided by the available amount. (Each trader "deposits" his initial supply in the market and then buys back any amounts he wants to consume from the market.) Decisions are ex ante independent in the sense that no trader attempts to take into account the impact of his spending on the other traders' decisions and on the resulting prices. In other words this is a noncooperative game where each trader takes every other trader's decisions as given.

bills and spend little on raw materials and semifinished goods, and conversely. Labor-intensive enterprises cannot postpone the expenditure of wages when they fall short of working capital because their customers are delaying payments. In these economies also the bank's decision to issue or to deny short-term credit is used to some extent as a means of controlling profligate enterprises. As a result of interenterprise crediting, carefully managed enterprises may have to resort to credit while their poorly managed customers finance their short-term needs by delaying payment. Also, in a market economy it may be more efficient to let banks instead of suppliers put pressure on debtors, especially in a "buyer's market" or "pressure economy," where greater bargaining power is generally lodged with the customer.

Janos Kornai in his important book on *Anti-Equilibrium* places great emphasis on the difference in behavior of consumers and enterprise managers in economies where there is, in some sense, surplus aggregate demand, or "suction," and in those where there is surplus supply, or "pressure." He argues persuasively that, although market economies tend to be characterized by "pressure" and centrally directed economies by "suction,"[8] differences in system structure become blurred when normally decentralized economies are in a suction phase. He points out that the number of enterprises in an industry may have less to do with their "market power"—their ability to set prices and quality standards—than with the basic suction-pressure alternatives.[9] The intensity and direction of invention and innovation are also, in Kornai's view, conditioned by these differences in the macroeconomic environment in which enterprises operate.[10] I have not dwelt on these important matters, largely because Kornai has treated the subject so extensively. I wonder, for all that, whether the Harsanyi model of bilateral power relations outlined in chapter 13 might not be used to arrive at a more precise analysis of the relative powers of suppliers and customers in suction and pressure environments than Kornai provides in his book.

Going down the list of lacunae, I must own up to a seriously deficient treatment of ruling organizations in alternative systems. The only functions systematically assigned to ruling organizations were (1) to set "rules of the game" restraining the decisions of enterprises and consumers in every system, (2) to preempt goods and services—directly or via taxes—for use as inputs in the production of public goods, and (3) in certain "centrally directed systems" to supervise and control the production programs of enterprises. In addition to fiscal and monetary policy, I also neglected or failed to treat in depth a number of other activities through which governments interact with

8. *Anti-Equilibrium*, p. 261.
9. Ibid., pp. 294–95.
10. Ibid., pp. 271–82.

the other participants in most systems. One of the more interesting system traits that we omitted to discuss is the collection, centralized processing, and dissemination by government agencies of information useful to producers and consumers. "Indicative planning," to the extent that it does not involve fiscal and monetary policy, consists chiefly in such information-gathering and -disseminating services. In France, for example, information is "collected and centrally processed" *inter alia* by bringing together representatives of trade and industrial associations who exchange notes on the future prospects, and documentation on the investment projects, of their respective sectors. These representatives then report back to members of their associations, who subsequently revise their expansion plans in the light of this information. By providing this service the government contributes to the adaptation of supply and demand in the long run. "Indicative planning," it may be argued, is a surrogate for organized futures markets, which, if they existed for all goods and services and functioned properly, might also be expected to bring about the long-run compatibility of supply and demand decisions.[11]

In chapter 14, we sought to model the interaction between supervisors and supervisees belonging to the same hierarchically structural organization. Ruling organizations may have a relationship with the organizations they supervise that may be modeled with a similar apparatus. In market economies local, regional, and national governmental agencies "regulate" public utilities and other more or less monopolistic enterprises by controlling the prices they charge customers for their products. We referred in passing (chapter 15) to the Averch and Johnson model, which assumes that regulated enterprise maximizes profits subject to the maximum rate of return on capital allowed by the regulatory agency. (This rate is generally greater than the cost of borrowing capital but less than the rate that would result from unconstrained profit maximization.) The model is unrealistic to the extent that it does not take into account the organizational behavior of the regulatory agency. Paul Joskow has collected evidence supporting the hypothesis that these agencies do not insist on a maximum rate of return when the regulated enterprise's costs and prices are declining. "Formal regulatory action," he writes, "is primarily triggered by firms attempting to raise the level of their rates or to make major changes in the structure of their rates."[12] In sum, regulators

11. On the relation between the development of futures markets and economic environment—level of development, standardization of goods, periodicity of deliveries and of customer requirements—the reader is referred to the theoretical and historical paper by H. S. Houthakker, "Scope and Limits of Futures Trading" in M. Abramovitz et al., eds. *The Allocation of Economic Resources: Essays in Honor of Bernard Francis Haley* (Stanford, Calif.: Stanford University Press, 1958), pp. 134–59.

12. Paul L. Joskow, "Inflation and Environmental Concern: Structural Change in the Process of Public Utility Price Regulation," Working Paper No. 128, Dept. of Economics, MIT, March 1974, p. 12.

satisfice, just as supervisors do. And the reason for so doing is similar: neither regulators nor supervisors can limit the options of a subordinate enterprise to a very narrow range because they (1) would have to check on the detailed performance of the enterprise very frequently and (2) would be bound to impose penalties (at a cost to themselves) for every derogation from this narrowly prescribed behavior, whether the enterprise was or was not at fault—a matter that is often very difficult to ascertain. (The regulator's acceptable set is admittedly rather peculiar. It includes every price or structure of prices set by the enterprise that either does not exceed the previous period's or, if it exceeds it, does not generate a rate of return higher than some maximum allowable rate.)

We conclude that the behavior neither of a supervisee nor of a regulated enterprise can be predicted only from its postulated maximand. Realistic models require an understanding of the motives of decision makers in both interacting organizations.

We have postulated that ruling organizations are made up of individuals with their own tastes and values. How do diverse systems ensure that the decisions they make that affect the incomes and other payoffs of a great many consumers and producers will not be influenced by these interested parties, many of whom would be glad to share their prospective earnings with members of these ruling organizations in exchange for special favors and dispensations? To the extent that ruling organizations comprise agencies specialized along those lines, pressure may be brought to bear on legislators ("lobbying"), members of the executive branch of government, and the courts. In many cases the individuals who are supposed to be insulated from these pressures are in one way or another directly concerned with the prospects of the enterprises whose fate lies in their hands—either because they are part owners of these enterprises through the obligations they hold in them or because they anticipate receiving leading positions therein upon their retirement from government service. This commingling of interests lies at the core of the theory of the "military-industrial complex," which, some economists claim, plays a decisive role in the government of many modern states—a role significant enough in any case to warrant the careful description and eventually the incorporation in systemic models of the conflicts of interests to which individuals with a stake in two or more organizations are liable.

As a matter of realism such conflicts are part and parcel of a more general phenomenon that has been glossed over. Except for our discussion of the efficient partitioning of an economy in chapter 11, we have more or less confined the decision making of individuals to their roles as "consumers," "producers," and "rulers," whereas in a complex modern economy they participate in a much greater variety of organizations with interdependent—positively or negatively correlated—payoffs. Individuals are not merely employees or bosses on the one hand and buyers of consumer goods on the other. They are often also members of labor unions, consumer action groups, and welfare organizations. Most of them are members of a family with a payoff in money or in kind that is almost sure to be at least partly pooled. In modern societies where political representatives are chosen through the polls, many of them will be voters. In less developed countries, and particularly in Africa, individuals belong to a clan or a tribe that commands their allegiance and loyalty. Membership in one or more of these organizations will often call for responses at variance with any mechanical conception of the individual maximizing his money income and bent on gratifying his own tastes.[13]

Here and there we have cited the influence of the environment on system rules and on the patterns of interaction that they affect. We briefly discussed in this connection the centrally directed "hydraulic societies" of ancient times (chap. 3), the development of rules on ownership in response to changes in population density (chap. 9), and the impact of tastes, values, and past traditions on hierarchic structures (chap. 12). These examples suggest that one might perhaps build up a systematic theory of the relation between economic institutions and economic development, a theory that would hopefully have better explanatory and predictive power than Karl Marx's "laws" relating the "level of the economic forces" to the "mode of production." One might start with the idea advanced by Neuberger and James on the "separability" of functions.[14] Economic development makes it possible to separate the hitherto jointly performed activities—entrepreneurship, the bearing of risk, investment, insurance, the choice of technology, and so forth—partly as a result of growing specialization within organizations and partly as a result of the creation of new specialized organizations for performing each function. In the course of development of market economies, for instance, financial intermediaries are created for performing increasingly narrow tasks. On behalf of their clients they choose investments associated with precisely the degree of expected risk that clients are willing to incur. They free investors from the time-consuming search for investment opportunities and from the

---

13. U.S. Labor Secretary Peter J. Brennan recently accounted for the absence of big strikes as follows: "The average worker today has a little better income, as he's probably able to save a few dollars.... He moves into a town and becomes a tax payer and active in the community and worried about the school cost. He finds now that he's on the other side, thinking like some of the people he was shouting at before" (cited in the New Haven *Journal-Courier*, July 25, 1973). If Brennan is right, the American union member's traditional reliance on collective bargaining backed up by the threat of strikes has lost some of its attractiveness now that his interests have been diffused as a result of his membership in a number of organizations with divergent goals. (Brennan did not say what happened to the worker's savings, but to the extent they were "invested" in corporate stock an even sharper conflict could emerge between his role as a union member and as part owner of a corporation.)

14. Egon Neuberger and Estelle James, "The Yugoslav Self-Managed Enterprise: A Systemic Approach," in M. Bornstein, ed., op. cit., pp. 249–65.

need to make managerial or entrepreneurial decisions they are not equipped or have no time to carry out. This proliferation of specialized institutions promotes efficiency both in production and distribution as long as "consumers' sovereignty" is accepted as the basic norm of the system.

In many systems, as Neuberger and James point out, existing rules have the effect of preventing this separation of functions. They fuse functions that individuals, if it were up to them, would prefer to have performed separately. In Yugoslavia, for example, members of collectives carry out production tasks, jointly bear the risk of investments, and may have to take part in policy making for the enterprise in the workers' council even though they may not have the qualifications or even the interest in so doing. This nonseparability is hard to reconcile with the sovereignty of individual decision makers unless one assumes that a transcendent public good is served by this fusion.[15]

In the course of this book we have dwelt at length on rules constraining individuals' decisions, but we had very little to say on the provisions in the system for interpreting the rules, deciding whether they had been transgressed, or pursuing the transgressors. We thus ignored the activities of the courts and of all other judicial or adjudicating agencies for the determination and punishment of violations. These activities, needless to say, are harder to model than rules and orders, but systemic differences in this area can be of paramount importance and they should somehow be accommodated in our descriptions. As Arthur Okun recently said about Phase IV of Federal Price Controls, it is not so much the rules of the game that will determine how effective these controls will be but "how the umpires call the shots."[16] The way the umpires are chosen and what formal or informal guidelines they will follow when apparent violations of controls are brought to their attention—the monitoring system itself being a significant component of the system structure—will be critical to the outcomes of this attempt to curb the inflation through direct government intervention.

So far most of the lapses and lacunae I have deplored in the present work are easy to talk about in a casual sort of way but hard to remedy because they are bound up with system traits that cannot readily be pinned down and formalized. Think of the difficulty, for instance, of building a model of labor allocation and wage determination that incorporates arbitration procedures by the court system! In one area that represents an important part of the subject of this book, however, it should be possible to develop more

15. Neuberger and James also observe that rules may prevent activities from being performed jointly that might be so performed in the absence of these rules. Again in Yugoslavia, communes until recently had a key role to play in founding new enterprises but were denied any responsibilities in their management (ibid., p. 257).

16. Paraphrase of an interview with Arthur Okun on CBS Radio after the announcement of Phase IV in July 1973.

realistic models. There is little doubt in my mind that hierarchies in general and the supervision relation in particular have been corseted too tightly in the descriptions and comparisons of the foregoing chapters. At least two extensions must be incorporated into models of hierarchic behavior if they are to have even a passing resemblance to their real-life counterparts. These two, closely related, extensions, which were briefly alluded to in chapter 10, concern what may be called "ultimate resort" and "delegation." An ultimate resort in a hierarchy may be an individual, a board, or any other association operating as a single person that has final authority to change personnel of the hierarchy, to formulate policies, or both, but that can only act either at stated intervals or under the most extraordinary circumstances. The body of voters in presidential elections in the United States, the association of stock-holders in a corporation, and the congresses of the Communist party of the USSR are instances of ultimate resorts. Immediately subordinate to the ultimate resorts are "executives" or "managers" responsible for all "interim decisions." In some systems the highest executive or manager may even decide when the ultimate resort will be consulted or appealed to. This is so in government by referendum and in practice in the case of the Politbureau of the Central Committee of the Communist Party (in most countries where this party is in power), which determines when party congresses will be held (whether or not the constitution of the party calls for such congresses at stated intervals). Ultimate resort differs from delegation in that the hierarch dele-gating power may take it back at any time or for any reason warranting his intrusion, whereas the rules of the organization normally deprive the ultimate resort of any ad hoc arrogation of decision-making powers. The person or body with ultimate-resort power exercises controls in a peculiarly aggregated man-ner: he or it will "accept" the record of an interim period on the basis of a judgment about average performance during this period or of another cri-terion that balances the desirable against the undesirable elements in this performance.

A realistic formalization of delegation in hierarchies should, in my view be integrated in a model of management by exception, of the type described in chapter 10, perhaps along the following lines. With each tier of the hierarchy we associate certain "critical states" of the environment and certain actions that if ordered and carried out would bring about outcomes with a payoff that is assumed to be absolutely larger with each higher tier.[17] Thus the critical states associated with the head's tier in conjunction with certain actions may be expected to trigger either very favorable or very unfavorable outcomes to the organization. We suppose that certain "ancillary

17. An action that successfully averts or mitigates the significant loss that would occur in case a routine action had been undertaken may also be said to have a positive payoff.

states," whether critical themselves or not, are correlated sequentially with the critical states in the sense that when one of these ancillary states crops up it is fairly probable that one or more of the critical states will soon make its appearance. It would be reasonable for the members of the organization collecting the most detailed information about the environment to communicate the news about the occurrence of any of these ancillary states in disaggregated form to the highest tier "concerned"—to the tier, that is, whose critical states have a high conditional probability of occurrence.

We referred in chapter 12 to the possibility that the members of a tier might wish to draw on more detailed information than that normally communicated to them from their supervisees. This may be done by field inspection, by auditing available records, or by any other means of obtaining disaggregated information. The information network of a hierarchy featuring a management-by-exception system suggested in the above sketch bears some resemblance to this inspection system. The chief difference resides in the fact that in the former detailed information is automatically sent up to higher tiers when particular states are observed in the lower tier, whereas in the latter this type of information is collected on the initiative of the higher tier, normally upon detection of some abnormality in the aggregated information.

So much for hierarchies, which I have trotted out for a last pirouette, not for the sake of comprehensiveness or to tie up loose ends—I know only too well how incomplete and loose ended the book is—but as a last illustration of my successive-approximations approach toward the realistic modeling of complex institutional phenomena.

Appendix: Information Theory

A.1 Partitions of the Set of States of an Individual's Environment

In several chapters of this book, reference has been made to the theory of information first developed by Jacob Marschak[1] and later elaborated by Marschak and Roy Radner.[2] A summary of this theory, illustrated by examples, follows.

Information, introduced as a primitive in chapter 2, may be regarded as the outcome of a particular type of action, called "perceiving" or "information gathering." We saw in chapter 2 that an action by individual i may be defined as a function from the set of states of i's environment to the set of possible outcomes. An information-gathering function η transforms states of i's environment into information signals. The function η is sometimes called an "information structure."

If η were a one-to-one function from the set of possible states of an individual's environment denoted E to the set of possible signals, denoted Y, information would be *complete*. Each state e in E would then generate a unique signal y, which in turn could have been generated only by e. But, owing to the imperfection of his senses and of his measuring instruments, man must normally resort to "simplified representations" of his environment. This may be interpreted to mean that a function such as η will map a well-defined subset E_y of E, where E_y contains elements other than e, into the signal y. Another subset of E, denoted E , will generate signal y', distinct from y. Clearly, there cannot be common elements to E_y and $E_{y'}$. The function η may thus be said to *partition* the set E into mutually exclusive subsets, one for each distinct signal in the set of possible signals Y. Both E and Y, for purposes of this exposition, will be considered finite.

Consider, for example, the following information-gathering functions η and η'. Function η generates signals by summing the coordinates of each

---

1. "Towards an Economic Theory of Organization and Information," in R. M. Thrall, C. H. Coombs, and R. L. Davis, eds., *Decision Processes* (New York: Wiley, 1954); "Problems in Information Economics," in C. P. Bonini, R. K. Jaedicke, and H. W. Wagner, eds., *Management Controls: New Directions in Basic Research* (New York: McGraw-Hill, 1969).

2. *Economic Theory of Teams* (New Haven: Yale University Press, 1972).

3. Let $\bar{e}$ be a common element of E_y and $E_{y'}$. Then the image set of $\bar{e}$ under the function η would be (y, y'), a two-element set if y and y' are distinct. This violates the functional definition of η.

state and η' by transmitting the first coordinate and omitting the others. Let there be two state variables x_1 and x_2, each of which can take on the values -1, 0, and $+1$. The set of possible states E contains nine elements:

$$\{(-1, -1), (-1, 0), (-1, 1), (0, -1), (0, 0), (0, 1), (1, -1), (1, 0), (1, 1)\}.$$

The set of distinct signals generated by η as the sum of two coordinates in each state is $\{(-2), (-1), (0), (1), (2)\}$. Note that signal (-2) is the image of the unique state $(-1, -1)$, whereas signal (0) is the image of three states: $(-1, 1)$, $(0, 0)$, and $(1, -1)$. Thus, function η induces a partition of E into five subsets: (1) $\{(-1, -1)\}$; (2) $\{(-1, 0), (0, -1)\}$; (3) $\{(-1, 1), (0, 0), (1, -1)\}$; (4) $\{(0, 1), (1, 0)\}$; and (5) $\{(1, 1)\}$. The image of the first subset under η is signal -2, of the second signal -1, and so on.

The sets of distinct signals generated by η' is $\{(-1), (0), (1)\}$. The partition of E_i into three subsets induced by η' is (1) $\{(-1, -1), (-1, 0), (-1, 1)\}$; (2) $\{(0, -1), (0, 0), (0, 1)\}$; and (3) $\{(1, -1), (1, 0), (1, 1)\}$. The first subset of E generates signal (-1), the second (0), and the third (1).

We now return to the general case. Let Z_1 be the partition of E induced by a given information-gathering function η_1 and let Z_2 be a distinct partition induced by η_2. Also let z_1 and z_2 be elements of Z_1 and Z_2, respectively (i.e., distinct subsets of E in the partitions induced by η_1 and η_2). We say that Z_1 is finer than Z_2 if for every z_1 in Z_1 there is a z_2 in Z_2 such that z_1 is contained in z_2. It can also be said in this case that Z_2 is *coarser* than Z_1. We may extend the concept of fineness from the partitions to the information-gathering functions or information structures generating these partitions. Thus we may say that the finest information structure is the one that induces a partition of E into subsets each of which contains a single state e. This is the complete-information structure already referred to.[4] The coarsest possible information structure ("no information") is one that induces a partition of E into a single element $\{E\}$ containing the entire set, which implies that every element of E generate the same signal y. (Whether this unique signal be y or y' of course makes no difference for any conceivable decision maker.)

It is manifest that both the partitions induced by η and η' in the numerical example above are coarser than the complete-information partition and finer than the no-information partition. On the other hand, η and η' are not comparable with respect to fineness. It is easily verified that some subsets of the partition of E induced by η are contained in no subsets of the partition induced by η', and conversely.

---

4. It should be recognized that the "finest partition" of E is a conventional concept. With enough research funds available · (for electronic microscopes, amplifiers, and other sensory aides), we may (almost always) increase the degree of detail in the description of our environment. The finest partition of the environment that we wish in some fashion to describe will of course always be at least as fine as any of the partitions induced by the information-gathering functions ("instruments") at our disposal.

A.2 INFORMATION AND DECISION MAKING[5]

In chapter 2, we sketched a model of rational behavior according to which an individual facing uncertainty will choose an action (out of his feasible set) that will maximize his expected utility. We suppose, or infer from such an action, that the individual assigns subjective probabilities ("priors") to the different possible states of his environment.

Let an individual's payoff for any state–action pair (e, a) be given by the payoff function $\omega(e, a)$. We call *payoff adequate* a partition Z of the set E that is sufficiently fine to satisfy the following condition: for every action a and for any pair of states e and e' in a subset z of E defined by Z, payoff $\omega(e, a)$ equals payoff $\omega(e', a)$. In other words the set of states is partitioned in such a way that an action a will yield the same payoff under any state belonging to a subset of E defined by this partition. Such subsets of E are called *events*.

The subjective probability that an individual attaches to state e is denoted $\phi(e)$. The probability he assigns to the event z containing e is $\pi(z) \equiv \sum_{e \in z} \phi(e)$.

In the basic model of rational behavior in chapter 2, the individual was viewed as maximizing the utility of his payoff, denoted $u(\omega)$. If $u(\omega)$ is a linear function of ω, there is no difference between maximizing the utility of ω or the payoff ω itself (which may be thought of as a sum of money). However if $u(\omega)$ is strictly concave, this will no longer be true. We shall assume henceforth that expected utility will be maximized for any decision that maximizes the expected payoff.

Thus, the individual maximizing the expected utility of his payoff will maximize $U \equiv \sum_{e \in E} \omega\{e, \alpha(\eta[e])\} \phi(e)$, where α is his decision-making function (whenever he receives the signal y $(\equiv \eta[e])$, he will choose the action a if $a = \alpha(y)$.)

Since $y = \eta(e)$, we may rewrite the above expression as

$$U = \sum_{y \in Y} \sum_{e \in E_y} \omega[e, \alpha(y)] \, \phi(e),$$

where E_y is the set of states generating signal y.

Since e is included in E_y, the joint probability of e and y is $\phi(e)$, and $\phi(e|y)$, the conditional probability of state e given signal y, is $\phi(e)/\pi(y)$. Hence, $\phi(e) = \phi(e|y)\pi(y)$. Substituting in the last expression for U, we conclude that in order to maximize U, the individual receiving signal y must maximize

$$\sum_{e \in E_y} \omega[e, \alpha(y)] \phi(e|y).$$

If Z is payoff adequate, we can reformulate the decision maker's payoff function as

$$\tilde{\omega}(z, a) \equiv \omega(e, a),$$

5. This section is summarized from Radner and Marschak, op. cit., pp. 51–64.

where $e \in z$ and $z \in \mathcal{Z}$. Thus, upon the receipt of y, he will choose the action maximizing

$$\sum_{z \in \mathcal{Z}} \tilde{\omega}[z, \alpha(y)] \pi(z|y).$$

Using the above expression, we may rewrite the expected payoff of a decision function α as

$$E(\omega) = \sum_{y \in Y} \pi(y) \sum_{z \in \mathcal{Z}} \omega[z, \alpha(y)] \pi(z|y).$$

In other words, for a decision rule α^* to be payoff maximizing, given the structure η, it is necessary and sufficient that, for every signal y with positive probability, $\alpha^*(y)$ be an action that maximizes the conditional expected payoff for that signal.[6] Once we substitute $\eta(e)$ for y in the above expression for $E(\omega)$ and consider the information structure to be subject to choice, we see that payoff maximization consists in selecting the pair (α, η) that simultaneously maximizes $E(\omega)$ for all possible messages generated by the probability distribution ϕ over E.

The maximization of expected utility (equations 2.1 and 2.2) may require the selection of a decision rule and an information structure differing from the pair maximizing the payoff if utility is a strictly concave function of ω.

The conditional probability $\pi(z|y)$ in the above expression is a posterior probability because it depends on the occurrence of y. It is related to the subjective conditional probabilities $\pi(y|z)$ and $\pi(z)$ by Bayes's theorem:

$$\pi(z|y) = \frac{\pi(y|z)\,\pi(z)}{\sum\limits_{z' \in \mathcal{Z}} \pi(y|z')\,\pi(z')},$$

where z' is any other event in the partition $\mathcal{Z}$.

This expression may be used to calculate the posterior conditional probabilities when only the priors are known. (It is often evident with what probability signal y will be emitted upon the occurrence of z, even though we may not be able to evaluate directly the probability that z actually occurred when signal y was received.)

We are now able to define a *noiseless information-gathering function*. An information-gathering function is noiseless if, for every z in $\mathcal{Z}$ (a payoff-adequate partition), the conditional probability distribution $\pi(\cdot|z)$ assigns the probability one to *some* signal in Y. Thus if η is noiseless and event z occurs, there will be some signal y in Y that will be emitted with probability one [i.e., $\pi(y|z) = 1$].

An example of a noiseless information-gathering function follows. Let every state e in E belong to the n space of reals and let the payoff be equal to

6. Ibid., p. 52.

$a\sum_{j=1}^{n} x_j$, where x_j is the number assumed by the jth state variable, and a, the action taken on any signal y, is confined to the interval of real numbers between -1 and $+1$ (i.e., $-1 \leqslant a \leqslant 1$).

A sufficient condition for the function η to be noiseless is that

$$y = \eta(e) = \sum_{j=1}^{n} x_j.$$

This can be seen as follows. Construct a partition $\mathcal{Z}$ of E such that any states e and e' in E with state variables x_1 to x_n and x'_1 to x'_n, respectively, belong to an element z in $\mathcal{Z}$ if and only if $\sum_{j=1}^{n} x_j = \sum_{j=1}^{n} x'_j$. It is clear that this partition is payoff adequate, since for any states e and e' in z, the payoff $a\sum_{j=1}^{n} x_j$ will be the same for any action a. Every subset z is then an event. By the definition of η, every state in z will generate the same signal y. Hence η is noiseless.

If on the other hand, under an alternative information structure $\bar{\eta}$, y were defined as $\sum_{j=1}^{m} x_j$ $(m < n)$, then e and e' in z might generate two distinct signals y and y'. If both e and e' have a positive probability, η will be noisy. An information system based on incomplete sampling is always noisy.

For a numerical example, consider again the information-gathering function η' at the beginning of this appendix, where n was equal to 2 and m to 1. The payoff-adequate partition of E is necessarily the same as the partition induced by function η in this first example, as the payoff has been assumed to be proportional to the sum of the coordinates. The second subset in the partition induced by η was $\{(-1, 0), (0, -1)\}$. But within this subset, denoted z^2, under η', the first state $(-1, 0)$ generates signal (-1) and the second state $(0, -1)$ signal (0). Hence if the prior probabilities of these two states are both positive, neither $\pi(-1|z^2)$ nor $\pi(0|z^2)$ is equal to unity. The function η' must be noisy.

Marschak and Radner stress that noise may always be conceived to originate in certain elements of the states of the environment—the condition of the recording instrument, defects in the observer's eyesight, the propensity of the person observing the phenomenon to lie, and so on—even though these elements may not appear as arguments in the payoff function. The methodological point to be kept in mind here is that a complete description of an environmental state should always include as distinct elements those characteristics of the individuals and of their sensory aids as they make the observation.

In general, if for some payoff function ω an information-gathering function η induces a payoff-adequate partition on E, then η is noiseless. But the converse proposition does not hold. A noiseless function η need not induce a payoff-adequate partition on E. However, in this case it is easily shown that any payoff-adequate partition Z on E must be finer than Z_η, the partition induced by η on E.

An example is

$$y = \eta(e) = \delta(\sum_{j=1}^{n} x_j),$$

where δ is the sign $(+$ or $-1)$ of $\sum_{j=1}^{n} x_j$, and $e \in R^n$. Payoff ω, as in our previous example, equals $a \sum_{j=1}^{n} x_j$, and a payoff-adequate partition Z of E is such that for any e and e' in a subset z of Z, the sum of the coordinates of e, $\sum_{j=n}^{n} x_j$, equals the sum of the coordinates of e', $\sum_{j=1}^{n} x_j'$.

Since the sign of both these sums must be the same, $y = \eta(e) = \eta(e')$, and η is noiseless. Clearly Z is at least as fine as Z_η (since every event z in Z generates the same signal y emitted by some subset z_η of Z_η). To show that Z is finer than Z_η, we need find only a second subset z' of Z' distinct from z that will generate the same signal y as z. It is easy to see that z' will fulfill this condition as long as the sum of its coordinates is of the same sign but different in magnitude from $\sum_{j=1}^{n} x_j$.

The value of an information-gathering function or structure depends on the payoff function and the set of actions open to the decision maker. We define structure η_1 to be at least as valuable η_2 for payoff function ω and probability distribution ϕ if

$$\max_\alpha \sum_e \omega[e, \alpha(\eta_1[e])]\phi(e) \geqslant \max_\alpha \sum_e \omega[e, \alpha(\eta_2[e])]\phi(e).$$

In other words, the maximum expected payoff under all possible decision rules α is at least as great for η_1 as it is for η_2. This formulation, however, ignores the cost of gathering the information. More precisely, we should say that η_1 has at least as high a "gross expected value" as η_2.

An important theorem states that if an information structure η is at least as fine as, η', it is at least as valuable (in gross terms) as η' *for every probability distribution* $\phi(e)$ *on* E *and every payoff function* ω.[7] It is also worthy of note that if η and η' are not comparable with respect to fineness, then for some payoff function ω, η will be more valuable than η' and for some other ω', η' will be more valuable than η.[8]

For our final definition we introduce a *sufficient* information structure. A structure η will be sufficient with respect to payoff function ω if for any

7. Theorem, ibid., p. 54.
8. Ibid., p. 55.

structure η' finer than η, the maximum expected payoff using η is equal to the maximum expected payoff using η'.

Given the greater cost of finer information structures, it should be advantageous to find the structure that is just sufficient with respect to the relevant payoff function. We have already referred, for example, to an information structure $\eta : y = \sum_{j=1}^{m} x_j (m < n)$, which was seen to be noisy with respect to the payoff function $\omega = a \sum_{j=1}^{n} x_j$, where $0 \leqslant a \leqslant 1$. Is η sufficient or would a coarser structure η' yield the same expected payoff for any given probability distribution over the set of states in E? It turns out that for any probability distribution over E such that the coordinates x_j of any state e are stochastically independent and have zero means $[E(x_j) = 0]$, the coarser structure η' will be sufficient. The expected payoff will be just as great if the choice of a is made on the basis of binary messages $(+, -)$ according to the sign of y as if y itself were transmitted.[9] It may be counterintuitive for some readers to discover that stronger restrictions must be placed on the class of admissible probability distributions to prove that this coarser information structure (the sign of y) will be sufficient in case the payoff function were given by $a \, \delta(\sum_{j=1}^{n} x_j)$, where δ again denotes the sign of the n coordinates of any state e.

In general, we should expect that a less "sensitive" (e.g., binary) payoff function would be associated with a sufficient information structure that was at least as coarse as the structure that would have been sufficient for a more "sensitive" (e.g., continuous) payoff function, but as we have just seen, this correspondence does not strictly hold for all probability distributions when both information structures compared are noisy.

9. Marschak, "Towards an Economic Theory," op. cit., pp. 56–57.

Index